Learn Docker – Fundamentals of Docker 19.x
Second Edition

Build, test, ship, and run containers with Docker and Kubernetes

Gabriel N. Schenker

BIRMINGHAM - MUMBAI

Learn Docker – Fundamentals of Docker 19.x
Second Edition

Commissioning Editor: Vijin Boricha
Acquisition Editor: Shrilekha Inani
Content Development Editor: Ronn Kurien
Senior Editor: Richard Brookes-Bland
Technical Editor: Sarvesh Jaywant
Copy Editor: Safis Editing
Project Coordinator: Neil Dmello
Proofreader: Safis Editing
Indexer: Tejal Daruwale Soni
Production Designer: Deepika Naik

First published: April 2018
Second edition: March 2020

Production reference: 1130320

Published by Packt Publishing Ltd.
Livery Place
35 Livery Street
Birmingham
B3 2PB, UK.

ISBN 978-1-83882-747-2

www.packt.com

Packt>

Subscribe to our online digital library for full access to over 7,000 books and videos, as well as industry leading tools to help you plan your personal development and advance your career. For more information, please visit our website.

Why subscribe?

- Spend less time learning and more time coding with practical eBooks and Videos from over 4,000 industry professionals

- Improve your learning with Skill Plans built especially for you

- Get a free eBook or video every month

- Fully searchable for easy access to vital information

- Copy and paste, print, and bookmark content

Did you know that Packt offers eBook versions of every book published, with PDF and ePub files available? You can upgrade to the eBook version at www.packt.com and as a print book customer, you are entitled to a discount on the eBook copy. Get in touch with us at customercare@packtpub.com for more details.

At www.packt.com, you can also read a collection of free technical articles, sign up for a range of free newsletters, and receive exclusive discounts and offers on Packt books and eBooks.

Contributors

About the author

Gabriel N. Schenker has more than 25 years of experience as an independent consultant, architect, leader, trainer, mentor, and developer. Currently, Gabriel works as Lead Solution Architect at Techgroup Switzerland. Prior to that, Gabriel worked as Lead Curriculum Developer at Docker and at Confluent. Gabriel has a Ph.D. in Physics, and he is a Docker Captain, a Certified Docker Associate, a Certified Kafka Developer and Operator, and an ASP Insider. When not working, Gabriel enjoys time with his wonderful wife Veronicah and his children.

I want to give special thanks to my editors, Ronn Kurien and Suzanne Coutinho, who patiently helped me to get this book done and get it done right.

About the reviewer

Francisco Javier Ramírez Urea is a technology enthusiast and professional, Docker Captain, casual developer, open source advocate, a certified trainer and solutions architect at HoplaSoftware, and a technical book writer and reviewer.

He is also a Kubernetes Certified Administrator, a Docker Certified Associate, a Docker Certified Instructor, and a Docker MTA program Consultant, as well as a Docker/Kubernetes and NGINX expert and a DevOps/CI-CD solutions integrator.

He currently works as a solutions architect focused on containers and microservices technologies. He is passionate to teach his students everything he know. Continuous learning is the main motivation of his career.

Packt is searching for authors like you

If you're interested in becoming an author for Packt, please visit authors.packtpub.com and apply today. We have worked with thousands of developers and tech professionals, just like you, to help them share their insight with the global tech community. You can make a general application, apply for a specific hot topic that we are recruiting an author for, or submit your own idea.

Table of Contents

Section 2: Containerization, from Beginner to Black Belt

Section 3: Orchestration Fundamentals and Docker Swarm

Preface

Developers are faced with ever-increasing pressure to build, modify, test, and deploy highly distributed applications in a high cadence. Operations engineers are looking for a uniform deployment strategy that encompasses most or all of their ever-growing portfolio of applications, and stakeholders want to keep their total cost of ownership low. Docker containers combined with a container orchestrator such as Kubernetes help them all to achieve these goals.

Docker containers accelerate and simplify the building, shipping, and running of highly distributed applications. Containers turbo-charge CI/CD pipelines, and containerized applications allow a company to standardize on one common deployment platform, such as Kubernetes. Containerized applications are more secure and can be run on any platform that's able to run containers, on premises or in the cloud.

Who this book is for

This book is targeted at system administrators, operations engineers, DevOps engineers, and developers or stakeholders who are interested in getting started with Docker from scratch.

What this book covers

Chapter 1, *What Are Containers and Why Should I Use Them?*, introduces the concept of containers and why they are so extremely useful in the software industry.

Chapter 2, *Setting Up a Working Environment*, discusses in detail how to set up an ideal environment for developers, DevOps, and operators that can be used when working with Docker containers.

Chapter 3, *Mastering Containers*, explains how to start, stop, and remove containers. We will also see how to inspect containers to retrieve additional metadata from them. Furthermore, we'll see how to run additional processes, how to attach to the main process in an already running container, and how to retrieve logging information from a container that is produced by the processes running inside it. Finally, the chapter introduces the inner workings of a container, including such things as Linux namespaces and groups.

Chapter 4, *Creating and Managing Container Images*, presents the different ways to create the container images that serve as the templates for containers. It introduces the inner structure of an image and how it is built. This chapter also explains how to lift and shift an existing legacy application so that it can run in containers.

Chapter 5, *Data Volumes and Configuration*, introduces data volumes, which can be used by stateful components running in containers. The chapter also shows how we can define individual environment variables for the application running inside the container, as well as how to use files containing whole sets of configuration settings.

Chapter 6, *Debugging Code Running in Containers*, discusses techniques commonly used to allow a developer to evolve, modify, debug, and test their code while running in a container. With these techniques at hand, the developer will enjoy a frictionless development process for applications running in a container, similar to what they experience when developing applications that run natively.

Chapter 7, *Using Docker to Supercharge Automation*, shows how we can use tools to perform administrative tasks without having to install those tools on the host computer. We will also see how to use containers that host and run test scripts or code used to test and validate application services running in containers. Finally, this chapter guides us through the task of building a simple Docker-based CI/CD pipeline.

Chapter 8, *Advanced Docker Usage Scenarios*, presents advanced tips, tricks, and concepts that are useful when containerizing complex distributed applications, or when using Docker to automate sophisticated tasks.

Chapter 9, *Distributed Application Architecture*, introduces the concept of a distributed application architecture and discusses the various patterns and best practices that are required to run a distributed application successfully. Finally, it discusses the additional requirements that need to be fulfilled to run such an application in production.

Chapter 10, *Single-Host Networking*, presents the Docker container networking model and its single-host implementation in the form of the bridge network. This chapter introduces the concept of software-defined networks and explains how they are used to secure containerized applications. It also discusses how container ports can be opened to the public and thus make containerized components accessible from the outside world. Finally, it introduces Traefik, a reverse proxy, to enable sophisticated HTTP application-level routing between containers.

Chapter 11, *Docker Compose*, addresses the concept of an application consisting of multiple services, each running in a container, and how Docker Compose allows us to easily build, run, and scale such an application using a declarative approach.

Chapter 12, *Orchestrators*, presents the concept of orchestrators. It explains why orchestrators are needed and how they work conceptually. The chapter will also provide an overview of the most popular orchestrators and name a few of their pros and cons.

Chapter 13, *Introduction to Docker Swarm*, introduces Docker's native orchestrator, SwarmKit. We will see all the concepts and objects SwarmKit uses to deploy and run a distributed, resilient, robust, and highly available application in a cluster on premises or in the cloud. The chapter also introduces how SwarmKit ensures secure applications using software-defined networks to isolate containers and secrets to protect sensitive information. Additionally, this chapter shows how to install a highly available Docker swarm in the cloud. It introduces the routing mesh, which provides Layer 4 routing and load balancing. Finally, it shows how to deploy an application consisting of multiple services onto the swarm.

Chapter 14, *Zero-Downtime Deployments and Secrets*, explains how to deploy services or applications onto a Docker swarm with zero downtime and automatic rollback capabilities. It also introduces secrets as a means to protect sensitive information.

Chapter 15, *Introduction to Kubernetes*, introduces the current most popular container orchestrator. It introduces the core Kubernetes objects that are used to define and run a distributed, resilient, robust, and highly available application in a cluster. Finally, it introduces MiniKube as a way to locally deploy a Kubernetes application, and also the integration of Kubernetes with Docker for Mac and Docker for Windows.

Chapter 16, *Deploying, Updating, and Securing an Application with Kubernetes*, explains how to deploy, update, and scale applications into a Kubernetes cluster. It also explains how to instrument your application services with liveness and readiness probes to support Kubernetes in its health and availability checking. Furthermore, the chapter explains how zero-downtime deployments are achieved to enable disruption-free updates and rollbacks of mission-critical applications. Finally, the chapter introduces Kubernetes secrets as a means to configure services and protect sensitive data.

Chapter 17, *Monitoring and Troubleshooting an App Running in Production*, teaches different techniques to monitor an individual service or a whole distributed application running on a Kubernetes cluster. It also shows how to troubleshoot an application service that is running in production without altering the cluster or the cluster nodes on which the service is running.

Chapter 18, *Running a Containerized App in the Cloud*, provides an overview of some of the most popular ways of running containerized applications in the cloud. We include self-hosting and hosted solutions and discuss their pros and cons. Fully managed offerings of vendors such as Microsoft Azure and Google Cloud Engine are briefly discussed.

To get the most out of this book

A solid understanding of distributed application architecture and an interest in accelerating and simplifying the building, shipping, and running of highly distributed applications are expected. No prior experience with Docker containers is required.

Access to a computer with Windows 10 Professional or macOS installed is highly recommended. The computer should have at least 16 GB of memory.

Software/Hardware covered in the book	OS Requirements
Docker for Desktop, Docker Toolbox, Visual Studio Code, Powershell or Bash Terminal.	Windows 10 Pro/macOS/ Linux minimum of 8GB RAM

If you are using the digital version of this book, we advise you to type the code yourself or access the code via the GitHub repository (link available in the next section). Doing so will help you avoid any potential errors related to copy/pasting of code.

Download the example code files

You can download the example code files for this book from your account at www.packt.com. If you purchased this book elsewhere, you can visit www.packtpub.com/support and register to have the files emailed directly to you.

You can download the code files by following these steps:

1. Log in or register at www.packt.com.
2. Select the **Support** tab.
3. Click on **Code Downloads**.
4. Enter the name of the book in the **Search** box and follow the onscreen instructions.

Once the file is downloaded, please make sure that you unzip or extract the folder using the latest version of:

- WinRAR/7-Zip for Windows
- Zipeg/iZip/UnRarX for Mac

- 7-Zip/PeaZip for Linux

The code bundle for the book is also hosted on GitHub
at `https://github.com/PacktPublishing/Learn-Docker---Fundamentals-of-Docker-19.x-Second-Edition`. In case there's an update to the code, it will be updated on the existing GitHub repository.

We also have other code bundles from our rich catalog of books and videos available at https://github.com/PacktPublishing/. Check them out!

Download the color images

We also provide a PDF file that has color images of the screenshots/diagrams used in this book. You can download it here: http://www.packtpub.com/sites/default/files/downloads/9781838827472_ColorImages.pdf.

Conventions used

There are a number of text conventions used throughout this book.

CodeInText: Indicates code words in text, database table names, folder names, filenames, file extensions, pathnames, dummy URLs, user input, and Twitter handles. Here is an example: "The container runtime on a Docker host consists of containerd and runc."

A block of code is set as follows:

```
{
  "name": "api",
  "version": "1.0.0",
  "description": "",
  "main": "index.js",
  "scripts": {
    "test": "echo \"Error: no test specified\" && exit 1"
  },
  "author": "",
  "license": "ISC"
}
```

When we wish to draw your attention to a particular part of a code block, the relevant lines or items are set in bold:

```
ARG BASE_IMAGE_VERSION=12.7-stretch
FROM node:${BASE_IMAGE_VERSION}
WORKDIR /app
COPY packages.json .
RUN npm install
COPY . .
CMD npm start
```

Any command-line input or output is written as follows:

```
$ /usr/bin/ruby -e "$(curl -fsSL
https://raw.githubusercontent.com/Homebrew/install/master/install)"
```

Bold: Indicates a new term, an important word, or words that you see onscreen. For example, words in menus or dialog boxes appear in the text like this. Here is an example: "Select **System info** from the **Administration** panel."

Warnings or important notes appear like this.

Tips and tricks appear like this.

Get in touch

Feedback from our readers is always welcome.

General feedback: If you have questions about any aspect of this book, mention the book title in the subject of your message and email us at customercare@packtpub.com.

Errata: Although we have taken every care to ensure the accuracy of our content, mistakes do happen. If you have found a mistake in this book, we would be grateful if you would report this to us. Please visit www.packtpub.com/support/errata, selecting your book, clicking on the Errata Submission Form link, and entering the details.

Piracy: If you come across any illegal copies of our works in any form on the Internet, we would be grateful if you would provide us with the location address or website name. Please contact us at copyright@packt.com with a link to the material.

If you are interested in becoming an author: If there is a topic that you have expertise in and you are interested in either writing or contributing to a book, please visit authors.packtpub.com.

Reviews

Please leave a review. Once you have read and used this book, why not leave a review on the site that you purchased it from? Potential readers can then see and use your unbiased opinion to make purchase decisions, we at Packt can understand what you think about our products, and our authors can see your feedback on their book. Thank you!

For more information about Packt, please visit packt.com.

Section 1: Motivation and Getting Started

The objective of *Part One* is to introduce you to the concept of containers and explain why they are so extremely useful in the software industry. You will also prepare your working environment for the use of Docker.

This section comprises the following chapters:

- `Chapter 1`, *What Are Containers and Why Should I Use Them?*
- `Chapter 2`, *Setting Up a Working Environment*

What Are Containers and Why Should I Use Them?

This first chapter will introduce you to the world of containers and their orchestration. This book starts from the very beginning, in that it assumes that you have no prior knowledge of containers, and will give you a very practical introduction to the topic.

In this chapter, we will focus on the software supply chain and the friction within it. Then, we'll present containers, which are used to reduce this friction and add enterprise-grade security on top of it. We'll also look into how containers and the ecosystem around them are assembled. We'll specifically point out the distinction between the upstream **Open Source Software** (**OSS**) components, united under the code name Moby, that form the building blocks of the downstream products of Docker and other vendors.

The chapter covers the following topics:

- What are containers?
- Why are containers important?
- What's the benefit for me or for my company?
- The Moby project
- Docker products
- Container architecture

After completing this module, you will be able to do the following:

- Explain what containers are, using an analogy such as physical containers, in a few simple sentences to an interested layman
- Justify why containers are so important using an analogy such as physical containers versus traditional shipping or apartment homes versus single-family homes, and so on, to an interested lay person
- Name at least four upstream open source components that are used by Docker products, such as Docker for Desktop
- Identify at least three Docker products

What are containers?

A software container is a pretty abstract thing, so it might help if we start with an analogy that should be pretty familiar to most of you. The analogy is a shipping container in the transportation industry. Throughout history, people have been transporting goods from one location to another by various means. Before the invention of the wheel, goods would most probably have been transported in bags, baskets, or chests on the shoulders of the humans themselves, or they might have used animals such as donkeys, camels, or elephants to transport them.

With the invention of the wheel, transportation became a bit more efficient as humans built roads that they could move their carts along. Many more goods could be transported at a time. When the first steam-driven machines, and later gasoline-driven engines, were introduced, transportation became even more powerful. We now transport huge amounts of goods on trains, ships, and trucks. At the same time, the types of goods became more and more diverse, and sometimes complex to handle.

In all these thousands of years, one thing didn't change, and that was the necessity to unload goods at a target location and maybe load them onto another means of transportation. Take, for example, a farmer bringing a cart full of apples to a central train station where the apples are then loaded onto a train, together with all the apples from many other farmers. Or think of a winemaker bringing his barrels of wine with a truck to the port where they are unloaded, and then transferred to a ship that will transport them overseas.

This unloading from one means of transportation and loading onto another means of transportation was a really complex and tedious process. Every type of product was packaged in its own way and thus had to be handled in its own particular way. Also, loose goods faced the risk of being stolen by unethical workers or damaged in the process of being handled.

Then, there came containers and they totally revolutionized the transportation industry. A container is just a metallic box with standardized dimensions. The length, width, and height of each container is the same. This is a very important point. Without the World agreeing on a standard size, the whole container thing would not have been as successful as it is now.

Now, with standardized containers, companies who want to have their goods transported from A to B package those goods into these containers. Then, they call a shipper, which comes with a standardized means for transportation. This can be a truck that can load a container or a train whose wagons can each transport one or several containers. Finally, we have ships that are specialized in transporting huge numbers of containers. Shippers never need to unpack and repackage goods. For a shipper, a container is just a black box, and they are not interested in what is in it, nor should they care in most cases. It is just a big iron box with standard dimensions. Packaging goods into containers is now fully delegated to the parties who want to have their goods shipped, and they should know how to handle and package those goods.

Since all containers have the same agreed-upon shape and dimensions, shippers can use standardized tools to handle containers; that is, cranes that unload containers, say from a train or a truck, and load them onto a ship and vice versa. One type of crane is enough to handle all the containers that come along over time. Also, the means of transportation can be standardized, such as container ships, trucks, and trains.

Because of all this standardization, all the processes in and around shipping goods could also be standardized and thus made much more efficient than they were before the age of containers.

Now, you should have a good understanding of why shipping containers are so important and why they revolutionized the whole transportation industry. I chose this analogy purposefully, since the software containers that we are going to introduce here fulfill the exact same role in the so-called software supply chain that shipping containers do in the supply chain of physical goods.

In the old days, developers would develop a new application. Once that application was completed in their eyes, they would hand that application over to the operations engineers, who were then supposed to install it on the production servers and get it running. If the operations engineers were lucky, they even got a somewhat accurate document with installation instructions from the developers. So far, so good, and life was easy.

But things get a bit out of hand when, in an enterprise, there are many teams of developers that create quite different types of application, yet all of them need to be installed on the same production servers and kept running there. Usually, each application has some external dependencies, such as which framework it was built on, what libraries it uses, and so on. Sometimes, two applications use the same framework but in different versions that might or might not be compatible with each other. Our operations engineer's life became much harder over time. They had to be really creative with how they could load their ship, (their servers,) with different applications without breaking something.

Installing a new version of a certain application was now a complex project on its own, and often needed months of planning and testing. In other words, there was a lot of friction in the software supply chain. But these days, companies rely more and more on software, and the release cycles need to become shorter and shorter. We cannot afford to just release twice a year or so anymore. Applications need to be updated in a matter of weeks or days, or sometimes even multiple times per day. Companies that do not comply risk going out of business, due to the lack of agility. So, what's the solution?

One of the first approaches was to use **virtual machines** (**VMs**). Instead of running multiple applications, all on the same server, companies would package and run a single application on each VM. With this, all the compatibility problems were gone and life seemed to be good again. Unfortunately, that happiness didn't last long. VMs are pretty heavy beasts on their own since they all contain a full-blown operating system such as Linux or Windows Server, and all that for just a single application. This is just as if you were in the transportation industry and were using a whole ship just to transport a single truckload of bananas. What a waste! That could never be profitable.

The ultimate solution to this problem was to provide something that is much more lightweight than VMs, but is also able to perfectly encapsulate the goods it needs to transport. Here, the goods are the actual application that has been written by our developers, plus – and this is important – all the external dependencies of the application, such as its framework, libraries, configurations, and more. This holy grail of a software packaging mechanism was the *Docker container*.

Developers use Docker containers to package their applications, frameworks, and libraries into them, and then they ship those containers to the testers or operations engineers. To testers and operations engineers, a container is just a black box. It is a standardized black box, though. All containers, no matter what application runs inside them, can be treated equally. The engineers know that, if any container runs on their servers, then any other containers should run too. And this is actually true, apart from some edge cases, which always exist.

Thus, Docker containers are a means to package applications and their dependencies in a standardized way. Docker then coined the phrase *Build, ship, and run anywhere*.

Why are containers important?

These days, the time between new releases of an application become shorter and shorter, yet the software itself doesn't become any simpler. On the contrary, software projects increase in complexity. Thus, we need a way to tame the beast and simplify the software supply chain.

Also, every day, we hear that cyber-attacks are on the rise. Many well-known companies are and have been affected by security breaches. Highly sensitive customer data gets stolen during such events, such as social security numbers, credit card information, and more. But not only customer data is compromised – sensitive company secrets are stolen too.

Containers can help in many ways. First of all, Gartner found that applications running in a container are more secure than their counterparts not running in a container. Containers use Linux security primitives such as Linux kernel *namespaces* to sandbox different applications running on the same computers and **control groups** (**cgroups**) in order to avoid the noisy-neighbor problem, where one bad application is using all the available resources of a server and starving all other applications.

Due to the fact that container images are immutable, it is easy to have them scanned for **common vulnerabilities and exposures** (**CVEs**), and in doing so, increase the overall security of our applications.

Another way to make our software supply chain more secure is to have our containers use a content trust. A content trust basically ensures that the author of a container image is who they pretend to be and that the consumer of the container image has a guarantee that the image has not been tampered with in transit. The latter is known as a **man-in-the-middle** (**MITM**) attack.

Everything I have just said is, of course, technically also possible without using containers, but since containers introduce a globally accepted standard, they make it so much easier to implement these best practices and enforce them.

OK, but security is not the only reason why containers are important. There are other reasons too.

One is the fact that containers make it easy to simulate a production-like environment, even on a developer's laptop. If we can containerize any application, then we can also containerize, say, a database such as Oracle or MS SQL Server. Now, everyone who has ever had to install an Oracle database on a computer knows that this is not the easiest thing to do, and it takes up a lot of precious space on your computer. You wouldn't want to do that to your development laptop just to test whether the application you developed really works end-to-end. With containers at hand, we can run a full-blown relational database in a container as easily as saying 1, 2, 3. And when we're done with testing, we can just stop and delete the container and the database will be gone, without leaving a trace on our computer.

Since containers are very lean compared to VMs, it is not uncommon to have many containers running at the same time on a developer's laptop without overwhelming the laptop.

A third reason why containers are important is that operators can finally concentrate on what they are really good at: provisioning the infrastructure and running and monitoring applications in production. When the applications they have to run on a production system are all containerized, then operators can start to standardize their infrastructure. Every server becomes just another Docker host. No special libraries or frameworks need to be installed on those servers, just an OS and a container runtime such as Docker.

Also, operators do not have to have intimate knowledge of the internals of applications anymore, since those applications run self-contained in containers that ought to look like black boxes to them, similar to how shipping containers look to the personnel in the transportation industry.

What's the benefit for me or for my company?

Somebody once said that, today, every company of a certain size has to acknowledge that they need to be a software company. In this sense, a modern bank is a software company that happens to specialize in the business of finance. Software runs all businesses, period. As every company becomes a software company, there is a need to establish a software supply chain. For the company to remain competitive, their software supply chain has to be secure and efficient. Efficiency can be achieved through thorough automation and standardization. But in all three areas – security, automation, and standardization – containers have been shown to shine. Large and well-known enterprises have reported that, when containerizing existing legacy applications (many call them traditional applications) and establishing a fully automated software supply chain based on containers, they can reduce the cost for the maintenance of those mission-critical applications by a factor of 50% to 60% and they can reduce the time between new releases of these traditional applications by up to 90%.

That being said, the adoption of container technologies saves these companies a lot of money, and at the same time it speeds up the development process and reduces the time to market.

The Moby project

Originally, when Docker (the company) introduced Docker containers, everything was open source. Docker didn't have any commercial products at this time. The Docker engine that the company developed was a monolithic piece of software. It contained many logical parts, such as the container runtime, a network library, a **RESTful (REST)** API, a command-line interface, and much more.

Other vendors or projects such as Red Hat or Kubernetes were using the Docker engine in their own products, but most of the time, they were only using part of its functionality. For example, Kubernetes did not use the Docker network library for the Docker engine but provided its own way of networking. Red Hat, in turn, did not update the Docker engine frequently and preferred to apply unofficial patches to older versions of the Docker engine, yet they still called it the Docker engine.

Out of all these reasons, and many more, the idea emerged that Docker had to do something to clearly separate the Docker open source part from the Docker commercial part. Furthermore, the company wanted to prevent competitors from using and abusing the name Docker for their own gains. This was the main reason why the Moby project was born. It serves as an umbrella for most of the open source components Docker developed and continues to develop. These open source projects do not carry the name Docker in them anymore.

The Moby project provides components that are used for image management, secret management, configuration management, and networking and provisioning, to name just a few. Also, part of the Moby project is special Moby tools that are, for example, used to assemble components into runnable artifacts.

Some components that technically belong to the Moby project have been donated by Docker to the Cloud-Native Computing Foundation (CNCF) and thus do not appear in the list of components anymore. The most prominent ones are `notary`, `containerd`, and `runc`, where the first is used for content trust and the latter two form the container runtime.

Docker products

Docker currently separates its product lines into two segments. There is the **Community Edition (CE)**, which is closed-source yet completely free, and then there is the **Enterprise Edition (EE)**, which is also closed-source and needs to be licensed on a yearly basis. These enterprise products are backed by 24/7 support and are supported by bug fixes.

Docker CE

Part of the Docker Community Edition are products such as the Docker Toolbox and Docker for Desktop with its editions for Mac and Windows. All these products are mainly targeted at developers.

Docker for Desktop is an easy-to-install desktop application that can be used to build, debug, and test Dockerized applications or services on a macOS or Windows machine. Docker for macOS and Docker for Windows are complete development environments that are deeply integrated with their respective hypervisor framework, network, and filesystem. These tools are the fastest and most reliable way to run Docker on a Mac or Windows.

Under the CE umbrella, there are also two products that are more geared toward operations engineers. These products are Docker for Azure and Docker for AWS.

For example, with Docker for Azure, which is a native Azure application, you can set up Docker in a few clicks, optimized for and integrated with underlying Azure **Infrastructure as a Service (IaaS)** services. It helps operations engineers accelerate time to productivity when building and running Docker applications in Azure.

Docker for AWS works very similarly but for Amazon's cloud.

Docker EE

The Docker Enterprise Edition consists of the **Universal Control Plane (UCP)** and the **Docker Trusted Registry (DTR)**, both of which run on top of Docker Swarm. Both are swarm applications. Docker EE builds on top of the upstream components of the Moby project and adds enterprise-grade features such as **role-based access control (RBAC)**, multi-tenancy, mixed clusters of Docker swarm and Kubernetes, web-based UI, and content trust, as well as image scanning on top.

Container architecture

Now, let's discuss how a system that can run Docker containers is designed at a high level. The following diagram illustrates what a computer that Docker has been installed on looks like. Note that a computer that has Docker installed on it is often called a Docker host because it can run or host Docker containers:

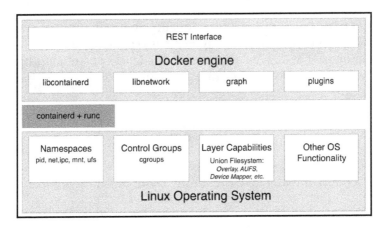

High-level architecture diagram of the Docker engine

In the preceding diagram, we can see three essential parts:

- On the bottom, we have the **Linux operating system**
- In the middle, in dark gray, we have the container runtime
- On the top, we have the **Docker engine**

Containers are only possible due to the fact that the Linux OS provides some primitives, such as namespaces, control groups, layer capabilities, and more, all of which are leveraged in a very specific way by the container runtime and the Docker engine. Linux kernel namespaces, such as **process ID (pid)** namespaces or **network (net)** namespaces, allow Docker to encapsulate or sandbox processes that run inside the container. **Control Groups** make sure that containers cannot suffer from the noisy-neighbor syndrome, where a single application running in a container can consume most or all of the available resources of the whole Docker host. **Control Groups** allow Docker to limit the resources, such as CPU time or the amount of RAM, that each container is allocated.

The container runtime on a Docker host consists of `containerd` and `runc`. `runc` is the low-level functionality of the container runtime, while `containerd`, which is based on `runc`, provides higher-level functionality. Both are open source and have been donated by Docker to the CNCF.

The container runtime is responsible for the whole life cycle of a container. It pulls a container image (which is the template for a container) from a registry if necessary, creates a container from that image, initializes and runs the container, and eventually stops and removes the container from the system when asked.

The **Docker engine** provides additional functionality on top of the container runtime, such as network libraries or support for plugins. It also provides a REST interface over which all container operations can be automated. The Docker command-line interface that we will use frequently in this book is one of the consumers of this REST interface.

Summary

In this chapter, we looked at how containers can massively reduce friction in the software supply chain and, on top of that, make the supply chain much more secure.

In the next chapter, we will learn how to prepare our personal or working environment such as that we can work efficiently and effectively with Docker. So, stay tuned.

Questions

Please answer the following questions to assess your learning progress:

1. Which statements are correct (multiple answers are possible)?

    A. A container is kind of a lightweight VM
    B. A container only runs on a Linux host
    C. A container can only run one process
    D. The main process in a container always has PID 1
    E. A container is one or more processes encapsulated by Linux namespaces and restricted by cgroups

2. In your own words, maybe by using analogies, explain what a container is.
3. Why are containers considered to be a game-changer in IT? Name three or four reasons.
4. What does it mean when we claim: *If a container runs on a given platform, then it runs anywhere...?* Name two to three reasons why this is true.
5. Docker containers are only really useful for modern greenfield applications based on microservices. Please justify your answer.

    A. True
    B. False

6. How much does a typical enterprise save when containerizing its legacy applications?

    A. 20%
    B. 33%
    C. 50%
    D. 75%

7. Which two core concepts of Linux are containers based on?

Further reading

The following is a list of links that lead to more detailed information regarding the topics we discussed in this chapter:

- Docker overview: `https://docs.docker.com/engine/docker-overview/`
- The Moby project: `https://mobyproject.org/`
- Docker products: `https://www.docker.com/get-started`
- Cloud-Native Computing Foundation: `https://www.cncf.io/`
- containerd – an industry-standard container runtime: `https://containerd.io/`

Setting Up a Working Environment

In the last chapter, we learned what Docker containers are and why they're important. We learned what kinds of problems containers solve in a modern software supply chain.

In this chapter, we are going to prepare our personal or working environment to work efficiently and effectively with Docker. We will discuss in detail how to set up an ideal environment for developers, DevOps, and operators that can be used when working with Docker containers.

This chapter covers the following topics:

- The Linux command shell
- PowerShell for Windows
- Installing and using a package manager
- Installing Git and cloning the code repository
- Choosing and installing a code editor
- Installing Docker for Desktop on macOS or Windows
- Installing Docker Toolbox
- Installing Minikube

Technical requirements

For this chapter, you will need a laptop or a workstation with either macOS or Windows, preferably Windows 10 Professional, installed. You should also have free internet access to download applications and permission to install those applications on your laptop.

It is also possible to follow along with this book if you have a Linux distribution as your operating system, such as Ubuntu 18.04 or newer. I will try to indicate where commands and samples differ significantly from the ones on macOS or Windows.

The Linux command shell

Docker containers were first developed on Linux for Linux. It is hence natural that the primary command-line tool used to work with Docker, also called a shell, is a Unix shell; remember, Linux derives from Unix. Most developers use the Bash shell. On some lightweight Linux distributions, such as Alpine, Bash is not installed and consequently one has to use the simpler Bourne shell, just called *sh*. Whenever we are working in a Linux environment, such as inside a container or on a Linux VM, we will use either /bin/bash or /bin/sh, depending on their availability.

Although Apple's macOS X is not a Linux OS, Linux and macOS X are both flavors of Unix and hence support the same set of tools. Among those tools are the shells. So, when working on macOS, you will probably be using the Bash shell.

In this book, we expect from you a familiarity with the most basic scripting commands in Bash and PowerShell, if you are working on Windows. If you are an absolute beginner, then we strongly recommend that you familiarize yourself with the following cheat sheets:

- *Linux Command Line Cheat Sheet* by Dave Child at http://bit.ly/2mTQr81
- *PowerShell Basic Cheat Sheet* at http://bit.ly/2EPHxze

PowerShell for Windows

On a Windows computer, laptop, or server, we have multiple command-line tools available. The most familiar is the command shell. It has been available on any Windows computer for decades. It is a very simple shell. For more advanced scripting, Microsoft has developed PowerShell. PowerShell is very powerful and very popular among engineers working on Windows. On Windows 10, finally, we have the so-called *Windows Subsystem for Linux*, which allows us to use any Linux tool, such as the Bash or Bourne shells. Apart from this, there are also other tools that install a Bash shell on Windows, for example, the Git Bash shell. In this book, all commands will use Bash syntax. Most of the commands also run in PowerShell.

Our recommendation for you is hence to either use PowerShell or any other Bash tool to work with Docker on Windows.

Using a package manager

The easiest way to install software on a macOS or Windows laptop is to use a good package manager. On macOS, most people use Homebrew, and on Windows, Chocolatey is a good choice. If you're using a Debian-based Linux distribution such as Ubuntu, then the package manager of choice for most is `apt`, which is installed by default.

Installing Homebrew on macOS

Homebrew is the most popular package manager on macOS, and it is easy to use and very versatile. Installing Homebrew on macOS is simple; just follow the instructions at `https://brew.sh/`:

1. In a nutshell, open a new Terminal window and execute the following command to install Homebrew:

   ```
   $ /usr/bin/ruby -e "$(curl -fsSL
   https://raw.githubusercontent.com/Homebrew/install/master/install)"
   ```

2. Once the installation is finished, test whether Homebrew is working by entering `brew --version` in the Terminal. You should see something like this:

   ```
   $ brew --version
   Homebrew 2.1.4
   Homebrew/homebrew-core (git revision 77d1b; last commit 2019-06-07)
   ```

3. Now, we are ready to use Homebrew to install tools and utilities. If we, for example, want to install the Vi text editor, we can do so like this:

```
$ brew install vim
```

This will then download and install the editor for you.

Installing Chocolatey on Windows

Chocolatey is a popular package manager for Windows, built on PowerShell. To install the Chocolatey package manager, please follow the instructions at https:// chocolatey.org/ or open a new PowerShell window in admin mode and execute the following command:

```
PS> Set-ExecutionPolicy Bypass -Scope Process -Force; iex ((New-Object
System.Net.WebClient).DownloadString('https://chocolatey.org/install.ps1'))
```

It is important to run the preceding command as an administrator, otherwise, the installation will not succeed.

1. Once Chocolatey is installed, test it with the `choco --version` command. You should see output similar to the following:

```
PS> choco --version
0.10.15
```

2. To install an application such as the Vi editor, use the following command:

```
PS> choco install -y vim
```

The `-y` parameter makes sure that the installation happens without asking for reconfirmation.

Please note that once Chocolatey has installed an application, you need to open a new PowerShell window to use that application.

Installing Git

We are using Git to clone the sample code accompanying this book from its GitHub repository. If you already have Git installed on your computer, you can skip this section:

1. To install Git on your macOS, use the following command in a Terminal window:

   ```
   $ choco install git
   ```

2. To install Git on Windows, open a PowerShell window and use Chocolatey to install it:

   ```
   PS> choco install git -y
   ```

3. Finally, on your Debian or Ubuntu machine, open a Bash console and execute the following command:

   ```
   $ sudo apt update && sudo apt install -y git
   ```

4. Once Git is installed, verify that it is working. On all platforms, use the following:

   ```
   $ git --version
   ```

   This should output something along the lines of the following:

   ```
   git version 2.16.3
   ```

5. Now that Git is working, we can clone the source code accompanying this book from GitHub. Execute the following command:

   ```
   $ cd ~
   $ git clone
   https://github.com/PacktPublishing/Learn-Docker---Fundamentals-of-D
   ocker-19.x-Second-Edition fod-solution
   ```

   This will clone the content of the master branch into your local folder, ~/fod-solution. This folder will now contain all of the sample solutions for the labs we are going to do together in this book. Refer to these sample solutions if you get stuck.

Now that we have installed the basics, let's continue with the code editor.

Choosing a code editor

Using a good code editor is essential to working productively with Docker. Of course, which editor is the best is highly controversial and depends on your personal preference. A lot of people use Vim, or others such as Emacs, Atom, Sublime, or **Visual Studio Code** (**VS Code**), to just name a few. VS Code is a completely free and lightweight editor, yet it is very powerful and is available for macOS, Windows, and Linux. According to Stack Overflow, it is currently by far the most popular code editor. If you are not yet sold on another editor, I highly recommend that you give VS Code a try.

But if you already have a favorite code editor, then please continue using it. As long as you can edit text files, you're good to go. If your editor supports syntax highlighting for Dockerfiles and JSON and YAML files, then even better. The only exception will be Chapter 6, *Debugging Code Running in a Container*. The examples presented in that chapter will be heavily tailored toward VS Code.

Installing VS Code on macOS

Follow these steps for installation:

1. Open a new Terminal window and execute the following command:

    ```
    $ brew cask install visual-studio-code
    ```

2. Once VS Code has been installed successfully, navigate to your home directory (~) and create a folder, `fundamentals-of-docker`; then navigate into this new folder:

    ```
    $ mkdir ~/fundamentals-of-docker && cd ~/fundamentals-of-docker
    ```

3. Now open VS Code from within this folder:

    ```
    $ code .
    ```

Don't forget the period (.) in the preceding command. VS will start and open the current folder (`~/fundamentals-of-docker`) as the working folder.

Installing VS Code on Windows

Follow these steps for installation:

1. Open a new PowerShell window in admin mode and execute the following command:

   ```
   PS> choco install vscode -y
   ```

2. Close your PowerShell window and open a new one, to make sure VS Code is in your path.
3. Now navigate to your home directory and create a folder, fundamentals-of-docker; then navigate into this new folder:

   ```
   PS> mkdir ~\fundamentals-of-docker; cd ~\fundamentals-of-docker
   ```

4. Finally open Visual Studio Code from within this folder:

   ```
   PS> code .
   ```

Don't forget the period (.) in the preceding command. VS will start and open the current folder (~\fundamentals-of-docker) as the working folder.

Installing VS Code on Linux

Follow these steps for installation:

1. On your Debian or Ubuntu-based Linux machine, open a Bash Terminal and execute the following statement to install VS Code:

   ```
   $ sudo snap install --classic code
   ```

2. If you're using a Linux distribution that's not based on Debian or Ubuntu, then please follow the following link for more details: https://code.visualstudio.com/docs/setup/linux
3. Once VS Code has been installed successfully, navigate to your home directory (~) and create a folder, fundamentals-of-docker; then navigate into this new folder:

   ```
   $ mkdir ~/fundamentals-of-docker && cd ~/fundamentals-of-docker
   ```

4. Now open Visual Studio Code from within this folder:

   ```
   $ code .
   ```

Don't forget the period (.) in the preceding command. VS will start and open the current folder (~/fundamentals-of-docker) as the working folder.

Installing VS Code extensions

Extensions are what make VS Code such a versatile editor. On all three platforms, macOS, Windows, and Linux, you can install VS Code extensions the same way:

1. Open a Bash console (or PowerShell in Windows) and execute the following group of commands to install the most essential extensions we are going to use in the upcoming examples in this book:

```
code --install-extension vscjava.vscode-java-pack
code --install-extension ms-vscode.csharp
code --install-extension ms-python.python
code --install-extension ms-azuretools.vscode-docker
code --install-extension eamodio.gitlens
```

We are installing extensions that enable us to work with Java, C#, .NET, and Python much more productively. We're also installing an extension built to enhance our experience with Docker.

2. After the preceding extensions have been installed successfully, restart VS Code to activate the extensions. You can now click the extensions icon in the activity pane on the left-hand side of VS Code to see all of the installed extensions.

Next, let's install Docker for Desktop.

Installing Docker for Desktop

If you are using macOS or have Windows 10 Professional installed on your laptop, then we strongly recommend that you install Docker for Desktop. This platform gives you the best experience when working with containers.

 Docker for Desktop is not supported on Linux at this time. Please refer to the *Installing Docker CE on Linux* section for more details.

Note that older versions of Windows or Windows 10 Home edition cannot run Docker for Windows. Docker for Windows uses Hyper-V to run containers transparently in a VM but Hyper-V is not available on older versions of Windows; nor is it available in the Home edition of Windows 10. In this case, we recommend that you use Docker Toolbox instead, which we will describe in the next section.

Follow these steps:

1. No matter what OS you're using, navigate to the Docker start page at `https://www.docker.com/get-started`.

2. On the right-hand side of the loaded page, you'll find a big blue button saying **Download Desktop and Take a Tutorial**. Click this button and follow the instructions. You will be redirected to Docker Hub. If you don't have an account on Docker Hub yet, then create one. It is absolutely free, but you need an account to download the software. Otherwise, just log in.

3. Once you're logged in, look out for this on the page:

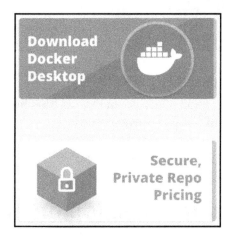

Download Docker Desktop on Docker Hub

4. Click the blue **Download Docker Desktop** button. You should then see a screen like the following:

Download screen for Docker for Desktop for macOS

 Note that if you're on a Windows PC, the blue button will say **Download Docker Desktop for Windows** instead.

Installing Docker for Desktop on macOS

Follow these steps for installation:

1. Once you have successfully installed Docker for Desktop for macOS, please open a Terminal window and execute the following command:

```
$ docker version
```

You should see something like this:

```
$ docker version
Client: Docker Engine - Community
 Version:           19.03.5
 API version:       1.40
 Go version:        go1.12.12
 Git commit:        633a0ea
 Built:             Wed Nov 13 07:22:37 2019
 OS/Arch:           windows/amd64
 Experimental:      false

Server: Docker Engine - Community
 Engine:
  Version:          19.03.5
  API version:      1.40 (minimum version 1.12)
  Go version:       go1.12.12
  Git commit:       633a0ea
  Built:            Wed Nov 13 07:29:19 2019
  OS/Arch:          linux/amd64
  Experimental:     false
 containerd:
  Version:          v1.2.10
  GitCommit:        b34a5c8af56e510852c35414db4c1f4fa6172339
 runc:
  Version:          1.0.0-rc8+dev
  GitCommit:        3e425f80a8c931f88e6d94a8c831b9d5aa481657
 docker-init:
  Version:          0.18.0
  GitCommit:        fec3683
```

Docker version on Docker for Desktop

2. To see whether you can run containers, enter the following command into the terminal window and hit *Enter*:

```
$ docker run hello-world
```

If all goes well, your output should look something like the following:

```
$ docker run hello-world
Unable to find image 'hello-world:latest' locally
latest: Pulling from library/hello-world
1b930d010525: Pull complete
Digest: sha256:0e11c388b664df8a27a901dce21eb89f11d8292f7fca1b3e3c4321bf7897bffe
Status: Downloaded newer image for hello-world:latest

Hello from Docker!
This message shows that your installation appears to be working correctly.

To generate this message, Docker took the following steps:
 1. The Docker client contacted the Docker daemon.
 2. The Docker daemon pulled the "hello-world" image from the Docker Hub.
    (amd64)
 3. The Docker daemon created a new container from that image which runs the
    executable that produces the output you are currently reading.
 4. The Docker daemon streamed that output to the Docker client, which sent it
    to your terminal.

To try something more ambitious, you can run an Ubuntu container with:
 $ docker run -it ubuntu bash

Share images, automate workflows, and more with a free Docker ID:
 https://hub.docker.com/

For more examples and ideas, visit:
 https://docs.docker.com/get-started/
```

Running Hello-World on Docker for Desktop for macOS

Next, we will install Docker on Windows.

Installing Docker for Desktop on Windows

Follow these steps for installation:

1. Once you have successfully installed Docker for Desktop for Windows, please open a PowerShell window and execute the following command:

```
PS> docker --version
Docker version 19.03.5, build 633a0ea
```

2. To see whether you can run containers, enter the following command into the PowerShell window and hit *Enter*:

```
PS> docker run hello-world
```

If all goes well, your output should look similar to the preceding figure.

Installing Docker CE on Linux

As mentioned earlier, Docker for Desktop is only available for macOS and Windows 10 Pro. If you're using a Linux machine, then you can use the Docker **Community Edition (CE)**, which consists of Docker Engine, plus a few additional tools, such as the Docker **Command Line Interface** (**CLI**) and `docker-compose`.

Please follow the instructions at the following link to install Docker CE for your particular Linux distribution—in this case, Ubuntu: `https://docs.docker.com/install/linux/docker-ce/ubuntu/`.

Installing Docker Toolbox

Docker Toolbox has been available for developers for a few years. It precedes newer tools such as Docker for Desktop. The Toolbox allows a user to work very elegantly with containers on any macOS or Windows computer. Containers must run on a Linux host. Neither Windows nor macOS can run containers natively. Hence, we need to run a Linux VM on our laptop, where we can then run our containers. Docker Toolbox installs VirtualBox on our laptop, which is used to run the Linux VMs we need.

As a Windows user, you might already be aware that there are so-called Windows containers that run natively on Windows, and you are right. Microsoft has ported Docker Engine to Windows and it is possible to run Windows containers directly on Windows Server 2016 or newer, without the need for a VM. So, now we have two flavors of containers, Linux containers and Windows containers. The former only runs on a Linux host and the latter only runs on a Windows server. In this book, we are exclusively discussing Linux containers, but most of the things we'll learn also apply to Windows containers.

If you are interested in Windows containers, we strongly recommend the book *Docker on Windows, Second Edition*: `https://www.packtpub.com/virtualization-and-cloud/docker-windows-second-edition`.

Let's start by installing the Docker Toolbox on a macOS.

Installing Docker Toolbox on macOS

Follow these steps for installation:

1. Open a new Terminal window and use Homebrew to install the toolbox:

   ```
   $ brew cask install docker-toolbox
   ```

   You should see something like this:

```
Updating Homebrew...
==> Auto-updated Homebrew!
Updated 1 tap (homebrew/core).
==> Updated Formulae
anyenv                   cointop                  hlint                    phpmyadmin
buildifier               dependency-check         jenkins

==> Satisfying dependencies
All Cask dependencies satisfied.
==> Downloading https://github.com/docker/toolbox/releases/download/v18.06.1-ce/DockerToolb
==> Downloading from https://github-production-release-asset-2e65be.s3.amazonaws.com/382749
######################################################################## 100.0%
==> Verifying SHA-256 checksum for Cask 'docker-toolbox'.
==> Installing Cask docker-toolbox
==> Running installer for docker-toolbox; your password may be necessary.
==> Package installers may write to any location; options such as --appdir are ignored.
Password:
installer: Package name is Docker Toolbox
installer: choices changes file '/var/folders/gr/mtd645cs3nxbtvszn7zfrvd40000gp/T/choices20
wtvmzm.xml' applied
installer: Installing at base path /
installer: The install was successful.
==> Changing ownership of paths required by docker-toolbox; your password may be necessary
🐳 docker-toolbox was successfully installed!
```

Installing Docker Toolbox on macOS

2. To verify that Docker Toolbox has been installed successfully, try to access `docker-machine` and `docker-compose`, two tools that are part of the installation:

```
$ docker-machine --version
docker-machine version 0.15.0, build b48dc28d
$ docker-compose --version
docker-compose version 1.22.0, build f46880f
```

Next, we will install Docker Toolbox on Windows.

Installing Docker Toolbox on Windows

Open a new Powershell window in admin mode and use Chocolatey to install Docker Toolbox:

```
PS> choco install docker-toolbox -y
```

The output should look similar to this:

```
  choco install docker-toolbox -y
Chocolatey v0.10.15
Installing the following packages:
docker-toolbox
By installing you accept licenses for the packages.
Progress: Downloading docker-toolbox 19.03.1... 100%

docker-toolbox v19.03.1 [Approved]
docker-toolbox package files install completed. Performing other installation steps.
Downloading docker-toolbox
  from 'https://github.com/docker/toolbox/releases/download/v19.03.1/DockerToolbox-19.03.1.exe'
Progress: 100% - Completed download of C:\Users\gnsch\AppData\Local\Temp\chocolatey\docker-toolbox\19.03.1\DockerToolbox-19.03.1.exe (231.29 MB).
Download of DockerToolbox-19.03.1.exe (231.29 MB) completed.
Hashes match.
Installing docker-toolbox...
docker-toolbox has been installed.
  docker-toolbox can be automatically uninstalled.
Environment Vars (like PATH) have changed. Close/reopen your shell to
 see the changes (or in powershell/cmd.exe just type 'refreshenv').
 The install of docker-toolbox was successful.
  Software installed to 'C:\Program Files\Docker Toolbox\'

Chocolatey installed 1/1 packages.
 See the log for details (C:\ProgramData\chocolatey\logs\chocolatey.log).

Enjoy using Chocolatey? Explore more amazing features to take your
experience to the next level at
 https://chocolatey.org/compare
```

Installing Docker Toolbox on Windows 10

We will now be setting up Docker Toolbox.

Setting up Docker Toolbox

Follow these steps for setup:

1. Let's use `docker-machine` to set up our environment. First, we list all Docker-ready VMs we have currently defined on our system. If you have just installed Docker Toolbox, you should see the following output:

List of all Docker-ready VMs

2. OK, we can see that there is a single VM called `default` installed, but it is currently in the STATE of `stopped`. Let's use `docker-machine` to start this VM so we can work with it:

   $ docker-machine start default

   This produces the following output:

```
$ docker-machine start default
Starting "default"...
(default) Check network to re-create if needed...
(default) Waiting for an IP...
Machine "default" was started.
Waiting for SSH to be available...
Detecting the provisioner...
Started machines may have new IP addresses. You may need to re-run the `docker-machine env` command.
$
```

Starting the default VM in Docker Toolbox

   If we now list the VMs again, we should see this:

Listing the running VMs in Docker Toolbox

The IP address used might be different in your case, but it will definitely be in the 192.168.0.0/24 range. We can also see that the VM has Docker version 18.06.1-ce installed.

3. If, for some reason, you don't have a default VM or you have accidentally deleted it, you can create it using the following command:

```
$ docker-machine create --driver virtualbox default
```

This will generate the following output:

```
$ docker-machine create --driver virtualbox default
Running pre-create checks...
(default) Default Boot2Docker ISO is out-of-date, downloading the latest release...
(default) Latest release for github.com/boot2docker/boot2docker is v18.09.6
(default) Downloading /Users/gabriel/.docker/machine/cache/boot2docker.iso from https://github.com/boot2d
ocker/boot2docker/releases/download/v18.09.6/boot2docker.iso...
(default) 0%....10%....20%....30%....40%....50%....60%....70%....80%....90%....100%
Creating machine...
(default) Copying /Users/gabriel/.docker/machine/cache/boot2docker.iso to /Users/gabriel/.docker/machine/
machines/default/boot2docker.iso...
(default) Creating VirtualBox VM...
(default) Creating SSH key...
(default) Starting the VM...
(default) Check network to re-create if needed...
(default) Waiting for an IP...
Waiting for machine to be running, this may take a few minutes...
Detecting operating system of created instance...
Waiting for SSH to be available...
Detecting the provisioner...
Provisioning with boot2docker...
Copying certs to the local machine directory...
Copying certs to the remote machine...
Setting Docker configuration on the remote daemon...
Checking connection to Docker...
Docker is up and running!
To see how to connect your Docker Client to the Docker Engine running on this virtual machine, run: docke
r-machine env default
$
```

Creating a new default VM in Docker Toolbox

If you carefully analyze the preceding output, you will see that docker-machine automatically downloaded the newest ISO file for the VM from Docker. It realized that my current version was outdated and replaced it with version v18.09.6.

4. To see how to connect your Docker client to the Docker Engine running on this virtual machine, run the following command:

```
$ docker-machine env default
```

This outputs the following:

```
export DOCKER_TLS_VERIFY="1"
export DOCKER_HOST="tcp://192.168.99.100:2376"
export
DOCKER_CERT_PATH="/Users/gabriel/.docker/machine/machines/default"
export DOCKER_MACHINE_NAME="default"
# Run this command to configure your shell:
# eval $(docker-machine env default)
```

5. We can execute the command listed on the last line in the preceding code snippet to configure our Docker CLI to use Docker running on the `default` VM:

```
$ eval $(docker-machine env default)
```

6. And now we can execute the first Docker command:

```
$ docker version
```

This should result in the following output:

```
$ docker version
Client:
 Version:           18.06.1-ce
 API version:       1.38
 Go version:        go1.10.3
 Git commit:        e68fc7a
 Built:             Tue Aug 21 17:21:31 2018
 OS/Arch:           darwin/amd64
 Experimental:      false

Server: Docker Engine - Community
 Engine:
  Version:          18.09.6
  API version:      1.39 (minimum version 1.12)
  Go version:       go1.10.8
  Git commit:       481bc77
  Built:            Sat May  4 02:41:08 2019
  OS/Arch:          linux/amd64
  Experimental:     false
$
```

Output of docker version

We have two parts here, the client and the server part. The client is the CLI running directly on your macOS or Windows laptop, while the server part is running on the `default` VM in VirtualBox.

7. Now, let's try to run a container:

```
$ docker run hello-world
```

This will produce the following output:

```
$ docker run hello-world
Unable to find image 'hello-world:latest' locally
latest: Pulling from library/hello-world
1b930d010525: Pull complete
Digest: sha256:0e11c388b664df8a27a901dce21eb89f11d8292f7fca1b3e3c4321bf7897bffe
Status: Downloaded newer image for hello-world:latest

Hello from Docker!
This message shows that your installation appears to be working correctly.

To generate this message, Docker took the following steps:
 1. The Docker client contacted the Docker daemon.
 2. The Docker daemon pulled the "hello-world" image from the Docker Hub.
    (amd64)
 3. The Docker daemon created a new container from that image which runs the
    executable that produces the output you are currently reading.
 4. The Docker daemon streamed that output to the Docker client, which sent it
    to your terminal.

To try something more ambitious, you can run an Ubuntu container with:
 $ docker run -it ubuntu bash

Share images, automate workflows, and more with a free Docker ID:
 https://hub.docker.com/

For more examples and ideas, visit:
 https://docs.docker.com/get-started/
```

The preceding output confirms that Docker Toolbox is working as expected and can run containers.

Docker Toolbox is a great addition even when you normally use Docker for Desktop for your development with Docker. Docker Toolbox allows you to create multiple Docker hosts (or VMs) in VirtualBox and connect them to a cluster, on top of which you can run Docker Swarm or Kubernetes.

Installing Minikube

If you cannot use Docker for Desktop or, for some reason, you only have access to an older version of the tool that does not yet support Kubernetes, then it is a good idea to install Minikube. Minikube provisions a single-node Kubernetes cluster on your workstation and is accessible through `kubectl`, which is the command-line tool used to work with Kubernetes.

Installing Minikube on macOS and Windows

To install Minikube for macOS or Windows, navigate to the following link: `https://kubernetes.io/docs/tasks/tools/install-minikube/`.

Follow the instructions carefully. If you have Docker Toolbox installed, then you already have a hypervisor on your system since the Docker Toolbox installer also installed VirtualBox. Otherwise, I recommend that you install VirtualBox first.

If you have Docker for macOS or Windows installed, then you already have `kubectl` installed with it, so you can skip that step too. Otherwise, follow the instructions on the site.

Testing Minikube and kubectl

Once Minikube is successfully installed on your workstation, open a Terminal and test the installation. First, we need to start Minikube. Enter `minikube start` at the command line. This command may take a few minutes or so to complete. The output should look similar to the following:

```
minikube start
* minikube v1.8.1 on Microsoft Windows 10 Pro 10.0.19041 Build 19041
* Using the hyperv driver based on existing profile
* Downloading VM boot image ...
* Reconfiguring existing host ...
* Starting existing hyperv VM for "minikube" ...
E0311 10:10:48.463030   13336 config.go:71] Failed to preload container runtime Docker: copying file: sudo test -d \ &&
sudo scp -t \ && sudo touch -d "2020-03-11 08:27:52.0791109 +0100" \/preloaded.tar.lz4: Process exited with status 1
output: , falling back to caching images
* Preparing Kubernetes v1.17.3 on Docker 19.03.6 ...
* Launching Kubernetes ...
* Enabling addons: default-storageclass, storage-provisioner
* Done! kubectl is now configured to use "minikube"
```

Starting Minikube

Note, your output may look slightly different. In my case, I am running Minikube on a Windows 10 Pro computer. On a Mac notifications are quite different, but this doesn't matter here.

Now, enter `kubectl version` and hit *Enter* to see something like the following screenshot:

```
$ kubectl version
Client Version: version.Info{Major:"1", Minor:"17", GitVersion:"v1.17.1", GitCommit:"d224476cd0730baca2b6e357d144171ed74
192d6", GitTreeState:"clean", BuildDate:"2020-01-14T21:04:32Z", GoVersion:"go1.13.5", Compiler:"gc", Platform:"windows/a
md64"}
Server Version: version.Info{Major:"1", Minor:"17", GitVersion:"v1.17.3", GitCommit:"06ad960bfd03b39c8310aaf92d1e7c12ce6
18213", GitTreeState:"clean", BuildDate:"2020-02-11T18:07:13Z", GoVersion:"go1.13.6", Compiler:"gc", Platform:"linux/amd
64"}
```

Determining the version of the Kubernetes client and server

If the preceding command fails, for example, by timing out, then it could be that your `kubectl` is not configured for the right context. `kubectl` can be used to work with many different Kubernetes clusters. Each cluster is called a context. To find out which context `kubectl` is currently configured for, use the following command:

```
$ kubectl config current-context
minikube
```

The answer should be `minikube`, as shown in the preceding output. If this is not the case, use `kubectl config get-contexts` to list all contexts that are defined on your system and then set the current context to `minikube`, as follows:

```
$ kubectl config use-context minikube
```

The configuration for `kubectl`, where it stores the contexts, is normally found in `~/.kube/config`, but this can be overridden by defining an environment variable called `KUBECONFIG`. You might need to unset this variable if it is set on your computer.

For more in-depth information about how to configure and use Kubernetes contexts, consult the link at `https://kubernetes.io/docs/concepts/configuration/organize-cluster-access-kubeconfig/`.

Assuming Minikube and `kubectl` work as expected, we can now use `kubectl` to get information about the Kubernetes cluster. Enter the following command:

```
$ kubectl get nodes
NAME STATUS ROLES AGE VERSION
minikube Ready master 47d v1.17.3
```

Evidently, we have a cluster of one node, which in my case has Kubernetes `v1.17.3` installed on it.

Summary

In this chapter, we set up and configured our personal or working environment so that we can productively work with Docker containers. This equally applies for developers, DevOps, and operations engineers. In that context, we make sure that we use a good editor, have Docker for macOS or Docker for Windows installed, and can use `docker-machine` to create VMs in VirtualBox or Hyper-V, which we can then use to run and test containers.

In the next chapter, we're going to learn all of the important facts about containers. For example, we will explore how we can run, stop, list, and delete containers, but more than that, we will also dive deep into the anatomy of containers.

Questions

Based on your reading of this chapter, please answer the following questions:

1. What is `docker-machine` used for? Name three to four scenarios.
2. With Docker for Windows, you can develop and run Linux containers.

   A. True
   B. False

3. Why are good scripting skills (such as Bash or PowerShell) essential for the productive use of containers?
4. Name three to four Linux distributions on which Docker is certified to run.
5. Name all of the Windows versions on which you can run Windows containers.

Further reading

Consider the following links for further reading:

- *Chocolatey - The Package Manager for Windows* at `https://chocolatey.org/`
- *Install Docker Toolbox on Windows:* `https://dockr.ly/2nuZUkU`
- *Run Docker on Hyper-V with Docker Machine* at `http://bit.ly/2HGMPiI`
- *Developing inside a Container* at `https://code.visualstudio.com/docs/remote/containers`

2
Section 2: Containerization, from Beginner to Black Belt

In this section, you will master all the essential aspects of building, shipping, and running a single container.

This section comprises the following chapters:

- Chapter 3, *Mastering Containers*
- Chapter 4, *Creating and Managing Container Images*
- Chapter 5, *Data Volumes and Configuration*
- Chapter 6, *Debugging Code Running in Containers*
- Chapter 7, *Using Docker to Supercharge Automation*
- Chapter 8, *Advanced Docker Usage Scenarios*

3
Mastering Containers

In the previous chapter, you learned how to optimally prepare your working environment for the productive and frictionless use of Docker. In this chapter, we are going to get our hands dirty and learn everything that is important to know when working with containers. Here are the topics we're going to cover in this chapter:

- Running the first container
- Starting, stopping, and removing containers
- Inspecting containers
- Exec into a running container
- Attaching to a running container
- Retrieving container logs
- Anatomy of containers

After finishing this chapter, you will be able to do the following things:

- Run, stop, and delete a container based on an existing image, such as Nginx, BusyBox, or Alpine.
- List all containers on the system.
- Inspect the metadata of a running or stopped container.
- Retrieve the logs produced by an application running inside a container.
- Run a process such as /bin/sh in an already-running container.
- Attach a Terminal to an already-running container.
- Explain in your own words to an interested lay person the underpinnings of a container.

Technical requirements

For this chapter, you should have installed Docker for Desktop on your macOS or Windows PC. If you are on an older version of Windows or are using Windows 10 Home Edition, then you should have Docker Toolbox installed and ready to use. On macOS, use the Terminal application, and on Windows, a PowerShell or Bash console, to try out the commands you will be learning.

Running the first container

Before we start, we want to make sure that Docker is installed correctly on your system and ready to accept your commands. Open a new Terminal window and type in the following command:

```
$ docker version
```

If you are using Docker Toolbox then use the Docker Quickstart Terminal that has been installed with the Toolbox, instead of the Terminal on macOS or Powershell on Windows.

If everything works correctly, you should see the version of Docker client and server installed on your laptop output in the Terminal. At the time of writing, it looks like this (shortened for readability):

```
Client: Docker Engine - Community
 Version: 19.03.0-beta3
 API version: 1.40
 Go version: go1.12.4
 Git commit: c55e026
 Built: Thu Apr 25 19:05:38 2019
 OS/Arch: darwin/amd64
 Experimental: false

Server: Docker Engine - Community
 Engine:
 Version: 19.03.0-beta3
 API version: 1.40 (minimum version 1.12)
 Go version: go1.12.4
 Git commit: c55e026
 Built: Thu Apr 25 19:13:00 2019
 OS/Arch: linux/amd64
 ...
```

You can see that I have `beta3` of version `19.03.0` installed on my macOS.

If this doesn't work for you, then something with your installation is not right. Please make sure that you have followed the instructions in the previous chapter on how to install Docker for Desktop or Docker Toolbox on your system.

So, you're ready to see some action. Please type the following command into your Terminal window and hit *Return*:

```
$ docker container run alpine echo "Hello World"
```

When you run the preceding command the first time, you should see an output in your Terminal window similar to this:

```
Unable to find image 'alpine:latest' locally
latest: Pulling from library/alpine
e7c96db7181b: Pull complete
Digest:
sha256:769fddc7cc2f0a1c35abb2f91432e8beecf83916c421420e6a6da9f8975464b6
Status: Downloaded newer image for alpine:latest
Hello World
```

Now that was easy! Let's try to run the very same command again:

```
$ docker container run alpine echo "Hello World"
```

The second, third, or n^{th} time you run the preceding command, you should see only this output in your Terminal:

```
Hello World
```

Try to reason about why the first time you run a command you see a different output than all of the subsequent times. But don't worry if you can't figure it out; we will explain the reasons in detail in the following sections of this chapter.

Starting, stopping, and removing containers

You have successfully run a container in the previous section. Now, we want to investigate in detail what exactly happened and why. Let's look again at the command we used:

```
$ docker container run alpine echo "Hello World"
```

This command contains multiple parts. First and foremost, we have the word `docker`. This is the name of the Docker **Command-Line Interface (CLI)** tool, which we are using to interact with the Docker engine that is responsible to run containers. Next, we have the word `container`, which indicates the context we are working with. As we want to run a container, our context is the word `container`. Next is the actual command we want to execute in the given context, which is `run`.

Let me recap—so far, we have `docker container run`, which means, *Hey Docker, we want to run a container.*

Now we also need to tell Docker which container to run. In this case, this is the so-called `alpine` container.

> `alpine` is a minimal Docker image based on Alpine Linux with a complete package index and is only 5 MB in size.

Finally, we need to define what kind of process or task shall be executed inside the container when it is running. In our case, this is the last part of the command, `echo "Hello World"`.

Maybe the following screenshot can help you to get a better idea of the whole thing:

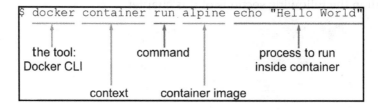

Anatomy of the docker container run expression

Now that we have understood the various parts of a command to run a container, let's try to run another container with a different process running inside it. Type the following command into your Terminal:

```
$ docker container run centos ping -c 5 127.0.0.1
```

You should see output in your Terminal window similar to the following:

```
Unable to find image 'centos:latest' locally
latest: Pulling from library/centos
8ba884070f61: Pull complete
Digest:
sha256:b5e66c4651870a1ad435cd75922fe2cb943c9e973a9673822d1414824a1d0475
Status: Downloaded newer image for centos:latest
PING 127.0.0.1 (127.0.0.1) 56(84) bytes of data.
64 bytes from 127.0.0.1: icmp_seq=1 ttl=64 time=0.104 ms
64 bytes from 127.0.0.1: icmp_seq=2 ttl=64 time=0.059 ms
64 bytes from 127.0.0.1: icmp_seq=3 ttl=64 time=0.081 ms
64 bytes from 127.0.0.1: icmp_seq=4 ttl=64 time=0.050 ms
64 bytes from 127.0.0.1: icmp_seq=5 ttl=64 time=0.055 ms
--- 127.0.0.1 ping statistics ---
5 packets transmitted, 5 received, 0% packet loss, time 4127ms
rtt min/avg/max/mdev = 0.050/0.069/0.104/0.022 ms
```

What changed is that this time, the container image we're using is `centos` and the process we're executing inside the `centos` container is `ping -c 5 127.0.0.1`, which pings the loopback address five times until it stops.

 `centos` is the official Docker image for CentOS Linux, which is a community-supported distribution derived from sources freely provided to the public by **Red Hat** for **Red Hat Enterprise Linux (RHEL)**.

Let's analyze the output in detail.

The first line is as follows:

```
Unable to find image 'centos:latest' locally
```

This tells us that Docker didn't find an image named `centos:latest` in the local cache of the system. So, Docker knows that it has to pull the image from some registry where container images are stored. By default, your Docker environment is configured so that images are pulled from Docker Hub at `docker.io`. This is expressed by the second line, as follows:

```
latest: Pulling from library/centos
```

The next three lines of output are as follows:

```
8ba884070f61: Pull complete
Digest:
sha256:b5e66c4651870a1ad435cd75922fe2cb943c9e973a9673822d1414824a1d0475
Status: Downloaded newer image for centos:latest
```

This tells us that Docker has successfully pulled the `centos:latest` image from Docker Hub.

All of the subsequent lines of the output are generated by the process we ran inside the container, which is the Ping tool in this case. If you have been attentive so far, then you might have noticed the `latest` keyword occurring a few times. Each image has a version (also called `tag`), and if we don't specify a version explicitly, then Docker automatically assumes it is `latest`.

If we run the preceding container again on our system, the first five lines of the output will be missing since, this time, Docker will find the container image cached locally and hence won't have to download it first. Try it out and verify what I just told you.

Running a random trivia question container

For the subsequent sections of this chapter, we need a container that runs continuously in the background and produces some interesting output. That's why we have chosen an algorithm that produces random trivia questions. The API that produces that free random trivia can be found at `http://jservice.io/`.

Now the goal is to have a process running inside a container that produces a new random trivia question every five seconds and outputs the question to `STDOUT`. The following script will do exactly that:

```
while :
do
  wget -qO- http://jservice.io/api/random | jq .[0].question
  sleep 5
done
```

Try it in a Terminal window. Stop the script by pressing *Ctrl + C*. The output should look similar to this:

```
"In 2004 Pitt alumna Wangari Maathai became the first woman from this
continent to win the Nobel Peace Prize"
"There are 86,400 of these in every day"
"For $5 million in 2013 an L.A. movie house became TCL Chinese Theatre, but
we bet many will still call it this, after its founder"
^C
```

Each response is a different trivia question.

 You may need to install jq first on your macOS or Windows computer. jq is a handy tool often used to nicely filter and format JSON output, which increases the readability of it on the screen.

Now, let's run this logic in an `alpine` container. Since this is not just a simple command, we want to wrap the preceding script in a script file and execute that one. To make things simpler, I have created a Docker image called `fundamentalsofdocker/trivia` that contains all of the necessary logic, so that we can just use it here. Later on, once we have introduced Docker images, we will analyze this container image further. For the moment, let's just use it as is. Execute the following command to run the container as a background service. In Linux, a background service is also called a daemon:

```
$ docker container run -d --name trivia fundamentalsofdocker/trivia:ed2
```

In the preceding expression, we have used two new command-line parameters, -d and --name. Now, -d tells Docker to run the process running in the container as a Linux daemon. The --name parameter, in turn, can be used to give the container an explicit name. In the preceding sample, the name we chose is `trivia`.

If we don't specify an explicit container name when we run a container, then Docker will automatically assign the container a random but unique name. This name will be composed of the name of a famous scientist and an adjective. Such names could be `boring_borg` or `angry_goldberg`. They're quite humorous, our Docker engineers, *aren't they?*

We are also using the tag ed2 for the container. This tag just tells us that this image has been created for the second edition of this book.

One important takeaway is that the container name has to be unique on the system. Let's make sure that the trivia container is up and running:

```
$ docker container ls -1
```

This should give us something like this (shortened for readability):

```
CONTAINER ID  IMAGE                            ... CREATED         STATUS
...
0ff3d7cf7634  fundamentalsofdocker/trivia:ed2  ... 11 seconds ago  Up 9
seconds ...
```

The important part of the preceding output is the STATUS column, which in this case is Up 9 seconds. That is, the container has been up and running for 9 seconds now.

Don't worry if the last Docker command is not yet familiar to you, we will come back to it in the next section.

To complete this section, let's stop and remove the trivia container with the following command:

```
$ docker rm -f trivia
```

Now it is time to learn how to list containers running or dangling on our system.

Listing containers

As we continue to run containers over time, we get a lot of them in our system. To find out what is currently running on our host, we can use the container ls command, as follows:

```
$ docker container ls
```

This will list all currently running containers. Such a list might look similar to this:

List of all containers running on the system

By default, Docker outputs seven columns with the following meanings:

Column	Description
Container ID	This is the unique ID of the container. It is an SHA-256.
Image	This is the name of the container image from which this container is instantiated.
Command	This is the command that is used to run the main process in the container.
Created	This is the date and time when the container was created.
Status	This is the status of the container (created, restarting, running, removing, paused, exited, or dead).
Ports	This is the list of container ports that have been mapped to the host.
Names	This is the name assigned to this container (multiple names are possible).

If we want to list not only the currently running containers but all containers that are defined on our system, then we can use the command-line parameter −a or −−all, as follows:

```
$ docker container ls -a
```

This will list containers in any state, such as `created`, `running`, or `exited`.

Sometimes, we want to just list the IDs of all containers. For this, we have the `-q` parameter:

```
$ docker container ls -q
```

You might wonder where this is useful. I will show you a command where it is very helpful right here:

```
$ docker container rm -f $(docker container ls -a -q)
```

Lean back and take a deep breath. Then, try to find out what the preceding command does. Don't read any further until you find the answer or give up.

The preceding command deletes all containers that are currently defined on the system, including the stopped ones. The `rm` command stands for remove, and it will be explained soon.

In the previous section, we used the `-l` parameter in the list command. Try to use Docker help to find out what the `-l` parameter stands for. You can invoke help for the list command as follows:

```
$ docker container ls -h
```

Next, let's learn how to stop and restart containers.

Stopping and starting containers

Sometimes, we want to (temporarily) stop a running container. Let's try this out with the trivia container we used previously:

1. Run the container again with this command:

   ```
   $ docker container run -d --name trivia
   fundamentalsofdocker/trivia:ed2
   ```

2. Now, if we want to stop this container, then we can do so by issuing this command:

   ```
   $ docker container stop trivia
   ```

When you try to stop the trivia container, you will probably note that it takes a while until this command is executed. To be precise, it takes about 10 seconds. *Why is this the case?*

Docker sends a Linux SIGTERM signal to the main process running inside the container. If the process doesn't react to this signal and terminate itself, Docker waits for 10 seconds and then sends SIGKILL, which will kill the process forcefully and terminate the container.

In the preceding command, we have used the name of the container to specify which container we want to stop. But we could have also used the container ID instead.

How do we get the ID of a container? There are several ways of doing so. The manual approach is to list all running containers and find the one that we're looking for in the list. From there, we copy its ID. A more automated way is to use some shell scripting and environment variables. If, for example, we want to get the ID of the trivia container, we can use this expression:

```
$ export CONTAINER_ID=$(docker container ls -a | grep trivia | awk '{print $1}')
```

 We are using the –a parameter with the Docker container ls command to list all containers, even the stopped ones. This is necessary in this case since we stopped the trivia container a moment ago.

Now, instead of using the container name, we can use the $CONTAINER_ID variable in our expression:

```
$ docker container stop $CONTAINER_ID
```

Once we have stopped the container, its status changes to Exited.

If a container is stopped, it can be started again using the docker container start command. Let's do this with our trivia container. It is good to have it running again, as we'll need it in the subsequent sections of this chapter:

```
$ docker container start trivia
```

It is now time to discuss what to do with stopped containers that we don't need anymore.

Removing containers

When we run the `docker container ls -a` command, we can see quite a few containers that are in the `Exited` status. If we don't need these containers anymore, then it is a good thing to remove them from memory; otherwise, they unnecessarily occupy precious resources. The command to remove a container is as follows:

```
$ docker container rm <container ID>
```

Another command to remove a container is the following:

```
$ docker container rm <container name>
```

Try to remove one of your exited containers using its ID.

Sometimes, removing a container will not work as it is still running. If we want to force a removal, no matter what the condition of the container currently is, we can use the command-line parameter `-f` or `--force`.

Inspecting containers

Containers are runtime instances of an image and have a lot of associated data that characterizes their behavior. To get more information about a specific container, we can use the `inspect` command. As usual, we have to provide either the container ID or name to identify the container of which we want to obtain the data. So, let's inspect our sample container:

```
$ docker container inspect trivia
```

The response is a big JSON object full of details. It looks similar to this:

```
[
    {
        "Id": "48630a3bf188...",
        ...
        "State": {
            "Status": "running",
            "Running": true,
            ...
        },
        "Image": "sha256:bbc92c8f014d605...",
        ...
        "Mounts": [],
        "Config": {
```

```
        "Hostname": "48630a3bf188",
        "Domainname": "",
        ...
    },
    "NetworkSettings": {
        "Bridge": "",
        "SandboxID": "82aed83429263ceb6e6e...",
        ...
    }
  }
]
```

The output has been shortened for readability.

Please take a moment to analyze what you got. You should see information such as the following:

- The ID of the container
- The creation date and time of the container
- The image from which the container is built

Many sections of the output, such as `Mounts` or `NetworkSettings`, don't make much sense right now, but we will certainly discuss those in the upcoming chapters of this book. The data you're seeing here is also named the metadata of a container. We will be using the `inspect` command quite often in the remainder of this book as a source of information.

Sometimes, we need just a tiny bit of the overall information, and to achieve this, we can either use the grep tool or a filter. The former method does not always result in the expected answer, so let's look into the latter approach:

```
$ docker container inspect -f "{{json .State}}" trivia | jq .
```

The `-f` or `--filter` parameter is used to define the filter. The filter expression itself uses the Go template syntax. In this example, we only want to see the state part of the whole output in the JSON format.

To nicely format the output, we pipe the result into the `jq` tool:

```
{
  "Status": "running",
  "Running": true,
  "Paused": false,
  "Restarting": false,
  "OOMKilled": false,
  "Dead": false,
  "Pid": 18252,
```

```
"ExitCode": 0,
"Error": "",
"StartedAt": "2019-06-16T13:30:15.776272Z",
"FinishedAt": "2019-06-16T13:29:38.6412298Z"
}
```

After we have learned how to retrieve loads of important and useful meta information about a container, we now want to investigate how we can execute it in a running container.

Exec into a running container

Sometimes, we want to run another process inside an already-running container. A typical reason could be to try to debug a misbehaving container. *How can we do this?* First, we need to know either the ID or the name of the container, and then we can define which process we want to run and how we want it to run. Once again, we use our currently running trivia container and we run a shell interactively inside it with the following command:

```
$ docker container exec -i -t trivia /bin/sh
```

The -i flag signifies that we want to run the additional process interactively, and -t tells Docker that we want it to provide us with a TTY (a Terminal emulator) for the command. Finally, the process we run is /bin/sh.

If we execute the preceding command in our Terminal, then we will be presented with a new prompt, /app #. We're now in a shell inside the trivia container. We can easily prove that by, for example, executing the ps command, which will list all running processes in the context:

```
/app # ps
```

The result should look somewhat similar to this:

```
/app # ps
PID    USER      TIME   COMMAND
   1 root       0:00 /bin/sh -c source script.sh
 618 root       0:00 /bin/sh
 654 root       0:00 sleep 5
 655 root       0:00 ps
```

List of processes running inside the trivia container

We can clearly see that the process with `PID 1` is the command that we have defined to run inside the trivia container. The process with `PID 1` is also named the main process.

Leave the container by pressing *Ctrl + D*. We cannot only execute additional processes interactive in a container. Please consider the following command:

```
$ docker container exec trivia ps
```

The output evidently looks very similar to the preceding output:

```
$ docker container exec trivia ps
PID   USER      TIME  COMMAND
    1 root      0:00  /bin/sh -c source script.sh
  760 root      0:00  sleep 5
  761 root      0:00  ps
$
```

List of processes running inside the trivia container

We can even run processes as a daemon using the −d flag and define environment variables using the −e flag variables, as follows:

```
$ docker container exec −it \
    −e MY_VAR="Hello World" \
    trivia /bin/sh
/app # echo $MY_VAR
Hello World
/app # <CTRL−d>
```

Great, we have learned how to execute into a running container and run additional processes. But there is another important way to mingle with a running container.

Attaching to a running container

We can use the `attach` command to attach our Terminal's standard input, output, and error (or any combination of the three) to a running container using the ID or name of the container. Let's do this for our trivia container:

```
$ docker container attach trivia
```

In this case, we will see every five seconds or so a new quote appearing in the output.

To quit the container without stopping or killing it, we can press the key combination *Ctrl + P+ Ctrl + Q*. This detaches us from the container while leaving it running in the background. On the other hand, if we want to detach and stop the container at the same time, we can just press *Ctrl + C*.

Let's run another container, this time an Nginx web server:

```
$ docker run -d --name nginx -p 8080:80 nginx:alpine
```

Here, we run the Alpine version of Nginx as a daemon in a container named `nginx`. The `-p 8080:80` command-line parameter opens port `8080` on the host for access to the Nginx web server running inside the container. Don't worry about the syntax here as we will explain this feature in more detail in Chapter 10, *Single-Host Networking*:

1. Let's see whether we can access Nginx using the `curl` tool and running this command:

   ```
   $ curl -4 localhost:8080
   ```

   If all works correctly, you should be greeted by the welcome page of Nginx (shortened for readability):

   ```
   <html>
   <head>
   <title>Welcome to nginx!</title>
   <style>
       body {
           width: 35em;
           margin: 0 auto;
           font-family: Tahoma, Verdana, Arial, sans-serif;
       }
   </style>
   </head>
   <body>
   <h1>Welcome to nginx!</h1>
   ...
   </html>
   ```

2. Now, let's attach our Terminal to the `nginx` container to observe what's happening:

   ```
   $ docker container attach nginx
   ```

3. Once you are attached to the container, you first will not see anything. But now open another Terminal, and in this new Terminal window, repeat the `curl` command a few times, for example, using the following script:

```
$ for n in {1..10}; do curl -4 localhost:8080; done
```

You should see the logging output of Nginx, which looks similar to this:

```
172.17.0.1 - - [16/Jun/2019:14:14:02 +0000] "GET / HTTP/1.1" 200
612 "-" "curl/7.54.0" "-"
172.17.0.1 - - [16/Jun/2019:14:14:02 +0000] "GET / HTTP/1.1" 200
612 "-" "curl/7.54.0" "-"
172.17.0.1 - - [16/Jun/2019:14:14:02 +0000] "GET / HTTP/1.1" 200
612 "-" "curl/7.54.0" "-"
...
```

4. Quit the container by pressing *Ctrl + C*. This will detach your Terminal and, at the same time, stop the `nginx` container.

5. To clean up, remove the `nginx` container with the following command:

```
$ docker container rm nginx
```

In the next section, we're going to learn how to work with container logs.

Retrieving container logs

It is a best practice for any good application to generate some logging information that developers and operators alike can use to find out what the application is doing at a given time, and whether there are any problems to help to pinpoint the root cause of the issue.

When running inside a container, the application should preferably output the log items to STDOUT and STDERR and not into a file. If the logging output is directed to STDOUT and STDERR, then Docker can collect this information and keep it ready for consumption by a user or any other external system:

1. To access the logs of a given container, we can use the `docker container logs` command. If, for example, we want to retrieve the logs of our `trivia` container, we can use the following expression:

```
$ docker container logs trivia
```

This will retrieve the whole log produced by the application from the very beginning of its existence.

 Stop, wait a second—this is not quite true, what I just said. By default, Docker uses the so-called `json-file` logging driver. This driver stores the logging information in a file. And if there is a file rolling policy defined, then `docker container logs` only retrieves what is in the current active log file and not what is in previous rolled files that might still be available on the host.

2. If we want to only get a few of the latest entries, we can use the `-t` or `--tail` parameter, as follows:

```
$ docker container logs --tail 5 trivia
```

This will retrieve only the last five items the process running inside the container produced.

Sometimes, we want to follow the log that is produced by a container. This is possible when using the `-f` or `--follow` parameter. The following expression will output the last five log items and then follow the log as it is produced by the containerized process:

```
$ docker container logs --tail 5 --follow trivia
```

Often using the default mechanism for container logging is not enough. We need a different way of logging. This is discussed in the following section.

Logging drivers

Docker includes multiple logging mechanisms to help us to get information from running containers. These mechanisms are named **logging drivers**. Which logging driver is used can be configured at the Docker daemon level. The default logging driver is `json-file`. Some of the drivers that are currently supported natively are as follows:

Driver	Description
none	No log output for the specific container is produced.
json-file	This is the default driver. The logging information is stored in files, formatted as JSON.
journald	If the journals daemon is running on the host machine, we can use this driver. It forwards logging to the `journald` daemon.

syslog	If the `syslog` daemon is running on the host machine, we can configure this driver, which will forward the log messages to the `syslog` daemon.
gelf	When using this driver, log messages are written to a **Graylog Extended Log Format** (**GELF**) endpoint. Popular examples of such endpoints are Graylog and Logstash.
fluentd	Assuming that the `fluentd` daemon is installed on the host system, this driver writes log messages to it.

 If you change the logging driver, please be aware that the `docker container logs` command is only available for the `json-file` and `journald` drivers.

Using a container-specific logging driver

We have seen that the logging driver can be set globally in the Docker daemon configuration file. But we can also define the logging driver on a container by container basis. In the following example, we are running a `busybox` container and use the `--log-driver` parameter to configure the `none` logging driver:

```
$ docker container run --name test -it \
    --log-driver none \
    busybox sh -c 'for N in 1 2 3; do echo "Hello $N"; done'
```

We should see the following:

```
Hello 1
Hello 2
Hello 3
```

Now, let's try to get the logs of the preceding container:

```
$ docker container logs test
```

The output is as follows:

```
Error response from daemon: configured logging driver does not support
reading
```

This is to be expected since the `none` driver does not produce any logging output. Let's clean up and remove the `test` container:

```
$ docker container rm test
```

Advanced topic – changing the default logging driver

Let's change the default logging driver of a Linux host:

1. The easiest way to do this is on a real Linux host. For this purpose, we're going to use Vagrant with an Ubuntu image:

```
$ vagrant init bento/ubuntu-17.04
$ vagrant up
$ vagrant ssh
```

 Vagrant is an open source tool developed by Hashicorp that is often used for building and maintaining portable virtual software development environments.

2. Once inside the Ubuntu VM, we want to edit the Docker daemon configuration file. Navigate to the `/etc/docker` folder and run `vi` as follows:

```
$ vi daemon.json
```

3. Enter the following content:

```
{
  "Log-driver": "json-log",
  "log-opts": {
    "max-size": "10m",
    "max-file": 3
  }
}
```

4. Save and exit `vi` by first pressing *Esc* and then typing `:w:q` and finally hitting the *Enter* key.

The preceding definition tells the Docker daemon to use the `json-log` driver with a maximum log file size of 10 MB before it is rolled, and the maximum number of log files that can be present on the system is 3 before the oldest file gets purged.

Now we have to send a `SIGHUP` signal to the Docker daemon so that it picks up the changes in the configuration file:

```
$ sudo kill -SIGHUP $(pidof dockerd)
```

Note that the preceding command only reloads the config file and does not restart the daemon.

Anatomy of containers

Many people wrongly compare containers to VMs. However, this is a questionable comparison. Containers are not just lightweight VMs. OK then, *what is the correct description of a container?*

Containers are specially encapsulated and secured processes running on the host system. Containers leverage a lot of features and primitives available in the Linux OS. The most important ones are *namespaces* and *cgroups*. All processes running in containers only share the same Linux kernel of the underlying host operating system. This is fundamentally different compared with VMs, as each VM contains its own full-blown operating system.

The startup times of a typical container can be measured in milliseconds, while a VM normally needs several seconds to minutes to start up. VMs are meant to be long-living. It is a primary goal of each operations engineer to maximize the uptime of their VMs. Contrary to that, containers are meant to be ephemeral. They come and go relatively quickly.

Let's first get a high-level overview of the architecture that enables us to run containers.

Architecture

Here, we have an architectural diagram on how this all fits together:

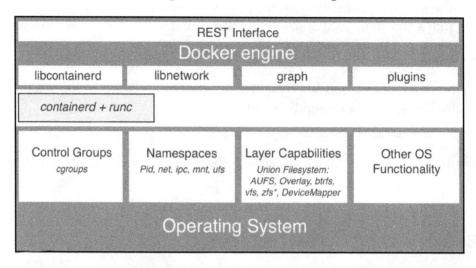

High-level architecture of Docker

In the lower part of the preceding diagram, we have the Linux operating system with its **cgroups**, **Namespaces**, and **Layer Capabilities** as well as **Other OS Functionality** that we do not need to explicitly mention here. Then, there is an intermediary layer composed of **containerd** and **runc**. On top of all that now sits the **Docker engine**. The **Docker engine** offers a RESTful interface to the outside world that can be accessed by any tool, such as the Docker CLI, Docker for macOS, and Docker for Windows or Kubernetes to name just a few.

Let's now describe the main building blocks in a bit more detail.

Namespaces

Linux namespaces had been around for years before they were leveraged by Docker for their containers. A namespace is an abstraction of global resources such as filesystems, network access, and process trees (also named PID namespaces) or the system group IDs and user IDs. A Linux system is initialized with a single instance of each namespace type. After initialization, additional namespaces can be created or joined.

The Linux namespaces originated in 2002 in the 2.4.19 kernel. In kernel version 3.8, user namespaces were introduced and with it, namespaces were ready to be used by containers.

If we wrap a running process, say, in a filesystem namespace, then this process has the illusion that it owns its own complete filesystem. This, of course, is not true; it is only a virtual filesystem. From the perspective of the host, the contained process gets a shielded subsection of the overall filesystem. It is like a filesystem in a filesystem:

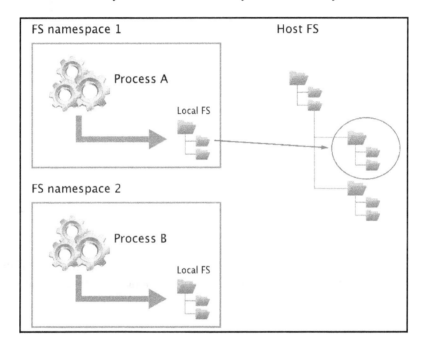

Filesystem namespaces on Linux

The same applies to all of the other global resources for which namespaces exist. The user ID namespace is another example. Having a user namespace, we can now define a jdoe user many times on the system as long as it is living in its own namespace.

The PID namespace is what keeps processes in one container from seeing or interacting with processes in another container. A process might have the apparent PID **1** inside a container, but if we examine it from the host system, it would have an ordinary PID, say **334**:

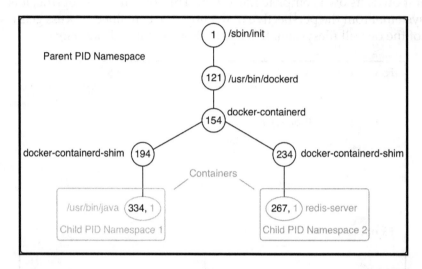

Process tree on a Docker host

In a given namespace, we can run one to many processes. That is important when we talk about containers, and we have experienced that already when we executed another process in an already-running container.

Control groups (cgroups)

Linux cgroups are used to limit, manage, and isolate resource usage of collections of processes running on a system. Resources are CPU time, system memory, network bandwidth, or combinations of these resources, and so on.

Engineers at Google originally implemented this feature in 2006. The cgroups functionality was merged into the Linux kernel mainline in kernel version 2.6.24, which was released in January 2008.

Using cgroups, administrators can limit the resources that containers can consume. With this, we can avoid, for example, the classical *noisy neighbor* problem, where a rogue process running in a container consumes all CPU time or reserves massive amounts of RAM and, as such, starves all of the other processes running on the host, whether they're containerized or not.

Union filesystem (Unionfs)

Unionfs forms the backbone of what is known as container images. We will discuss container images in detail in the next chapter. At this time, we want to just understand a bit better what Unionfs is, and how it works. Unionfs is mainly used on Linux and allows files and directories of distinct filesystems to be overlaid to form a single coherent filesystem. In this context, the individual filesystems are called branches. Contents of directories that have the same path within the merged branches will be seen together in a single merged directory, within the new virtual filesystem. When merging branches, the priority between the branches is specified. In that way, when two branches contain the same file, the one with the higher priority is seen in the final filesystem.

Container plumbing

The basement on top of which the Docker engine is built; is the **container plumbing** and is formed by two components, **runc** and **containerd**.

Originally, Docker was built in a monolithic way and contained all of the functionality necessary to run containers. Over time, this became too rigid and Docker started to break out parts of the functionality into their own components. Two important components are runc and containerd.

runC

runC is a lightweight, portable container runtime. It provides full support for Linux namespaces as well as native support for all security features available on Linux, such as SELinux, AppArmor, seccomp, and cgroups.

runC is a tool for spawning and running containers according to the **Open Container Initiative** (**OCI**) specification. It is a formally specified configuration format, governed by the **Open Container Project** (**OCP**) under the auspices of the Linux Foundation.

Containerd

runC is a low-level implementation of a container runtime; containerd builds on top of it and adds higher-level features, such as image transfer and storage, container execution, and supervision as well as network and storage attachments. With this, it manages the complete life cycle of containers. Containerd is the reference implementation of the OCI specifications and is by far the most popular and widely used container runtime.

Containerd was donated to and accepted by the CNCF in 2017. There exist alternative implementations of the OCI specification. Some of them are rkt by CoreOS, CRI-O by RedHat, and LXD by Linux Containers. However, containerd at this time is by far the most popular container runtime and is the default runtime of Kubernetes 1.8 or later and the Docker platform.

Summary

In this chapter, you learned how to work with containers that are based on existing images. We showed how to run, stop, start, and remove a container. Then, we inspected the metadata of a container, extracted the logs of it, and learned how to run an arbitrary process in an already-running container. Last but not least, we dug a bit deeper and investigated how containers work and what features of the underlying Linux operating system they leverage.

In the next chapter, you're going to learn what container images are and how we can build and share our own custom images. We'll also be discussing the best practices commonly used when building custom images, such as minimizing their size and leveraging the image cache. Stay tuned!

Questions

To assess your learning progress, please answer the following questions:

1. What are the states of a container?
2. Which command helps us to find out what is currently running on our Docker host?
3. Which command is used to list the IDs of all containers?

Further reading

The following articles give you some more information related to the topics we discussed in this chapter:

- Docker containers at `http://dockr.ly/2iLBV2I`
- Getting started with containers at `http://dockr.ly/2gmxKWB`
- Isolating containers with a user namespace at `http://dockr.ly/2gmyKdf`
- Limiting a container's resources at `http://dockr.ly/2wqN5Nn`

4
Creating and Managing Container Images

In the previous chapter, we learned what containers are and how to run, stop, remove, list, and inspect them. We extracted the logging information of some containers, ran other processes inside an already running container, and finally, we dived deep into the anatomy of containers. Whenever we ran a container, we created it using a container image. In this chapter, we will be familiarizing ourselves with these container images. We will learn in detail what they are, how to create them, and how to distribute them.

This chapter will cover the following topics:

- What are images?
- Creating images
- Lift and shift: Containerizing a legacy app
- Sharing or shipping images

After completing this chapter, you will be able to do the following:

- Name three of the most important characteristics of a container image.
- Create a custom image by interactively changing the container layer and committing it.
- Author a simple `Dockerfile` to generate a custom image.
- Export an existing image using `docker image save` and import it into another Docker host using `docker image load`.
- Write a two-step Dockerfile that minimizes the size of the resulting image by only including the resulting artifacts in the final image.

What are images?

In Linux, everything is a file. The whole operating system is basically a filesystem with files and folders stored on the local disk. This is an important fact to remember when looking at what container images are. As we will see, an image is basically a big tarball containing a filesystem. More specifically, it contains a layered filesystem.

The layered filesystem

Container images are templates from which containers are created. These images are not made up of just one monolithic block but are composed of many layers. The first layer in the image is also called the base layer. We can see this in the following graphic:

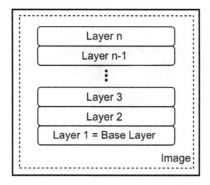

The image as a stack of layers

Each individual layer contains files and folders. Each layer only contains the changes to the filesystem with respect to the underlying layers. Docker uses a Union filesystem—as discussed in Chapter 3, *Mastering Containers* — to create a virtual filesystem out of the set of layers. A storage driver handles the details regarding the way these layers interact with each other. Different storage drivers are available that have advantages and disadvantages in different situations.

The layers of a container image are all immutable. Immutable means that once generated, the layer cannot ever be changed. The only possible operation affecting the layer is its physical deletion. This immutability of layers is important because it opens up a tremendous amount of opportunities, as we will see.

In the following screenshot, we can see what a custom image for a web application, using Nginx as a web server, could look like:

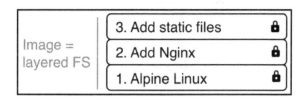

A sample custom image based on Alpine and Nginx

Our base layer here consists of the **Alpine Linux** distribution. Then, on top of that, we have an **Add Nginx** layer where Nginx is added on top of Alpine. Finally, the third layer contains all the files that make up the web application, such as HTML, CSS, and JavaScript files.

As has been said previously, each image starts with a base image. Typically, this base image is one of the official images found on Docker Hub, such as a Linux distro, Alpine, Ubuntu, or CentOS. However, it is also possible to create an image from scratch.

 Docker Hub is a public registry for container images. It is a central hub ideally suited for sharing public container images.

Each layer only contains the delta of changes in regard to the previous set of layers. The content of each layer is mapped to a special folder on the host system, which is usually a subfolder of `/var/lib/docker/`.

Since layers are immutable, they can be cached without ever becoming stale. This is a big advantage, as we will see.

The writable container layer

As we have discussed, a container image is made of a stack of immutable or read-only layers. When the Docker Engine creates a container from such an image, it adds a writable container layer on top of this stack of immutable layers. Our stack now looks as follows:

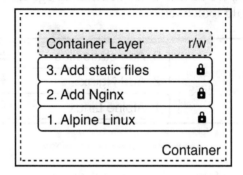

The writable container layer

The **Container Layer** is marked as read/write. Another advantage of the immutability of image layers is that they can be shared among many containers created from this image. All that is needed is a thin, writable container layer for each container, as shown in the following screenshot:

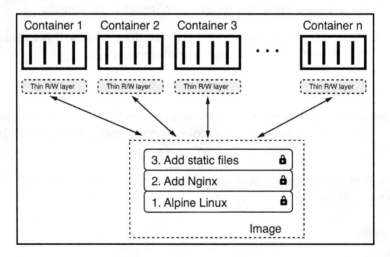

Multiple containers sharing the same image layers

This technique, of course, results in a tremendous reduction in the resources that are consumed. Furthermore, this helps to decrease the loading time of a container since only a thin container layer has to be created once the image layers have been loaded into memory, which only happens for the first container.

Copy-on-write

Docker uses the copy-on-write technique when dealing with images. Copy-on-write is a strategy for sharing and copying files for maximum efficiency. If a layer uses a file or folder that is available in one of the low-lying layers, then it just uses it. If, on the other hand, a layer wants to modify, say, a file from a low-lying layer, then it first copies this file up to the target layer and then modifies it. In the following screenshot, we can see a glimpse of what this means:

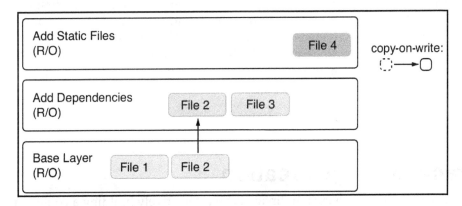

Docker image using copy-on-write

The second layer wants to modify **File 2**, which is present in the **Base Layer**. Thus, it copies it up and then modifies it. Now, let's say that we're sitting in the top layer of the preceding screenshot. This layer will use **File 1** from the **Base Layer** and **File 2** and **File 3** from the second layer.

Graph drivers

Graph drivers are what enable the Union filesystem. Graph drivers are also called storage drivers and are used when dealing with layered container images. A graph driver consolidates multiple image layers into a root filesystem for the mount namespace of the container. Or, put differently, the driver controls how images and containers are stored and managed on the Docker host.

Docker supports several different graph drivers using a pluggable architecture. The preferred driver is `overlay2`, followed by `overlay`.

Creating images

There are three ways to create a new container image on your system. The first one is by interactively building a container that contains all the additions and changes one desires, and then committing those changes into a new image. The second, and most important, way is to use a `Dockerfile` to describe what's in the new image, and then build the image using that `Dockerfile` as a manifest. Finally, the third way of creating an image is by importing it into the system from a tarball.

Now, let's look at these three ways in detail.

Interactive image creation

The first way we can create a custom image is by interactively building a container. That is, we start with a base image that we want to use as a template and run a container of it interactively. Let's say that this is the Alpine image.

To interactively create an image follow along:

1. The command to run the container would be as follows:

    ```
    $ docker container run -it \
        --name sample \
        alpine:3.10 /bin/sh
    ```

    The preceding command runs a container based on the `alpine:3.10` image.

    We run the container interactively with an attached **teletypewriter** (**TTY**) using the `-it` parameter, name it `sample` with the `--name` parameter, and—finally—run a shell inside the container using `/bin/sh`.

In the Terminal window where you run the preceding command, you should see something similar to this:

```
Unable to find image 'alpine:3.10' locally
3.10: Pulling from library/alpine
921b31ab772b: Pull complete
Digest:
sha256:ca1c944a4f8486a153024d9965aafbe24f5723c1d5c02f4964c045a16d19
dc54
Status: Downloaded newer image for alpine:3.10
/ #
```

By default, the alpine container does not have the ping tool installed. Let's assume we want to create a new custom image that has ping installed.

2. Inside the container, we can then run the following command:

    / # apk update && apk add iputils

    This uses the apk Alpine package manager to install the iputils library, of which ping is a part. The output of the preceding command should look approximately like this:

```
/ # apk update && apk add iputils
fetch http://dl-cdn.alpinelinux.org/alpine/v3.10/main/x86_64/APKINDEX.tar.gz
fetch http://dl-cdn.alpinelinux.org/alpine/v3.10/community/x86_64/APKINDEX.tar.gz
v3.10.0-9-gf0bd10f20b [http://dl-cdn.alpinelinux.org/alpine/v3.10/main]
v3.10.0-8-gf1f49be1c7 [http://dl-cdn.alpinelinux.org/alpine/v3.10/community]
OK: 10327 distinct packages available
(1/2) Installing libcap (2.27-r0)
(2/2) Installing iputils (20180629-r1)
Executing busybox-1.30.1-r2.trigger
OK: 6 MiB in 16 packages
/ #
```

Installing ping on Alpine

3. Now, we can indeed use `ping`, as the following code snippet shows:

```
/ # ping -c 3 127.0.0.1
PING 127.0.0.1 (127.0.0.1) 56(84) bytes of data.
64 bytes from 127.0.0.1: icmp_seq=1 ttl=64 time=0.057 ms
64 bytes from 127.0.0.1: icmp_seq=2 ttl=64 time=0.064 ms
64 bytes from 127.0.0.1: icmp_seq=3 ttl=64 time=0.063 ms

--- 127.0.0.1 ping statistics ---
3 packets transmitted, 3 received, 0% packet loss, time 98ms
rtt min/avg/max/mdev = 0.057/0.061/0.064/0.007 ms
/ #
```

Using ping from within the container

4. Once we have finished our customization, we can quit the container by typing `exit` at the prompt.

   If we now list all containers with the `ls -a` Docker container, we can see that our sample container has a status of `Exited`, but still exists on the system, as shown in the following code block:

```
$ docker container ls -a | grep sample
040fdfe889a6 alpine:3.10 "/bin/sh" 8 minutes ago Exited (0) 4
seconds ago
```

5. If we want to see what has changed in our container in relation to the base image, we can use the `docker container diff` command, as follows:

```
$ docker container diff sample
```

   The output should present a list of all modifications done on the filesystem of the container, as follows:

```
C /usr
C /usr/sbin
A /usr/sbin/getcap
A /usr/sbin/ipg
A /usr/sbin/tftpd
A /usr/sbin/ninfod
A /usr/sbin/rdisc
A /usr/sbin/rarpd
A /usr/sbin/tracepath
...
A /var/cache/apk/APKINDEX.d8b2a6f4.tar.gz
A /var/cache/apk/APKINDEX.00740ba1.tar.gz
```

```
C /bin
C /bin/ping
C /bin/ping6
A /bin/traceroute6
C /lib
C /lib/apk
C /lib/apk/db
C /lib/apk/db/scripts.tar
C /lib/apk/db/triggers
C /lib/apk/db/installed
```

We have shortened the preceding output for better readability. In the list, A stands for *added*, and C stands for *changed*. If we had any deleted files, then those would be prefixed with a D.

6. We can now use the `docker container commit` command to persist our modifications and create a new image from them, like this:

```
$ docker container commit sample my-alpine
sha256:44bca4141130ee8702e8e8efd1beb3cf4fe5aadb62a0c69a6995afd49c2e
7419
```

With the preceding command, we have specified that the new image will be called `my-alpine`. The output generated by the preceding command corresponds to the ID of the newly generated image.

7. We can verify this by listing all images on our system, as follows:

```
$ docker image ls
```

We can see this image ID (shortened) as follows:

```
REPOSITORY     TAG       IMAGE ID       CREATED              SIZE
my-alpine      latest    44bca4141130   About a minute ago   7.34MB
...
```

We can see that the image named `my-alpine` has the expected ID of `44bca4141130` and automatically got a `latest` tag assigned. This happens since we did not explicitly define a tag ourselves. In this case, Docker always defaults to the `latest` tag.

8. If we want to see how our custom image has been built, we can use the `history` command as follows:

    `$ docker image history my-alpine`

    This will print a list of the layers our image consists of, as follows:

```
$ docker image history my-alpine
IMAGE              CREATED              CREATED BY                                          SIZE
ea57e53a92e5       5 minutes ago        /bin/sh                                             1.76MB
4d90542f0623       10 days ago          /bin/sh -c #(nop)  CMD ["/bin/sh"]                  0B
<missing>          10 days ago          /bin/sh -c #(nop) ADD file:fef3b00b3ae63967d…       5.58MB
$
```

History of the my-alpine Docker image

The first layer in the preceding output is the one that we just created by adding the `iputils` package.

Using Dockerfiles

Manually creating custom images, as shown in the previous section of this chapter, is very helpful when doing exploration, creating prototypes, or authoring feasibility studies. But it has a serious drawback: it is a manual process and thus is not repeatable or scalable. It is also as error-prone as any other task executed manually by humans. There must be a better way.

This is where the so-called `Dockerfile` comes into play. A `Dockerfile` is a text file that is usually literally called `Dockerfile`. It contains instructions on how to build a custom container image. It is a declarative way of building images.

Declarative versus imperative:
In computer science, in general, and with Docker specifically, one often uses a declarative way of defining a task. One describes the expected outcome and lets the system figure out how to achieve this goal, rather than giving step-by-step instructions to the system on how to achieve this desired outcome. The latter is an imperative approach.

Let's look at a sample `Dockerfile`, as follows:

```
FROM python:2.7
RUN mkdir -p /app
WORKDIR /app
COPY ./requirements.txt /app/
RUN pip install -r requirements.txt
CMD ["python", "main.py"]
```

This is a `Dockerfile` as it is used to containerize a Python 2.7 application. As we can see, the file has six lines, each starting with a keyword such as FROM, RUN, or COPY. It is a convention to write the keywords in all caps, but that is not a must.

Each line of the `Dockerfile` results in a layer in the resulting image. In the following screenshot, the image is drawn upside down compared to the previous illustrations in this chapter, showing an image as a stack of layers. Here, the **Base Layer** is shown on top. Don't let yourself be confused by this. In reality, the base layer is always the lowest layer in the stack:

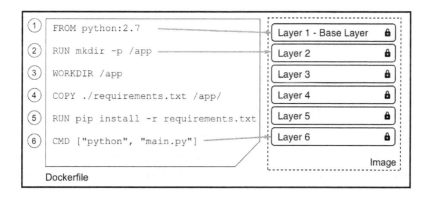

The relation of Dockerfile and layers in an image

Now, let's look at the individual keywords in more detail.

The FROM keyword

Every `Dockerfile` starts with the FROM keyword. With it, we define which base image we want to start building our custom image from. If we want to build starting with CentOS 7, for example, we would have the following line in the `Dockerfile`:

```
FROM centos:7
```

On Docker Hub, there are curated or official images for all major Linux distros, as well as for all important development frameworks or languages, such as Python, Node.js, Ruby, Go, and many more. Depending on our needs, we should select the most appropriate base image.

For example, if I want to containerize a Python 3.7 application, I might want to select the relevant official `python:3.7` image.

If we really want to start from scratch, we can also use the following statement:

```
FROM scratch
```

This is useful in the context of building super-minimal images that only—for example—contain a single binary: the actual statically linked executable, such as `Hello-World`. The `scratch` image is literally an empty base image.

`FROM scratch` is a `no-op` in the `Dockerfile`, and as such does not generate a layer in the resulting container image.

The RUN keyword

The next important keyword is `RUN`. The argument for `RUN` is any valid Linux command, such as the following:

```
RUN yum install -y wget
```

The preceding command is using the `yum` CentOS package manager to install the `wget` package into the running container. This assumes that our base image is CentOS or **Red Hat Enterprise Linux (RHEL)**. If we had Ubuntu as our base image, then the command would look similar to the following:

```
RUN apt-get update && apt-get install -y wget
```

It would look like this because Ubuntu uses `apt-get` as a package manager. Similarly, we could define a line with `RUN`, like this:

```
RUN mkdir -p /app && cd /app
```

We could also do this:

```
RUN tar -xJC /usr/src/python --strip-components=1 -f python.tar.xz
```

Here, the former creates an /app folder in the container and navigates to it, and the latter untars a file to a given location. It is completely fine, and even recommended, for you to format a Linux command using more than one physical line, such as this:

```
RUN apt-get update \
    && apt-get install -y --no-install-recommends \
      ca-certificates \
      libexpat1 \
      libffi6 \
      libgdbm3 \
      libreadline7 \
      libsqlite3-0 \
      libssl1.1 \
    && rm -rf /var/lib/apt/lists/*
```

If we use more than one line, we need to put a backslash (\) at the end of the lines to indicate to the shell that the command continues on the next line.

Try to find out what the preceding command does.

The COPY and ADD keywords

The COPY and ADD keywords are very important since, in the end, we want to add some content to an existing base image to make it a custom image. Most of the time, these are a few source files of—say—a web application, or a few binaries of a compiled application.

These two keywords are used to copy files and folders from the host into the image that we're building. The two keywords are very similar, with the exception that the ADD keyword also lets us copy and unpack TAR files, as well as providing a URL as a source for the files and folders to copy.

Let's look at a few examples of how these two keywords can be used, as follows:

```
COPY . /app
COPY ./web /app/web
COPY sample.txt /data/my-sample.txt
ADD sample.tar /app/bin/
ADD http://example.com/sample.txt /data/
```

In the preceding lines of code, the following applies:

- The first line copies all files and folders from the current directory recursively to the `app` folder inside the container image.
- The second line copies everything in the `web` subfolder to the target folder, `/app/web`.
- The third line copies a single file, `sample.txt`, into the target folder, `/data`, and at the same time, renames it to `my-sample.txt`.
- The fourth statement unpacks the `sample.tar` file into the target folder, `/app/bin`.
- Finally, the last statement copies the remote file, `sample.txt`, into the target file, `/data`.

Wildcards are allowed in the source path. For example, the following statement copies all files starting with `sample` to the `mydir` folder inside the image:

```
COPY ./sample* /mydir/
```

From a security perspective, it is important to know that, by default, all files and folders inside the image will have a **user ID (UID)** and a **group ID (GID)** of 0. The good thing is that for both `ADD` and `COPY`, we can change the ownership that the files will have inside the image using the optional `--chown` flag, as follows:

```
ADD --chown=11:22 ./data/web* /app/data/
```

The preceding statement will copy all files starting with the name `web` and put them into the `/app/data` folder in the image, and at the same time assign user `11` and group `22` to these files.

Instead of numbers, one could also use names for the user and group, but then these entities would have to be already defined in the root filesystem of the image at `/etc/passwd` and `/etc/group` respectively; otherwise, the build of the image would fail.

The WORKDIR keyword

The `WORKDIR` keyword defines the working directory or context that is used when a container is run from our custom image. So, if I want to set the context to the `/app/bin` folder inside the image, my expression in the `Dockerfile` would have to look as follows:

```
WORKDIR /app/bin
```

All activity that happens inside the image after the preceding line will use this directory as the working directory. It is very important to note that the following two snippets from a `Dockerfile` are not the same:

```
RUN cd /app/bin
RUN touch sample.txt
```

Compare the preceding code with the following code:

```
WORKDIR /app/bin
RUN touch sample.txt
```

The former will create the file in the root of the image filesystem, while the latter will create the file at the expected location in the `/app/bin` folder. Only the `WORKDIR` keyword sets the context across the layers of the image. The `cd` command alone is not persisted across layers.

The CMD and ENTRYPOINT keywords

The `CMD` and `ENTRYPOINT` keywords are special. While all other keywords defined for a `Dockerfile` are executed at the time the image is built by the Docker builder, these two are actually definitions of what will happen when a container is started from the image we define. When the container runtime starts a container, it needs to know what the process or application will be that has to run inside that container. That is exactly what `CMD` and `ENTRYPOINT` are used for—to tell Docker what the start process is and how to start that process.

Now, the differences between `CMD` and `ENTRYPOINT` are subtle, and honestly, most users don't fully understand them or use them in the intended way. Luckily, in most cases, this is not a problem and the container will run anyway; it's just the handling of it that is not as straightforward as it could be.

To better understand how to use the two keywords, let's analyze what a typical Linux command or expression looks like. Let's take the `ping` utility as an example, as follows:

```
$ ping -c 3 8.8.8.8
```

In the preceding expression, `ping` is the command and `-c 3 8.8.8.8` are the parameters to this command. Let's look at another expression here:

```
$ wget -O - http://example.com/downloads/script.sh
```

Again, in the preceding expression, `wget` is the command and `-O -` `http://example.com/downloads/script.sh` are the parameters.

Now that we have dealt with this, we can get back to `CMD` and `ENTRYPOINT`. `ENTRYPOINT` is used to define the command of the expression, while `CMD` is used to define the parameters for the command. Thus, a `Dockerfile` using Alpine as the base image and defining `ping` as the process to run in the container could look like this:

```
FROM alpine:3.10
ENTRYPOINT ["ping"]
CMD ["-c","3","8.8.8.8"]
```

For both `ENTRYPOINT` and `CMD`, the values are formatted as a JSON array of strings, where the individual items correspond to the tokens of the expression that are separated by whitespace. This is the preferred way of defining `CMD` and `ENTRYPOINT`. It is also called the *exec* form.

Alternatively, one can also use what's called the shell form, as shown here:

```
CMD command param1 param2
```

We can now build an image called `pinger` from the preceding `Dockerfile`, as follows:

```
$ docker image build -t pinger .
```

Then, we can run a container from the `pinger` image we just created, like this:

```
$ docker container run --rm -it pinger
PING 8.8.8.8 (8.8.8.8): 56 data bytes
64 bytes from 8.8.8.8: seq=0 ttl=37 time=19.298 ms
64 bytes from 8.8.8.8: seq=1 ttl=37 time=27.890 ms
64 bytes from 8.8.8.8: seq=2 ttl=37 time=30.702 ms
```

The beauty of this is that I can now override the `CMD` part that I have defined in the `Dockerfile` (remember, it was `["-c", "3","8.8.8.8"]`) when I create a new container by adding the new values at the end of the `docker container run` expression, like this:

```
$ docker container run --rm -it pinger -w 5 127.0.0.1
```

This will now cause the container to ping the loopback for 5 seconds.

If we want to override what's defined in the ENTRYPOINT in the Dockerfile, we need to use the --entrypoint parameter in the docker container run expression. Let's say we want to execute a shell in the container instead of the ping command. We could do so by using the following command:

```
$ docker container run --rm -it --entrypoint /bin/sh pinger
```

We will then find ourselves inside the container. Type exit to leave the container.

As I already mentioned, we do not necessarily have to follow best practices and define the command through ENTRYPOINT and the parameters through CMD; we can instead enter the whole expression as a value of CMD and it will work, as shown in the following code block:

```
FROM alpine:3.10
CMD wget -O - http://www.google.com
```

Here, I have even used the shell form to define the CMD. But what does really happen in this situation where ENTRYPOINT is undefined? If you leave ENTRYPOINT undefined, then it will have the default value of /bin/sh -c, and whatever the value of CMD is will be passed as a string to the shell command. The preceding definition would thereby result in entering the following code to run the process inside the container:

```
/bin/sh -c "wget -O - http://www.google.com"
```

Consequently, /bin/sh is the main process running inside the container, and it will start a new child process to run the wget utility.

A complex Dockerfile

We have discussed the most important keywords commonly used in Dockerfiles. Let's look at a realistic, and somewhat complex example of a Dockerfile. The interested reader might note that it looks very similar to the first Dockerfile that we presented in this chapter. Here is the content:

```
FROM node:12.5-stretch
RUN mkdir -p /app
WORKDIR /app
COPY package.json /app/
RUN npm install
COPY . /app
ENTRYPOINT ["npm"]
CMD ["start"]
```

OK; so, what is happening here? Evidently, this is a `Dockerfile` that is used to build an image for a Node.js application; we can deduce this from the fact that the `node:12.5-stretch` base image is used. Then, the second line is an instruction to create an `/app` folder in the filesystem of the image. The third line defines the working directory or context in the image to be this new `/app` folder. Then, on line four, we copy a `package.json` file into the `/app` folder inside the image. After this, on line five, we execute the `npm install` command inside the container; remember, our context is the `/app` folder, and thus, `npm` will find the `package.json` file there that we copied on line four.

After all the Node.js dependencies are installed, we copy the rest of the application files from the current folder of the host into the `/app` folder of the image.

Finally, on the last two lines, we define what the startup command will be when a container is run from this image. In our case, it is `npm start`, which will start the Node.js application.

Building an image

Let's look at a concrete example and build a simple Docker image, as follows:

1. In your home directory, create a `fod` folder (short for **Fundamentals of Docker**) with a `ch04` subfolder in it, and navigate to this folder, like this:

   ```
   $ mkdir -p ~/fod/ch04 && cd ~/fod/ch04
   ```

2. In the preceding folder, create a `sample1` subfolder and navigate to it, like this:

   ```
   $ mkdir sample1 && cd sample1
   ```

3. Use your favorite editor to create a file called `Dockerfile` inside this sample folder, with the following content:

   ```
   FROM centos:7
   RUN yum install -y wget
   ```

4. Save the file and exit your editor.

5. Back in the Terminal window, we can now build a new container image using the preceding `Dockerfile` as a manifest or construction plan, like this:

   ```
   $ docker image build -t my-centos .
   ```

Please note that there is a period at the end of the preceding command. This command means that the Docker builder is creating a new image called my-centos using the `Dockerfile` that is present in the current directory. Here, the period at the end of the command stands for *current directory*. We could also write the preceding command as follows, with the same result:

```
$ docker image build -t my-centos -f Dockerfile .
```

But we can omit the `-f` parameter, since the builder assumes that the `Dockerfile` is literally called `Dockerfile`. We only ever need the `-f` parameter if our `Dockerfile` has a different name or is not located in the current directory.

The preceding command gives us this (shortened) output:

```
Sending build context to Docker daemon 2.048kB
Step 1/2 : FROM centos:7
7: Pulling from library/centos
af4b0a2388c6: Pull complete
Digest:
sha256:2671f7a3eea36ce43609e9fe7435ade83094291055f1c96d9d1d1d7c0b98
6a5d
Status: Downloaded newer image for centos:7
---> ff426288ea90
Step 2/2 : RUN yum install -y wget
---> Running in bb726903820c
Loaded plugins: fastestmirror, ovl
Determining fastest mirrors
 * base: mirror.dal10.us.leaseweb.net
 * extras: repos-tx.psychz.net
 * updates: pubmirrors.dal.corespace.com
Resolving Dependencies
--> Running transaction check
---> Package wget.x86_64 0:1.14-15.el7_4.1 will be installed
...
Installed:
  wget.x86_64 0:1.14-15.el7_4.1
Complete!
Removing intermediate container bb726903820c
---> bc070cc81b87
Successfully built bc070cc81b87
Successfully tagged my-centos:latest
```

Let's analyze this output, as follows:

1. First, we have the following line:

   ```
   Sending build context to Docker daemon 2.048kB
   ```

   The first thing the builder does is package the files in the current build context, excluding the files and folder mentioned in the .dockerignore file (if present), and sends the resulting .tar file to the Docker daemon.

2. Next, we have the following lines:

   ```
   Step 1/2 : FROM centos:7
   7: Pulling from library/centos
   af4b0a2388c6: Pull complete
   Digest: sha256:2671f7a...
   Status: Downloaded newer image for centos:7
   ---> ff426288ea90
   ```

   The first line tells us which step of the Dockerfile the builder is currently executing. Here, we only have two statements in the Dockerfile, and we are on *Step 1* of 2. We can also see what the content of that section is. Here, it is the declaration of the base image, on top of which we want to build our custom image. What the builder then does is pull this image from Docker Hub, if it is not already available in the local cache. The last line of the preceding code snippet indicates which ID the just-built image layer gets assigned by the builder.

3. Now, follow the next step. I have shortened it even more than the preceding one to concentrate on the essential part:

   ```
   Step 2/2 : RUN yum install -y wget
   ---> Running in bb726903820c
   . . .
   . . .
   Removing intermediate container bb726903820c
   ---> bc070cc81b87
   ```

   Here, again, the first line indicates to us that we are in *Step 2* of 2. It also shows us the respective entry from the Dockerfile. On line two, we can see Running in bb726903820c, which tells us that the builder has created a container with ID bb726903820c, inside which it executes the RUN command.

We have omitted the output of the `yum install -y wget` command in the snippet since it is not important in this section. When the command is finished, the builder stops the container, commits it to a new layer, and then removes the container. The new layer has ID `bc070cc81b87`, in this particular case.

4. At the very end of the output, we encounter the following two lines:

```
Successfully built bc070cc81b87
Successfully tagged my-centos:latest
```

This tells us that the resulting custom image has been given the ID `bc070cc81b87`, and has been tagged with the name `my-centos:latest`.

So, how does the builder work, exactly? It starts with the base image. From this base image, once downloaded into the local cache, the builder creates a container and runs the first statement of the `Dockerfile` inside this container. Then, it stops the container and persists the changes made in the container into a new image layer. The builder then creates a new container from the base image and the new layer and runs the second statement inside this new container. Once again, the result is committed to a new layer. This process is repeated until the very last statement in the `Dockerfile` is encountered. After having committed the last layer of the new image, the builder creates an ID for this image and tags the image with the name we provided in the `build` command, as shown in the following screenshot:

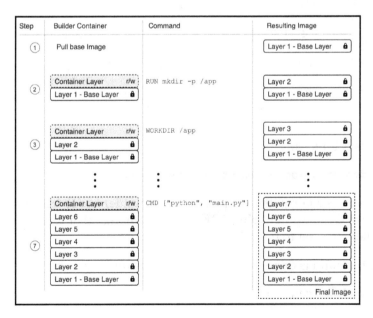

The image build process visualized

Now that we have analyzed how the build process of a Docker image works and what steps are involved, let's talk about how to further improve this by introducing multi-step builds.

Multi-step builds

To demonstrate why a `Dockerfile` with multiple build steps is useful, let's make an example `Dockerfile`. Let's take a Hello World application written in C. Here is the code found inside the `hello.c` file:

```
#include <stdio.h>
int main (void)
{
    printf ("Hello, world!\n");
    return 0;
}
```

Follow along to experience the advantages of a multi-step build:

1. To containerize this application we first write a `Dockerfile` with the following content:

```
FROM alpine:3.7
RUN apk update &&
apk add --update alpine-sdk
RUN mkdir /app
WORKDIR /app
COPY . /app
RUN mkdir bin
RUN gcc -Wall hello.c -o bin/hello
CMD /app/bin/hello
```

2. Next, let's build this image:

```
$ docker image build -t hello-world .
```

This gives us a fairly long output since the builder has to install the Alpine **Software Development Kit** (**SDK**), which, among other tools, contains the C++ compiler we need to build the application.

3. Once the build is done, we can list the image and see its size shown, as follows:

```
$ docker image ls | grep hello-world
hello-world    latest    e9b...    2 minutes ago    176MB
```

With a size of 176 MB, the resulting image is way too big. In the end, it is just a Hello World application. The reason for it being so big is that the image not only contains the Hello World binary but also all the tools to compile and link the application from the source code. But this is really not desirable when running the application, say, in production. Ideally, we only want to have the resulting binary in the image and not a whole SDK.

It is precisely for this reason that we should define Dockerfiles as multi-stage. We have some stages that are used to build the final artifacts, and then a final stage, where we use the minimal necessary base image and copy the artifacts into it. This results in very small Docker images. Have a look at this revised `Dockerfile`:

```
FROM alpine:3.7 AS build
RUN apk update && \
    apk add --update alpine-sdk
RUN mkdir /app
WORKDIR /app
COPY . /app
RUN mkdir bin
RUN gcc hello.c -o bin/hello

FROM alpine:3.7
COPY --from=build /app/bin/hello /app/hello
CMD /app/hello
```

Here, we have the first stage with a `build` alias that is used to compile the application, and then the second stage uses the same `alpine:3.7` base image but does not install the SDK, and only copies the binary from the `build` stage, using the `--from` parameter, into this final image:

1. Let's build the image again, as follows:

   ```
   $ docker image build -t hello-world-small .
   ```

2. When we compare the sizes of the images, we get the following output:

   ```
   $ docker image ls | grep hello-world
   hello-world-small   latest   f98...   20 seconds ago   4.16MB
   hello-world         latest   469...   10 minutes ago   176MB
   ```

We have been able to reduce the size from 176 MB down to 4 MB. This is a reduction in size by a factor of 40. A smaller image has many advantages, such as a smaller attack surface area for hackers, reduced memory and disk consumption, faster startup times of the corresponding containers, and a reduction of the bandwidth needed to download the image from a registry, such as Docker Hub.

Dockerfile best practices

There are a few recommended best practices to consider when authoring a `Dockerfile`, which are as follows:

- First and foremost, we need to consider that containers are meant to be ephemeral. By ephemeral, we mean that a container can be stopped and destroyed, and a new one built and put in place with an absolute minimum of setup and configuration. That means that we should try hard to keep the time that is needed to initialize the application running inside the container at a minimum, as well as the time needed to terminate or clean up the application.

- The next best practice tells us that we should order the individual commands in the `Dockerfile` so that we leverage caching as much as possible. Building a layer of an image can take a considerable amount of time—sometimes many seconds, or even minutes. While developing an application, we will have to build the container image for our application multiple times. We want to keep the build times at a minimum.

When we're rebuilding a previously built image, the only layers that are rebuilt are the ones that have changed, but if one layer needs to be rebuilt, all subsequent layers also need to be rebuilt. This is very important to remember. Consider the following example:

```
FROM node:9.4
RUN mkdir -p /app
WORKIR /app
COPY . /app
RUN npm install
CMD ["npm", "start"]
```

In this example, the npm install command on line five of the Dockerfile usually takes the longest. A classical Node.js application has many external dependencies, and those are all downloaded and installed in this step. This can take minutes until it is done. Therefore, we want to avoid running npm install each time we rebuild the image, but a developer changes their source code all the time during the development of an application. That means that line four, the result of the COPY command, changes every time, and thus this layer has to be rebuilt. But as we discussed previously, that also means that all subsequent layers have to be rebuilt, which—in this case—includes the npm install command. To avoid this, we can slightly modify the Dockerfile and have the following:

```
FROM node:9.4
RUN mkdir -p /app
WORKIR /app
COPY package.json /app/
RUN npm install
COPY . /app
CMD ["npm", "start"]
```

What we have done here is, on line four, we only copied the single file that the npm install command needs as a source, which is the package.json file. This file rarely changes in a typical development process. As a consequence, the npm install command also has to be executed only when the package.json file changes. All the remaining, frequently changed content is added to the image after the npm install command.

- A further best practice is to keep the number of layers that make up your image relatively small. The more layers an image has, the more the graph driver needs to work to consolidate the layers into a single root filesystem for the corresponding container. Of course, this takes time, and thus the fewer layers an image has, the faster the startup time for the container can be.

But how can we keep our number of layers low? Remember that in a Dockerfile, each line that starts with a keyword such as FROM, COPY, or RUN creates a new layer. The easiest way to reduce the number of layers is to combine multiple individual RUN commands into a single one. For example, say that we had the following in a Dockerfile:

```
RUN apt-get update
RUN apt-get install -y ca-certificates
RUN rm -rf /var/lib/apt/lists/*
```

We could combine these into a single concatenated expression, as follows:

```
RUN apt-get update \
    && apt-get install -y ca-certificates \
    && rm -rf /var/lib/apt/lists/*
```

The former will generate three layers in the resulting image, while the latter only creates a single layer.

The next three best practices all result in smaller images. Why is this important? Smaller images reduce the time and bandwidth needed to download the image from a registry. They also reduce the amount of disk space needed to store a copy locally on the Docker host and the memory needed to load the image. Finally, smaller images also mean a smaller attack surface for hackers. Here are the best practices mentioned:

- The first best practice that helps to reduce the image size is to use a `.dockerignore` file. We want to avoid copying unnecessary files and folders into an image, to keep it as lean as possible. A `.dockerignore` file works in exactly the same way as a `.gitignore` file, for those who are familiar with Git. In a `.dockerignore` file, we can configure patterns to exclude certain files or folders from being included in the context when building the image.
- The next best practice is to avoid installing unnecessary packages into the filesystem of the image. Once again, this is to keep the image as lean as possible.
- Last but not least, it is recommended that you use multi-stage builds so that the resulting image is as small as possible and only contains the absolute minimum needed to run your application or application service.

Saving and loading images

The third way to create a new container image is by importing or loading it from a file. A container image is nothing more than a tarball. To demonstrate this, we can use the `docker image save` command to export an existing image to a tarball, like this:

```
$ docker image save -o ./backup/my-alpine.tar my-alpine
```

The preceding command takes our `my-alpine` image that we previously built and exports it into a file called `./backup/my-alpine.tar`.

If, on the other hand, we have an existing tarball and want to import it as an image into our system, we can use the `docker image load` command, as follows:

```
$ docker image load -i ./backup/my-alpine.tar
```

In the next section, we will discuss how we can create Docker images for existing legacy applications, and thus run them in a container, and profit from this.

Lift and shift: Containerizing a legacy app

We can't always start from scratch and develop a brand new application. More often than not, we find ourselves with a huge portfolio of traditional applications that are up and running in production and provide mission-critical value to the company or the customers of the company. Often, those applications are organically grown and very complex. Documentation is sparse, and nobody really wants to touch such an application. Often, the saying *Never touch a running system* applies. Yet, market needs change, and with that arises the need to update or rewrite those apps. Often, a complete rewrite is not possible due to the lack of resources and time, or due to the excessive cost. What are we going to do about those applications? Could we possibly Dockerize them and profit from benefits introduced by containers?

It turns out we can. In 2017, Docker introduced a program called **Modernize Traditional Apps (MTA)** to their enterprise customers, which in essence promised to help those customers to take their existing or traditional Java and .NET applications and containerize them, without the need to change a single line of code. The focus of MTA was on Java and .NET applications since those made up the lion's share of the traditional applications in a typical enterprise. But the same is possible for any application that was written in—say—C, C++, Python, Node.js, Ruby, PHP, or Go, to just name a few other languages and platforms.

Let's imagine such a legacy application for a moment. Assume we have an old Java application written 10 years ago, and continuously updated during the following 5 years. The application is based on Java SE 6, which came out in December 2006. It uses environment variables and property files for configuration. Secrets such as username and passwords used in the database connection strings are pulled from a secrets keystore, such as HashiCorp's Vault.

Analysis of external dependencies

One of the first steps in the modernization process is to discover and list all external dependencies of the legacy application.

We need to ask ourselves questions like the following:

1. Does it use a database? If yes, which one? What does the connection string look like?
2. Does it use external APIs such as credit card approval or geo-mapping APIs? What are the API keys and key secrets?
3. Is it consuming from or publishing to an **Enterprise Service Bus (ESB)**?

These are just a few possible dependencies that come to mind. Many more exist. These are the seams of the application to the outer world, and we need to be aware of them and create an inventory.

Source code and build instructions

The next step is to locate all the source code and other assets, such as images and CSS and HTML files that are part of the application. Ideally, they should be located in a single folder. This folder will be the root of our project and can have as many subfolders as needed. This project root folder will be the context during the build of the container image we want to create for our legacy application. Remember, the Docker builder only includes files in the build that are part of that context; in our case, that is the root project folder.

There is, though, an option to download or copy files during the build from different locations, using the `COPY` or `ADD` commands. Please refer to the online documentation for the exact details on how to use these two commands. This option is useful if the sources for your legacy application cannot be easily contained in a single, local folder.

Once we are aware of all the parts that are contributing to the final application, we need to investigate how the application is built and packaged. In our case, this is most probably done by using Maven. Maven is the most popular build automation tool for Java, and has been—and still is—used in most enterprises that are developing Java applications. In the case of a legacy .NET application, it is most probably done by using the MSBuild tool; and in the case of a C/C++ application, Make would most likely be used.

Once again, let's extend our inventory and write down the exact build commands used. We will need this information later on when authoring the `Dockerfile`.

Configuration

Applications need to be configured. Information provided during configuration can be—for example— the type of application logging to use, connection strings to databases, hostnames to services such as ESBs or URIs to external APIs, to name just a few.

We can differentiate a few types of configurations, as follows:

- **Build time**: This is the information needed during the build of the application and/or its Docker image. It needs to be available when we create the Docker images.
- **Environment**: This is configuration information that varies with the environment in which the application is running—for example, DEVELOPMENT versus STAGING or PRODUCTION. This kind of configuration is applied to the application when a container with the app starts—for example, in production.
- **Runtime**: This is information that the application retrieves during runtime, such as secrets to access an external API.

Secrets

Every mission-critical enterprise application needs to deal with secrets in some form or another. The most familiar secrets are part of the connection information needed to access databases that are used to persist the data produced by or used by the application. Other secrets include the credentials needed to access external APIs, such as a credit score lookup API. It is important to note that, here, we are talking about secrets that have to be provided by the application itself to the service providers the application uses or depends on, and not secrets provided by the users of the application. The actor here is our application, which needs to be authenticated and authorized by external authorities and service providers.

There are various ways traditional applications got their secrets. The worst and most insecure way of providing secrets is by hardcoding them or reading them from configuration files or environment variables, where they are available in cleartext. A much better way is to read the secrets during runtime from a special secrets store that persists the secrets encrypted and provides them to the application over a secure connection, such as **Transport Layer Security (TLS)**.

Once again, we need to create an inventory of all secrets that our application uses and the way it procures them. Is it through environment variable or configuration files, or is it by accessing an external keystore, such as HashiCorp's Vault?

Authoring the Dockerfile

Once we have a complete inventory of all the items discussed in the previous few sections, we are ready to author our `Dockerfile`. But I want to warn you: don't expect this to be a one-shot-and-go task. You may need several iterations until you have crafted your final `Dockerfile`. The `Dockerfile` may be rather long and ugly-looking, but that's not a problem, as long as we get a working Docker image. We can always fine-tune the `Dockerfile` once we have a working version.

The base image

Let's start by identifying the base image we want to use and build our image from. Is there an official Java image available that is compatible with our requirements? Remember that our imaginary application is based on Java SE 6. If such a base image is available, then let's use that one. Otherwise, we want to start with a Linux distro such as Red Hat, Oracle, or Ubuntu. In the latter case, we will use the appropriate package manager of the distro (`yum`, `apt`, or another) to install the desired versions of Java and Maven. For this, we use the `RUN` keyword in the `Dockerfile`. Remember, `RUN` gives us the possibility to execute any valid Linux command in the image during the build process.

Assembling the sources

In this step, we make sure all source files and other artifacts needed to successfully build the application are part of the image. Here, we mainly use the two keywords of the `Dockerfile`: `COPY` and `ADD`. Initially, the structure of the source inside the image should look exactly the same as on the host, to avoid any build problems. Ideally, you would have a single `COPY` command that copies all of the root project folder from the host into the image. The corresponding `Dockerfile` snippet could then look as simple as this:

```
WORKDIR /app
COPY . .
```

 Don't forget to also provide a `.dockerignore` file located in the project root folder, which lists all the files and (sub-) folders of the project root folder that should not be part of the build context.

As mentioned earlier, you can also use the ADD keyword to download sources and other artifacts into the Docker image that are not located in the build context but somewhere reachable by a URI, as shown here:

```
ADD http://example.com/foobar ./
```

This would create a `foobar` folder in the image's working folder and copy all the contents from the URI.

Building the application

In this step, we make sure to create the final artifacts that make up our executable legacy application. Often, this is a JAR or WAR file, with or without some satellite JARs. This part of the `Dockerfile` should exactly mimic the way you traditionally used to build an application before containerizing them. Thus, if using Maven as the build automation tool, the corresponding snippet of the `Dockerfile` could look as simple as this:

```
RUN mvn --clean install
```

In this step, we may also want to list the environment variables the application uses, and provide sensible defaults. But never provide default values for environment variables that provide secrets to the application such as the database connection string! Use the ENV keyword to define your variables, like this:

```
ENV foo=bar
ENV baz=123
```

Also, declare all ports that the application is listening on and that need to be accessible from outside of the container via the EXPOSE keyword, like this:

```
EXPOSE 5000
EXPOSE 15672/tcp
```

Defining the start command

Usually, a Java application is started with a command such as `java -jar <main application jar>` if it is a standalone application. If it is a WAR file, then the start command may look a bit different. We can thus either define the ENTRYPOINT or the CMD to use this command. Thus, the final statement in our `Dockerfile` could look like this:

```
ENTRYPOINT java -jar pet-shop.war
```

Often, though, this is too simplistic, and we need to execute a few pre-run tasks. In this case, we can craft a script file that contains the series of commands that need to be executed to prepare the environment and run the application. Such a file is often called `docker-entrypoint.sh`, but you are free to name it however you want. Make sure the file is executable— for example, with the following:

```
chmod +x ./docker-entrypoint.sh
```

The last line of the `Dockerfile` would then look like this:

```
ENTRYPOINT ./docker-entrypoint.sh
```

Now that you have been given hints on how to containerize a legacy application, it is time to recap and ask ourselves: *Is it really worth the whole effort?*

Why bother?

At this point, I can see you scratching your head and asking yourself: *Why bother?* Why should you take on all this seemingly huge effort just to containerize a legacy application? What are the benefits?

It turns out that the **return on investment (ROI)** is huge. Enterprise customers of Docker have publicly disclosed at conferences such as DockerCon 2018 and 2019 that they are seeing these two main benefits of Dockerizing traditional applications:

- More than a 50% saving in maintenance costs.
- Up to a 90% reduction in the time between the deployments of new releases.

The costs saved by reducing the maintenance overhead can be directly reinvested and used to develop new features and products. The time saved during new releases of traditional applications makes a business more agile and able to react to changing customer or market needs more quickly.

Now that we have discussed at length how to build Docker images, it is time to learn how we can ship those images through the various stages of the software delivery pipeline.

Sharing or shipping images

To be able to ship our custom image to other environments, we need to first give it a globally unique name. This action is often called *tagging* an image. We then need to publish the image to a central location from which other interested or entitled parties can pull it. These central locations are called *image registries*.

Tagging an image

Each image has a so-called *tag*. A tag is often used to version images, but it has a broader reach than just being a version number. If we do not explicitly specify a tag when working with images, then Docker automatically assumes we're referring to the `latest` tag. This is relevant when pulling an image from Docker Hub, as in the following example:

```
$ docker image pull alpine
```

The preceding command will pull the `alpine:latest` image from Docker Hub. If we want to explicitly specify a tag, we do so like this:

```
$ docker image pull alpine:3.5
```

This will now pull the `alpine` image that has been tagged with `3.5`.

Image namespaces

So far, we have been pulling various images and haven't been worrying so much about where those images originated from. Your Docker environment is configured so that, by default, all images are pulled from Docker Hub. We also only pulled so-called official images from Docker Hub, such as `alpine` or `busybox`.

Now, it is time to widen our horizon a bit and learn about how images are namespaced. The most generic way to define an image is by its fully qualified name, which looks as follows:

```
<registry URL>/<User or Org>/<name>:<tag>
```

Let's look at this in a bit more detail:

- `<registry URL>`: This is the URL to the registry from which we want to pull the image. By default, this is `docker.io`. More generally, this could be `https://registry.acme.com`.

  Other than Docker Hub, there are quite a few public registries out there that you could pull images from. The following is a list of some of them, in no particular order:

  - Google, at `https://cloud.google.com/container-registry`
  - Amazon AWS **Amazon Elastic Container Registry (ECR)**, at `https://aws.amazon.com/ecr/`
  - Microsoft Azure, at `https://azure.microsoft.com/en-us/services/container-registry/`
  - Red Hat, at `https://access.redhat.com/containers/`
  - Artifactory, at `https://jfrog.com/integration/artifactory-docker-registry/`

- `<User or Org>`: This is the private Docker ID of either an individual or an organization defined on Docker Hub—or any other registry, for that matter—such as `microsoft` or `oracle`.
- `<name>`: This is the name of the image, which is often also called a repository.
- `<tag>`: This is the tag of the image.

Let's look at an example, as follows:

```
https://registry.acme.com/engineering/web-app:1.0
```

Here, we have an image, `web-app`, that is tagged with version `1.0` and belongs to the `engineering` organization on the private registry at `https://registry.acme.com`.

Now, there are some special conventions:

- If we omit the registry URL, then Docker Hub is automatically taken.
- If we omit the tag, then `latest` is taken.
- If it is an official image on Docker Hub, then no user or organization namespace is needed.

Here are a few samples in tabular form:

Image	Description
alpine	Official alpine image on Docker Hub with the latest tag.
ubuntu:19.04	Official ubuntu image on Docker Hub with the 19.04 tag or version.
microsoft/nanoserver	nanoserver image of Microsoft on Docker Hub with the latest tag.
acme/web-api:12.0	web-api image version 12.0 associated with the acme org. The image is on Docker Hub.
gcr.io/gnschenker/sample-app:1.1	sample-app image with the 1.1 tag belonging to an individual with the gnschenker ID on Google's container registry.

Now that we know how the fully qualified name of a Docker image is defined and what its parts are, let's talk about some special images we can find on Docker Hub.

Official images

In the preceding table, we mentioned *official image* a few times. This needs an explanation. Images are stored in repositories on the Docker Hub registry. Official repositories are a set of repositories hosted on Docker Hub that are curated by individuals or organizations that are also responsible for the software packaged inside the image. Let's look at an example of what that means. There is an official organization behind the Ubuntu Linux distro. This team also provides official versions of Docker images that contain their Ubuntu distros.

Official images are meant to provide essential base OS repositories, images for popular programming language runtimes, frequently used data storage, and other important services.

Docker sponsors a team whose task it is to review and publish all those curated images in public repositories on Docker Hub. Furthermore, Docker scans all official images for vulnerabilities.

Pushing images to a registry

Creating custom images is all well and good, but at some point, we want to actually share or ship our images to a target environment, such as a test, **quality assurance (QA)**, or production system. For this, we typically use a container registry. One of the most popular and public registries out there is Docker Hub. It is configured as a default registry in your Docker environment, and it is the registry from which we have pulled all our images so far.

On a registry, one can usually create personal or organizational accounts. For example, my personal account at Docker Hub is `gnschenker`. Personal accounts are good for personal use. If we want to use the registry professionally, then we'll probably want to create an organizational account, such as `acme`, on Docker Hub. The advantage of the latter is that organizations can have multiple teams. Teams can have differing permissions.

To be able to push an image to my personal account on Docker Hub, I need to tag it accordingly:

1. Let's say I want to push the latest version of Alpine to my account and give it a tag of `1.0`. I can do this in the following way:

   ```
   $ docker image tag alpine:latest gnschenker/alpine:1.0
   ```

2. Now, to be able to push the image, I have to log in to my account, as follows:

   ```
   $ docker login -u gnschenker -p <my secret password>
   ```

3. After a successful login, I can then push the image, like this:

```
$ docker image push gnschenker/alpine:1.0
```

I will see something similar to this in the Terminal:

```
The push refers to repository [docker.io/gnschenker/alpine]
04a094fe844e: Mounted from library/alpine
1.0: digest: sha256:5cb04fce... size: 528
```

For each image that we push to Docker Hub, we automatically create a repository. A repository can be private or public. Everyone can pull an image from a public repository. From a private repository, an image can only be pulled if one is logged in to the registry and has the necessary permissions configured.

Summary

In this chapter, we have discussed in detail what container images are and how we can build and ship them. As we have seen, there are three different ways that an image can be created—either manually, automatically, or by importing a tarball into the system. We also learned some of the best practices commonly used when building custom images.

In the next chapter, we're going to introduce Docker volumes that can be used to persist the state of a container. We'll also show how to define individual environment variables for the application running inside the container, as well as how to use files containing whole sets of configuration settings.

Questions

Please try to answer the following questions to assess your learning progress:

1. How would you create a Dockerfile that inherits from Ubuntu version `19.04`, and that installs `ping` and runs `ping` when a container starts? The default address to `ping` will be `127.0.0.1`.
2. How would you create a new container image that uses `alpine:latest` and installs `curl`? Name the new image `my-alpine:1.0`.
3. Create a `Dockerfile` that uses multiple steps to create an image of a Hello World app of minimal size, written in C or Go.

4. Name three essential characteristics of a Docker container image.

5. You want to push an image named `foo:1.0` to your `jdoe` personal account on Docker Hub. Which of the following is the right solution?

A. `$ docker container push foo:1.0`

B. `$ docker image tag foo:1.0 jdoe/foo:1.0`
`$ docker image push jdoe/foo:1.0`

C. `$ docker login -u jdoe -p <your password>`
`$ docker image tag foo:1.0 jdoe/foo:1.0`
`$ docker image push jdoe/foo:1.0`

D. `$ docker login -u jdoe -p <your password>`
`$ docker container tag foo:1.0 jdoe/foo:1.0`
`$ docker container push jdoe/foo:1.0`

E. `$ docker login -u jdoe -p <your password>`
`$ docker image push foo:1.0 jdoe/foo:1.0`

Further reading

The following list of references gives you some material that dives more deeply into the topic of authoring and building container images:

- Best practices for writing Dockerfiles, at `http://dockr.ly/22WiJiO`
- Using multi-stage builds, at `http://dockr.ly/2ewcUY3`
- About storage drivers, at `http://dockr.ly/1TuWndC`
- Graphdriver plugins, at `http://dockr.ly/2eIVCab`
- User-guided caching in Docker for Mac, at `http://dockr.ly/2xKafPf`

5
Data Volumes and Configuration

In the last chapter, we learned how to build and share our own container images. Particular focus was placed on how to build images that are as small as possible by only containing artifacts that are really needed by the containerized application.

In this chapter, we are going to learn how we can work with stateful containers—that is, containers that consume and produce data. We will also learn how to configure our containers at runtime and at image build time, using environment variables and config files.

Here is a list of the topics we're going to discuss:

- Creating and mounting data volumes
- Sharing data between containers
- Using host volumes
- Defining volumes in images
- Configuring containers

After working through this chapter, you will be able to do the following:

- Create, delete, and list data volumes.
- Mount an existing data volume into a container.
- Create durable data from within a container using a data volume.
- Share data between multiple containers using data volumes.
- Mount any host folder into a container using data volumes.
- Define the access mode (read/write or read-only) for a container when accessing data in a data volume.
- Configure environment variables for applications running in a container.
- Parametrize a `Dockerfile` by using build arguments.

Technical requirements

For this chapter, you need either Docker Toolbox installed on your machine or access to a Linux **virtual machine** (**VM**) running Docker on your laptop or in the cloud. Furthermore, it is advantageous to have Docker for Desktop installed on your machine. There is no code accompanying this chapter.

Creating and mounting data volumes

All meaningful applications consume or produce data. Yet containers are, preferably, meant to be stateless. How are we going to deal with this? One way is to use Docker volumes. Volumes allow containers to consume, produce, and modify a state. Volumes have a life cycle that goes beyond the life cycle of containers. When a container that uses a volume dies, the volume continues to exist. This is great for the durability of the state.

Modifying the container layer

Before we dive into volumes, let's first discuss what happens if an application in a container changes something in the filesystem of the container. In this case, the changes are all happening in the writable container layer that we introduced in Chapter 3, *Mastering Containers*. Let's quickly demonstrate this by running a container, and execute a script in it that is creating a new file, like this:

```
$ docker container run --name demo \
    alpine /bin/sh -c 'echo "This is a test" > sample.txt'
```

The preceding command creates a container named demo, and, inside this container, creates a file called sample.txt with the content This is a test. The container exits after running the echo command but remains in memory, available for us to do our investigations. Let's use the diff command to find out what has changed in the container's filesystem in relation to the filesystem of the original image, as follows:

```
$ docker container diff demo
```

The output should look like this:

```
A /sample.txt
```

Evidently, a new file, as indicated by the A, has been added to the filesystem of the container, as expected. Since all layers that stem from the underlying image (alpine, in this case) are immutable, the change could only happen in the writeable container layer.

Files that have changed compared to the original image will be marked with a C, and those that have been deleted, with a D.

If we now remove the container from memory, its container layer will also be removed, and with it, all the changes will be irreversibly deleted. If we need our changes to persist even beyond the lifetime of the container, this is not a solution. Luckily, we have better options, in the form of Docker volumes. Let's get to know them.

Creating volumes

Since at this time, when using Docker for Desktop on a macOS or Windows computer, containers are not running natively on macOS or Windows but rather in a (hidden) VM created by Docker for Desktop, for illustrative purposes it is best we use `docker-machine` to create and use an explicit VM running Docker. At this point, we assume that you have Docker Toolbox installed on your system. If not, then please go back to `Chapter 2`, *Setting up a Working Environment,* where we provide detailed instructions on how to install Toolbox:

1. Use `docker-machine` to list all VMs currently running in VirtualBox, as follows:

   $ docker-machine ls

2. If you do not have a VM called `node-1` listed, then please create one with the following command:

   $ docker-machine create --driver virtualbox node-1

Refer back to `Chapter 2`, *Setting up a Working Environment,* on how to create a Hyper-V-based VM with `docker-machine` if you are running on Windows with Hyper-V enabled.

3. If, on the other hand, you have a VM called `node-1` but it is not running, then please start it, as follows:

   $ docker-machine start node-1

4. Now that everything is ready, use `docker-machine` to SSH into this VM, like this:

   $ docker-machine ssh node-1

5. You should be greeted by this welcome image:

```
$ docker-machine ssh node-1
   ( '>')
  /) TC (\    Core is distributed with ABSOLUTELY NO WARRANTY.
 (/-_--_-\)            www.tinycorelinux.net

docker@node-1:~$ █
```

docker-machine VM welcome message

6. To create a new data volume, we can use the `docker volume create` command. This will create a named volume that can then be mounted into a container and used for persistent data access or storage. The following command creates a volume called `sample`, using the default volume driver:

```
$ docker volume create sample
```

The default volume driver is the so-called local driver, which stores the data locally in the host filesystem.

7. The easiest way to find out where the data is stored on the host is by using the `docker volume inspect` command on the volume we just created. The actual location can differ from system to system, and so, this is the safest way to find the target folder. You can see this command in the following code block:

```
$ docker volume inspect sample
[
    {
        "CreatedAt": "2019-08-02T06:59:13Z",
        "Driver": "local",
        "Labels": {},
        "Mountpoint":
"/mnt/sda1/var/lib/docker/volumes/sample/_data",
        "Name": "my-data",
        "Options": {},
        "Scope": "local"
    }
]
```

The host folder can be found in the output under `Mountpoint`. In our case, when using `docker-machine` with a LinuxKit-based VM running in VirtualBox, the folder is `/mnt/sda1/var/lib/docker/volumes/sample/_data`.

The target folder is often a protected folder, and we thus might need to use `sudo` to navigate to this folder and execute any operations in it.

On our LinuxKit-based VM in Docker Toolbox, access is also denied, yet we don't have `sudo` available either. Is that the end of our exploration?

Luckily not; I have prepared a `fundamentalsofdocker/nsenter` utility container that allows us to access the backing folder of our `sample` volume we created earlier.

8. We need to run this container in `privileged` mode to get access to this protected part of the filesystem, like this:

```
$ docker run -it --rm --privileged --pid=host \
    fundamentalsofdocker/nsenter
/ #
```

We are running the container with the `--privileged` flag. This means that any app running in the container gets access to the devices of the host. The `--pid=host` flag signifies that the container is allowed to access the process tree of the host (the hidden VM in which the Docker daemon is running). Now, the preceding container runs the Linux `nsenter` tool to enter the Linux namespace of the host and then runs a shell within there. From this shell, we are thus granted access to all resources managed by the host.

When running the container, we basically execute the following command inside the container:

```
nsenter -t 1 -m -u -n -i sh
```

If that sounds complicated to you, don't worry; you will understand more as we proceed through this book. If there is one takeaway for you out of this, then it is to realize how powerful the right use of containers can be.

9. From within this container, we can now navigate to the folder representing the mount point of the volume, and then list its content, as follows:

```
/ # cd /mnt/sda1/var/lib/docker/volumes/sample/_data
/ # ls -l
total 0
```

The folder is currently empty since we have not yet stored any data in the volume.

10. Exit the tool container by pressing *Ctrl + D*.

There are other volume drivers available from third parties, in the form of plugins. We can use the `--driver` parameter in the `create` command to select a different volume driver. Other volume drivers use different types of storage systems to back a volume, such as cloud storage, **Network File System** (**NFS**) drives, software-defined storage, and more. The discussion of the correct usage of other volume drivers is beyond the scope of this book, though.

Mounting a volume

Once we have created a named volume, we can mount it into a container by following these steps:

1. For this, we can use the `-v` parameter in the `docker container run` command, like this:

```
$ docker container run --name test -it \
    -v sample:/data \
    alpine /bin/sh

Unable to find image 'alpine:latest' locally
latest: Pulling from library/alpine
050382585609: Pull complete
Digest:
sha256:6a92cd1fcdc8d8cdec60f33dda4db2cb1fcdcacf3410a8e05b3741f44a9b
5998
Status: Downloaded newer image for alpine:latest
/ #
```

The preceding command mounts the `sample` volume to the `/data` folder inside the container.

2. Inside the container, we can now create files in the `/data` folder and then exit, as follows:

```
/ # cd /data / # echo "Some data" > data.txt
/ # echo "Some more data" > data2.txt
/ # exit
```

3. If we navigate to the host folder that contains the data of the volume and list its content, we should see the two files we just created inside the container (remember: we need to use the `fundamentalsofdocker/nsenter` tool container to do so), as follows:

```
$ docker run -it --rm --privileged --pid=host \
  fundamentalsofdocker/nsenter
/ # cd /mnt/sda1/var/lib/docker/volumes/sample/_data
/ # ls -l
total 8
-rw-r--r-- 1 root root 10 Jan 28 22:23 data.txt
-rw-r--r-- 1 root root 15 Jan 28 22:23 data2.txt
```

4. We can even try to output the content of, say, the second file, like this:

```
/ # cat data2.txt
```

5. Let's try to create a file in this folder from the host, and then use the volume with another container, like this:

```
/ # echo "This file we create on the host" > host-data.txt
```

6. Exit the tool container by pressing *Ctrl + D*.

7. Now, let's delete the `test` container, and run another one based on CentOS. This time, we are even mounting our volume to a different container folder, `/app/data`, like this:

```
$ docker container rm test
$ docker container run --name test2 -it \
    -v my-data:/app/data \
    centos:7 /bin/bash

Unable to find image 'centos:7' locally
7: Pulling from library/centos
8ba884070f61: Pull complete
Digest:
sha256:a799dd8a2ded4a83484bbae769d97655392b3f86533ceb7dd96bbac92980
9f3c
Status: Downloaded newer image for centos:7
[root@275c1fe31ec0 /]#
```

8. Once inside the `centos` container, we can navigate to the `/app/data` folder to which we have mounted the volume, and list its content, as follows:

```
[root@275c1fe31ec0 /]# cd /app/data
[root@275c1fe31ec0 /]# ls -l
```

As expected, we should see these three files:

```
-rw-r--r-- 1 root root 10 Aug 2 22:23 data.txt
-rw-r--r-- 1 root root 15 Aug 2 22:23 data2.txt
-rw-r--r-- 1 root root 32 Aug 2 22:31 host-data.txt
```

This is the definitive proof that data in a Docker volume persists beyond the lifetime of a container, and also, that volumes can be reused by other, even different, containers from the one that used it first.

It is important to note that the folder inside the container to which we mount a Docker volume is excluded from the Union filesystem. That is, each change inside this folder and any of its subfolders will not be part of the container layer, but will be persisted in the backing storage provided by the volume driver. This fact is really important since the container layer is deleted when the corresponding container is stopped and removed from the system.

9. Exit the `centos` container with *Ctrl + D*. Now, exit the `node-1` VM by pressing *Ctrl + D* again.

Removing volumes

Volumes can be removed using the `docker volume rm` command. It is important to remember that removing a volume destroys the containing data irreversibly, and thus is to be considered a dangerous command. Docker helps us a bit in this regard, as it does not allow us to delete a volume that is still in use by a container. Always make sure before you remove or delete a volume that you either have a backup of its data or you really don't need this data anymore. Let's see how to remove volumes by following these steps:

1. The following command deletes our `sample` volume that we created earlier:

```
$ docker volume rm sample
```

2. After executing the preceding command, double-check that the folder on the host has been deleted.

3. To remove all running containers in order to clean up the system, run the following command:

```
$ docker container rm -f $(docker container ls -aq)
```

Note that by using the -v or --volume flag in the command you use to remove a container, you can ask the system to also remove any volume associated with that particular container. Of course, that will only work if the particular volume is only used by this container.

In the next section, we will show how we can access the backing folder of a volume when working with Docker for Desktop.

Accessing volumes created with Docker for Desktop

Follow these steps:

1. Let's create a sample volume and inspect it using Docker for Desktop on our macOS or Windows machine, like this:

```
$ docker volume create sample
$ docker volume inspect sample
[
    {
        "CreatedAt": "2019-08-02T07:44:08Z",
        "Driver": "local",
        "Labels": {},
        "Mountpoint": "/var/lib/docker/volumes/sample/_data",
        "Name": "sample",
        "Options": {},
        "Scope": "local"
    }
]
```

The Mountpoint is shown as /var/lib/docker/volumes/sample/_data, but you will discover that there is no such folder on your macOS or Windows machine. The reason is that the path shown is in relation to the hidden VM that Docker for Windows uses to run containers. At this time, Linux containers cannot run natively on macOS, nor on Windows.

2. Next, let's generate two files with data in the volume from within an `alpine` container. To run the container and mount the sample `volume` to the `/data` folder of the container, use the following code:

```
$ docker container run --rm -it -v sample:/data alpine /bin/sh
```

3. Generate two files in the `/data` folder inside the container, like this:

```
/ # echo "Hello world" > /data/sample.txt
/ # echo "Other message" > /data/other.txt
```

4. Exit the `alpine` container by pressing *Ctrl + D*.

As mentioned earlier, we cannot directly access the backing folder of the `sample` volume from our macOS or from Windows. This is because the volume is in the hidden VM running on macOS or Windows that is used to run the Linux container in Docker for Desktop.

To access that hidden VM from our macOS, we have two options. We can either use a special container and run it in privileged mode, or we can use the `screen` utility to screen into the Docker driver. The first method is also applicable to Docker for Windows.

5. Let's start with the first method mentioned, by running a container from the `fundamentalsofdocker/nsenter` image. We have been using this container already in the previous section. Run the following code:

```
$ docker run -it --rm --privileged --pid=host
fundamentalsofdocker/nsenter
/ #
```

6. We can now navigate to the folder backing our `sample` volume, like this:

```
/ # cd /var/lib/docker/volumes/sample/_data
```

Let's see what is in this folder by running this code:

```
/ # ls -l
total 8
-rw-r--r-- 1 root root 14 Aug 2 08:07 other.txt
-rw-r--r-- 1 root root 12 Aug 2 08:07 sample.txt
```

7. Let's try to create a file from within this special container, and then list the content of the folder, as follows:

```
/ # echo "I love Docker" > docker.txt
/ # ls -l
total 12
-rw-r--r-- 1 root root 14 Aug 2 08:08 docker.txt
-rw-r--r-- 1 root root 14 Aug 2 08:07 other.txt
-rw-r--r-- 1 root root 12 Aug 2 08:07 sample.txt
```

And now, we have the files in the backing folder of the sample volume.

8. To exit our special privileged container, we can just press *Ctrl + D*.

9. Now that we have explored the first option, and if you're using macOS, let's try the screen tool, as follows:

```
$ screen
~/Library/Containers/com.docker.docker/Data/com.docker.driver.amd64
-linux/tty
```

10. By doing so, we will be greeted by an empty screen. Hit *Enter*, and a docker-desktop:~# command-line prompt will be displayed. We can now navigate to the volume folder, like this:

```
docker-desktop:~# cd /var/lib/docker/volumes/sample/_data
```

11. Let's create another file with some data in it, and then list the content of the folder, as follows:

```
docker-desktop:~# echo "Some other test" > test.txt
docker-desktop:~# ls -l
total 16
-rw-r--r-- 1 root root 14 Aug 2 08:08 docker.txt
-rw-r--r-- 1 root root 14 Aug 2 08:07 other.txt
-rw-r--r-- 1 root root 12 Aug 2 08:07 sample.txt
-rw-r--r-- 1 root root 16 Aug 2 08:10 test.txt
```

12. To exit this session with the Docker VM, press *Ctrl + A + K*.

We have now created data using three different methods, as follows:

- From within a container that has a `sample` volume mounted.
- Using a special privileged folder to access the hidden VM used by Docker for Desktop, and directly writing into the backing folder of the `sample` volume.
- Only on macOS, using the `screen` utility to enter into the hidden VM, and also directly writing into the backing folder of the `sample` volume.

Sharing data between containers

Containers are like sandboxes for the applications running inside them. This is mostly beneficial and wanted, in order to protect applications running in different containers from each other. It also means that the whole filesystem visible to an application running inside a container is private to this application, and no other application running in a different container can interfere with it.

At times, though, we want to share data between containers. Say an application running in container A produces some data that will be consumed by another application running in container B. *How can we achieve this?* Well, I'm sure you've already guessed it—we can use Docker volumes for this purpose. We can create a volume and mount it to container A, as well as to container B. In this way, both applications A and B have access to the same data.

Now, as always when multiple applications or processes concurrently access data, we have to be very careful to avoid inconsistencies. To avoid concurrency problems such as race conditions, we ideally have only one application or process that is creating or modifying data, while all other processes concurrently accessing this data only read it. We can enforce a process running in a container to only be able to read the data in a volume by mounting this volume as read-only. Have a look at the following command:

```
$ docker container run -it --name writer \
    -v shared-data:/data \
    alpine /bin/sh
```

Here, we create a container called `writer` that has a volume, `shared-data`, mounted in default read/write mode:

1. Try to create a file inside this container, like this:

   ```
   # / echo "I can create a file" > /data/sample.txt
   ```

   It should succeed.

2. Exit this container, and then execute the following command:

   ```
   $ docker container run -it --name reader \
       -v shared-data:/app/data:ro \
       ubuntu:19.04 /bin/bash
   ```

   And we have a container called `reader` that has the same volume mounted as **read-only** (`ro`).

3. Firstly, make sure you can see the file created in the first container, like this:

   ```
   $ ls -l /app/data
   total 4
   -rw-r--r-- 1 root root 20 Jan 28 22:55 sample.txt
   ```

4. Then, try to create a file, like this:

   ```
   # / echo "Try to break read/only" > /app/data/data.txt
   ```

   It will fail with the following message:

   ```
   bash: /app/data/data.txt: Read-only file system
   ```

5. Let's exit the container by typing `exit` at the Command Prompt. Back on the host, let's clean up all containers and volumes, as follows:

   ```
   $ docker container rm -f $(docker container ls -aq)
   $ docker volume rm $(docker volume ls -q)
   ```

6. Once this is done, exit the `docker-machine` VM by also typing `exit` at the Command Prompt. You should be back on your Docker for Desktop. Use `docker-machine` to stop the VM, like this:

   ```
   $ docker-machine stop node-1
   ```

Next, we will show how to mount arbitrary folders from the Docker host into a container.

Using host volumes

In certain scenarios, such as when developing new containerized applications or when a containerized application needs to consume data from a certain folder produced—say—by a legacy application, it is very useful to use volumes that mount a specific host folder. Let's look at the following example:

```
$ docker container run --rm -it \
    -v $(pwd)/src:/app/src \
    alpine:latest /bin/sh
```

The preceding expression interactively starts an `alpine` container with a shell and mounts the `src` subfolder of the current directory into the container at `/app/src`. We need to use `$(pwd)` (or `` `pwd` ``, for that matter), which is the current directory, as when working with volumes, we always need to use absolute paths.

Developers use these techniques all the time when they are working on their application that runs in a container, and want to make sure that the container always contains the latest changes they make to the code, without the need to rebuild the image and rerun the container after each change.

Let's make a sample to demonstrate how that works. Let's say we want to create a simple static website using nginx as our web server as follows:

1. First, let's create a new folder on the host, where we will put our web assets—such as HTML, CSS, and JavaScript files—and navigate to it, like this:

    ```
    $ mkdir ~/my-web
    $ cd ~/my-web
    ```

2. Then, we create a simple web page, like this:

    ```
    $ echo "<h1>Personal Website</h1>" > index.html
    ```

3. Now, we add a `Dockerfile` that will contain instructions on how to build the image containing our sample website.

4. Add a file called `Dockerfile` to the folder, with this content:

    ```
    FROM nginx:alpine
    COPY . /usr/share/nginx/html
    ```

The `Dockerfile` starts with the latest Alpine version of nginx, and then copies all files from the current host directory into the `/usr/share/nginx/html` containers folder. This is where nginx expects web assets to be located.

5. Now, let's build the image with the following command:

```
$ docker image build -t my-website:1.0 .
```

6. And finally, we run a container from this image. We will run the container in detached mode, like this:

```
$ docker container run -d \
    --name my-site \
    -p 8080:80 \
    my-website:1.0
```

Note the `-p 8080:80` parameter. We haven't discussed this yet, but we will do it in detail in `Chapter 10`, *Single-Host Networking*. At the moment, just know that this maps the container port `80` on which nginx is listening for incoming requests to port `8080` of your laptop, where you can then access the application.

7. Now, open a browser tab and navigate to `http://localhost:8080/index.html`, and you should see your website, which currently consists only of a title, `Personal Website`.

8. Now, edit the `index.html` file in your favorite editor, to look like this:

```
<h1>Personal Website</h1>
<p>This is some text</p>
```

9. Now, save it, and then refresh the browser. Oh! That didn't work. The browser still displays the previous version of the `index.html` file, which consists only of the title. So, let's stop and remove the current container, then rebuild the image, and rerun the container, as follows:

```
$ docker container rm -f my-site
$ docker image build -t my-website:1.0 .
$ docker container run -d \
    --name my-site \
    -p 8080:80 \
    my-website:1.0
```

This time, when you refresh the browser, the new content should be shown. Well, it worked, but there is way too much friction involved. Imagine you have to do this each and every time that you make a simple change to your website. That's not sustainable.

10. Now is the time to use host-mounted volumes. Once again, remove the current container and rerun it with the volume mount, like this:

```
$ docker container rm -f my-site
$ docker container run -d \
    --name my-site \
    -v $(pwd):/usr/share/nginx/html \
    -p 8080:80 \
    my-website:1.0
```

11. Now, append some more content to the `index.html` file, and save it. Then, refresh your browser. You should see the changes. And this is exactly what we wanted to achieve; we also call this an *edit-and-continue* experience. You can make as many changes in your web files and always immediately see the result in the browser, without having to rebuild the image and restart the container containing your website.

It is important to note that the updates are now propagated bi-directionally. If you make changes on the host, they will be propagated to the container, and vice versa. Also important is the fact that when you mount the current folder into the container target folder, `/usr/share/nginx/html`, the content that is already there is replaced by the content of the host folder.

Defining volumes in images

If we go for a moment back to what we have learned about containers in Chapter 3, *Mastering Containers,* then we have this: the filesystem of each container, when started, is made up of the immutable layers of the underlying image, plus a writable container layer specific to this very container. All changes that the processes running inside the container make to the filesystem will be persisted in this container layer. Once the container is stopped and removed from the system, the corresponding container layer is deleted from the system and irreversibly lost.

Some applications, such as databases running in containers, need to persist their data beyond the lifetime of the container. In this case, they can use volumes. To make things a bit more explicit, let's look at a concrete example. MongoDB is a popular open source document database. Many developers use MongoDB as a storage service for their applications. The maintainers of MongoDB have created an image and published it on Docker Hub, which can be used to run an instance of the database in a container. This database will be producing data that needs to be persisted long term, but the MongoDB maintainers do not know who uses this image and how it is used. So, they have no influence over the `docker container run` command with which the users of the database will start this container. *How can they now define volumes?*

Luckily, there is a way of defining volumes in the `Dockerfile`. The keyword to do so is VOLUME, and we can either add the absolute path to a single folder or a comma-separated list of paths. These paths represent folders of the container's filesystem. Let's look at a few samples of such volume definitions, as follows:

```
VOLUME /app/data
VOLUME /app/data, /app/profiles, /app/config
VOLUME ["/app/data", "/app/profiles", "/app/config"]
```

The first line in the preceding snippet defines a single volume to be mounted at /app/data. The second line defines three volumes as a comma-separated list. The last one defines the same as the second line, but this time, the value is formatted as a JSON array.

When a container is started, Docker automatically creates a volume and mounts it to the corresponding target folder of the container for each path defined in the `Dockerfile`. Since each volume is created automatically by Docker, it will have an SHA-256 as its ID.

At container runtime, the folders defined as volumes in the `Dockerfile` are excluded from the Union filesystem, and thus any changes in those folders do not change the container layer but are persisted to the respective volume. It is now the responsibility of the operations engineers to make sure that the backing storage of the volumes is properly backed up.

We can use the `docker image inspect` command to get information about the volumes defined in the `Dockerfile`. Let's see what MongoDB gives us by following these steps:

1. First, we pull the image with the following command:

```
$ docker image pull mongo:3.7
```

2. Then, we inspect this image, and use the `--format` parameter to only extract the essential part from the massive amount of data, as follows:

```
$ docker image inspect \
    --format='{{json .ContainerConfig.Volumes}}' \
    mongo:3.7 | jq .
```

Note the `| jq .` at the end of the command. We are piping the output of `docker image inspect` into the `jq` tool, which nicely formats the output. If you haven't installed `jq` yet on your system, you can do so with `brew install jq` on your macOS, or with `choco install jq` on Windows.

The preceding command will return the following result:

```
{
    "/data/configdb": {},
    "/data/db": {}
}
```

Evidently, the `Dockerfile` for MongoDB defines two volumes at /data/configdb and /data/db.

3. Now, let's run an instance of MongoDB in the background as a daemon, as follows:

```
$ docker run --name my-mongo -d mongo:3.7
```

4. We can now use the `docker container inspect` command to get information about the volumes that have been created, among other things.

Use this command to just get the volume information:

```
$ docker inspect --format '{{json .Mounts}}' my-mongo | jq .
```

The preceding command should output something like this (shortened):

```
[
    {
        "Type": "volume",
        "Name": "b9ea0158b5...",
        "Source": "/var/lib/docker/volumes/b9ea0158b.../_data",
        "Destination": "/data/configdb",
        "Driver": "local",
        ...
    },
    {
```

```
            "Type": "volume",
            "Name": "5becf84b1e...",
            "Source": "/var/lib/docker/volumes/5becf84b1.../_data",
            "Destination": "/data/db",
            ...
        }
    ]
```

Note that the values of the `Name` and `Source` fields have been trimmed for readability. The `Source` field gives us the path to the host directory, where the data produced by the MongoDB inside the container will be stored.

That's it for the moment about volumes. In the next section, we will explore how we can configure applications running in containers, and the container image build process itself.

Configuring containers

More often than not, we need to provide some configuration to the application running inside a container. The configuration is often used to allow one and the same container to run in very different environments, such as in development, test, staging, or production environments.

In Linux, configuration values are often provided via environment variables.

We have learned that an application running inside a container is completely shielded from its host environment. Thus, the environment variables that we see on the host are different from the ones that we see from within a container.

Let's prove that by first looking at what is defined on our host:

1. Use this command:

   ```
   $ export
   ```

   On my macOS, I see something like this (shortened):

   ```
   ...
   COLORFGBG '7;0'
   COLORTERM truecolor
   HOME /Users/gabriel
   ITERM_PROFILE Default
   ITERM_SESSION_ID w0t1p0:47EFAEFE-BA29-4CC0-B2E7-8C5C2EA619A8
   LC_CTYPE UTF-8
   LOGNAME gabriel
   ...
   ```

2. Next, let's run a shell inside an `alpine` container, and list the environment variables we see there, as follows:

```
$ docker container run --rm -it alpine /bin/sh
/ # export
```

```
export HOME='/root'
export HOSTNAME='91250b722bc3'
export
PATH='/usr/local/sbin:/usr/local/bin:/usr/sbin:/usr/bin:/sbin:/bin'
export PWD='/'
export SHLVL='1'
export TERM='xterm'
```

The preceding output we see from the `export` command is evidently totally different than what we saw directly on the host.

3. Hit *Ctrl + D* to leave the `alpine` container.

Next, let's define environment variables for containers.

Defining environment variables for containers

Now, the good thing is that we can actually pass some configuration values into the container at start time. We can use the `--env` (or the short form, `-e`) parameter in the form `--env <key>=<value>` to do so, where `<key>` is the name of the environment variable and `<value>` represents the value to be associated with that variable. Let's assume we want the app that is to be run in our container to have access to an environment variable called `LOG_DIR`, with the value `/var/log/my-log`. We can do so with this command:

```
$ docker container run --rm -it \
    --env LOG_DIR=/var/log/my-log \
    alpine /bin/sh
/ #
```

The preceding code starts a shell in an `alpine` container and defines the requested environment inside the running container. To prove that this is true, we can execute this command inside the `alpine` container:

```
/ # export | grep LOG_DIR
```

```
export LOG_DIR='/var/log/my-log'
```

The output looks as expected. We now indeed have the requested environment variable with the correct value available inside the container.

We can, of course, define more than just one environment variable when we run a container. We just need to repeat the `--env` (or `-e`) parameter. Have a look at this sample:

```
$ docker container run --rm -it \
    --env LOG_DIR=/var/log/my-log \
    --env MAX_LOG_FILES=5 \
    --env MAX_LOG_SIZE=1G \
  alpine /bin/sh
/ #
```

If we do a list of the environment variables now, we see the following:

```
/ # export | grep LOG
```

```
export LOG_DIR='/var/log/my-log'
export MAX_LOG_FILES='5'
export MAX_LOG_SIZE='1G'
```

Let's now look at situations where we have many environment variables to configure.

Using configuration files

Complex applications can have many environment variables to configure, and thus our command to run the corresponding container can quickly become unwieldy. For this purpose, Docker allows us to pass a collection of environment variable definitions as a file, and we have the `--env-file` parameter in the `docker container run` command.

Let's try this out, as follows:

1. Create a `fod/05` folder and navigate to it, like this:

   ```
   $ mkdir -p ~/fod/05 && cd ~/fod/05
   ```

2. Use your favorite editor to create a file called `development.config` in this folder. Add the following content to the file, and save it, as follows:

   ```
   LOG_DIR=/var/log/my-log
   MAX_LOG_FILES=5
   MAX_LOG_SIZE=1G
   ```

Notice how we have the definition of a single environment variable per line in the format <key>=<value>, where, once again, <key> is the name of the environment variable, and <value> represents the value to be associated with that variable.

3. Now, from within the fod/05 folder, let's run an alpine container, pass the file as an environment file, and run the export command inside the container to verify that the variables listed inside the file have indeed been created as environment variables inside the container, like this:

```
$ docker container run --rm -it \
    --env-file ./development.config \
    alpine sh -c "export"
```

And indeed, the variables are defined, as we can see in the output generated:

```
export HOME='/root'
export HOSTNAME='30ad92415f87'
export LOG_DIR='/var/log/my-log'
export MAX_LOG_FILES='5'
export MAX_LOG_SIZE='1G'
export
PATH='/usr/local/sbin:/usr/local/bin:/usr/sbin:/usr/bin:/sbin:/bin'
export PWD='/'
export SHLVL='1'
export TERM='xterm'
```

Next, let's look at how to define default values for environment variables that are valid for all container instances of a given Docker image.

Defining environment variables in container images

Sometimes, we want to define some default value for an environment variable that must be present in each container instance of a given container image. We can do so in the `Dockerfile` that is used to create that image by following these steps:

1. Use your favorite editor to create a file called `Dockerfile` in the `~/fod/05` folder. Add the following content to the file, and save it:

   ```
   FROM alpine:latest
   ENV LOG_DIR=/var/log/my-log
   ENV  MAX_LOG_FILES=5
   ENV MAX_LOG_SIZE=1G
   ```

2. Create a container image called `my-alpine` using the preceding `Dockerfile`, as follows:

   ```
   $ docker image build -t my-alpine .
   ```

   Run a container instance from this image that outputs the environment variables defined inside the container, like this:

   ```
   $ docker container run --rm -it \
       my-alpine sh -c "export | grep LOG"

   export LOG_DIR='/var/log/my-log'
   export MAX_LOG_FILES='5'
   export MAX_LOG_SIZE='1G'
   ```

   This is exactly what we would have expected.

   The good thing, though, is that we are not stuck with those variable values at all. We can override one or many of them, using the `--env` parameter in the `docker container run` command. Have a look at the following command and its output:

   ```
   $ docker container run --rm -it \
       --env MAX_LOG_SIZE=2G \
       --env MAX_LOG_FILES=10 \
       my-alpine sh -c "export | grep LOG"

   export LOG_DIR='/var/log/my-log'
   export MAX_LOG_FILES='10'
   export MAX_LOG_SIZE='2G'
   ```

We can also override default values, using environment files together with the `--env-file` parameter in the `docker container run` command. Please try it out for yourself.

Environment variables at build time

Sometimes, we would want to have the possibility to define some environment variables that are valid at the time when we build a container image. Imagine that you want to define a `BASE_IMAGE_VERSION` environment variable that shall then be used as a parameter in your `Dockerfile`. Imagine the following `Dockerfile`:

```
ARG BASE_IMAGE_VERSION=12.7-stretch
FROM node:${BASE_IMAGE_VERSION}
WORKDIR /app
COPY packages.json .
RUN npm install
COPY . .
CMD npm start
```

We are using the `ARG` keyword to define a default value that is used each time we build an image from the preceding `Dockerfile`. In this case, that means that our image uses the `node:12.7-stretch` base image.

Now, if we want to create a special image for—say—testing purposes, we can override this variable at image build time using the `--build-arg` parameter, as follows:

```
$ docker image build \
    --build-arg BASE_IMAGE_VERSION=12.7-alpine \
    -t my-node-app-test .
```

In this case, the resulting `my-node-test:latest` image will be built from the `node:12.7-alpine` base image and not from the `node:12.7-stretch` default image.

To summarize, environment variables defined via `--env` or `--env-file` are valid at container runtime. Variables defined with `ARG` in the `Dockerfile` or `--build-arg` in the `docker container build` command are valid at container image build time. The former are used to configure an application running inside a container, while the latter are used to parametrize the container image build process.

Summary

In this chapter, we have introduced Docker volumes that can be used to persist states produced by containers and make them durable. We can also use volumes to provide containers with data originating from various sources. We have learned how to create, mount, and use volumes. We have learned various techniques of defining volumes such as by name, by mounting a host directory, or by defining volumes in a container image.

In this chapter, we have also discussed how we can configure environment variables that can be used by applications running inside a container. We have shown how to define those variables in the `docker container run` command, either explicitly, one by one, or as a collection in a configuration file. We have also shown how to parametrize the build process of container images by using build arguments.

In the next chapter, we are going to introduce techniques commonly used to allow a developer to evolve, modify, debug, and test their code while running in a container.

Questions

Please try to answer the following questions to assess your learning progress:

1. How would you create a named data volume with a name—for example, `my-products`—using the default driver?
2. How would you run a container using the `alpine` image and mount the `my-products` volume in read-only mode into the `/data` container folder?
3. How would you locate the folder that is associated with the `my-products` volume and navigate to it? Also, how will you create a file, `sample.txt`, with some content?
4. How would you run another `alpine` container in to which you mount the `my-products` volume to the `/app-data` folder, in read/write mode? Inside this container, navigate to the `/app-data` folder and create a `hello.txt` file with some content.
5. How would you mount a host volume—for example, `~/my-project`—into a container?

6. How would you remove all unused volumes from your system?

7. The list of environment variables that an application running in a container sees is the same as if the application were to run directly on the host.

   A. True
   B. False

8. Your application that shall run in a container needs a huge list of environment variables for configuration. What is the simplest method to run a container with your application and provide all this information to it?

Further reading

The following articles provide more in-depth information:

- Use volumes, at `http://dockr.ly/2EUjTml`
- Manage data in Docker, at `http://dockr.ly/2EhBpzD`
- Docker volumes on **Play with Docker (PWD)**, at `http://bit.ly/2sjIfDj`
- `nsenter` —Linux man page, at `https://bit.ly/2MEPG0n`
- Set environment variables, at `https://dockr.ly/2HxMCjS`
- Understanding how `ARG` and `FROM` interact, at `https://dockr.ly/2OrhZgx`

6
Debugging Code Running in Containers

In the previous chapter, we learned how to work with stateful containers, that is, containers that consume and produce data. We also learned how to configure our containers at runtime and at image build time using environment variables and config files.

In this chapter, we're going to introduce techniques commonly used to allow a developer to evolve, modify, debug, and test their code while running in a container. With these techniques at hand, you will enjoy a frictionless development process for applications running in a container, similar to what you experience when developing applications that run natively.

Here is a list of the topics we're going to discuss:

- Evolving and testing code running in a container
- Auto restarting code upon changes
- Line-by-line code debugging inside a container
- Instrumenting your code to produce meaningful logging information
- Using Jaeger to monitor and troubleshoot

After finishing this chapter, you will be able to do the following:

- Mount source code residing on the host in a running container
- Configure an application running in a container to auto-restart after a code change
- Configure Visual Studio Code to debug applications written in Java, Node.js, Python, or .NET running inside a container line by line
- Log important events from your application code

Technical requirements

In this chapter, if you want to follow along with the code, you need Docker for Desktop on macOS or Windows and a code editor—preferably Visual Studio Code. The sample will also work on a Linux machine with Docker and VS Code installed.

Evolving and testing code running in a container

When developing code that will eventually be running in a container, it is often the best approach to run the code in the container from the very beginning, to make sure there will be no unexpected surprises. But, we have to do this in the right way in order not to introduce any unnecessary friction into our development process. Let's first look at a naive way that we could run and test code in a container:

1. Create a new project folder and navigate to it:

   ```
   $ mkdir -p ~/fod/ch06 && cd ~/fod/ch06
   ```

2. Let's use npm to create a new Node.js project:

   ```
   $ npm init
   ```

3. Accept all the defaults. Notice that a package.json file is created with the following content:

   ```
   {
     "name": "ch06",
     "version": "1.0.0",
     "description": "",
     "main": "index.js",
     "scripts": {
       "test": "echo \"Error: no test specified\" && exit 1"
     },
     "author": "",
     "license": "ISC"
   }
   ```

4. We want to use the Express.js library in our Node application; thus, use npm to install it:

   ```
   $ npm install express --save
   ```

This will install the newest version of Express.js on our machine and, because of the --save parameter, add a reference to our package.json file that looks similar to this:

```
"dependencies": {
  "express": "^4.17.1"
}
```

5. Start VS Code from within this folder:

   ```
   $ code .
   ```

6. In VS Code, create a new index.js file and add this code snippet to it. Do not forget to save:

   ```
   const express = require('express');
   const app = express();

   app.listen(3000, '0.0.0.0', ()=>{
       console.log('Application listening at 0.0.0.0:3000');
   })

   app.get('/', (req, res)=>{
       res.send('Sample Application: Hello World!');
   })
   ```

7. From back within your terminal window, start the application:

   ```
   $ node index.js
   ```

   You should see this as the output:

   ```
   Application listening at 0.0.0.0:3000
   ```

This means that the application is running and ready to listen at 0.0.0.0:3000. You may ask yourself what the meaning of the host address 0.0.0.0 is and why we have chosen it. We will come back to that later, when we run the application inside a container. For the moment, just know that 0.0.0.0 is a reserved IP address with a special meaning, similar to the loopback address 127.0.0.1. The 0.0.0.0 address simply means *all IPv4 addresses on the local machine*. If a host has two IP addresses, say 52.11.32.13 and 10.11.0.1, and a server running on the host listens on 0.0.0.0, it will be reachable at both of those IPs.

8. Now open a new tab in your favorite browser and navigate to `localhost:3000`. You should see this:

Sample Node.js app running in a browser

Great—our Node.js application is running on our developer machine. Stop the application by pressing *Ctrl + C* in the terminal.

9. Now we want to test the application we have developed so far by running it inside a container. To do this, we have to create a `Dockerfile` first, so that we can build a container image, from which we can then run a container. Let's use VS Code again to add a file called `Dockerfile` to our project folder and give it the following content:

```
FROM node:latest
WORKDIR /app
COPY package.json ./
RUN npm install
COPY . .
CMD node index.js
```

10. We can then use this `Dockerfile` to build an image called `sample-app` as follows:

```
$ docker image build -t sample-app .
```

11. After building, run the application in the container with this command:

```
$ docker container run --rm -it \
    --name my-sample-app \
    -p 3000:3000 \
    sample-app
```

The preceding command runs a container with the name `my-sample-app` from the container image `sample-app` and maps the container port `3000` to the equivalent host port. The port mapping is necessary; otherwise, we could not access the application running inside the container from outside the container. We will learn more about port mapping in `Chapter 10`, *Single-Host Networking*.

Similar to when we ran the application directly on our host, the output is as follows:

```
Application listening at 0.0.0.0:3000
```

12. Refresh the browser tab from before (or open a new browser tab and navigate to `localhost:3000`, if you closed it). You should see that the application still runs and produces the same output as when running natively. This is good. We have just shown that our application not only runs on our host but also inside a container.
13. Stop and remove the container by pressing *Ctrl + C* in the terminal.
14. Now let's modify our code and add some additional functionality. We will define another `HTTP GET` endpoint at `/hobbies`. Please add the following code snippet to your `index.js` file:

```
const hobbies = [
  'Swimming', 'Diving', 'Jogging', 'Cooking', 'Singing'
];

app.get('/hobbies', (req, res)=>{
  res.send(hobbies);
})
```

We can first test the new functionality on our host by running the app with `node index.js` and navigating to `localhost:3000/hobbies` in the browser. We should see the expected output in the browser window. Don't forget to stop the application with *Ctrl + C* when done testing.

15. Next, we need to test the code when it runs inside the container. Thus, first, we create a new version of the container image:

```
$ docker image build -t sample-app .
```

16. Next, we run a container from this new image:

```
$ docker container run --rm -it \
    --name my-sample-app \
    -p 3000:3000 \
    sample-app
```

Now, we can navigate to `localhost:3000/hobbies` in our browser and confirm that the application works as expected inside the container too. Once again, don't forget to stop the container when done by pressing *Ctrl + C*.

We can repeat this sequence of tasks over and over again for each feature we add or any existing features we improve. It turns out that this is a lot of added friction compared to times when all the applications we developed always ran directly on the host.

However, we can do better. In the next section, we will look at a technique that allows us to remove most of the friction.

Mounting evolving code into the running container

What if, after a code change, we do not have to rebuild the container image and rerun a container? Wouldn't it be great if the changes would immediately, as we save them in an editor such as VS Code, be available inside the container too? Well, exactly that is possible with volume mapping. In the last chapter, we learned how to map an arbitrary host folder into an arbitrary location inside a container. We want to leverage exactly that in this section.

We saw in *Chapter 5*, *Data Volumes and Configuration*, how we can map host folders as volumes in a container. If I want, for example, to mount a host folder, `/projects/sample-app`, into a container at `/app`, the syntax for this looks as follows:

```
$ docker container run --rm -it \
    --volume /projects/sample-app:/app \
    alpine /bin/sh
```

Notice the line `--volume <host-folder>:<container-folder>`. The path to the host folder needs to be an absolute path, as in the example, `/projects/sample-app`.

If we now want to run a container from our `sample-app` container image, and, if we do that from the project folder, then we can map the current folder into the `/app` folder of the container as follows:

```
$ docker container run --rm -it \
    --volume $(pwd):/app \
    -p 3000:3000 \
```

Please note the `$ (pwd)` in place of the host folder path. `$ (pwd)` evaluates to the absolute path of the current folder, which comes in very handy.

Now, if we do mount the current folder into the container as described above, then whatever was in the `/app` folder of the `sample-app` container image will be overridden by the content of the mapped host folder, that is, in our case, the current folder. That's exactly what we want—we want the current source to be mapped from the host in the container.

Let's test whether it works:

1. Stop the container if you have started it by pressing *Ctrl + C*.
2. Then add the following snippet to the end of the `index.js` file:

```
app.get('/status', (req, res)=>{
  res.send('OK');
})
```

Do not forget to save.

3. Then run the container again – this time without rebuilding the image first – to see what happens:

```
$ docker container run --rm -it \
    --name my-sample-app \
    --volume $(pwd):/app \
    -p 3000:3000 \
    sample-app
```

4. In your browser, navigate to `localhost:3000/status` and expect to see the OK output in the browser window. Alternatively, you could use `curl` in another terminal window:

```
$ curl localhost:3000/status
OK
```

For all those working on Windows and/or Docker for Windows, you can use the PowerShell command `Invoke-WebRequest` or `iwr` for short instead of `curl`. The equivalent to the preceding command would then be `iwr -Url localhost:3000/status`.

5. Leave the application in the container running for the moment and make yet another change. Instead of just returning OK when navigating to /status, we want the message OK, all good to be returned. Make your modification and save the changes.

6. Then execute the curl command again or, if you did use the browser, refresh the page. What do you see? Right—nothing happened. The change we made is not reflected in the running application.

7. Well, let's double-check whether the change has been propagated in the running container. To do this, let's execute the following command:

```
$ docker container exec my-sample-app cat index.js
```

We should see something like this—I have shortened the output for readability:

```
...
app.get('/hobbies', (req, res)=>{
 res.send(hobbies);
})

app.get('/status', (req, res)=>{
 res.send('OK, all good');
})
...
```

Evidently, our changes have been propagated into the container as expected. Why, then, are the changes not reflected in the running application? Well, the answer is simple: for changes to be applied to the application, the application has to be restarted.

8. Let's try that. Stop the container with the application running by pressing *Ctrl + C*. Then re-execute the preceding docker container run command and use curl to probe the endpoint localhost:3000/status. Now, the following new message should be displayed:

```
$ curl localhost:3000/status
 OK, all good
```

So, we have achieved a significant reduction in the friction in the development process by mapping the source code in the running container. We can now add new or modify existing code and test it without having to build the container image first. Yet, there is still a bit of friction left in play. We have to manually restart the container every time we want to test some new or modified code. Can we automate this? The answer is yes! We will demonstrate exactly this in the next section.

Auto restarting code upon changes

Cool—in the last section, we showed how we can massively reduce friction by volume mapping the source code folder in the container, thus avoiding having to rebuild the container image and rerun the container over and over again.

Yet we still feel some remaining friction. The application running inside the container does not automatically restart when a code change happens. Thus, we have to manually stop and restart the container to pick up the new changes.

Auto-restarting for Node.js

If you have been coding for a while, you will certainly have heard about helpful tools that can run your applications and restart them automatically whenever they discover a change in the code base. For Node.js applications, the most popular such tool is nodemon. We can install nodemon globally on our system with the following command:

```
$ npm install -g nodemon
```

Now, having nodemon available, instead of starting our application (for example, on the host) with node index.js, we can just execute nodemon and we should see the following:

```
$ nodemon
[nodemon] 1.17.2
[nodemon] to restart at any time, enter `rs`
[nodemon] watching: *.*
[nodemon] starting `node index.js`
Application listening at 0.0.0.0:3000
```

Using nodemon to run a Node.js application

Evidently, nodemon has recognized, from parsing our package.json file, that it should use node index.js as the start command.

Now try to change some code, for example, add the following code snippet at the end of index.js and then save the file:

```
app.get('/colors', (req,res)=>{
  res.send(['red','green','blue']);
})
```

Look at the terminal window. Did you see something happening? You should see this additional output:

```
[nodemon] restarting due to changes...
[nodemon] starting `node index.js`
Application listening at 0.0.0.0:3000
```

This clearly indicates that nodemon has recognized some changes and automatically restarted the application. Try it out with your browser by navigating to localhost:3000/colors. You should see the following expected output in the browser:

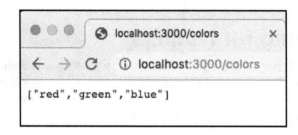

Getting colors

This is cool—you got this result without having to manually restart the application. This makes us yet another bit more productive. Now, can we do the same within the container? Yes, we can. We won't use the start command node index.js, as defined in the last line of our Dockerfile:

```
CMD node index.js
```

We will use nodemon instead.

Do we have to modify our Dockerfile? Or do we need two different Dockerfiles, one for development and one for production?

Our original Dockerfile creates an image that unfortunately does not contain nodemon. Thus, we need to create a new Dockerfile. Let's call it Dockerfile-dev. It should look like this:

```
FROM node:latest
RUN npm install -g nodemon
WORKDIR /app
COPY package.json ./
RUN npm install
COPY . .
CMD nodemon
```

Comparing with our original Dockerfile, we have added line 2 where we install `nodemon`. We have also changed the last line and are now using `nodemon` as our start command.

Let's build our development image as follows:

```
$ docker image build -t sample-app-dev .
```

We'll run a container like this:

```
$ docker container run --rm -it \
    -v $(pwd):/app \
    -p 3000:3000 \
    sample-app-dev
```

Now, while the application is running in the container, change some code, save, and notice that the application inside the container is automatically restarted. Thus, we have achieved the same reduction in friction running in a container as we did when running directly on the host.

You may ask, does this only apply to Node.js? No, fortunately many of the popular languages support similar concepts.

Auto-restarting for Python

Let's look at how the same thing works for Python:

1. First, create a new project folder for our sample Python application and navigate to it:

```
$ mkdir -p ~/fod/ch06/python && cd ~/fod/ch06/python
```

2. Open VS Code from within this folder with the command `code ..`
3. We will create a sample Python application that uses the popular Flask library. Thus, add a `requirements.txt` file with the `flask` content to this folder.

4. Next, add a `main.py` file and give it this content:

```python
from flask import Flask
app = Flask(__name__)

@app.route("/")
def hello():
    return "Hello World!"

if __name__ == "__main__":
    app.run()
```

This is a simple **Hello World** type app that implements a single RESTful endpoint at `localhost:5000/`.

5. Before we can run and test this application, we need to install the dependencies—Flask in our case. In the terminal, run the following:

```
$ pip install -r requirements.txt
```

This should install Flask on your host. We are now ready to go.

6. When using Python, we can also use `nodemon` to have our application auto restart upon any changes to the code. For example, assume that your command to start the Python application is `python main.py`. Then you would just use `nodemon` as follows:

```
$ nodemon main.py
```

You should see this:

```
$ nodemon main.py
[nodemon] 1.17.2
[nodemon] to restart at any time, enter `rs`
[nodemon] watching: *.*
[nodemon] starting `python main.py`
 * Serving Flask app "main" (lazy loading)
 * Environment: production
   WARNING: Do not use the development server in a production environment.
   Use a production WSGI server instead.
 * Debug mode: off
 * Running on http://127.0.0.1:5000/ (Press CTRL+C to quit)
```

7. Using `nodemon` to start and monitor a Python application, we can test the application by using `curl` and should see this:

```
$ curl localhost:5000/
Hello World!
```

8. Let's now modify the code by adding this snippet to `main.py`, right after the definition of the `/` endpoint, and save:

```
from flask import jsonify

@app.route("/colors")
def colors():
    return jsonify(["red", "green", "blue"])
```

nodemon will discover the changes and restart the Python app, as we can see in the output produced in the terminal:

```
[nodemon] restarting due to changes...
[nodemon] starting `python main.py`
 * Serving Flask app "main" (lazy loading)
 * Environment: production
   WARNING: Do not use the development server in a production environment.
   Use a production WSGI server instead.
 * Debug mode: off
 * Running on http://127.0.0.1:5000/ (Press CTRL+C to quit)
```

nodemon discovering a change in the Python code

9. Once again, believing is good, testing is better. Thus, let's use our friend `curl` once again to probe the new endpoint and see what we get:

```
$ curl localhost:5000/colors
["red", "green", "blue"]
```

Nice—it works! With that, we have covered Python. .NET is another popular platform. Let's see if we can do something similar to this when developing a C# application on .NET.

Auto-restarting for .NET

Our next candidate is a .NET application written in C#. Let's look at how auto-restart works in .NET.

1. First, create a new project folder for our sample C# application and navigate to it:

   ```
   $ mkdir -p ~/fod/ch06/csharp && cd ~/fod/ch06/csharp
   ```

    If you have not done so before, please install .NET Core on your laptop or workstation. You can get it at https://dotnet.microsoft.com/download/dotnet-core. At the time of writing, version 2.2 is the current stable version. Once it's installed, check the version with dotnet --version. It is 2.2.401 for me.

2. Navigate to the source folder for this chapter:

   ```
   $ cd ~/fod/ch06
   ```

3. From within this folder, use the dotnet tool to create a new Web API and have it placed in the dotnet subfolder:

   ```
   $ dotnet new webapi -o dotnet
   ```

4. Navigate to this new project folder:

   ```
   $ cd dotnet
   ```

5. Once again, use the code . command to open VS Code from within the dotnet folder.

    If this is the first time you have opened a .NET Core 2.2 project with VS Code, then the editor will start to download some C# dependencies. Wait until all dependencies have been downloaded. The editor may also display a popup asking you to add the missing dependencies for our dotnet project. Click the Yes button in this case.

In the project explorer of VS Code, you should see this:

DotNet Web API project in the VS Code Project Explorer

6. Please note the `Controllers` folder with the `ValuesController.cs` file in it. Open this file and analyze its content. It contains the definition for a `ValuesController` class, which implements a simple RESTful controller with `GET`, `PUT`, `POST`, and `DELETE` endpoints at `api/values`.

7. From your terminal, run the application with `dotnet run`. You should see something like this:

```
$ dotnet run
info: Microsoft.AspNetCore.DataProtection.KeyManagement.XmlKeyManager[0]
      User profile is available. Using '/Users/gabriel/.aspnet/DataProtection-Keys' as key
repository; keys will not be encrypted at rest.
Hosting environment: Development
Content root path: /Users/gabriel/fod/ch06/dotnet
Now listening on: https://localhost:5001
Now listening on: http://localhost:5000
Application started. Press Ctrl+C to shut down.
```

Running the .NET sample Web API on the host

8. We can use `curl` to test the application as follows, for example:

```
$ curl --insecure https://localhost:5001/api/values
["value1","value2"]
```

The application runs and returns the expected result.

 Please note that the application is configured to redirect `http://localhost:5000` to `https://localhost:5001` by default. But, this is an insecure endpoint and to suppress the warning, we use the `--insecure` switch.

9. We can now try to modify the code in `ValuesController.cs` and return, say, three items instead of two from the first `GET` endpoint:

```
[HttpGet]
public ActionResult<IEnumerable<string>> Get()
{
    return new string[] { "value1", "value2", "value3" };
}
```

10. Save your changes and rerun the `curl` command. Notice how the result does not contain the new added value. It is the same problem as we observed for Node.js and Python. To see the new updated return value, we need to (manually) restart the application.

11. Thus, in your terminal, stop the application with *Ctrl + C* and restart it with `dotnet run`. Try the `curl` command again. The result should now reflect your changes.

12. Luckily for us, the `dotnet` tool has the `watch` command. Stop the application by pressing *Ctrl + C* and execute `dotnet watch run`. You should see output resembling the following:

```
$ dotnet watch run
watch : Started
info: Microsoft.AspNetCore.DataProtection.KeyManagement.XmlKeyManager[0]
      User profile is available. Using '/Users/gabriel/.aspnet/DataProtection-Keys' as key
repository; keys will not be encrypted at rest.
Hosting environment: Development
Content root path: /Users/gabriel/fod/ch06/dotnet
Now listening on: https://localhost:5001
Now listening on: http://localhost:5000
Application started. Press Ctrl+C to shut down.
```

Running the .NET sample application with the watch task

Notice the second line in the preceding output, which states that the running application is now watched for changes.

13. Make another change in `ValuesController.cs`; for example, add a fourth item to the return value of the first `GET` endpoint and save. Observe the output in the terminal. It should look something like this:

```
Application is shutting down...
watch : Exited
watch : File changed: /Users/gabriel/fod/ch06/dotnet/Controllers/ValuesController.cs
watch : Started
info: Microsoft.AspNetCore.DataProtection.KeyManagement.XmlKeyManager[0]
      User profile is available. Using '/Users/gabriel/.aspnet/DataProtection-Keys' as key
repository; keys will not be encrypted at rest.
Hosting environment: Development
Content root path: /Users/gabriel/fod/ch06/dotnet
Now listening on: https://localhost:5001
Now listening on: http://localhost:5000
Application started. Press Ctrl+C to shut down.
```

Auto restarting the running sample .NET Core application

14. With that automatic restart of the application upon changes to the code, the result is immediately available to us and we can easily test it by running the `curl` command:

```
$ curl --insecure https://localhost:5001/api/values
["value1","value2","value3","value4"]
```

15. Now that we have auto restart working on the host, we can author a Dockerfile that does the same for the application running inside a container. In VS Code, add a new file called `Dockerfile-dev` to the project and add the following content to it:

```
FROM mcr.microsoft.com/dotnet/core/sdk:2.2
WORKDIR /app
COPY dotnet.csproj ./
RUN dotnet restore
COPY . .
CMD dotnet watch run
```

16. Before we can continue and build the container image, we need to add a slight modification to the startup configuration of the .NET application, such that the web server (Kestrel in this case) listens, for example, at `0.0.0.0:3000` and will thus be able to run inside a container and be accessible from outside of the container. Open the `Program.cs` file and make the following modification to the `CreateWebHostBuilder` method:

```
public static IWebHostBuilder CreateWebHostBuilder(string[] args)
=>
    WebHost.CreateDefaultBuilder(args)
    .UseUrls("http://0.0.0.0:3000")
    .UseStartup<Startup>();
```

With the `UseUrls` method, we tell the web server to listen to the desired endpoints.

Now we're ready to build the container image:

1. To build the image use the following command:

```
$ docker image build -f Dockerfile-dev -t sample-app-dotnet .
```

2. Once the image is built, we can run a container from it:

```
$ docker container run --rm -it \
    -p 3000:3000 \
    -v $(pwd):/app \
    sample-app-dotnet
```

We should see a similar output to that seen when running natively:

```
$ docker container run --rm -it \
>    -p 3000:3000 \
>    -v $(pwd):/app \
>    sample-app-dotnet
    Polling file watcher is enabled
    Started
: Microsoft.AspNetCore.DataProtection.KeyManagement.XmlKeyManager[0]
    User profile is available. Using '/root/.aspnet/DataProtection-Keys' as key repositor
y; keys will not be encrypted at rest.
info: Microsoft.AspNetCore.DataProtection.KeyManagement.XmlKeyManager[58]
    Creating key {313859e0-5e04-4ffc-84c6-35695a63df3d} with creation date 2019-08-26 07:
46:02Z, activation date 2019-08-26 07:46:02Z, and expiration date 2019-11-24 07:46:02Z.
warn: Microsoft.AspNetCore.DataProtection.KeyManagement.XmlKeyManager[35]
    No XML encryptor configured. Key {313859e0-5e04-4ffc-84c6-35695a63df3d} may be persis
ted to storage in unencrypted form.
info: Microsoft.AspNetCore.DataProtection.Repositories.FileSystemXmlRepository[39]
    Writing data to file '/root/.aspnet/DataProtection-Keys/key-313859e0-5e04-4ffc-84c6-3
5695a63df3d.xml'.
Hosting environment: Development
Content root path: /app
Now listening on: http://0.0.0.0:3000
Application started. Press Ctrl+C to shut down.
```

A .NET sample application running in a container

3. Let's test the application with our friend `curl`:

```
$ curl localhost:3000/api/values
["value1","value2","value3","value4"]
$
$ curl localhost:3000/api/values/1
value
```

No surprises here—it works as expected.

4. Now let's do a code change in the controller and then save. Observe what's happening in the terminal window. We should see an output similar to this:

```
Application is shutting down...
        Exited
        File changed: /app/Controllers/ValuesController.cs
        Started
info: Microsoft.AspNetCore.DataProtection.KeyManagement.XmlKeyManager[0]
        User profile is available. Using '/root/.aspnet/DataProtection-Keys' as key repositor
y; keys will not be encrypted at rest.
Hosting environment: Development
Content root path: /app
Now listening on: http://0.0.0.0:3000
Application started. Press Ctrl+C to shut down.
```

Auto restart happening to the .NET sample application running inside the container

Well, that's exactly what we expected. With this, we have removed most of the friction introduced by using containers when developing a .NET application.

Line-by-line code debugging inside a container

Before we dive into this section about the line-by-line debugging of code running inside a container, let me make a disclaimer. What you will learn here should usually be your last resort, if nothing else works. Ideally, when following a test-driven approach when developing your application, the code is mostly guaranteed to work due to the fact that you have written unit and integration tests for it and run them against your code, which also runs in a container. Alternatively, if unit or integration tests don't provide you with enough insight and you really need to debug your code line by line, you can do so having your code running directly on your host, thus leveraging the support of development environments such as Visual Studio, Eclipse, or IntelliJ, to name just a few IDEs.

With all this preparation, you should rarely need to have to manually debug your code as it is running inside a container. That said, let's see how you can do it!

In this section, we are going to concentrate exclusively on how to debug when using Visual Studio Code. Other editors and IDEs may or may not offer similar capabilities.

Debugging a Node.js application

We'll start with the easiest one—a Node.js application. We will use our sample application in folder `~/fod/ch06/node`, which we worked with earlier in this chapter:

1. Make sure that you navigate to this project folder and open VS Code from within it:

```
$ cd ~/fod/ch06/node
$ code .
```

2. In the terminal window, from within the project folder, run a container with our sample Node.js application:

```
$ docker container run --rm -it \
    --name my-sample-app \
    -p 3000:3000 \
    -p 9229:9229 \
    -v $(pwd):/app \
    sample-app node --inspect=0.0.0.0 index.js
```

Note how I map port `9229` to the host. This port is used by the debugger, and VS Studio will communicate with our Node application via this port. Thus it is important that you open this port—but only during a debugging session! Also note that we override the standard start command defined in the Dockerfile (`node index.js`) with `node --inspect=0.0.0.0 index.js`. `--inspect=0.0.0.0` tells Node to run in debug mode and listen on all IP4 addresses in the container.

Now we are ready to define a VS Code launch task for the scenario at hand, that is, our code running inside a container:

1. To open the `launch.json` file, press *Ctrl+Shift+P* (or *Ctrl+Shift+P* on Windows) to open the command palette and look for `Debug:Open launch.json` and select it. The `launch.json` file should open in the editor.

2. Click the blue **Add Configuration...** button to add the new configuration we need to debug inside the container.

3. From the options, select `Docker: Attach to Node`. A new entry will be added to the configurations list in the `launch.json` file. It should look similar to this:

```
{
    "type": "node",
    "request": "attach",
    "name": "Docker: Attach to Node",
    "remoteRoot": "/usr/src/app"
},
```

Since we have our code in the `/app` folder, inside the container, we need to change the value of `remoteRoot` accordingly. Change the `/usr/src/app` value to just `/app`. Do not forget to save your change. That's it, we are ready to roll.

4. Open the Debug view in VS Code by pressing *command + Shift + D* (*Ctrl + Shift + D* on Windows).

5. Make sure you select the correct launch task in the dropdown right next to the green start button at the top of the view. Select `Docker: Attach to Node` as shown here:

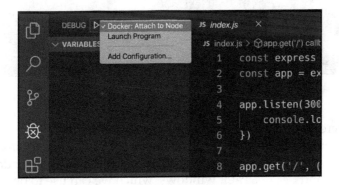

Selecting the correct launch task for debugging in VS Code

6. Next click on the green start button to attach VS Code to the Node application running in the container.

7. Open `index.js` in the editor and put a breakpoint on the line that returns the message `"Sample Application: Hello World!"` when calling the endpoint `'/'`.

8. In another terminal window, use `curl` to navigate to `localhost:3000/` and observe that the code execution stops at the breakpoint:

The code execution stops at the breakpoint

In the preceding screenshot, we can see the yellow bar indicating that the code execution has stopped at the breakpoint. In the upper-right corner, we have a toolbar that allows us to navigate through the code, for example, step by step. On the left-hand side, we see the `VARIABLES`, `WATCH`, and `CALL STACK` windows, which we can use to observe the details of our running application. The fact that we are really debugging the code running inside the container can be verified by the fact that in the terminal windows where we started the container, we see the output `Debugger attached.`, which was generated the moment we started debugging inside VS Code.

Let's look how we can further improve the debugging experience:

1. To stop the container, enter the following command in the terminal:

```
$ docker container rm -f my-sample-app
```

2. If we want to use `nodemon` for even more flexibility, then we have to change the `container run` command slightly:

```
$ docker container run --rm -it \
    --name my-sample-app \
    -p 3000:3000 \
    -p 9229:9229 \
    -v $(pwd):/app \
    sample-app-dev nodemon --inspect=0.0.0.0 index.js
```

Note how we use the start command, `nodemon --inspect=0.0.0.0 index.js`. This will have the benefit that, upon any code changes, the application running inside the container will restart automatically, as we learned earlier in this chapter. You should see the following:

```
$ docker container run --rm -it \
>       --name my-sample-app \
>       -p 3000:3000 \
>       -p 9229:9229 \
>       -v $(pwd):/app \
>       sample-app-dev nodemon --inspect=0.0.0.0 index.js
[nodemon] 1.19.1
[nodemon] to restart at any time, enter `rs`
[nodemon] watching: *.*
[nodemon] starting `node --inspect=0.0.0.0 index.js`
Debugger listening on ws://0.0.0.0:9229/6605853f-d28f-4d95-85b0-3aa17af83481
For help, see: https://nodejs.org/en/docs/inspector
Application listening at 0.0.0.0:3000
```

Starting the Node.js application with nodemon and debugging turned on

3. Unfortunately, the consequence of an application restart is that the debugger loses the connection with VS Code. But no worries—we can mitigate this by adding `"restart": true` to our launch task in the `launch.json` file. Modify the task such that it looks like this:

```
{
    "type": "node",
    "request": "attach",
    "name": "Docker: Attach to Node",
    "remoteRoot": "/app",
    "restart": true
},
```

4. After saving your changes, start the debugger in VS Code by clicking the green start button in the debug window. In the terminal, you should again see that the `Debugger attached.` message is output. In addition to that, VS Code shows an orange status bar at the bottom, indicating that the editor is in debug mode.

5. In a different terminal window, use `curl` and try to navigate to `localhost:3000/` to test that line-by-line debugging still works. Make sure code execution stops at any breakpoint you have set in the code.

6. Once you have verified that debugging still works, try to modify some code; for example, change the message `"Sample Application: Hello World!"` to `"Sample Application: Message from within container"` and save your changes. Observe how `nodemon` restarts the application and the debugger is automatically re-attached to the application running inside the container:

```
[nodemon] restarting due to changes...
[nodemon] starting `node --inspect=0.0.0.0 index.js`
Debugger listening on ws://0.0.0.0:9229/39da95bc-ca6e-4132-b6ea-e7f8c4aa5673
For help, see: https://nodejs.org/en/docs/inspector
Debugger attached.
Application listening at 0.0.0.0:3000
```

nodemon restarting the application and the debugger automatically re-attaching to application

With that, we have everything assembled and can now work with code running inside a container as if the same code were running natively on the host. We have removed pretty much all of the friction that the introduction of containers brought into the development process. We can now just enjoy the benefits of deploying our code in containers.

To clean up, stop the container by pressing *Ctrl* + *C*.

Debugging a .NET application

Now we want to give a quick run-through on how you can debug a .NET application line-by-line. We will use the sample .NET application that we created earlier in this chapter.

1. Navigate to the project folder and open VS Code from within there:

```
$ cd ~/fod/ch06/dotnet
$ code .
```

2. To work with the debugger, we need to first install the debugger in the container. Thus, let's create a new Dockerfile in the project directory. Call it Dockerfile-debug and add the following content:

```
FROM mcr.microsoft.com/dotnet/core/sdk:2.2
RUN apt-get update && apt-get install -y unzip && \
    curl -sSL https://aka.ms/getvsdbgsh | \
        /bin/sh /dev/stdin -v latest -l ~/vsdbg
WORKDIR /app
COPY dotnet.csproj ./
RUN dotnet restore
COPY . .
CMD dotnet watch run
```

Please note the second line of the Dockerfile, which uses apt-get to install the unzip tool and then uses curl to download and install the debugger.

3. We can build an image called sample-app-dotnet-debug from this Dockerfile as follows:

```
$ docker image build -t sample-app-dotnet-debug .
```

This command can take a moment to execute since, among other things, the debugger has to be downloaded and installed.

4. Once this is done, we can run a container from this image interactively:

```
$ docker run --rm -it \
    -v $(pwd):/app \
    -w /app \
    -p 3000:3000 \
    --name my-sample-app \
    --hostname sample-app \
    sample-app-dotnet-debug
```

We will see something like this:

```
root@sdk:/app# dotnet run
: Microsoft.AspNetCore.DataProtection.KeyManagement.XmlKeyManager[0]
      User profile is available. Using '/root/.aspnet/DataProtection-Keys' as key repository; keys will not |
info: Microsoft.AspNetCore.DataProtection.KeyManagement.XmlKeyManager[58]
      Creating key {4e83d14c-8e31-4c73-a6b5-189cc6c6505e} with creation date 2019-08-29 13:51:36Z, activatior
tion date 2019-11-27 13:51:36Z.
warn: Microsoft.AspNetCore.DataProtection.KeyManagement.XmlKeyManager[35]
      No XML encryptor configured. Key {4e83d14c-8e31-4c73-a6b5-189cc6c6505e} may be persisted to storage in
info: Microsoft.AspNetCore.DataProtection.Repositories.FileSystemXmlRepository[39]
      Writing data to file '/root/.aspnet/DataProtection-Keys/key-4e83d14c-8e31-4c73-a6b5-189cc6c6505e.xml'.
Hosting environment: Development
Content root path: /app
Now listening on: http://0.0.0.0:3000
Application started. Press Ctrl+C to shut down.
```

Sample .NET application started interactively inside the SDK container

5. In VS Code, open the `launch.json` file and add the following launch task:

```
{
    "name": ".NET Core Docker Attach",
    "type": "coreclr",
    "request": "attach",
    "processId": "${command:pickRemoteProcess}",
    "pipeTransport": {
        "pipeProgram": "docker",
        "pipeArgs": [ "exec", "-i", "my-sample-app" ],
        "debuggerPath": "/root/vsdbg/vsdbg",
        "pipeCwd": "${workspaceRoot}",
        "quoteArgs": false
    },
    "sourceFileMap": {
        "/app": "${workspaceRoot}"
    },
    "logging": {
        "engineLogging": true
    }
},
```

6. Save your changes and switch to the debug window of VS Code (use *command +
Shift + D* or *Ctrl + Shift + D* to open it). Make sure you have selected the correct
debug launch task—its name is .NET Core Docker Attach:

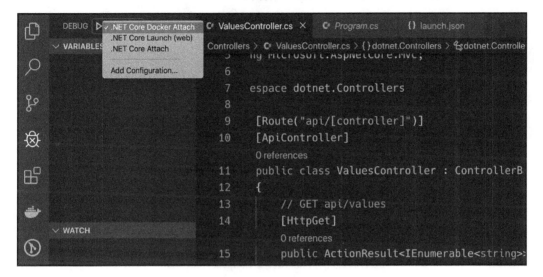

Select the correct debug launch task in VS Code

7. Now click the green start button to start the debugger. As a consequence, the
popup to select the process shows up with the list of potential processes to attach
to. Select the process that looks like the one marked in the following screenshot:

Select the process to attach the debugger to

8. Let's put a breakpoint in the first `GET` request of the `ValuesController.cs` file and then execute a `curl` command:

```
$ curl localhost:3000/api/values
```

The code execution should stop at the breakpoint, as shown here:

```
 7   namespace dotnet.Controllers
 8   {
 9       [Route("api/[controller]")]
10       [ApiController]
11       public class ValuesController : ControllerBase
12       {
13           // GET api/values
14           [HttpGet]
15           public ActionResult<IEnumerable<string>> Get()
16           {
17               return new string[] { "value1", "value2", "value3", "value4" };
18           }
19
```

Line-by-line debugging a .NET Core application running inside a container

9. We can now step through the code, define watches, or analyze the call stack of the application, similar to what we did with the sample Node.js application. Hit the **Continue** button on the debug toolbar or press *F5* to continue the code execution.

10. Now change some code and save the changes. Observe in the terminal window how the application is automatically restarted.

11. Use `curl` again to test whether your changes are visible to the application. Indeed, the changes are available, but have you noticed something? Yes—the code execution did not start at the breakpoint. Unfortunately, restarting the application caused the debugger to disconnect. You have to re-attach the debugger afresh by clicking the start button in the debug view of VS Code and selecting the right process.

12. To stop the application, press *Ctrl + C* in the terminal window where you started the container.

Now that we know how to debug code running in a container line by line, it is time to instrument our code such that it produces meaningful logging information.

Instrumenting your code to produce meaningful logging information

Once an application is running in production, it is impossible or strongly discouraged to interactively debug the application. Thus, we need to come up with other ways to find the root cause when the system is behaving unexpectedly or causing errors. The best way is to have the application generate detailed logging information that can then be used by the developers that need to track down any errors. Since logging is such a common task, all relevant programming languages or frameworks offer libraries that make the task of producing logging information inside an application straightforward.

It is common to categorize the information output by an application as logs into so-called severity levels. Here is the list of those severity levels with a short description of each:

Security levels	Explanation
TRACE	Very fine-grained information. At this level, you are looking at capturing every detail possible about your application's behavior.
DEBUG	Relatively granular and mostly diagnostic information helping to pin down potential problems if they occur.
INFO	Normal application behavior or milestones.
WARN	The application might have encountered a problem or you detected an unusual situation.
ERROR	The application encountered a serious issue. This most probably represents the failure of an important application task.
FATAL	The catastrophic failure of your application. The immediate shutdown of the application is advised.

List of the severity levels used when generating logging information

Logging libraries usually allow a developer to define different log sinks, that is, destinations for the logging information. Popular sinks are file sinks or a stream to the console. When working with containerized applications, it is strongly recommended to always direct logging output to the console or `STDOUT`. Docker will then make this information available to you via the `docker container logs` command. Other log collectors, such as Prometheus, can also be used to scrape this information.

Instrumenting a Python application

Let's now try to instrument our existing Python sample application:

1. First, in your terminal, navigate to the project folder and open VS Code:

   ```
   $ cd ~/fob/ch06/python
   $ code .
   ```

2. Open the `main.py` file and add the following code snippet to the top of it:

```
1    import logging
2
3    logger = logging.getLogger("Sample App")
4    logger.setLevel(logging.WARN)
5    # create a console handler
6    ch = logging.StreamHandler()
7    # create a formatter and add it to the handlers
8    formatter = logging.Formatter('%(asctime)s - %(name)s - %(levelname)s - %(message)s')
9    ch.setFormatter(formatter)
10   logger.addHandler(ch)
```

Defining a logger for our Python sample application

On line 1, we import the standard `logging` library. We then define a `logger` for our sample application of line 3. On line 4, we define the filter for logging to be used. In this case, we set it to WARN. That means that all logging messages produced by the application with a severity equal to or higher than WARN will be output to the defined `logging` handlers or sinks as we called them at the beginning of this section. In our case, only log messages with a log level of WARN, ERROR, or FATAL will be output.

On line 6, we create a logging sink or handler. In our case, it is `StreamHandler`, which outputs to `STDOUT`. Then, on line 8, we define how we want the `logger` to format the messages it outputs. Here, the format that we chose will output the time and date, the application (or `logger`) name, the log severity level, and finally, the actual message that we developers define in code. On line 9, we add the formatter to the log handler, and, on line 10, we add the handler to the `logger`. Note that we can define more than one handler per logger. Now we are ready to use the `logger`.

3. Let's instrument the `hello` function, which is called when we navigate to the endpoint `/`:

```
15    @app.route("/")
16    def hello():
17        logger.info("Accessing endpoint '/'")
18        return "Hello World!"
```

Instrumenting a method with logging

As you can see in the preceding screenshot, we have added line 17, where we use the `logger` object to produce a logging message with log level `INFO`. The message is: `"Accessing endpoint '/'"`.

4. Let's instrument another function and output a message with the log level `WARN`:

```
22    @app.route("/colors")
23    def colors():
24        logger.warning("Warning, you are accessing /colors")
25        return jsonify(["red", "green", "blue"])
```

Generating a warning

This time, we produce a message with the log level `WARN` on line 24 in the `colors` function. So far, so good—that wasn't hard!

5. Let's now run the application and see what output we get:

```
$ python main.py
```

6. Then, in your browser, navigate to `localhost:5000/` first and then to `localhost:5000/colors`. You should see an output similar to this:

```
$ python main.py
 * Serving Flask app "main" (lazy loading)
 * Environment: production
   WARNING: Do not use the development server in a production environment.
   Use a production WSGI server instead.
 * Debug mode: off
 * Running on http://127.0.0.1:5000/ (Press CTRL+C to quit)
127.0.0.1 - - [06/Sep/2019 11:06:57] "GET / HTTP/1.1" 200 -
2019-09-06 11:07:04,466 - Sample App - WARNING - Warning, you are accessing /colors
127.0.0.1 - - [06/Sep/2019 11:07:04] "GET /colors HTTP/1.1" 200 -
```

Running the instrumented sample Python application

As you can see, only the warning is output to the console; the INFO message is not. This is due to the filter we set when defining the logger. Also note how our logging message is formatted with the date and time at the beginning, then the name of the logger, the log level, and finally, our actual message defined on line 24 of our application. When done, please stop the application by pressing *Ctrl + C*.

Instrumenting a .NET C# application

Let's now instrument our sample C# application:

1. First, navigate to the project folder, from where you'll open VS Code:

   ```
   $ cd ~/fod/ch06/dotnet
   $ code .
   ```

2. Next, we need to add a NuGet package containing the logging library to the project:

   ```
   $ dotnet add package Microsoft.Extensions.Logging
   ```

   This should add the following line to your `dotnet.csproj` project file:

   ```
   <PackageReference Include="Microsoft.Extensions.Logging"
   Version="2.2.0" />
   ```

3. Open the `Program.cs` class and notice that we call
   the `CreateDefaultBuilder(args)` method on line `21`:

```
1 reference
20    public static IWebHostBuilder CreateWebHostBuilder(string[] args) =>
21        WebHost.CreateDefaultBuilder(args)
22            .UseUrls("http://0.0.0.0:3000")
23            .UseStartup<Startup>();
```

Configuring logging in ASP.NET Core 2.2

This method, by default, adds a few logging providers to the application, among
them the console logging provider. This comes in very handy and frees us from
having to do any complicated configuration first. You can, of course, override the
default setting any time with your own settings.

4. Next, open the `ValuesController.cs` file in the `Controllers` folder and add
   the following `using` statement to the top of the file:

   using Microsoft.Extensions.Logging;

5. Then, in the class body, add an instance variable, `_logger`, of type `ILogger` and
   add a constructor that has a parameter of type `ILogger<T>`. Assign this
   parameter to the instance variable `_logger`:

```
10    [Route("api/[controller]")]
11    [ApiController]
      1 reference
12    public class ValuesController : ControllerBase
13    {
          1 reference
14        private readonly ILogger _logger;
          0 references
15        public ValuesController(ILogger<ValuesController> logger){
16            _logger = logger;
17        }
18
```

Defining a logger for the Web API controller

6. Now we're ready to use the logger in the controller methods. Let's instrument the `Get` method with an `INFO` message:

```
19          // GET api/values
20          [HttpGet]
            0 references
21          public ActionResult<IEnumerable<string>> Get()
22          {
23              _logger.LogInformation("Getting a list of values");
24              return new string[] { "value1", "value2", "value3", "value4" };
25          }
```

Logging an INFO message from the API controller

7. Let's now instrument the `Get(int id)` method:

```
29          public ActionResult<string> Get(int id)
30          {
31              _logger.LogDebug($"Entering endpoint api/values/{id}");
32              if(id > 4 || id < 1){
33                  _logger.LogError($"You entered an invalid id ({id})");
34                  return NotFound("Value not found!");
35              }
36              return "value" + id;
37          }
```

Logging messages with log levels WARN and ERROR

On line `31`, we have the logger generate a `DEBUG` message and then we have some logic on line `32` to catch unexpected values for `id` and producing `ERROR` messages and returning an HTTP response status of `404` (not found).

8. Let's run the application with the following:

```
$ dotnet run
```

9. We should see this when navigating to `localhost:3000/api/values`:

```
Application started. Press Ctrl+C to shut down.
info: Microsoft.AspNetCore.Hosting.Internal.WebHost[1]
      Request starting HTTP/1.1 GET http://localhost:3000/api/values
warn: Microsoft.AspNetCore.HttpsPolicy.HttpsRedirectionMiddleware[3]
      Failed to determine the https port for redirect.
info: Microsoft.AspNetCore.Routing.EndpointMiddleware[0]
      Executing endpoint 'dotnet.Controllers.ValuesController.Get (dotnet)'
info: Microsoft.AspNetCore.Mvc.Internal.ControllerActionInvoker[3]
      Route matched with {action = "Get", controller = "Values"}. Executing controller action with signature M
lections.Generic.IEnumerable`1[System.String]] Get() on controller dotnet.Controllers.ValuesController (dotnet
info: Microsoft.AspNetCore.Mvc.Internal.ControllerActionInvoker[1]
      Executing action method dotnet.Controllers.ValuesController.Get (dotnet) - Validation state: Valid
info: dotnet.Controllers.ValuesController[0]
      Getting a list of values
info: Microsoft.AspNetCore.Mvc.Internal.ControllerActionInvoker[2]
      Executed action method dotnet.Controllers.ValuesController.Get (dotnet), returned result Microsoft.AspNe
info: Microsoft.AspNetCore.Mvc.Infrastructure.ObjectResultExecutor[1]
      Executing ObjectResult, writing value of type 'System.String[]'.
info: Microsoft.AspNetCore.Mvc.Internal.ControllerActionInvoker[2]
      Executed action dotnet.Controllers.ValuesController.Get (dotnet) in 58.769ms
info: Microsoft.AspNetCore.Routing.EndpointMiddleware[1]
      Executed endpoint 'dotnet.Controllers.ValuesController.Get (dotnet)'
info: Microsoft.AspNetCore.Hosting.Internal.WebHost[2]
      Request finished in 115.4346ms 200 application/json; charset=utf-8
```

Log of our sample .NET application when accessing endpoint `/api/values`

We can see the output of our log message of type `INFO`. All the other log items have been produced by the ASP.NET Core library. You can see that there is a lot of helpful information available if you need to debug the application.

10. Now let's try to access the endpoint `/api/values/{id}` with an invalid value for `{id}`. We should see something along the lines of this:

```
      Route matched with {action = "Get", controller = "Values"}. Executing controller action with signature M
ing] Get(Int32) on controller dotnet.Controllers.ValuesController (dotnet).
info: Microsoft.AspNetCore.Mvc.Internal.ControllerActionInvoker[1]
      Executing action method dotnet.Controllers.ValuesController.Get (dotnet) - Validation state: Valid
dbug: dotnet.Controllers.ValuesController[0]
      Entering endpoint api/values/10
fail: dotnet.Controllers.ValuesController[0]
      You entered an invalid id (10)
info: Microsoft.AspNetCore.Mvc.Internal.ControllerActionInvoker[2]
      Executed action method dotnet.Controllers.ValuesController.Get (dotnet), returned result Microsoft.AspNe
info: Microsoft.AspNetCore.Mvc.Infrastructure.ObjectResultExecutor[1]
      Executing ObjectResult, writing value of type 'System.String'.
```

Debug and error log items generated by our .NET sample application

We can clearly first see the log item with the level `DEBUG` and then the one with the level `ERROR`. The latter in the output is marked in red as `fail`.

11. When done, please end the application with *Ctrl* + C.

Now that we have learned about instrumenting, we will look at Jaeger in the next section.

Using Jaeger to monitor and troubleshoot

When we want to monitor and troubleshoot transactions in a complex distributed system, we need something a bit more powerful than what we have just learned. Of course, we can and should continue to instrument our code with meaningful logging messages, yet we need something more on top of that. This *more* is the capability to trace a single request or transaction end to end, as it flows through the system consisting of many application services. Ideally, we would also want to capture other interesting metrics such as the time spent on each component versus the total time that the request took.

Luckily, we do not have to reinvent the wheel. There is battle-tested open source software out there that helps us to achieve exactly the aforementioned goals. One example of such an infrastructure component or software is Jaeger (`https://www.jaegertracing.io/`). When using Jaeger, you run a central Jaeger server component and each application component uses a Jaeger client that will forward debug and tracing information transparently to the Jaeger server component. There are Jaeger clients for all major programming languages and frameworks, such as Node.js, Python, Java, and .NET.

We will not go into all the intimate details of how to use Jaeger in this book, but will give a high-level overview of how it works conceptually:

1. First, we define a Jaeger `tracer` object. This object basically coordinates the whole process of tracing a request through our distributed application. We can use this `tracer` object and also create a `logger` object from it, which our application code can use to generate log items, similar to what we did in the previous Python and .NET examples.
2. Next, we have to wrap each method in the code that we want to trace with what Jaeger calls a `span`. The `span` has a name and provides us with a `scope` object. Let's look at some C# pseudo-code that illustrates that:

```csharp
public void SayHello(string helloTo) {
    using(var scope = _tracer.BuildSpan("say-
hello").StartActive(true)) {
        // here is the actual logic of the method
        ...
        var helloString = FormatString(helloTo);
        ...
    }
}
```

As you can see, we're instrumenting the `SayHello` method. With a `using` statement creating a span, we're wrapping the whole application code of this method. We call the span `"say-hello"`, and this will be the ID with which we can identify the method in the trace log produced by Jaeger.

Note that the method calls another nested method, `FormatString`. This method will look quite similar in regard to the code needed for instrumenting it:

```
public void string Format(string helloTo) {
    using(var scope = _tracer.BuildSpan("format-string").StartActive(true))
    {
        // here is the actual logic of the method
        ...
        _logger.LogInformation(helloTo);
        return
        ...
    }
}
```

The span that our `tracer` object builds in this method will be a child span of the calling method. This child span here is called `"format-string"`. Also note that we are using the `logger` object in the preceding method to explicitly generate a log item of level `INFO`.

In the code included with this chapter, you can find a complete sample application written in C# consisting of a Jaeger server container and two application containers called client and library that use the Jaeger client library to instrument the code.

1. Navigate to the project folder:

   ```
   $ cd ~/fod/ch06/jaeger-sample
   ```

2. Next, start the Jaeger server container:

   ```
   $ docker run -d --name jaeger \
       -e COLLECTOR_ZIPKIN_HTTP_PORT=9411 \
       -p 5775:5775/udp \
       -p 6831:6831/udp \
       -p 6832:6832/udp \
       -p 5778:5778 \
       -p 16686:16686 \
       -p 14268:14268 \
       -p 9411:9411 \
       jaegertracing/all-in-one:1.13
   ```

3. Next, we need to run the API, which is implemented as an ASP.NET Core 2.2 Web API component. Navigate to the `api` folder and start the component:

```
$ cd ~/fod/ch06/jaeger-sample/api/
$ dotnet run
info: Jaeger.Configuration[0]
      Initialized Tracer(ServiceName=Webservice, Version=CSharp-0.3.4.0, Reporter=CompositeReporter(Reporters
ftUdpTransport(Client=127.0.0.1:6831))), LoggingReporter(Logger=Microsoft.Extensions.Logging.Logger`1[J
ampler(True), IPv4=-1062731412, Tags=[jaeger.version, CSharp-0.3.4.0], [hostname, gabriel.home], [ip, 192.168
nLogs=False, UseTraceId128Bit=False)
info: Microsoft.AspNetCore.DataProtection.KeyManagement.XmlKeyManager[0]
      User profile is available. Using '/Users/gabriel/.aspnet/DataProtection-Keys' as key repository; keys
Hosting environment: Development
Content root path: /Users/gabriel/fod/ch06/jaeger-sample/api
Now listening on: http://0.0.0.0:5000
Application started. Press Ctrl+C to shut down.
```

Starting the API component of the Jaeger sample

4. Now open a new terminal window and navigate into the `client` subfolder and then run the application:

```
$ cd ~/fod/ch06/jaeger-sample/client
$ dotnet run Gabriel Bonjour
```

Please note the two parameters I am passing—`Gabriel` and `Bonjour`—which correspond with `<name>` and `<greeting>`. You should see something along the lines of this:

Running the client component of the Jaeger sample application

In the preceding output, you can see the three spans marked with red arrows, starting from the innermost to the outermost span. We can also use the graphical UI of Jaeger to see more details:

1. In your browser, navigate to `http://localhost:16686` to access the Jaeger UI.
2. In the **Search** panel, make sure the `hello-world` service is selected. Leave **Operation** as `all` and click the **Find Traces** button. You should see the following:

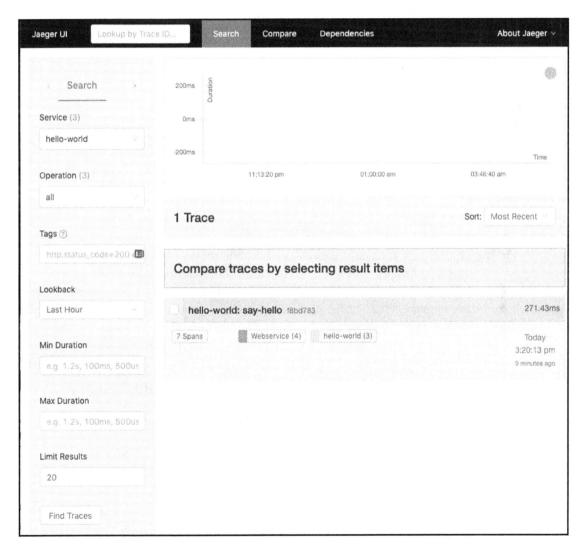

The Search view of the Jaeger UI

2. Now click on the (only) entry `hello-world: say-hello` to see the details of that request:

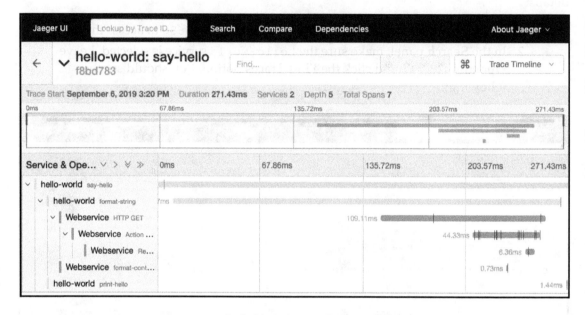

Details of the request as reported by Jaeger

In the preceding screenshot, we can see how the request starts in the `hello-world` component in the `say-hello` method, then navigates to the `format-string` method in the same component, which, in turn, calls an endpoint in `Webservice`, whose logic is implemented in the `FormatController` controller. For each and every step, we see the exact timings as well as other interesting information. You can drill down in this view to see even more details.

Before you continue, you may want to take some time and browse through the code of the API and the `client` component that we just used for this demo.

3. To clean up, stop the Jaeger server container:

```
$ docker container rm -f jaeger
```

Also stop the API with *Ctrl + C*.

Summary

In this chapter, we have learned how to debug Node.js, Python, Java, and .NET code running inside a container. We first started by mounting the source code from the host into the container to avoid a rebuild of the container image each time the code changes. Then, we smoothed out the development process further by enabling automatic application restart inside the container upon code changes. Next, we learned how to configure Visual Studio Code to enable the full interactive debugging of code running inside a container. Finally, we learned how we can instrument our applications such that they generate logging information that can help us to do root cause analysis on failures or misbehaving applications or application services running in production.

In the next chapter, we are going to show how using Docker containers can super-charge your automation, from running a simple automation task in a container, to using containers to build up CI/CD pipelines.

Questions

Please try to answer the following questions to assess your learning progress:

1. Name two methods that help to reduce the friction in the development process introduced by the use of containers.

2. How can you achieve a live update of code inside a container?

3. When and why would you use the line-by-line debugging of code running inside a container?

4. Why is instrumenting code with good debugging information paramount?

Further reading

- **Live debugging with Docker:** `https://www.docker.com/blog/live-debugging-docker/`
- **Debug apps in a local Docker container:** `https://docs.microsoft.com/en-us/visualstudio/containers/edit-and-refresh?view=vs-2019`
- **Debug your java applications in Docker using IntelliJ IDEA:** `https://blog.jetbrains.com/idea/2019/04/debug-your-java-applications-in-docker-using-intellij-idea/`

7
Using Docker to Supercharge Automation

In the last chapter, we introduced techniques commonly used to allow a developer to evolve, modify, debug, and test their code while running in a container. We also learned how to instrument applications so that they generate logging information that can help us to do root cause analysis of failures or misbehaviors of applications or application services that are running in production.

In this chapter, we will show how you can use tools to perform administrative tasks without having to install those tools on the host computer. We will also illustrate the use of containers that host and run test scripts or code used to test and validate application services running in containers. Finally, we will guide the reader through the task of building a simple Docker-based CI/CD pipeline.

This is a quick overview of all of the subjects we are going to touch on in this chapter:

- Executing simple admin tasks in a container
- Using test containers
- Using Docker to power a CI/CD pipeline

After finishing this chapter, you will be able to do the following:

- Run a tool not available on the host in a container
- Use a container to run test scripts or code against an application service
- Build a simple CI/CD pipeline using Docker

Technical requirements

In this section, if you want to follow along with the code, you need Docker for Desktop on your macOS or Windows machine and a code editor, preferably Visual Studio Code. The sample will also work on a Linux machine with Docker and VS Code installed.

Executing simple admin tasks in a container

Let's assume you need to strip all leading whitespaces from a file and you found the following handy Perl script to do exactly that:

```
$ cat sample.txt | perl -lpe 's/^\s*//'
```

As it turns out, you don't have Perl installed on your working machine. What can you do? Install Perl on the machine? Well, that would certainly be an option, and it's exactly what most developers or system admins do. But wait a second, you already have Docker installed on your machine. Can't we use Docker to circumvent the need to install Perl? Yes, we can. This is how we're going to do it:

1. Create a folder, ch07/simple-task, and navigate to it:

   ```
   $ mkdir -p ~/fod/ch07/simple-task && cd ~/fod/ch07/simple-task
   ```

2. Open VS Code from within this folder:

   ```
   $ code .
   ```

3. In this folder, create a sample.txt file with the following content:

   ```
   1234567890
     This is some text
      another line of text
   more text
        final line
   ```

   Please note the whitespaces at the beginning of each line. Save the file.

4. Now, we can run a container with Perl installed in it. Thankfully, there is an official Perl image on Docker Hub. We are going to use the slim version of the image:

```
$ docker container run --rm -it \
    -v $(pwd):/usr/src/app \
    -w /usr/src/app \
    perl:slim sh -c "cat sample.txt | perl -lpe 's/^\s*//'"
```

The preceding command runs a Perl container (`perl:slim`) interactively, maps the content of the current folder into the `/usr/src/app` folder of the container, and sets the working folder inside the container to `/usr/src/app`. The command that is run inside the container is `sh -c "cat sample.txt | perl -lpe 's/^\s*//'"`, basically spawning a Bourne shell and executing our desired Perl command.

The output generated by the preceding command should look like this:

```
1234567890
This is some text
another line of text
more text
final line
```

5. Without needing to install Perl on our machine, we were able to achieve our goal.

If that doesn't convince you yet because if you're on macOS, you already have Perl installed, then consider you're looking into running a Perl script named `your-old-perl-script.pl` that is old and not compatible with the newest release of Perl that you happen to have installed on your system. Do you try to install multiple versions of Perl on your machine and potentially break something? No, you just run a container with the (old) version of Perl that is compatible with your script, as in this example:

```
$ docker container run -it --rm \
    -v $(pwd):/usr/src/app \
    -w /usr/src/app \
    perl:<old-version> perl your-old-perl-script.pl
```

Here, `<old-version>` corresponds to the tag of the version of Perl that you need to run your script. The nice thing is that, after the script has run, the container is removed from your system without leaving any traces because we used the `--rm` flag in the `docker container run` command.

A lot of people use quick and dirty Python scripts or mini apps to automate tasks that are not easily coded with, say, Bash. Now if the Python script has been written in Python 3.7 and you only happen to have Python 2.7 installed, or no version at all on your machine, then the easiest solution is to execute the script inside a container. Let's assume a simple example where the Python script counts lines, words, and letters in a given file and outputs the result to the console:

1. Still in the `ch07/simple-task` folder add a `stats.py` file and add the following content:

```python
import sys

fname = sys.argv[1]
lines = 0
words = 0
letters = 0

for line in open(fname):
    lines += 1
    letters += len(line)

    pos = 'out'
    for letter in line:
        if letter != ' ' and pos == 'out':
            words += 1
            pos = 'in'
        elif letter == ' ':
            pos = 'out'

print("Lines:", lines)
print("Words:", words)
print("Letters:", letters)
```

2. After saving the file, you can run it with the following command:

```
$ docker container run --rm -it \
    -v $(pwd):/usr/src/app \
    -w /usr/src/app \
    python:3.7.4-alpine python stats.py sample.txt
```

Note that, in this example, we are reusing the `sample.txt` file from before. The output in my case is as follows:

```
Lines: 5
Words: 13
Letters: 81
```

The beauty of this approach is that this Python script will now run on any computer with any OS installed, as long as the machine is a Docker host and, hence, can run containers.

Using test containers

For each serious software project out there, it is highly recommended to have plenty of tests in place. There are various test categories such as unit tests, integration tests, stress and load tests, and end-to-end tests. I have tried to visualize the different categories in the following screenshot:

Categories of application tests

Unit tests assert the correctness and quality of an individual, isolated piece of the overall application or application service. Integration tests make sure that pieces that are closely related work together as expected. Stress and load tests often take the application or service as a whole and assert a correct behavior under various edge cases such as high load through multiple concurrent requests handled by the service, or by flooding the service with a huge amount of data. Finally, end-to-end tests simulate a real user working with the application or application service. The typical tasks that a user would do are automated.

The code or component under test is often called a **System Under Test (SUT)**.

Unit tests are in their nature tightly coupled to the actual code or SUT. It is, hence, necessary that those tests run in the same context as the code under test. Hence, the test code lives in the same container as the SUT. All external dependencies of the SUT are either mocked or stubbed.

Integration tests, stress and load tests, and end-to-end tests, on the other hand, act on public interfaces of the system under test and it is, hence, most common to run that test code in a separate container:

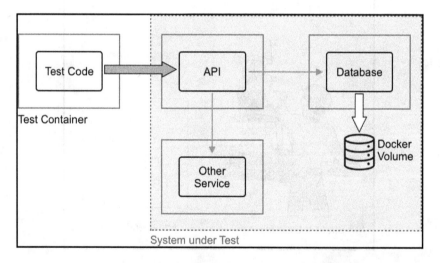

Integration tests using containers

In the preceding diagram, we can see the **Test Code** running in its own **Test Container**. The **Test Code** accesses the public interface of the **API** component that also runs in a dedicated container. The **API** component has external dependencies such as **Other Service** and **Database** that each run in their dedicated container. In this case, the whole ensemble of **API**, **Other Service**, and **Database** is our system under test, or SUT.

What exactly would stress and load tests look like? Imagine a situation where we have a Kafka Streams application we want to put under test. The following diagram gives an idea of what exactly we could test, from a high level:

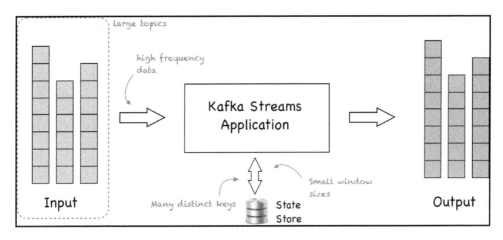

Stress and load test a Kafka Streams application

In a nutshell, a **Kafka Streams application** consumes data from one or more topics stored in Apache Kafka(R). The application filters, transforms, or aggregates the data. The resulting data is written back to one or several topics in Kafka. Typically, when working with Kafka, we deal with real-time data streaming into Kafka. Tests could now simulate the following:

- Large topics with a huge amount of records
- Data flowing into Kafka with a very high frequency
- Data being grouped by the application under test, where there is a lot of distinct keys, each one with low cardinality
- Data aggregated by time windows where the size of the window is small, for example, each only a few seconds long

End-to-end tests automate the users that interact with an application by the use of tools such as the Selenium Web Driver, which provides a developer means to automate actions on a given web page such as filling out fields in a form or clicking buttons.

Integration tests for a Node.js application

Let's now have a look at a sample integration test implemented in Node.js. Here is the setup that we are going to look into:

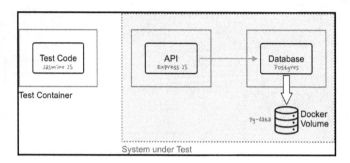

Integration tests for an Express JS Application

Following are the steps to create such an integration test:

1. Let's first prepare our project folder structure. We create the project root and navigate to it:

   ```
   $ mkdir ~/fod/ch07/integration-test-node && \
       cd ~/fod/ch07/integration-test-node
   ```

2. Within this folder, we create three subfolders, tests, api, and database:

   ```
   $ mkdir tests api database
   ```

3. Now, we open VS Code from the project root:

   ```
   $ code .
   ```

4. To the database folder, add an init-script.sql file with the following content:

   ```
   CREATE TABLE hobbies(
       hobby_id serial PRIMARY KEY,
       hobby VARCHAR (255) UNIQUE NOT NULL
   );

   insert into hobbies(hobby) values('swimming');
   insert into hobbies(hobby) values('diving');
   insert into hobbies(hobby) values('jogging');
   insert into hobbies(hobby) values('dancing');
   insert into hobbies(hobby) values('cooking');
   ```

The preceding script will create a `hobbies` table in our Postgres database that we are going to use and fill it with some seed data. Save the file.

5. Now we can start the database. Of course, we are going to use the official Docker image for Postgres to run the database in a container. But first, we will create a Docker volume where the database will store its files. We will call the volume `pg-data`:

```
$ docker volume create pg-data
```

6. Now, it's time to run the database container. From within the project root folder (`integration-test-node`), run the following:

```
$ docker container run -d \
    --name postgres \
    -p 5432:5432 \
    -v $(pwd)/database:/docker-entrypoint-initdb.d \
    -v pg-data:/var/lib/postgresql/data \
    -e POSTGRES_USER=dbuser \
    -e POSTGRES_DB=sample-db \
    postgres:11.5-alpine
```

Note that the folder from which you run the preceding command matters, due to the volume mounting we are using for the database initialization script, `init-script.sql`. Also note that we are using environment variables to define the name and user of the database in Postgres, and we are mapping port 5432 of Postgres to the equivalent port on our host machine.

7. After you have started the database container, double-check that it runs as expected by retrieving its logs:

```
$ docker container logs postgres
```

You should see something similar to this:

```
...
server started
CREATE DATABASE

/usr/local/bin/docker-entrypoint.sh: running /docker-entrypoint-
initdb.d/init-db.sql
CREATE TABLE
INSERT 0 1
INSERT 0 1
INSERT 0 1
INSERT 0 1
```

```
INSERT 0 1

...

PostgreSQL init process complete; ready for start up.

2019-09-07 17:22:30.056 UTC [1] LOG: listening on IPv4 address
"0.0.0.0", port 5432
...
```

Note, we have shortened the output for better readability. The important parts of the preceding output are the first few lines, where we can see that the database has picked up our initialization script, created the `hobbies` table and seeded it with five records. Also important is the last line, telling us that the database is ready to work. The container logs are always your first stop when troubleshooting problems!

With that, our first piece of the SUT is ready. Let's move on to the next one, which is our API implemented in Express JS:

1. In the Terminal window, navigate to the `api` folder:

   $ cd ~/fod/ch07/integration-test-node/api

2. Then, run `npm init` to initialize the API project. Just accept all defaults:

   $ npm init

   The resulting `package.json` file should look like this:

```
{
  "name": "api",
  "version": "1.0.0",
  "description": "",
  "main": "index.js",
  "scripts": {
    "test": "echo \"Error: no test specified\" && exit 1"
  },
  "author": "",
  "license": "ISC"
}
```

3. Modify the `scripts` node of the preceding file so that it contains a start command:

```
6    "scripts": {
7        "start": "node index.js",
8        "test": "echo \"Error: no test specified\" && exit 1"
9    },
```

Adding a start script to the package.json file

4. We then have to install Express JS and can do so with the following command:

```
$ npm install express --save
```

This will install the library and all of its dependencies and add a dependencies node to our `package.json` file that looks similar to this:

```
12    "dependencies": {
13        "express": "^4.17.1"
14    }
```

Adding Express JS as a dependency to the API

5. In the `api` folder, create a `server.js` file and add the following code snippet:

```
1    const express = require('express');
2    const app = express();
3
4    app.listen(3000, '0.0.0.0', () => {
5        console.log('Application listening at 0.0.0.0:3000');
6    })
7
8    app.get('/', (req, res) => {
9        res.send('Sample API');
10   })
```

Simple Express JS API

This is a simple Express JS API with only the / endpoint implemented. It serves as a starting point for our exploration into integration testing. Note that the API will be listening at port 3000, on all endpoints inside the container (0.0.0.0).

6. Now we can start the API with `npm start` and then test the home endpoint, for example, with `curl`:

```
$ curl localhost:3000
Sample API
```

After all of these steps, we're ready to scaffold the test environment.

7. We will be using `jasmine` to write our tests. Navigate to the `tests` folder and run `npm init` to initialize the test project:

```
$ cd ~/fod/ch07/integration-test-node/tests && \
    npm init
```

Accept all of the defaults.

8. Next, add `jasmine` to the project:

```
$ npm install --save-dev jasmine
```

9. Then initialize `jasmine` for this project:

```
$ node node_modules/jasmine/bin/jasmine init
```

10. We also need to change our `package.json` file so that the scripts block looks like this:

```
6    "scripts": {
7      "test": "jasmine"
8    },
```

Adding a test script for our integration tests

11. We cannot run the tests any time by executing `npm test` from within the `tests` folder. The first time we run it, we will get an error since we have not yet added any tests:

```
$ npm test

> tests@1.0.0 test /Users/gabriel/fod/ch07/integration-test-node/tests
> jasmine

Randomized with seed 07145
Started


No specs found
Finished in 0.002 seconds
Incomplete: No specs found
Randomized with seed 07145 (jasmine --random=true --seed=07145)
npm ERR! Test failed.  See above for more details.
```

The first run fails since no tests were found

12. Now in the `spec/support` subfolder of the project, let's create a `jasmine.json` file. This will contain the configuration settings for the `jasmine` test framework. Add the following code snippet to this file and save:

```
{
  "spec_dir": "spec",
  "spec_files": [
    "**/*[sS]pec.js"
  ],
  "stopSpecOnExpectationFailure": false,
  "random": false
}
```

13. Since we are going to author integration tests we will want to access the SUT via its public interface, which, in our case, is a RESTful API. Hence, we need a client library that allows us to do so. My choice is the Requests library. Let's add it to our project:

```
$ npm install request --save-dev
```

14. Add an `api-spec.js` file to the `spec` subfolder of the project. It will contain our test functions. Let's start with the first one:

```
 1   var request = require("request");
 2
 3   const base_url = process.env.BASE_URL || 'http://localhost:3000'
 4
 5   describe("API test suite", () => {
 6       desc any "GET /", () => {
 7           it("returns status code 200", function(done) {
 8               request.get(base_url, (error, response, body) => {
 9                   expect(response.statusCode).toBe(200);
10                   done();
11               });
12           });
13           it("returns description", () => {
14               request.get(base_url, (error, response, body) => {
15                   expect(body).toBe("Sample API");
16                   done();
17               });
18           });
19       });
20   });
```

Sample test suite for the API

We are using the `request` library to make RESTful calls to our API (line 1). Then, on line 3, we're defining the base URL on which the API is listening. Note, the code that we use allows us to override the default of `http://localhost:3000` with whatever we define in an environment variable called `BASE_URL`. Line 5 defines our test suite, which, on line 6, has a test for `GET /`. We then assert two outcomes, namely that the status code of a `GET` call to / is `200` (OK) and that the text returned in the body of the response is equal to `Sample API`.

15. If we run the test now, we get the following outcome:

```
$ npm test

> tests@1.0.0 test /Users/gabriel/fod/ch07/integration-test-node/tests
> jasmine

Started
..

2 specs, 0 failures
Finished in 0.023 seconds
```

Successfully running Jasmine-based integration tests

We have two specifications—another word for tests—running; all of them are successful since we have zero failures reported.

16. Before we continue, please stop the API and remove the Postgres container with `docker container rm -f postgres`.

So far so good, but now let's bring containers to the table. That's what we are most excited about, isn't it? We're excited to run everything, including test code in containers. If you recall, we are going to deal with three containers, the database, the API, and the container with the test code. For the database, we are just using the standard Postgres Docker image, but, for the API and tests, we will create our own images:

1. Let's start with the API. To the `api` folder, add a `Dockerfile` file with this content:

   ```
   FROM node:alpine
   WORKDIR /usr/src/app
   COPY package.json ./
   RUN npm install
   COPY . .
   EXPOSE 3000
   CMD npm start
   ```

   This is just a very standard way of creating a container image for a Node.js based application. There's nothing special here.

2. To the `tests` folder, also add a Dockerfile with this content:

   ```
   FROM node:alpine
   WORKDIR /usr/src/app
   COPY package.json ./
   ```

```
RUN npm install
COPY . .
CMD npm test
```

3. Now, we're ready to run all three containers, in the right sequence. To simplify this task, let's create a shell script that does exactly that. Add a `test.sh` file to the `integration-test-node` folder, our project root folder. Add the following content to this file and save:

```
docker image build -t api-node api
docker image build -t tests-node tests

docker network create test-net

docker container run --rm -d \
    --name postgres \
    --net test-net \
    -v $(pwd)/database:/docker-entrypoint-initdb.d \
    -v pg-data:/var/lib/postgresql/data \
    -e POSTGRES_USER=dbuser \
    -e POSTGRES_DB=sample-db \
    postgres:11.5-alpine

docker container run --rm -d \
    --name api \
    --net test-net \
    api-node

echo "Sleeping for 5 sec..."
sleep 5

docker container run --rm -it \
    --name tests \
    --net test-net \
    -e BASE_URL="http://api:3000" \
    tests-node
```

On the first two lines of the script, we make sure that the two container images for API and tests are built with the newest code. Then, we create a Docker network called `test-net` on which we will run all three containers. Don't worry about the details of this as we will explain networks in detail in Chapter 10, *Single Host Networking*. For the moment, suffice to say that if all containers run on the same network, then the applications running inside those containers can see each other as if they were running natively on the host, and they can call each other by name.

The next command starts the database container, followed by the command that starts the API. Then, we pause for a few seconds to give the database and the API time to completely start up and initialize, before we start the third and final container, the tests container.

4. Make this file an executable with the following:

    $ chmod +x ./test.sh

5. Now you can run it:

    $ ./test.sh

    If everything works as expected, you should see something along these lines (shortened for readability):

    ```
    . . .
    Successfully built 44e0900aaae2
    Successfully tagged tests-node:latest
    b4f233c3578898ae851dc6facaa310b014ec86f4507afd0a5afb10027f10c79d
    728eb5a573d2c3c1f3a44154e172ed9565606af8e7653afb560ee7e99275ecf6
    0474ea5e0afbcc4d9cd966de17e991a6e9a3cec85c53a934545c9352abf87bc6
    Sleeping for 10 sec...

    > tests@1.0.0 test /usr/src/app
    > jasmine

    Started

    ..


    2 specs, 0 failures
    Finished in 0.072 seconds
    ```

6. We can also create a script that cleans up after testing. For this, add a file called cleanup.sh and make it an executable the same way as you've done with the test.sh script. Add the following code snippet to this file:

    ```
    docker container rm -f postgres api
    docker network rm test-net
    docker volume rm pg-data
    ```

Line one removes the postgres and api containers. Line 2 removes the network we used for the third container, and finally, line 3 removes the volume used by Postgres. After each test run, execute this file with ./cleanup.sh.

Now you can start adding more code to your API component and more integration tests. Each time you want to test new or modified code, just run the `test.sh` script.

Challenge: How can you optimize this process further, so that fewer manual steps are required?
Use what we have learned in `Chapter 6`, *Debugging Code Running in Containers*.

The Testcontainers project

If you're a Java developer, then there is a nice project called Testcontainers (`https://testcontainers.org`). In their own words, the project can be summarized as follows:

> *"Testcontainers is a Java library that supports JUnit tests, providing lightweight, throwaway instances of common databases, Selenium web browsers, or anything else that can run in Docker container."*

To experiment with Testcontainer follow along:

1. First create a `testcontainer-node` folder and navigate to it:

   ```
   $ mkdir ~/fod/ch07/testcontainer-node && cd
   ~/fod/ch07/testcontainer-node
   ```

2. Next open VS Code from within that folder with `code ..` Create three subfolders, `database`, `api`, and `tests`, within the same folder. To the `api` folder, add a `package.json` file with the following content:

   ```
    1  {
    2      "name": "testcontainers-node",
    3      "version": "1.0.0",
    4      "main": "server.js",
    5      "scripts": {
    6          "start": "node server.js"
    7      },
    8      "license": "ISC",
    9      "dependencies": {
   10          "express": "^4.17.1",
   11          "pg": "^7.12.1"
   12      }
   13  }
   ```

   Content of package.json for the API

3. Add a `server.js` file to the `api` folder with this content:

```
1    const express = require('express');
2    const app = express();
3
4    const host = process.env.DB_HOST || 'localhost'
5    const port = process.env.DB_PORT || '5432'
6    console.log("Database is at: %s:%s", host,  port)
7
8    const { Pool } = require('pg')
9    const pool = new Pool({
10       user: 'dbuser',
11       host: host,
12       database: 'sample-db',
13       password: 'secretpassword',
14       port: parseInt(port),
15   })
16
17   app.listen(3000, '0.0.0.0', () => {
18       console.log('Application listening at 0.0.0.0:3000');
19   })
20
21   app.get('/hobbies', async (req, res) => {
22       const result = await pool.query('SELECT hobby FROM hobbies')
23       res.send(result.rows );
24   })
```

The sample API using the pg library to access Postgres

Here, we create an Express JS application listening at port 3000. The application uses the pg library, which is a client library for Postgres, to access our database. On lines 8 through 15, we are defining a connection pool object that will allow us to connect to Postgres and retrieve or write data. On lines 21 through 24, we're defining a GET method on the /hobbies endpoint, which returns the list of hobbies that are retrieved from the database via the SQL query, SELECT hobby FROM hobbies.

4. Now add a Dockerfile to the same folder with this content:

```
1  FROM node:alpine
2  WORKDIR /usr/src/app
3  COPY package.json ./
4  RUN npm install
5  COPY . .
6  EXPOSE 3000
7  CMD npm start
```

Dockerfile for the API

This is exactly the same definition as we used in the previous example. With this, the API is ready to be used. Let's now continue with the tests that will use the `testcontainer` library to simplify container-based testing.

5. In your Terminal, navigate to the `tests` folder that we created earlier and use `npm init` to initialize it as a Node.js project. Accept all of the defaults. Next, use `npm` to install the `request` library and the `testcontainers` library:

```
$ npm install request --save-dev
$ npm install testcontainers --save-dev
```

The result of this is a `package.json` file that should look similar to this:

```
{} package.json ×

ch07 > testcontainers-node > tests > {} package.json > {} scripts
1  {
2    "name": "tests",
3    "version": "1.0.0",
4    "description": "",
5    "main": "tests.js",
6    "scripts": {
7      "test": "echo \"Error: no test specified\" && exit 1"
8    },
9    "author": "Gabriel N. Schenker",
10   "license": "ISC",
11   "devDependencies": {
12     "testcontainers": "^2.0.0",
13     "request": "^2.88.0"
14   }
15 }
16
```

The package.json file for the tests project

6. Now, still in the `tests` folder, create a `tests.js` file and add the following code snippet:

```
const request = require("request");
const path = require('path');
const dns = require('dns');
const os = require('os');
const { GenericContainer } = require("testcontainers");

(async () => {
// TODO
})();
```

Note how we're requesting a new object such as the `request` object, which will help us to access the RESTful interface of our sample API component. We are also requesting the `GenericContainer` object from the `testcontainers` library that will allow us to build and run any container.

We then define an async self-invoking function, which will be the wrapper for our setup and test code. It has to be an async function since, inside it, we will be awaiting other async functions, such as the various methods used from the `testcontainers` library.

7. As a very first step, we want to use the `testcontainers` library to create a Postgres container with the necessary seed data loaded. Let's add this code snippet after `//TODO`:

```
const localPath = path.resolve(__dirname, "../database");
const dbContainer = await new GenericContainer("postgres")
    .withName("postgres")
    .withExposedPorts(5432)
    .withEnv("POSTGRES_USER", "dbuser")
    .withEnv("POSTGRES_DB", "sample-db")
    .withBindMount(localPath, "/docker-entrypoint-initdb.d")
    .withTmpFs({ "/temp_pgdata": "rw,noexec,nosuid,size=65536k" })
    .start();
```

The preceding snippet has some similarities with a Docker `run` command. That is no accident since we are instructing the `testcontainers` library to do exactly that and run an instance of PostgreSQL for us.

8. Next, we need to find out to which host port the exposed port `5432` is mapped. We can do that with the following logic:

```
const dbPort = dbContainer.getMappedPort(5432);
```

We will need this information since the API component will have to access Postgres via this port.

9. We also need to know which IP address the host is reachable from within a container—note, localhost won't work from within a container since that would map to the loopback adapter of the container's own network stack. We can get this host IP address like this:

```
const myIP4 = await lookupPromise();
```

The `lookupPromise` function is a wrapper function to make the normal async `dns.lookup` function return a promise so that we can `await` it. Here is its definition:

```
async function lookupPromise() {
    return new Promise((resolve, reject) => {
        dns.lookup(os.hostname(), (err, address, family) => {
            if (err) throw reject(err);
            resolve(address);
        });
    });
};
```

10. Now, with this information, we are ready to instruct the `testcontainer` library to first build the container image for the API and then run a container from this image. Let's start with the build:

```
const buildContext = path.resolve(__dirname, "../api");
const apiContainer = await GenericContainer
    .fromDockerfile(buildContext)
    .build();
```

Note how this command uses the Dockerfile that we defined in the `api` subfolder.

11. Once we have the `apiContainer` variable referencing the new image, we can use this to run a container from it:

```
const startedApiContainer = await apiContainer
    .withName("api")
    .withExposedPorts(3000)
    .withEnv("DB_HOST", myIP4)
    .withEnv("DB_PORT", dbPort)
    .start();
```

12. Once again, we need to find out to which host port the exposed port `3000` of the API component has been mapped. The `testcontainer` library makes this a breeze:

```
const apiPort = startedApiContainer.getMappedPort(3000);
```

13. With this last line, we have finished the test setup code and can now finally start implementing some tests. We start by defining the base URL for the API component that we want to access. Then, we use the `request` library to make an HTTP GET request to the `/hobbies` endpoint:

```
const base_url = `http://localhost:${apiPort}`
request.get(base_url + "/hobbies", (error, response, body) => {
    //Test code here...
})
```

14. Let's now implement some assertions right after the `//Test code here...` comment:

```
console.log("> expecting status code 200");
if(response.statusCode != 200){
    logError(`Unexpected status code ${response.statusCode}`);
}
```

First, we log our expectation to the console as a feedback when running tests. Then, we assert that the returned status code is `200`, and, if not, we log an error. The `logError` helper function just writes the given message in red to the console, and prefixes it with `***ERR`. Here is the definition of this function:

```
function logError(message){
    console.log('\x1b[31m%s\x1b[0m', `***ERR: ${message}`);
}
```

15. Let's add two more assertions:

```
const hobbies = JSON.parse(body);
console.log("> expecting length of hobbies == 5");
if(hobbies.length != 5){
    logError(`${hobbies.length} != 5`);
}
console.log("> expecting first hobby == swimming");
if(hobbies[0].hobby != "swimming"){
    logError(`${hobbies[0].hobby} != swimming`);
}
```

I leave it up to you, dear reader, to find out what these assertions do exactly.

16. At the end of the assertions, we have to clean up so that we're ready for a next run:

```
await startedApiContainer.stop()
await dbContainer.stop();
```

What we're doing is just stopping the API and the database container. This will automatically remove them from memory too.

17. Now we can run this test suite using the following command from within the `tests` subfolder:

```
$ node tests.js
```

The output in my case looks like this (note, I have sprinkled a few `console.log` statements in the code to more easily follow along what exactly is happening at a give time):

```
$ node tests.js
Starting Postgres...
Postgres listening at host port: 51726
My IP4 is: 192.168.1.108
Building API container image...
Image name is: 4ea3ddfbd4f2e9ce6957cf4b4d96f929:fd16b1ece26e863be4884c13a09a1d17
Starting API container...
API listening at host port 51728
API base URL: http://localhost:51728
> expecting status code 200
> expecting length of hobbies == 5
> expecting first hobby == swimming
Cleaning up...
```

Running the testcontainer-based integration tests

The full code is given in the sample code repository that you cloned from GitHub. If you have problems running your tests, please compare your implementation to the given sample solution.

Now that we have a good understanding of how to use containers to run our integration tests, we'll move on to another very popular use case for container based automation, namely, building a Continuous Integration and Continuous Deployment or Delivery (CI/CD) pipeline.

Using Docker to power a CI/CD pipeline

The goal of this section is to build a CI/CD pipeline that looks like this:

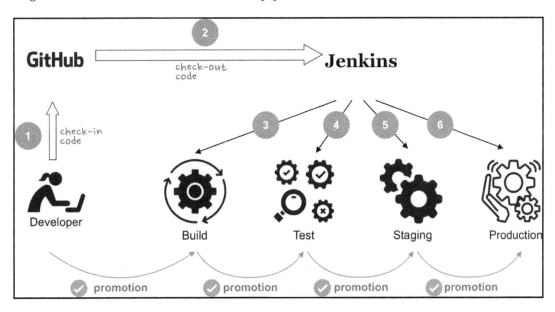

A simple CI/CD pipeline using Jenkins

We are going to use Jenkins (`https://jenkins.io`) as our automation server. Other automation servers such as TeamCity (`https://www.jetbrains.com/teamcity`) work equally well. When using Jenkins, the central document is the `Jenkinsfile`, which will contain the definition of the pipeline with its multiple stages.

A simple `Jenkinsfile` with the `Build, Test, Deploy to Staging,` and `Deploy to Production` stages could look like this:

```
pipeline {
    agent any
    options {
        skipStagesAfterUnstable()
    }
    stages {
        stage('Build') {
            steps {
                echo 'Building'
            }
        }
        stage('Test') {
            steps {
                echo 'Testing'
            }
        }
        stage('Deploy to Staging') {
            steps {
                echo 'Deploying to Staging'
            }
        }
        stage('Deploy to Production') {
            steps {
                echo 'Deploying to Production'
            }
        }
    }
}
```

Of course, the preceding pipeline just outputs a message during each stage and does nothing else. It is useful though as a starting point from which to build up our pipeline:

1. Create a project folder named `jenkins-pipeline` and navigate to it:

   ```
   $ mkdir ~/fod/ch07/jenkins-pipeline && cd ~/fod/ch07/jenkins-
   pipeline
   ```

2. Now, let's run Jenkins in a Docker container. Use the following command to do so:

```
$ docker run --rm -d \
    --name jenkins \
    -u root \
    -p 8080:8080 \
    -v jenkins-data:/var/jenkins_home \
    -v /var/run/docker.sock:/var/run/docker.sock \
    -v "$HOME":/home \
    jenkinsci/blueocean
```

Note that we are running as the `root` user inside the container and that we are mounting the Docker socket into the container (`-v /var/run/docker.sock:/var/run/docker.sock`) so that Jenkins can access Docker from within the container. Data produced and used by Jenkins will be stored in the Docker volume, `jenkins-data`.

3. We can find the initial admin password generated automatically by Jenkins with the following command:

```
$ docker container exec jenkins cat
/var/jenkins_home/secrets/initialAdminPassword
```

In my case, this outputs `7f449293de5443a2bbcb0918c8558689`. Save this password as you will be using it in the next step.

4. In your browser, navigate to `http://localhost:8080` to access the graphical UI of Jenkins.

5. Unlock Jenkins with the admin password that you retrieved with the previous command.

6. Next, choose **Install suggested plugins** to have Jenkins automatically install the most useful plugins. Plugins include the GitHub integration, an email extension, Maven and Gradle integration, and so on.

7. As soon as the plugins are installed, create your first admin account. When asked to restart Jenkins, do so.

8. Once you have configured your Jenkins server, start by creating a new project; you may need to click **New Item** in the main menu:

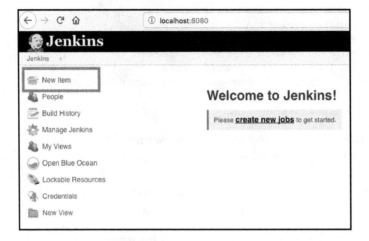

Add a new project in Jenkins

9. Give the project the name `sample-pipeline`, select the `Pipeline` type, and click **OK**.

10. In the configuration view, select the **Pipeline** tab and add the pipeline definition from the preceding into the **Script** textbox:

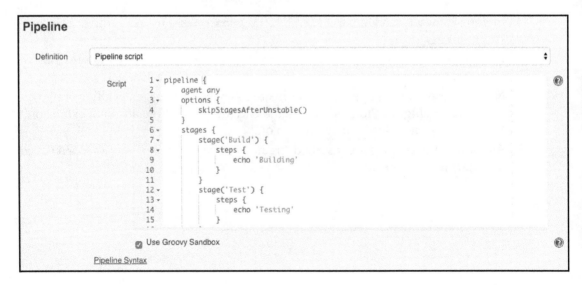

Defining the pipeline in our Jenkins project called sample-pipeline

11. Click **Save** and then, in the main menu of Jenkins, select **Build Now**. After a short moment, you should see this:

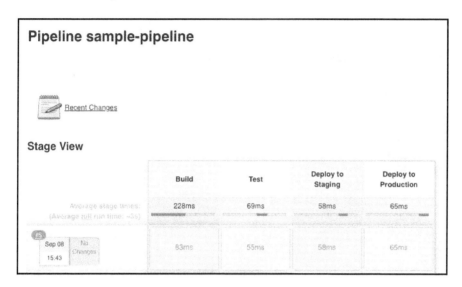

Running our sample pipeline in Jenkins

12. Now that we have prepared Jenkins, we can start to integrate our sample application. Let's start with the build step. First, we initialize the `jenkins-pipeline` project folder as a Git project:

```
$ cd ~/fod/ch07/jenkins-pipeline && git init
```

13. Add a `package.json` file to this folder with this content:

```
{
  "name": "jenkins-pipeline",
  "version": "1.0.0",
  "main": "server.js",
  "scripts": {
    "start": "node server.js",
    "test": "jasmine"
  },
  "dependencies": {
    "express": "^4.17.1"
  },
  "devDependencies": {
    "jasmine": "^3.4.0"
  }
}
```

There is nothing exceptional in this file other the usual list of external dependencies, express and jasmine, in this case. Also, note the two scripts start and test that we define for use with npm.

14. Add a hobbies.js file to the project, which implements the logic to retrieve hobbies as a JavaScript module called hobbies:

```
const hobbies =
["jogging","cooking","diving","swimming","reading"];

exports.getHobbies = () => {
    return hobbies;
}

exports.getHobby = id => {
    if(id<1 || id > hobbies.length)
        return null;
    return hobbies[id-1];
}
```

This code evidently is simulating a database by serving pre-canned data stored in the hobbies array. We do this for simplicity.

15. Next add a server.js file to the folder that defines a RESTful API with the three endpoints, GET /, GET /hobbies, and GET /hobbies/:id. The code uses the logic defined in the hobbies module to retrieve data:

```
const hobbies = require('./hobbies');
const express = require('express');
const app = express();

app.listen(3000, '0.0.0.0', () => {
    console.log('Application listening at 0.0.0.0:3000');
})

app.get('/', (req, res) => {
    res.send('Sample API');
})

app.get('/hobbies', async (req, res) => {
    res.send(hobbies.getHobbies());
})

app.get('/hobbies/:id', async (req, res) => {
    const id = req.params.id;
    const hobby = hobbies.getHobby(id);
    if(!hobby){
```

```
            res.status(404).send("Hobby not found");
            return;
        }
        res.send();
    })
```

16. Now we need to define some unit tests. Create a `spec` subfolder in the project and add the `hobbies-spec.js` file to it with the following code that tests the `hobbies` module:

```
const hobbies = require('../hobbies');
describe("API unit test suite", () => {
    describe("getHobbies", () => {
        const list = hobbies.getHobbies();
        it("returns 5 hobbies", () => {
            expect(list.length).toEqual(5);
        });
        it("returns 'jogging' as first hobby", () => {
            expect(list[0]).toBe("jogging");
        });
    })
})
```

17. The last step is to add a `support/jasmine.json` file to configure our test framework, Jasmine. Add the following code snippet:

```
{
    "spec_dir": "spec",
    "spec_files": [
      "**/*[sS]pec.js"
    ],
    "stopSpecOnExpectationFailure": false,
    "random": false
}
```

This is all the code that we need for the moment.

We can now start to build the CI/CD pipeline:

1. Commit the code just created locally with the following command:

   ```
   $ git add -A && git commit -m "First commit"
   ```

2. To avoid all of the node modules being saved to GitHub, add a `.gitignore` file to the project `root` folder with the following content:

   ```
   node_modules
   ```

3. Now, we need to define a repository on GitHub. Log in to your account on GitHub at `https://github.com`.

4. Create a new repository there and call it `jenkins-pipeline`:

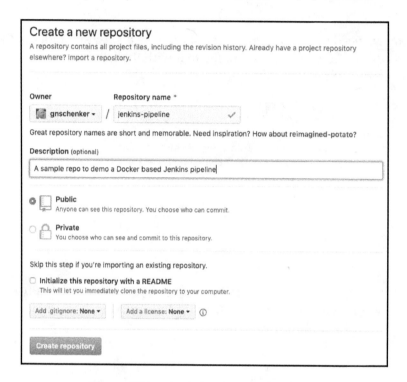

Create a new GitHub repository for the Jenkins pipeline sample application

 Note that my GitHub account is `gnschenker`. In your case, it will be your own account.

5. After you have clicked the green button, **Create repository**, go back to you project and execute the following two commands from within the project `root` folder:

```
$ git remote add origin
https://github.com/gnschenker/jenkins-pipeline.git
$ git push -u origin master
```

Make sure you replace `gnschenker` in the first line with your own GitHub account name. After this step, your code will be available on GitHub for further use. One of the users will be Jenkins, which will pull the code from this repository as we will show shortly.

6. The next thing is to go back to Jenkins (`localhost:8080`) and modify the configuration of the project. Log in to Jenkins if needed and select your project, `sample-pipeline`.

7. Then, select **Configure** in the main menu. Select the **Pipeline** tab and modify the settings so that they look similar to this:

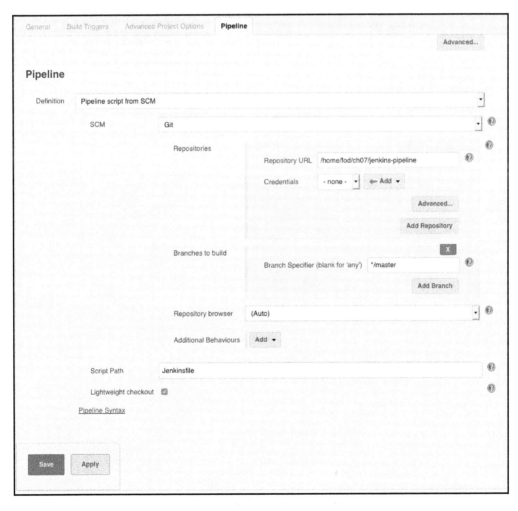

Configuring Jenkins to pull source from GitHub

With this, we configure Jenkins to pull code from GitHub and use a `Jenkinsfile` to define the pipeline. `Jenkinsfile` is expected to be found in the `root` of the project. Note that for the repository URL path, we need to give the relative path to the `/home` directory where our project is located. Remember that, when running the Jenkins container, we mapped our own home folder on the host to the `/home` folder inside the Jenkins container with this: `-v "$HOME":/home`.

8. Hit the green **Save** button to accept the changes.
9. We have defined that `Jenkinsfile` needs to be in the project `root` folder. This is the foundation of **Pipeline-as-Code**, since the pipeline definition file will be committed to the GitHub repository along with the rest of the code. Hence, add a file called `Jenkinsfile` to the `jenkins-pipeline` folder and add this code to it:

```
pipeline {
    environment {
        registry = "gnschenker/jenkins-docker-test"
        DOCKER_PWD = credentials('docker-login-pwd')
    }
    agent {
        docker {
            image 'gnschenker/node-docker'
            args '-p 3000:3000'
            args '-w /app'
            args '-v /var/run/docker.sock:/var/run/docker.sock'
        }
    }
    options {
        skipStagesAfterUnstable()
    }
    stages {
        stage("Build"){
            steps {
                sh 'npm install'
            }
        }
        stage("Test"){
            steps {
                sh 'npm test'
            }
        }
        stage("Build & Push Docker image") {
            steps {
                sh 'docker image build -t $registry:$BUILD_NUMBER
.'
```

```
                    sh 'docker login -u gnschenker -p $DOCKER_PWD'
                    sh 'docker image push $registry:$BUILD_NUMBER'
                    sh "docker image rm $registry:$BUILD_NUMBER"
                }
            }
        }
    }
```

OK, let's dive into this file one part at a time. At the top, we're defining two environment variables that will be available throughout every stage of the pipeline. We will be using those variables in the `Build & Push Docker image` stage:

```
environment {
    registry = "gnschenker/jenkins-docker-test"
    DOCKER_PWD = credentials('docker-login-pwd')
}
```

The first variable, `registry`, just contains the full name of the container image we will eventually produce and push to Docker Hub. Replace `gnschenker` with your own GitHub username. The second variable, `DOCKER_PWD`, is a bit more interesting. It will contain the password to log in to my Docker Hub account. Of course, I don't want to have the value hardcoded here in code, hence, I use the credentials function of Jenkins that gives me access to a secret stored under the name `docker-login-pwd` in Jenkins.

Next, we define the agent we want to use to run the Jenkins pipeline on. In our case, it is based on a Docker image. We are using the `gnschenker/node-docker` image for this purpose. This is an image based on `node:12.10-alpine`, which has Docker and `curl` installed, as we will need these two tools in some of the stages:

```
agent {
    docker {
        image 'gnschenker/node-docker'
        args '-v /var/run/docker.sock:/var/run/docker.sock'
    }
}
```

With the `args` parameter, we are also mapping the Docker socket into the container so that we can use Docker from within the agent.

Ignore the options part for the moment. We then are defining three stages:

```
stages {
    stage("Build"){
        steps {
            sh 'npm install'
        }
```

```
        }
        stage("Test"){
            steps {
                sh 'npm test'
            }
        }
        stage("Build & Push Docker image") {
            steps {
                sh 'docker image build -t $registry:$BUILD_NUMBER .'
                sh 'docker login -u gnschenker -p $DOCKER_PWD'
                sh 'docker image push $registry:$BUILD_NUMBER'
                sh "docker image rm $registry:$BUILD_NUMBER"
            }
        }
    }
}
```

The first stage, `Build`, just runs `npm install` to make sure all external dependencies of our app can be installed. If this were, for example, a Java application, we would probably also compile and package the application in this step.

In the second stage, `Test`, we run `npm test`, which runs our unit tests that we have defined for the sample API.

The third stage, `Build & Push Docker image`, is a bit more interesting. Now that we have successfully built and tested our application, we can create a Docker image for it and push it to a registry. We are using Docker Hub as our registry, but any private or public registry would work. In this stage, we define four steps:

1. We use Docker to build the image. We use the `$registry` environment variable we have defined in the first part of the Jenkinsfile. The `$BUILD_NUMBER` variable is defined by Jenkins itself.
2. Before we can push something to the registry, we need to log in. Here, I am using the `$DOCKER_PWD` variable that I defined earlier on.
3. Once we're successfully logged in to the registry, we can push the image.
4. Since the image is now in the registry, we can delete it from the local cache to avoid wasting space.

Remember that all of the stages run inside our `gnschenker/node-docker` builder container. Hence, we're running Docker inside Docker. But, since we have mapped the Docker socket into the builder, the Docker commands act on the host.

Let's add two more stages to the pipeline. The first one looks like this:

```
stage('Deploy and smoke test') {
    steps{
```

```
            sh './jenkins/scripts/deploy.sh'
        }
    }
```

Add it just after the `Build & Push Docker image` stage. This stage just executes a `deploy.sh` script located in the `jenkins/scripts` subfolder. We do not yet have such a file in our project.

Hence, add this file to your project with the following content:

```
#!/usr/bin/env sh

echo "Removing api container if it exists..."
docker container rm -f api || true
echo "Removing network test-net if it exists..."
docker network rm test-net || true

echo "Deploying app ($registry:$BUILD_NUMBER)..."
docker network create test-net

docker container run -d \
    --name api \
    --net test-net \
    $registry:$BUILD_NUMBER

# Logic to wait for the api component to be ready on port 3000

read -d '' wait_for << EOF
echo "Waiting for API to listen on port 3000..."
while ! nc -z api 3000; do
  sleep 0.1 # wait for 1/10 of the second before check again
  printf "."
done
echo "API ready on port 3000!"
EOF

docker container run --rm \
    --net test-net \
    node:12.10-alpine sh -c "$wait_for"

echo "Smoke tests..."
docker container run --name tester \
    --rm \
    --net test-net \
    gnschenker/node-docker sh -c "curl api:3000"
```

OK, so this code does the following. First, it tries to remove any artifacts that might have been left over from an earlier, failed run of the pipeline. Then, it creates a Docker network called `test-net`. Next, it runs a container from the image we built in the previous step. This container is our Express JS API and is called `api` accordingly.

This container and the application within it may take a moment to be ready. Hence, we define some logic that uses the `netcat` or `nc` tool to probe port `3000`. Once the application is listening at port `3000`, we continue with the smoke test. In our case, the smoke test is just making sure it can access the / endpoint of our API. We are using `curl` for this task. In a more realistic setup, you would run some more sophisticated tests here.

As a last stage, we are adding a `Cleanup` step:

1. Add the following snippet as a last stage to your `Jenkinsfile`:

   ```
   stage('Cleanup') {
       steps{
           sh './jenkins/scripts/cleanup.sh'
       }
   }
   ```

   Once again, this `Cleanup` stage uses a script located in the `jenkins/script` subfolder.

2. Please add such a file to your project with the following content:

   ```
   #!/usr/bin/env sh

   docker rm -f api
   docker network rm test-net
   ```

   This script removes the `api` container and the Docker network, `test-net`, that we used to run our containers on.

3. Now, we are ready to roll. Use `git` to commit your changes and push them to your repository:

   ```
   $ git -a . && git commit -m "Defined code based Pipeline"
   $ git push origin master
   ```

   Once the code is pushed to GitHub, go back to Jenkins.

4. Select your `sample-pipeline` project and click **Build now** in the main menu. Jenkins will start to build the pipeline. If everything goes well, you should see something like this:

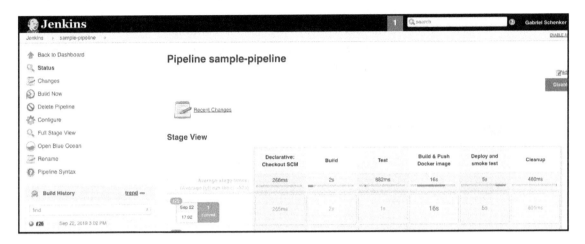

Running our full code-based pipeline in Jenkins

Our pipeline is executed successfully and now has six steps. The checkout from GitHub has been automatically added as a first enabling step. To access the logs generated during the pipeline execution, you can click the little ball icon on the left side of the run under **Build History**. In the preceding screenshot, it is the bluish icon on the left of **#26**. This is especially helpful if the pipeline step fails to quickly find the root cause of the failure.

To summarize, we have built a simple CI/CD pipeline where everything, including the automation server, Jenkins, is running in containers. We have only scratched the surface of what is possible.

Summary

In this chapter, we learned how to use Docker containers to optimize various kinds of automation tasks, from running a simple one-off task to building up a containerized CI/CD pipeline.

In the next chapter, we will introduce advanced tips, tricks, and concepts useful when containerizing complex distributed applications or when using Docker to automate sophisticated tasks.

Questions

1. Name a few pros and cons for running a one-off task in a container instead of directly on the host machine.
2. List two or three advantages of running tests in containers.
3. Sketch a high-level diagram of a containerized CI/CD pipeline, starting from the user producing code till the code being deployed into production.

Further reading

- Write Maintainable Integration Tests with Docker at `https://www.docker.com/blog/maintainable-integration-tests-with-docker/`
- A Docker Workflow for .NET Developer - Part 2 (Integration Tests) at `https://gabrielschenker.com/index.php/2019/10/09/a-docker-workflow-for-net-developers-part-2/`
- Jenkins on Docker Hub at `https://hub.docker.com/_/jenkins/`
- Jenkins Tutorial Overview at `https://jenkins.io/doc/tutorials/`

8
Advanced Docker Usage Scenarios

In the last chapter, we showed you how you can use tools to perform administrative tasks without having to install those tools on the host computer. We also illustrated the use of containers that host and run test scripts or code used to test and validate application services running in containers. Finally, we guided you through the task of building a simple Docker-based CI/CD pipeline using Jenkins as the automation server.

In this chapter, we will introduce advanced tips, tricks, and concepts that are useful when containerizing complex distributed applications, or when using Docker to automate sophisticated tasks.

This is a quick overview of all of the subjects we are going to touch on in this chapter:

- All of the tips and tricks of a Docker pro
- Running your Terminal in a remote container and accessing it via HTTPS
- Running your development environment inside a container
- Running your code editor in a remote container and accessing it via HTTPS

After finishing this chapter, you will be able to do the following:

- Successfully restore your Docker environment after it has been messed up completely
- Run a remote Terminal in a container and access it with your browser via HTTPS
- Edit code remotely with Visual Studio Code with your browser via HTTPS

Technical requirements

In this chapter, if you want to follow along with the code, you need Docker for Desktop on your Mac or Windows machine and the Visual Studio Code editor. The example will also work on a Linux machine with Docker and Visual Studio Code installed. Docker Toolbox is not supported in this chapter.

All of the tips and tricks of a Docker pro

In this section, I will present a few very useful tips and tricks that make the lives of advanced Docker users so much easier. We will start with some guidance on how to keep your Docker environment clean.

Keeping your Docker environment clean

First, we want to learn how we can delete dangling images. According to Docker, dangling images are layers that have no relationship to any tagged images. Such image layers are certainly useless to us and can quickly fill up our disk—it's better to remove them from time to time. Here is the command:

```
$ docker image prune -f
```

Please note that I have added the -f parameter to the prune command. This is to prevent the CLI from asking for a confirmation that we really want to delete those superfluous layers.

Stopped containers can waste precious resources too. If you're sure that you don't need these containers anymore, then you should remove them, either individually with the following:

```
$ docker container rm <container-id>
```

Or, you can remove them as a batch with the following:

```
$ docker container prune --force
```

It is worth mentioning once again that, instead of <container-id>, we can also use <container-name> to identify a container.

Unused Docker volumes too can quickly fill up disk space. It is a good practice to tender your volumes, specifically in a development or CI environment where you create a lot of mostly temporary volumes. But I have to warn you, Docker volumes are meant to store data. Often, this data must live longer than the life cycle of a container. This is specifically true in a production or production-like environment where the data is often mission-critical. Hence, be 100% sure of what you're doing when using the following command to prune volumes on your Docker host:

```
$ docker volume prune
WARNING! This will remove all local volumes not used by at least one
container.
Are you sure you want to continue? [y/N]
```

I recommend using this command without the `-f` (or `--force`) flag. It is a dangerous and terminal operation and it's better to give yourself a second chance to reconsider your action. Without the flag, the CLI outputs the warning you see in the preceding. You have to explicitly confirm by typing `y` and pressing the *Enter* key.

On production or production-like systems, you should abstain from the preceding command and rather delete unwanted volumes one at a time by using this command:

```
$ docker volume rm <volume-name>
```

I should also mention that there is a command to prune Docker networks. But since we have not yet officially introduced networks, I will defer this to `chapter 10`, *Single-Host Networking*.

In the next section, we are going to show how we can automate Docker from within a container.

Running Docker in Docker

At times, we may want to run a container hosting an application that automates certain Docker tasks. How can we do that? The Docker Engine and the Docker CLI are installed on the host, yet the application runs inside the container. Well, from early on, Docker has provided a means to bind-mount Linux sockets from the host into the container. On Linux, sockets are used as very efficient data communications endpoints between processes that run on the same host. The Docker CLI uses a socket to communicate with the Docker Engine; it is often called the Docker socket. If we can give access to the Docker socket to an application running inside a container then we can just install the Docker CLI inside this container, and we will then be able to run an application in the same container that uses this locally installed Docker CLI to automate container-specific tasks.

It is important to note that here we are not talking about running the Docker Engine inside the container but rather only the Docker CLI and bind-mount the Docker socket from the host into the container so that the CLI can communicate with the Docker Engine running on the host computer. This is an important distinction. Running the Docker Engine inside a container, although possible, is not recommended.

Let's assume we have the following script, called `pipeline.sh`, automating the building, testing, and pushing of a Docker image:

```
#! /bin/bash
# *** Sample script to build, test and push containerized Node.js
applications ***
# build the Docker image
docker image build -t $HUB_USER/$REPOSITORY:$TAG .
# Run all unit tests
docker container run $HUB_USER/$REPOSITORY:$TAG npm test
# Login to Docker Hub
docker login -u $HUB_USER -p $HUB_PWD
# Push the image to Docker Hub
docker image push $HUB_USER/$REPOSITORY:$TAG
```

Note that we're using four environment variables: $HUB_USER and $HUB_PWD being the credentials for Docker Hub and $REPOSITORY and $TAG being the name and tag of the Docker image we want to build. Eventually, we will have to pass values for those environment variables in the docker run command.

We want to run that script inside a builder container. Since the script uses the Docker CLI, our builder container must have the Docker CLI installed, and to access the Docker Engine, the builder container must have the Docker socket bind-mounted. Let's start creating a Docker image for such a builder container:

1. First, create a `builder` folder and navigate to it:

   $ mkdir builder && cd builder

2. Inside this folder, create a `Dockerfile` that looks like this:

   ```
   FROM alpine:latest
   RUN apk update && apk add docker
   WORKDIR /usr/src/app
   COPY . .
   CMD ./pipeline.sh
   ```

3. Now create a `pipeline.sh` file in the `builder` folder and add as content the pipeline script we have presented in the preceding file.

4. Save and make the file an executable:

```
$ chmod +x ./pipeline.sh
```

5. Building an image is straightforward:

```
$ docker image build -t builder .
```

We are now ready to try `builder` out with a real Node.js application, for example, the sample app we defined in the `ch08/sample-app` folder. Make sure you replace <user> and <password> with your own credentials for Docker Hub:

```
$ cd ~/fod/ch08/sample-app
$ docker container run --rm \
    --name builder \
    -v /var/run/docker.sock:/var/run/docker.sock \
    -v "$PWD":/usr/src/app \
    -e HUB_USER=<user> \
    -e HUB_PWD=<password>@j \
    -e REPOSITORY=ch08-sample-app \
    -e TAG=1.0 \
    builder
```

Notice how, in the preceding command, we mounted the Docker socket into the container with `-v /var/run/docker.sock:/var/run/docker.sock`. If everything goes well, you should have a container image built for the sample application, the test should have been run, and the image should have been pushed to Docker Hub. This is only one of the many use cases where it is very useful to be able to bind-mount the Docker socket.

A special notice to all those of you who want to try Windows containers. On Docker for Windows, you can create a similar environment by bind-mounting Docker's **named pipe** instead of a socket. A named pipe on Windows is roughly the same as a socket on a Unix-based system. Assuming you're using a PowerShell Terminal, the command to bind-mount a named pipe when running a Windows container hosting Jenkins looks like this:

```
PS> docker container run `
--name jenkins `
-p 8080:8080 `
-v \\.\pipe\docker_engine:\\.\pipe\docker_engine `
friism/jenkins
```

Note the special syntax, \\.\pipe\docker_engine, to access Docker's named pipe.

Formatting the output of common Docker commands

Have you at times wished that your Terminal window was infinitely wide since the output of a Docker command such as docker container ps is scrambled across several lines per item? Worry not, as you can customize the output to your liking. Almost all commands that produce an output have a --format argument, which accepts a so-called Go template as a parameter. If you wonder why a Go template, it's because most of Docker is written in this popular low-level language. Let's look at an example. Assume we want to only show the name of the container, the name of the image, and the state of the container, separated by tabs, output by the docker container ps command. The format would then look like this:

```
$ docker container ps -a \
--format "table {{.Names}}\t{{.Image}}\t{{.Status}}"
```

Please be aware that the format string is case sensitive. Also, note the addition of the -a parameter to include stopped containers in the output. A sample output could look like this:

```
NAMES               IMAGE         STATUS
elated_haslett      alpine        Up 2 seconds
brave_chebyshev     hello-world   Exited (0) 3 minutes ago
```

This is definitely nicer to display even on a narrow Terminal window than the unformatted one scattering wildly over multiple lines.

Filtering the output of common Docker commands

Similar to what we have done in the previous section by pretty-printing the output of Docker commands, we can also filter what is output. There are quite a few filters that are supported. Please find the full list for each command in the Docker online documentation. The format of filters is straightforward and of the type `--filter <key>=<value>`. If we need to combine more than one filter, we can just combine multiple of these statements. Let's do an example with the `docker image ls` command as I have a lot of images on my workstation:

```
$ docker image ls --filter dangling=false --filter "reference=*/*/*:latest"
```

The preceding filter only outputs images that are not dangling, that is, real images whose fully qualified name is of the form `<registry>/<user|org><repository>:<tag>`, and the tag is equal to `latest`. The output on my machine looks like this:

```
REPOSITORY                                    TAG     IMAGE ID      CREATED
SIZE
docker.bintray.io/jfrog/artifactory-cpp-ce  latest  092f11699785  9 months
ago 900MB
docker.bintray.io/jfrog/artifactory-oss      latest  a8a8901c0230  9 months
ago 897MB
```

Having shown how to pretty print and filter output generated by the Docker CLI, it is now time to talk once more about building Docker images and how to optimize this process.

Optimizing your build process

Many Docker beginners make the following mistake when crafting their first `Dockerfile`:

```
FROM node:12.10-alpine
WORKDIR /usr/src/app
COPY . .
RUN npm install
CMD npm start
```

Can you spot the weak point in this typical `Dockerfile` for a Node.js application? In `Chapter 4`, *Creating and Managing Container Images*, we have learned that an image consists of a series of layers. Each (logical) line in a `Dockerfile` creates a layer, except the lines with the `CMD` and/or `ENTRYPOINT` keyword. We have also learned that the Docker builder tries to do its best by caching layers and reusing them if they have not changed between subsequent builds. But the caching only uses cached layers that occur before the first changed layer. All subsequent layers need to be rebuilt. That said, the preceding structure of the `Dockerfile` busts the image layer cache!

Why? Well, from experience, you certainly know that `npm install` can be a pretty expensive operation in a typical Node.js application with many external dependencies. The execution of this command can take from seconds to many minutes. That said, each time one of the source files changes, and we know that happens frequently during development, line 3 in the `Dockerfile` causes the corresponding image layer to change. Hence, the Docker builder cannot reuse this layer from cache, nor can it reuse the subsequent layer created by `RUN npm install`. Any minor change in code causes a complete rerun of `npm install`. That can be avoided. The `package.json` file containing the list of external dependencies rarely changes. With all of that information, let's fix the `Dockerfile`:

```
FROM node:12.10-alpine
WORKDIR /usr/src/app
COPY package.json ./
RUN npm install
COPY . .
CMD npm start
```

This time, on line 3, we only copy the `package.json` file into the container, which rarely changes. Hence, the subsequent `npm install` command has to be executed equally rarely. The `COPY` command on line 5 then is a very fast operation and hence rebuilding an image after some code has changed only needs to rebuild this last layer. Build times reduce to merely a fraction of a second.

The very same principle applies to most languages or frameworks, such as Python, .NET, or Java. Avoid busting your image layer cache!

Limiting resources consumed by a container

One of the great features of a container, apart from encapsulating application processes, is the possibility of limiting the resources a single container can consume at. This includes CPU and memory consumption. Let's have a look at how limiting the amount of memory (RAM) works:

```
$ docker container run --rm -it \
    --name stress-test \
    --memory 512M \
    ubuntu:19.04 /bin/bash
```

Once inside the container, install the `stress` tool, which we will use to simulate memory pressure:

```
/# apt-get update && apt-get install -y stress
```

Open another Terminal window and execute the `docker stats` command. You should see something like this:

CONTAINER ID	NAME	CPU %	MEM USAGE / LIMIT	MEM %	NET I/O	BLOCK I/O
8e00c974ae6e	stress-test	0.00%	1.871MiB / 512MiB	0.37%	16MB / 271kB	0B / 111MB

docker stats showing a resource-limited container

Look at MEM USAGE and LIMIT. Currently, the container uses only 1.87MiB memory and has a limit of 512MB. The latter corresponds to what we have configured for this container. Now, let's use `stress` to simulate four workers, which try to `malloc()` memory in blocks of 256MB. Run this command inside the container to do so:

```
/# stress -m 4
```

In the Terminal running Docker stats, observe how the value for MEM USAGE approaches but never exceeds LIMIT. This is exactly the behavior we expected from Docker. Docker uses Linux `cgroups` to enforce those limits.

We could similarly limit the amount of CPU a container can consume with the `--cpu` switch.

With this operation, engineers can avoid the noisy neighbor problem on a busy Docker host, where a single container starves all of the others by consuming an excessive amount of resources.

Read-only filesystem

To protect your applications against malicious hacker attacks, it is often advised to define the filesystem of the container or part of it as read-only. This makes the most sense for stateless services. Assume that you have a billing service running in a container as part of your distributed, mission-critical application. You could run your billing service as follows:

```
$ docker container run -d --rm \
  --name billing \
  --read-only \
  acme/billing:2.0
```

The `--read-only` flag mounts the container's filesystem as read-only. If a hacker succeeds in entering your billing container and tries to change an application maliciously by, say, replacing one of the binaries with a compromised one, then this operation would fail. We can easily demonstrate that with the following commands:

```
$ docker container run --tty -d \
    --name billing \
    --read-only \
    alpine /bin/sh

$ docker container exec -it billing \
    sh -c 'echo "You are doomed!" > ./sample.txt'
sh: can't create ./sample.txt: Read-only file system
```

The first command runs a container with a read-only filesystem and the second command tries to execute another process in this container, which is supposed to write something to the filesystem—in this case, a simple text file. This fails, as we can see in the preceding output, with the error message `Read-only file system`.

Another means to tighten the security of your applications running in containers is to avoid running them as `root`.

Avoid running a containerized app as root

Most applications or application services that run inside a container do not need root access. To tighten security, it is helpful in those scenarios to run these processes with minimal necessary privileges. These applications should not be run as `root` nor assume that they have `root`-level privileges.

Once again, let's illustrate what we mean with an example. Assume we have a file with top-secret content. We want to secure this file on our Unix-based system using the chmod tool so that only users with root permission can access it. Let's assume I am logged in as gabriel on the dev host and hence my prompt is gabriel@dev $. I can use sudo su to impersonate a superuser. I have to enter the superuser password though:

```
gabriel@dev $ sudo su
Password: <root password>
root@dev $
```

Now, as the root user, I can create this file called top-secret.txt and secure it:

```
root@dev $ echo "You should not see this." > top-secret.txt
root@dev $ chmod 600 ./top-secret.txt
root@dev $ exit
gabriel@dev $
```

If I try to access the file as gabriel, the following happens:

```
gabriel@dev $ cat ./top-secret.txt
cat: ./top-secret.txt: Permission denied
```

I get Permission denied, which is what we wanted. No other user except root can access this file. Now, let's build a Docker image that contains this secured file and when a container is created from it, tries to output its content. The Dockerfile could look like this:

```
FROM ubuntu:latest
COPY ./top-secret.txt /secrets/
# simulate use of restricted file
CMD cat /secrets/top-secret.txt
```

We can build an image from that Dockerfile (as root!) with the following:

```
gabriel@dev $ sudo su
Password: <root password>
root@dev $ docker image build -t demo-image .
root@dev $ exit
gabriel@dev $
```

Then, when running a container from that image we get:

```
gabriel@dev $ docker container run demo-image
You should not see this.
```

OK, so although I am impersonating the `gabriel` user on the host and running the container under this user account, the application running inside the container automatically runs as `root`, and hence has full access to protected resources. That's bad, so let's fix it! Instead of running with the default, we define an explicit user inside the container. The modified `Dockerfile` looks like this:

```
FROM ubuntu:latest
RUN groupadd -g 3000 demo-group |
    && useradd -r -u 4000 -g demo-group demo-user
USER demo-user
COPY ./top-secret.txt /secrets/
# simulate use of restricted file
CMD cat /secrets/top-secret.txt
```

We use the `groupadd` tool to define a new group, `demo-group`, with the ID `3000`. Then, we use the `useradd` tool to add a new user, `demo-user`, to this group. The user has the ID `4000` inside the container. Finally, with the `USER demo-user` statement, we declare that all subsequent operations should be executed as `demo-user`.

Rebuild the image—again as `root`—and then try to run a container from it:

```
gabriel@dev $ sudo su
Password: <root password>
root@dev $ docker image build -t demo-image .
root@dev $ exit
gabriel@dev $ docker container run demo-image
cat: /secrets/top-secret.txt: Permission denied
```

And as you can see on the last line, the application running inside the container runs with restricted permissions and cannot access resources that need root-level access. By the way, what do you think would happen if I ran the container as `root`? Try it out!

These have been a few tips and tricks for pros that are useful in the day-to-day usage of containers. There are many more. Google them. It is worth it.

Running your Terminal in a remote container and accessing it via HTTPS

There are situations where you need to access a remote server and only have the option to use a browser for that. Your laptop may be locked down by your employer so that you are not allowed to, for example, `ssh` into a server outside of the company's domain.

To test this scenario proceed as follows:

1. Create a free account on Microsoft Azure, GCP, or AWS. Then, create a VM, preferably with Ubuntu 18.04 or higher as the operating system, to follow along more easily.

2. Once your VM is ready, SSH into it. The command to do so should look similar to this:

   ```
   $ ssh gnschenker@40.115.4.249
   ```

   To get access, you may need to open port 22 for ingress first for the VM.

   The user I have defined during the provisioning of the VM is gnschenker and the public IP address of my VM is 40.115.4.249.

3. Install Docker on this VM using the description found here: https://docs.docker.com/install/linux/docker-ce/ubuntu/.

4. On a special note, do not forget to add your user (gnschenker, in my case) to the docker group on the VM with the following command:

   ```
   $ sudo usermod -aG docker <user-name>
   ```

   With this, you avoid having to constantly use sudo for all Docker commands. You need to log out from and log in to the VM to make this change work.

5. Now, we are ready to run **Shell in a Box** (https://github.com/shellinabox/shellinabox) in a container on the VM. There are quite a few people who have containerized Shell in a Box. We are using the Docker image, sspreitzer/shellinabox. At the time of writing, it is the most popular version by far on Docker Hub. With the following command, we are running the application with a user, gnschenker; password, top-secret; sudo for the user enabled; and with self-signed certificates:

   ```
   $ docker container run --rm \
       --name shellinabox \
       -p 4200:4200 \
       -e SIAB_USER=gnschenker \
       -e SIAB_PASSWORD=top-secret \
       -e SIAB_SUDO=true \
       -v `pwd`/dev:/usr/src/dev \
       sspreitzer/shellinabox:latest
   ```

Note that initially, we recommend running the container in interactive mode so that you can follow what's happening. Once you are more familiar with the service, consider running it in the background with the -d flag. Also, note that we are mounting the ~/dev folder from the host to the /usr/src/dev folder inside the container. This is useful if we want to remotely edit code that we have, for example, cloned from GitHub into the ~/dev folder.

Also, notice that we are mapping port 4200 of Shell in a Box to host port 4200. This is the port over which we will be able to access the shell using a browser and HTTPS. Hence, you need to open port 4200 for ingress on your VM. As a protocol, select TCP.

6. Once the container is running and you have opened port 4200 for ingress, open a new browser window and navigate to https://<public-IP>:4200, where <public-IP> is the public IP address of your VM. Since we're using a self-signed certificate, you will be greeted with a warning, here shown when using Firefox:

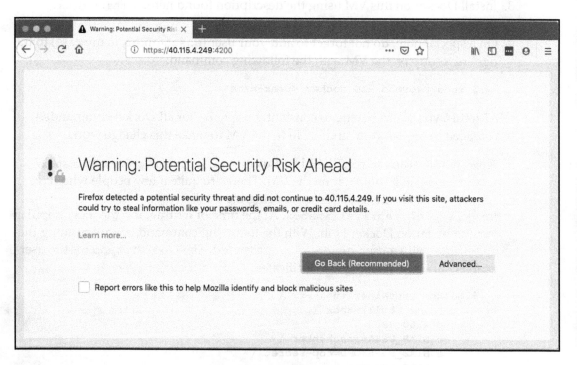

Browser warning due to the use of self-signed certificates

7. In our case, this is not a problem; we know the cause—it's the self-signed certificate. Hence, click the **Advanced...** button and then **Accept Risk and Continue**. Now, you will be redirected to the login screen. Log in with your username and password:

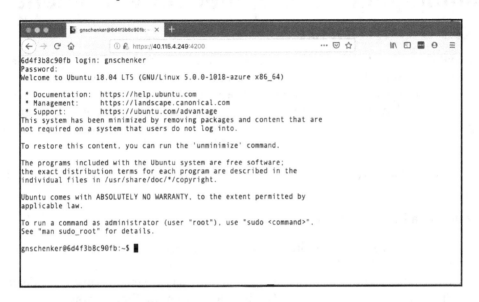

Log in to the remote VM from your browser using HTTPS

We are logged in to the **Shell in a Box** application running on our remote VM, using the HTTPS protocol.

8. Now, we have full access to, for example, the files and folder mapped from the host VM to `/usr/src/dev`. We can, for example, use the `vi` text editor to create and edit files, although we have to first install vi with this:

```
$ sudo apt-get update && sudo apt-get install -y vim
```

9. The possibilities are nearly endless. Please experiment with this setup.For example, run the Shell in a Box container with the Docker socket mounted, install Docker inside the container, and then try to use the Docker CLI from within the container. It is really cool because you can do all of this from within your browser!

10. If you intend to use this Shell in a Box container often and need some additional software installed, do not hesitate to create your own custom Docker image inheriting from `sspreitzer/shellinabox`.

Next, we will see how to run your development environment inside a container.

Running your development environment inside a container

Imagine that you only have access to a workstation with Docker for Desktop installed, but no possibility to add or change anything else on this workstation. Now you want to do some proof of concepts and code some sample application using Python. Unfortunately, Python is not installed on your computer. What can you do? What if you could run a whole development environment inside a container, including code editor and debugger? What if, at the same time, you could still have your code files on your host machine?

Containers are awesome and genius engineers have come up with solutions for exactly this kind of problem.

Let's try this for a Python application:

1. We will be using Visual Studio Code, our favorite code editor, to show how to run a complete Python development environment inside a container. But first, we need to install the necessary Visual Studio Code extension. Open Visual StudioCode and install the extension called **Remote Development**:

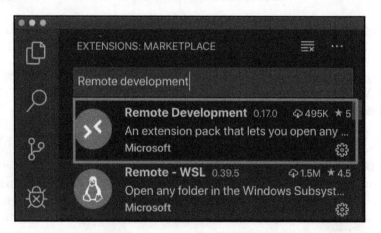

Remote Development extension for Visual Studio Code

2. Then, click the green quick actions status bar item in the lower-left of the Visual Studio Code window. In the popup, select **Remote-Containers: Open Folder in Container...**:

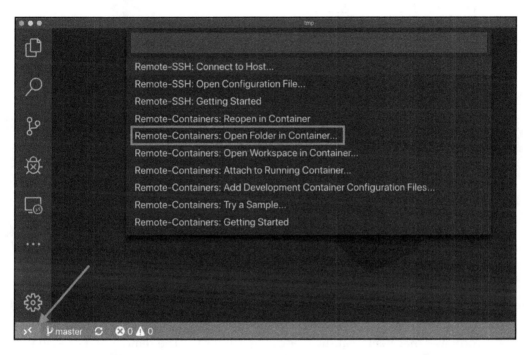

Opening a project in a remote container

3. Select the project folder you want to work with in the container. In our case, we selected the `~/fod/ch08/remote-app` folder. Visual StudioCode will start preparing the environment, which, the very first time, can take a couple of minutes or so. You will see a message like this while this is happening:

Visual Studio Code preparing the development container

By default, this development container runs as a non-root user—called `python` in our case. We learned, in a prior section, that this is a highly recommended best practice. You can change though, and run as `root` by commenting out the line with `"runArgs": [ "-u", "python" ]`, in the `.devcontainer/devcontainer.json` file.

4. Open a Terminal inside Visual Studio Code with *Shift + Ctrl + `* and run the Flask app with the `env FLASK_APP=main.py flask run` command. You should see output like this:

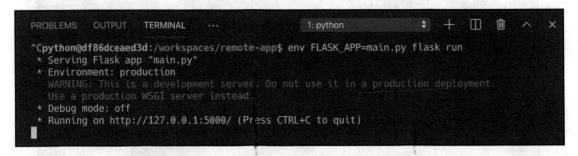

Starting a Python Flask app from Visual Studio Code running inside a container

The `python@df86dceaed3d:/workspaces/remote-app$` prompt indicates that we are **not** running directly on our Docker host but from within a development container that Visual Studio Code spun up for us. The remote part of Visual Studio Code itself also runs inside that container. Only the client part of Visual Studio Code—the UI—continues to run on our host.

5. Open another Terminal window inside Visual Studio Code by pressing *Shift+Ctrl+`*. Then, use `curl` to test the application:

Testing the remote Flask app

6. Press *Ctrl + C* to stop the Flask application.

7. We can also debug the application like we're used when working directly on the host. Open the `.vscode/launch.json` file to understand how the Flask app is started and how the debugger is attached.

8. Open the `main.py` file and set a breakpoint on the `return` statement of the `home()` function.

9. Then, switch to the Debug view of Visual Studio Code and make sure the launch task, `Python: Flask`, is selected in the drop-down menu.

10. Next, press the green start arrow to start debugging. The output in the Terminal should look like this:

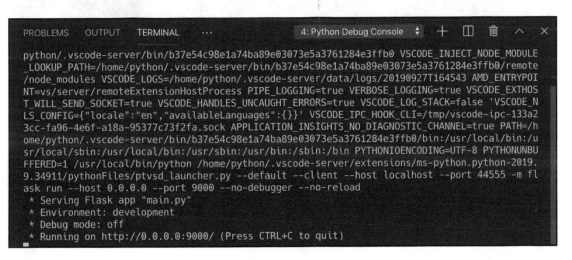

Start debugging a remote app running in a container

11. Open another Terminal with *Shift + Ctrl + `* and test the application by running the `curl localhost:9000/` command. The debugger should hit the breakpoint and you can start analyzing:

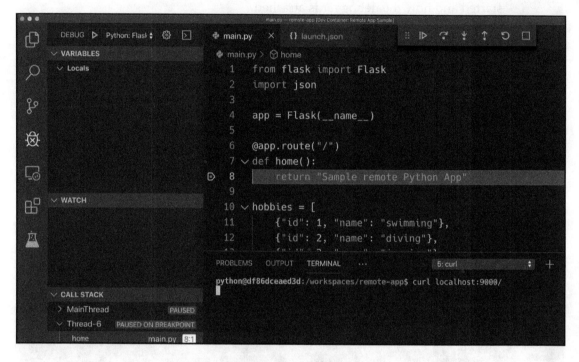

Line-by-line debugging in Visual Studio Code running inside a container

I cannot say strongly enough how cool that is. The backend (non-UI part) of Visual Studio Code is running inside a container, as is Python, the Python debugger, and the Python Flask application itself. At the same time, the source code is mounted from the host into the container and the UI part of Visual Studio Code also runs on the host. This opens up unlimited possibilities for developers even on the most restricted workstations. You can do the same for all popular languages and frameworks, such as .NET, C#, Java, Go, Node.js, and Ruby. If one language is not supported out of the box, you can craft your own development container that will then work the same way as what we have shown with Python.

What if you are working on a workstation that does not have Docker for Desktop installed and is locked down even further? What are your options there?

Running your code editor in a remote container and accessing it via HTTPS

In this section, we will show how you can use Visual Studio Code to enable remote development inside a container. This is interesting when you are limited in what you can run on your workstation. Let's follow these steps:

1. Download and extract the latest version of `code-server`. You can find out the URL by navigating to `https://github.com/cdr/code-server/releases/latest`. At the time of writing, it is `1.1156-vsc1.33.1`:

   ```
   $ VERSION=<version>
   $ wget
   https://github.com/cdr/code-server/releases/download/${VERSION}/cod
   e-server${VERSION}-linux-x64.tar.gz
   $ tar -xvzf code-server${VERSION}-linux-x64.tar.gz
   ```

   Make sure to replace `<version>` with your specific version.

2. Navigate to the folder with the extracted binary, make it executable, and start it:

   ```
   $ cd code-server${VERSION}-linux-x64
   $ chmod +x ./code-server
   $ sudo ./code-server -p 4200
   ```

   The output should look similar to this:

```
(node:15596) [DEP0005] DeprecationWarning: Buffer() is deprecated due to security and usability issues. Please
cUnsafe(), or Buffer.from() methods instead.
INFO  code-server v1.1156-vsc1.33.1
INFO  Additional documentation: http://github.com/cdr/code-server
INFO  Initializing {"data-dir":"/home/gnschenker/.local/share/code-server","extensions-dir":"/home/gnschenker/.
,"working-dir":"/home/gnschenker/code-server1.1156-vsc1.33.1-linux-x64","log-dir":"/home/gnschenker/.cache/code
INFO  Starting webserver... {"host":"0.0.0.0","port":"4200"}
WARN  No certificate specified. This could be insecure.
WARN  Documentation on securing your setup: https://github.com/cdr/code-server/blob/master/doc/security/ssl.md
INFO
INFO  Password: 63ab13ac759c5e4afd92c9d2
INFO
INFO  Started (click the link below to open):
INFO  https://localhost:4200/
INFO
INFO  Starting shared process [1/5]...
WARN  stderr {"data":"(node:15608) [DEP0005] DeprecationWarning: Buffer() is deprecated due to security and usab
r.alloc(), Buffer.allocUnsafe(), or Buffer.from() methods instead.\n"}
INFO  Connected to shared process
```

Starting Visual Studio Code remote-server on a remote VM

Code Server is using self-signed certificates to secure communication, so we can access it over HTTPS. Please make sure you note down the `Password` output on the screen since you need it when accessing Code Server from within your browser. Also note that we are using port `4200` to expose Code Server on the host, the reason being that we already opened that port for ingress on our VM. You can, of course, select any port you want—just make sure you open it for ingress.

3. Open a new browser page and navigate to `https://<public IP>:4200`, where `<public IP>` is the public IP address of your VM. Since we are using self-signed certificates once again, the browser will greet you with a warning similar to what happened when we were using Shell in a Box earlier in this chapter. Accept the warning and you will be redirected to the login page of Code Server:

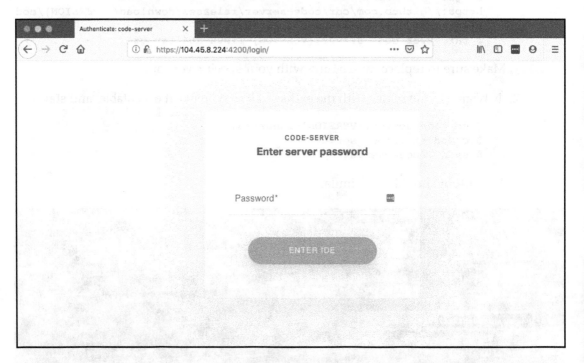

Login page of Code Server

4. Enter the password that you noted down before and click **ENTER IDE**. Now you will be able to use Visual Studio Code remotely via your browser over a secure HTTPS connection:

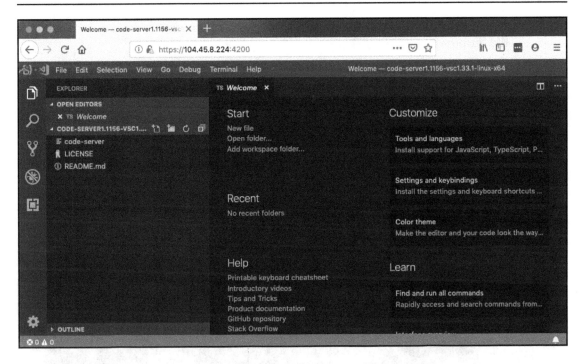

Visual Studio Code running in the browser over HTTPS

5. Now you can do your development from, for example, a Chrome Book or a locked-down workstation, without restrictions. But wait a minute, you may say now! What does this have to do with containers? You're right—so far, there are no containers involved. I could say, though, that if your remote VM has Docker installed, you can use Code Server to do any container-specific development, and I would have saved the day. But that would be a cheap answer.

6. Let's run Code Server itself in a container. That should be easy, shouldn't it? Try using this command, which maps the internal port `8080` to the host port `4200` and mounts host folders containing Code Server settings and possibly your projects into the container:

```
$ docker container run -it \
    -p 4200:8080 \
    -v "${HOME}/.local/share/code-
server:/home/coder/.local/share/code-server" \
    -v "$PWD:/home/coder/project" \
    codercom/code-server:v2
```

Note, the preceding command runs Code Server in insecure mode as indicated in the output:

```
info Server listening on http://0.0.0.0:8080
info  - No authentication
info  - Not serving HTTPS
```

7. You can now access Visual Studio Code in your browser at `http://<public IP>:4200`. Please note the `HTTP` in the URL instead of `HTTPS`! Similarly to when running Code Server natively on the remote VM, you can now use Visual Studio Code from within your browser:

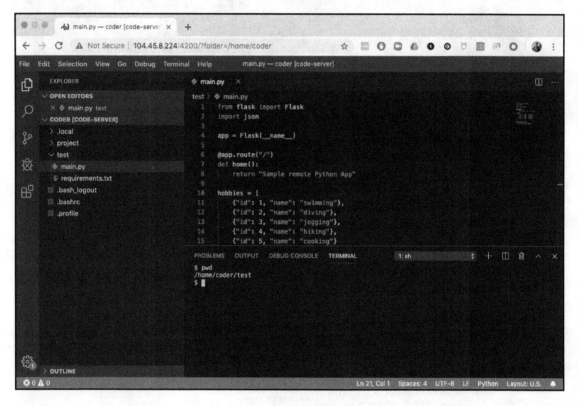

Developing within your browser

With this, I hope you have got a feel for the near-unlimited possibilities that the use of containers offers to you.

Summary

In this chapter, we have shown a few tips and tricks for the advanced Docker user that can make your life much more productive. We have also shown how you can leverage containers to serve whole development environments that run on remote servers and can be accessed from within a browser over a secure HTTPS connection.

In the next chapter, we will introduce the concept of a distributed application architecture and discuss the various patterns and best practices that are required to run a distributed application successfully. In addition to that, we will list some of the concerns that need to be fulfilled to run such an application in production or a production-like environment.

Questions

1. Name the reasons why you would want to run a complete development environment inside a container.
2. Why should you avoid to run applications inside a container as `root`?
3. Why would you ever bind-mount the Docker socket into a container?
4. When pruning your Docker resources to make space, why do you need to handle volumes with special care?

Further reading

- Using Docker in Docker at `http://jpetazzo.github.io/2015/09/03/do-not-use-docker-in-docker-for-ci/`
- Shell in a Box at `https://github.com/shellinabox/shellinabox`
- Remote development using SSH at `https://code.visualstudio.com/docs/remote/ssh`
- Developing inside a container at `https://code.visualstudio.com/docs/remote/containers`

3
Section 3: Orchestration Fundamentals and Docker Swarm

In this section, you will get familiar with the concepts of a dockerized distributed application, as well as container orchestrators, and use Docker Swarm to deploy and run your applications.

This section comprises the following chapters:

- Chapter 9, *Distributed Application Architecture*
- Chapter 10, *Single-Host Networking*
- Chapter 11, *Docker Compose*
- Chapter 12, *Orchestrators*
- Chapter 13, *Introduction to Docker Swarm*
- Chapter 14, *Zero-Downtime Deployments and Secrets*

Distributed Application Architecture

9

In the previous chapter, we discussed advanced tips, tricks, and concepts that are useful when containerizing complex distributed applications, or when using Docker to automate sophisticated tasks.

In this chapter, we'll introduce the concept of a distributed application architecture and discuss the various patterns and best practices that are required to run a distributed application successfully. Finally, we will discuss the additional requirements that need to be fulfilled to run such an application in production.

In this chapter, we will cover the following topics:

- Understanding the distributed application architecture
- Patterns and best practices
- Running in production

After finishing this chapter, you will be able to do the following:

- Name at least four characteristics of a distributed application architecture
- List three to four patterns that need to be implemented for a production-ready distributed application

Understanding the distributed application architecture

In this section, we are going to explain what we mean when we talk about a distributed application architecture. First, we need to make sure that all words or acronyms we use have a meaning and that we are all talking the same language.

Defining the terminology

In this and subsequent chapters, we will talk about a lot about concepts that might not be familiar to everyone. To make sure we're all talking the same language,
let's briefly introduce and describe the most important of these concepts or words:

Terminology	Explanation
VM	The acronym for virtual machine. This is a virtual computer.
Node	An individual server used to run applications. This can be a physical server, often called bare-metal, or a VM. A can be a mainframe, supercomputer, standard business server, or even a Raspberry Pi. Nodes can be computers in a company's own data center or in the cloud. Normally, a node is part of a cluster.
Cluster	A group of nodes connected by a network that are used to run distributed applications.
Network	Physical and software-defined communication paths between individual nodes of a cluster and programs running on those nodes.
Port	A channel on which an application such as a web server listens for incoming requests.
Service	This, unfortunately, is a very overloaded term and its real meaning depends on the context that it is used in. If we use the term *service* in the context of an application such as an application service, then it usually means that this is a piece of software that implements a limited set of functionality that is then used by other parts of the application. As we progress through this book, other types of services that have a slightly different definition will be discussed.

Naively said, a distributed application architecture is the opposite of a monolithic application architecture, but it's not unreasonable to look at this monolithic architecture first. Traditionally, most business applications have been written in such a way that the result can be seen as one single, tightly coupled program that runs on a named server somewhere in a data center. All its code is compiled into a single binary or a few very tightly coupled binaries that need to be co-located when running the application. The fact that the server, or more general host, that the application is running on has a well-defined name or static IP address is also important in this context. Let's look at the following diagram to illustrate this type of application architecture a bit more clearly:

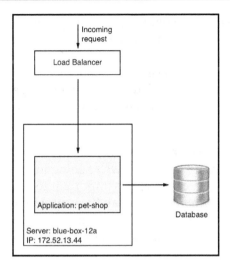

Monolithic application architecture

In the preceding diagram, we can see a **Server** named `blue-box-12a` with an **IP** address of `172.52.13.44` running an application called `pet-shop`, which is a monolith consisting of a main module and a few tightly coupled libraries.

Now, let's look at the following diagram:

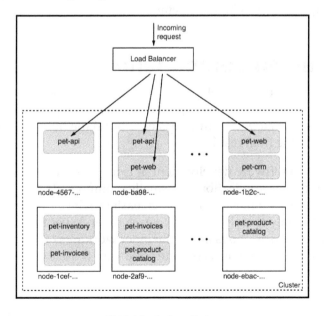

Distributed application architecture

Here, all of a sudden, we don't have only a single named server anymore; instead, we have a lot of them, and they don't have human-friendly names, but rather some unique IDs that can be something like a **Universal Unique Identifier** (**UUID**). The pet shop application, all of a sudden, also does not consist of a single monolithic block anymore, but rather a plethora of interacting, yet loosely coupled, services such as **pet-api**, **pet-web**, and **pet-inventory**. Furthermore, each service runs in multiple instances in this cluster of servers or hosts.

You might be wondering why we are discussing this in a book about Docker containers, and you are right to ask. While all the topics we're going to investigate apply equally to a world where containers do not (yet) exist, it is important to realize that containers and container orchestration engines help address all these problems in a much more efficient and straightforward way. Most of the problems that used to be very hard to solve in a distributed application architecture become quite simple in a containerized world.

Patterns and best practices

A distributed application architecture has many compelling benefits, but it also has one very significant drawback compared to a monolithic application architecture – the former is way more complex. To tame this complexity, the industry has come up with some important best practices and patterns. In the following sections, we are going to look into some of the most important ones in more detail.

Loosely coupled components

The best way to address a complex subject has always been to divide it into smaller subproblems that are more manageable. As an example, it would be insanely complex to build a house in one single step. It is much easier to build the house from simple parts that are then combined into the final result.

The same also applies to software development. It is much easier to develop a very complex application if we divide this application into smaller components that interoperate and make up the overall application. Now, it is much easier to develop these components individually if they are only loosely coupled to each other. What this means is that component A makes no assumptions about the inner workings of, say, components B and C, and is only interested in how it can communicate with those two components across a well-defined interface.

If each component has a well-defined and simple public interface through which communication with the other components in the system and the outside world happens, then this enables us to develop each component individually, without implicit dependencies to other components. During the development process, other components in the system can easily be replaced by stubs or mocks to allow us to test our components.

Stateful versus stateless

Every meaningful business application creates, modifies, or uses data. In IT, a synonym for data is *state*. An application service that creates or modifies persistent data is called a stateful component. Typical stateful components are database services or services that create files. On the other hand, application components that do not create or modify persistent data are called stateless components.

In a distributed application architecture, stateless components are much simpler to handle than stateful components. Stateless components can be easily scaled up and down. Furthermore, they can be quickly and painlessly torn down and restarted on a completely different node of the cluster – all of this because they have no persistent data associated with them.

Given that fact, it is helpful to design a system in a way that most of the application services are stateless. It is best to push all the stateful components to the boundary of the application and limit their number. Managing stateful components is hard.

Service discovery

As we build applications that consist of many individual components or services that communicate with each other, we need a mechanism that allows the individual components to find each other in the cluster. Finding each other usually means that you need to know on which node the target component is running and on which port it is listening for communication. Most often, nodes are identified by an IP address and a port, which is just a number in a well-defined range.

Technically, we could tell **Service A**, which wants to communicate with a target, **Service B**, what the **IP** address and **port** of the target are. This could happen, for example, through an entry in a configuration file:

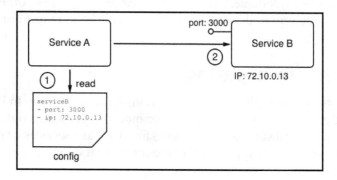

Components are hardwired

While this might work very well in the context of a monolithic application that runs on one or only a few well-known and curated servers, it totally falls apart in a distributed application architecture. First of all, in this scenario, we have many components, and keeping track of them manually becomes a nightmare. This is definitely not scalable. Furthermore, **Service A** typically should or will never know on which node of the cluster the other components run. Their location may not even be stable as component B could be moved from node X to another node Y, due to various reasons external to the application. Thus, we need another way in which **Service A** can locate **Service B**, or any other service, for that matter. What is most commonly used is an external authority that is aware of the topology of the system at any given time.

This external authority or service knows all the nodes and their IP addresses that currently pertain to the cluster; it knows about all the services that are running and where they are running. Often, this kind of service is called a **DNS service**, where **DNS** stands for **Domain Name System**. As we will see, Docker has a DNS service implemented as part of the underlying engine. Kubernetes – the number one container orchestration system, which we'll discuss in `Chapter 12`, *Orchestrators* – also uses a **DNS service** to facilitate communication between components running in the cluster:

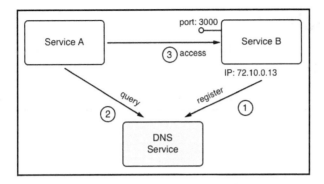

Components consulting an external locator service

In the preceding diagram, we can see how **Service A** wants to communicate with **Service B**, but it can't do this directly. First, it has to query the external authority, a registry service (here, called a **DNS Service**), about the whereabouts of **Service B**. The registry service will answer with the requested information and hand out the IP address and port number that **Service A** can use to reach **Service B**. **Service A** then uses this information and establishes a communication with **Service B**. Of course, this is a naive picture of what's really happening on a low level, but it is a good picture to help us understand the architectural pattern of service discovery.

Routing

Routing is the mechanism of sending packets of data from a source component to a target component. Routing is categorized into different types. The so-called OSI model (see the reference to this in the *Further reading* section of this chapter for more information) is used to distinguish between different types of routing. In the context of containers and container orchestration, routing at layers 2, 3, 4, and 7 is relevant. We will dive into more detail about routing in subsequent chapters. Here, let's just say that layer 2 routing is the most low-level type of routing, which connects a MAC address to another MAC address, while layer 7 routing, which is also called application-level routing, is the most high-level one. The latter is, for example, used to route requests that have a target identifier, that is, a URL such as `https://acme.com/pets`, to the appropriate target component in our system.

Load balancing

Load balancing is used whenever **Service A** needs to communicate with **Service B**, say in a request-response pattern, but the latter is running in more than one instance, as shown in the following diagram:

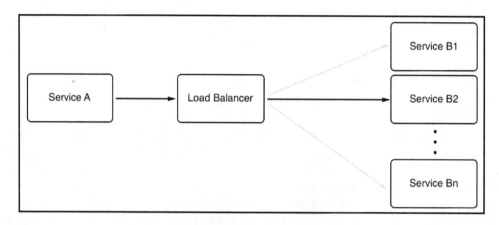

The request of Service A being load balanced to Service B

If we have multiple instances of a service such as **Service B** running in our system, we want to make sure that every one of those instances gets an equal amount of workload assigned to it. This task is a generic one, which means that we don't want the caller to have to do the load balancing, but rather an external service that intercepts the call and takes over the part of deciding which of the target service instances to forward the call to. This external service is called a load balancer. Load balancers can use different algorithms to decide how to distribute incoming calls to target service instances. The most common algorithm that's used is called round-robin. This algorithm just assigns requests in a repetitive way, starting with instance 1, then 2, until instance n. After the last instance has been served, the load balancer starts over with instance number 1.

In the preceding example, a **load balancer** also facilitates high availability since a request from **service A** will be forwarded to a healthy instance of **Service B**. The **load balancer** also takes the role of periodically checking the health of each instance of B.

Defensive programming

When developing a service for a distributed application, it is important to remember that this service is not going to be standalone and that it's dependent on other application services or even on external services provided by third parties, such as credit card validation services or stock information services, to just name two. All these other services are external to the service we are developing. We have no control over their correctness or their availability at any given time. Thus, when coding, we always need to assume the worst and hope for the best. Assuming the worst means that we have to deal with potential failures explicitly.

Retries

When there is a possibility that an external service might be temporarily unavailable or not responsive enough, then the following procedure can be used. When the call to the other service fails or times out, the calling code should be structured in such a way that the same call is repeated after a short wait time. If the call fails again, the wait should be a bit longer before the next trial. The calls should be repeated up until a maximum number of times, each time increasing the wait time. After that, the service should give up and provide a degraded service, which could mean returning some stale cached data or no data at all, depending on the situation.

Logging

Important operations that are performed on a service should always be logged. Logging information needs to be categorized to be of any real value. A common list of categories includes debug, info, warning, error, and fatal. Logging information should be collected by a central log aggregation service and not be stored on an individual node of the cluster. Aggregated logs are easy to parse and filter for relevant information. This information is essential to quickly pinpoint the root cause of a failure or unexpected behavior in a distributed system consisting of many moving parts, running in production.

Error handling

As we mentioned earlier, each application service in a distributed application is dependent on other services. As developers, we should always expect the worst and have appropriate error handling in place. One of the most important best practices is to fail fast. Code the service in such a way that unrecoverable errors are discovered as early as possible and, if such an error is detected, have the service fail immediately. But don't forget to log meaningful information to STDERR or STDOUT, which can be used by developers or system operators later to track malfunctions of the system. Also, return a helpful error to the caller, indicating as precisely as possible why the call failed.

One sample of fail fast is to always check the input values provided by the caller. Are the values in the expected ranges and complete? If not, then do not try to continue processing; instead, immediately abort the operation.

Redundancy

A mission-critical system has to be available at all times, around the clock, 365 days a year. Downtime is not acceptable since it might result in a huge loss of opportunities or reputation for the company. In a highly distributed application, the likelihood of a failure of at least one of the many involved components is non-neglectable. We can say that the question is not whether a component will fail, but rather when a failure will occur.

To avoid downtime when one of the many components in the system fails, each individual part of the system needs to be redundant. This includes the application components, as well as all infrastructure parts. What that means is that if we, say, have a payment service as part of our application, then we need to run this service redundantly. The easiest way to do that is to run multiple instances of this very service on different nodes of our cluster. The same applies, say, for an edge router or a load balancer. We cannot afford for this to ever go down. Thus, the router or load balancer must be redundant.

Health checks

We have mentioned various times that in a distributed application architecture, with its many parts, the failure of an individual component is highly likely and that it is only a matter of time until it happens. For that reason, we run every single component of the system redundantly. Proxy services then load balance the traffic across the individual instances of a service.

But now, there is another problem. How does the proxy or router know whether a certain service instance is available? It could have crashed or it could be unresponsive. To solve this problem, we can use so-called health checks. The proxy, or some other system service on behalf of the proxy, periodically polls all the service instances and checks their health. The questions are basically, Are you still there? Are you healthy? The answer to each service is either Yes or No, or the health check times out if the instance is not responsive anymore.

If the component answers with No or a timeout occurs, then the system kills the corresponding instance and spins up a new instance in its place. If all this happens in a fully automated way, then we say that we have an auto-healing system in place.

Instead of the proxy periodically polling the status of the components, responsibility can also be turned around. The components could be required to periodically send live signals to the proxy. If a component fails to send live signals over a predefined, extended period of time, it is assumed to be unhealthy or dead.

There are situations where either of the described ways is more appropriate.

Circuit breaker pattern

A circuit breaker is a mechanism that is used to avoid a distributed application going down due to the cascading failure of many essential components. Circuit breakers help to avoid one failing component tearing down other dependent services in a domino effect. Like circuit breakers in an electrical system, which protect a house from burning down due to the failure of a malfunctioning plugged-in appliance by interrupting the power line, circuit breakers in a distributed application interrupt the connection from **Service A** to **Service B** if the latter is not responding or is malfunctioning.

This can be achieved by wrapping a protected service call in a circuit breaker object. This object monitors for failures. Once the number of failures reaches a certain threshold, the circuit breaker trips. All subsequent calls to the circuit breaker will return with an error, without the protected call being made at all:

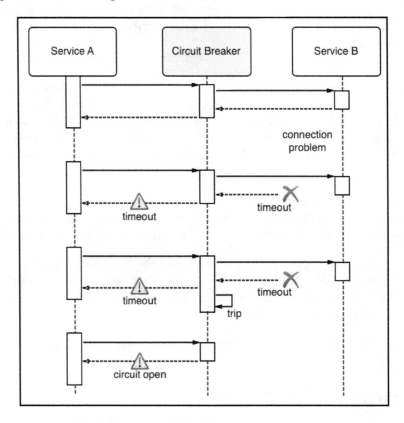

Circuit breaker pattern

In the preceding diagram, we have a circuit breaker that tips over after the second timeout is received when calling **Service B**.

Running in production

To successfully run a distributed application in production, we need to consider a few more aspects beyond the best practices and patterns presented in the preceding sections. One specific area that comes to mind is introspection and monitoring. Let's go through the most important aspects in detail.

Logging

Once a distributed application is in production, it is not possible to live debug it. But how can we then find out what exactly is the root cause of the application malfunctioning? The solution to this problem is that the application produces abundant and meaningful logging information while running. Developers need to instrument their application services in such a way that they output helpful information, such as when an error happens or a potentially unexpected or unwanted situation is encountered. Often, this information is output to STDOUT and STDERR, where it is then collected by system daemons that write the information to local files or forward it to a central log aggregation service.

If there is sufficient information in the logs, developers can use those logs to track down the root cause of the errors in the system.

In a distributed application architecture, with its many components, logging is even more important than in a monolithic application. The paths of execution of a single request through all the components of the application can be very complex. Also, remember that the components are distributed across a cluster of nodes. Thus, it makes sense to log everything of importance, and to add things to each log entry such as the exact time when it happened, the component in which it happened, and the node on which the component ran, to name just a few. Furthermore, the logging information should be aggregated in a central location so that it is readily available for developers and system operators to analyze.

Tracing

Tracing is used to find out how an individual request is funneled through a distributed application and how much time is spent overall for the request and in every individual component. This information, if collected, can be used as one of the sources for dashboards that shows the behavior and health of the system.

Monitoring

Operation engineers like to have dashboards showing live key metrics of the system, which show them the overall health of the application at a glance. These metrics can be non-functional metrics, such as memory and CPU usage, the number of crashes of a system or application component, and the health of a node, as well as functional and, hence, application-specific metrics, such as the number of checkouts in an ordering system or the number of items out of stock in an inventory service.

Most often, the base data that's used to aggregate the numbers that are used for a dashboard is extracted from logging information. This can either be system logs, which will mostly be used for non-functional metrics, or application-level logs, for functional metrics.

Application updates

One of the competitive advantages for a company is to be able to react in a timely manner to changing market situations. Part of this is to be able to quickly adjust an application to fulfill new and changed needs or to add new functionality. The faster we can update our applications, the better. Many companies these days roll out new or changed features multiple times per day.

Since application updates are so frequent, these updates have to be non-disruptive. We cannot allow the system to go down for maintenance when upgrading. It all has to happen seamlessly and transparently.

Rolling updates

One way of updating an application or an application service is to use rolling updates. The assumption here is that the particular piece of software that has to be updated runs in multiple instances. Only then can we use this type of update.

What happens is that the system stops one instance of the current service and replaces it with an instance of the new service. As soon as the new instance is ready, it will be served traffic. Usually, the new instance is monitored for some time to see whether or not it works as expected and, if it does, the next instance of the current service is taken down and replaced with a new instance. This pattern is repeated until all the service instances have been replaced.

Since there are always a few instances running at any given time, current or new, the application is operational all the time. No downtime is needed.

Blue-green deployments

In blue-green deployments, the current version of the application service, called **blue**, handles all the application traffic. We then install the new version of the application service, called **green**, on the production system. The new service is not wired with the rest of the application yet.

Once **green** is installed, we can execute **smoke tests** against this new service and, if those succeed, the router can be configured to funnel all traffic that previously went to **blue** to the new service, **green**. The behavior of **green** is then observed closely and, if all success criteria are met, **blue** can be decommissioned. But if, for some reason, **green** shows some unexpected or unwanted behavior, the router can be reconfigured to return all traffic to blue. Green can then be removed and fixed, and a new blue-green deployment can be executed with the corrected version:

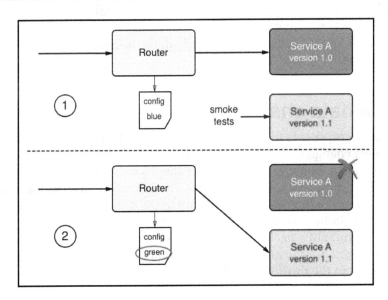

Blue-green deployment

Next, let's look at canary releases.

Canary releases

Canary releases are releases where we have the current version of the application service and the new version installed on the system in parallel. As such, they resemble blue-green deployments. At first, all traffic is still routed through the current version. We then configure a router so that it funnels a small percentage, say 1%, of the overall traffic to the new version of the application service. Subsequently, the behavior of the new service is monitored closely to find out whether it works as expected. If all the criteria for success are met, then the router is configured to funnel more traffic, say 5% this time, through the new service. Again, the behavior of the new service is closely monitored and, if it is successful, more and more traffic is routed to it until we reach 100%. Once all the traffic has been routed to the new service and it has been stable for some time, the old version of the service can be decommissioned.

Why do we call this a canary release? It is named after the coal miners who would use canary birds as an early warning system in the mines. Canary birds are particularly sensitive to toxic gas and if such a canary bird died, the miners knew they had to abandon the mine immediately.

Irreversible data changes

If part of our update process is to execute an irreversible change in our state, such as an irreversible schema change in a backing relational database, then we need to address this with special care. It is possible to execute such changes without downtime if we use the right approach. It is important to recognize that, in such a situation, we cannot deploy the code changes that require the new data structure in the data store at the same time as the changes to the data. Rather, the whole update has to be separated into three distinct steps. In the first step, we roll out a backward-compatible schema and data change. If this is successful, then we roll out the new code in the second step. Again, if that is successful, we clean up the schema in the third step and remove the backward compatibility:

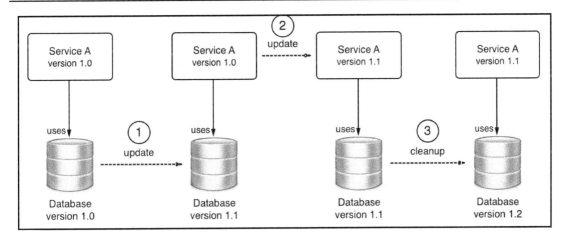

Rolling out an irreversible data or schema change

The preceding diagram shows how the data and its structure are updated, then how the application code is updated, and finally, in the third step, how the data and data structure are cleaned up.

Rollback

If we have frequent updates for our application services that run in production, sooner or later, there will be a problem with one of those updates. Maybe a developer, while fixing a bug, introduced a new one, which was not caught by all the automated, and maybe manual, tests, so the application is misbehaving and it is imperative that we roll back the service to the previous good version. In this regard, a rollback is a recovery from a disaster.

Again, in a distributed application architecture, it is not a question of whether a rollback will ever be needed, but rather when a rollback will have to occur. Thus, we need to be absolutely sure that we can always roll back to a previous version of any service that makes up our application. Rollbacks cannot be an afterthought; they have to be a tested and proven part of our deployment process.

If we are using blue-green deployments to update our services, then rollbacks should be fairly simple. All we need to do is switch the router from the new green version of the service back to the previous blue version.

Summary

In this chapter, we learned what a distributed application architecture is and what patterns and best practices are helpful or needed to successfully run a distributed application. Lastly, we discussed what more is needed to run such an application in production.

In the next chapter, we will dive into networking limited to a single host. We're going to discuss how containers living on the same host can communicate with each other and how external clients can access containerized applications if necessary.

Questions

Please answer the following questions to assess your understanding of this chapter's content:

1. When and why does every part in a distributed application architecture have to be redundant? Explain in a few short sentences.
2. Why do we need DNS services? Explain in three to five sentences.
3. What is a circuit breaker and why is it needed?
4. What are some of the important differences between a monolithic application and a distributed or multi-service application?
5. What is a blue-green deployment?

Further reading

The following articles provide more in-depth information regarding what was covered in this chapter:

- Circuit breakers: http://bit.ly/1NU1sgW
- The OSI model explained: http://bit.ly/1UCcvMt
- Blue-green deployments: http://bit.ly/2r2IxNJ

10
Single-Host Networking

In the previous chapter, we learned about the most important architectural patterns and best practices that are used when dealing with a distributed application architecture.

In this chapter, we will introduce the Docker container networking model and its single-host implementation in the form of the bridge network. This chapter also introduces the concept of software-defined networks and how they are used to secure containerized applications. Furthermore, we will demonstrate how container ports can be opened to the public and thus make containerized components accessible to the outside world. Finally, we will introduce Traefik, a reverse proxy, which can be used to enable sophisticated HTTP application-level routing between containers.

This chapter covers the following topics:

- Dissecting the container network model
- Network firewalling
- Working with the bridge network
- The host and null network
- Running in an existing network namespace
- Managing container ports
- HTTP-level routing using a reverse proxy

After completing this chapter, you will be able to do the following:

- Create, inspect, and delete a custom bridge network
- Run a container attached to a custom bridge network
- Isolate containers from each other by running them on different bridge networks
- Publish a container port to a host port of your choice
- Add Traefik as a reverse proxy to enable application-level routing

Technical requirements

For this chapter, the only thing you will need is a Docker host that is able to run Linux containers. You can use your laptop with either Docker for macOS or Windows or have Docker Toolbox installed.

Dissecting the container network model

So far, we have been mostly working with single containers. But in reality, a containerized business application consists of several containers that need to collaborate to achieve a goal. Therefore, we need a way for individual containers to communicate with each other. This is achieved by establishing pathways that we can use to send data packets back and forth between containers. These pathways are called **networks**. Docker has defined a very simple networking model, the so-called **container network model** (**CNM**), to specify the requirements that any software that implements a container network has to fulfill. The following is a graphical representation of the CNM:

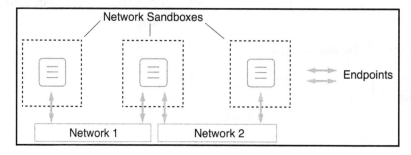

The Docker CNM

The CNM has three elements – sandbox, endpoint, and network:

- **Sandbox:** The sandbox perfectly isolates a container from the outside world. No inbound network connection is allowed into the sandboxed container. But, it is very unlikely that a container will be of any value in a system if absolutely no communication with it is possible. To work around this, we have element number two, which is the endpoint.

- **Endpoint:** An endpoint is a controlled gateway from the outside world into the network's sandbox that shields the container. The endpoint connects the network sandbox (but not the container) to the third element of the model, which is the network.
- **Network:** The network is the pathway that transports the data packets of an instance of communication from endpoint to endpoint or, ultimately, from container to container.

It is important to note that a network sandbox can have zero to many endpoints, or, said differently, each container living in a network sandbox can either be attached to no network at all or it can be attached to multiple different networks at the same time. In the preceding diagram, the middle of the three **Network Sandboxes** is attached to both **Network 1** and **Network 2** through an **endpoint**.

This networking model is very generic and does not specify where the individual containers that communicate with each other over a network run. All containers could, for example, run on one and the same host (local) or they could be distributed across a cluster of hosts (global).

Of course, the CNM is just a model describing how networking works among containers. To be able to use networking with our containers, we need real implementations of the CNM. For both local and global scope, we have multiple implementations of the CNM. In the following table, we've given a short overview of the existing implementations and their main characteristics. The list is in no particular order:

Network	Company	Scope	Description
Bridge	Docker	Local	Simple network based on Linux bridges to allow networking on a single host
Macvlan	Docker	Local	Configures multiple layer 2 (that is, MAC) addresses on a single physical host interface
Overlay	Docker	Global	Multinode-capable container network based on **Virtual Extensible LAN (VXLan)**

Weave Net	Weaveworks	Global	Simple, resilient, multi-host Docker networking
Contiv Network Plugin	Cisco	Global	Open source container networking

All network types not directly provided by Docker can be added to a Docker host as a plugin.

Network firewalling

Docker has always had the mantra of security first. This philosophy had a direct influence on how networking in a single and multi-host Docker environment was designed and implemented. Software-defined networks are easy and cheap to create, yet they perfectly firewall containers that are attached to this network from other non-attached containers, and from the outside world. All containers that belong to the same network can freely communicate with each other, while others have no means to do so.

In the following diagram, we have two networks called **front** and **back**. Attached to the front network, we have containers **c1** and **c2**, and attached to the back network, we have containers **c3** and **c4**. **c1** and **c2** can freely communicate with each other, as can **c3** and **c4**. But **c1** and **c2** have no way to communicate with either **c3** or **c4**, and vice versa:

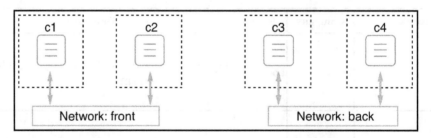

Docker networks

Now, what about the situation where we have an application consisting of three services: **webAPI**, **productCatalog**, and **database**? We want **webAPI** to be able to communicate with **productCatalog**, but not with the **database**, and we want **productCatalog** to be able to communicate with the **database** service. We can solve this situation by placing **webAPI** and the database on different networks and attaching **productCatalog** to both of these networks, as shown in the following diagram:

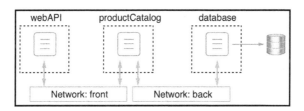

Container attached to multiple networks

Since creating SDNs is cheap, and each network provides added security by isolating resources from unauthorized access, it is highly recommended that you design and run applications so that they use multiple networks and only run services on the same network that absolutely need to communicate with each other. In the preceding example, there is absolutely no need for the **webAPI** component to ever communicate directly with the **database** service, so we have put them on different networks. If the worst-case scenario happens and a hacker compromises the **webAPI**, they cannot access the **database** from there without also hacking the **productCatalog** service.

Working with the bridge network

The Docker bridge network is the first implementation of the container network model that we're going to look at in detail. This network implementation is based on the Linux bridge. When the Docker daemon runs for the first time, it creates a Linux bridge and calls it docker0. This is the default behavior and can be changed by changing the configuration. Docker then creates a network with this Linux bridge and calls the network bridge. All the containers that we create on a Docker host and that we do not explicitly bind to another network leads to Docker automatically attaching to this bridge network.

To verify that we indeed have a network called bridge of the bridge type defined on our host, we can list all the networks on the host with the following command:

```
$ docker network ls
```

This should provide an output similar to the following:

```
$ docker network ls
NETWORK ID      NAME      DRIVER      SCOPE
928c8ce47bf2    bridge    bridge      local
bdb36adcf70c    host      host        local
af82006f2f2d    none      null        local
$
```

Listing all the Docker networks available by default

In your case, the IDs will be different, but the rest of the output should look the same. We do indeed have a first network called `bridge` using the `bridge` driver. The scope being `local` just means that this type of network is restricted to a single host and cannot span multiple hosts. In `Chapter 13`, *Introduction to Docker Swarm*, we will also discuss other types of networks that have a global scope, meaning they can span whole clusters of hosts.

Now, let's look a little bit deeper into what this bridge network is all about. For this, we are going to use the Docker `inspect` command:

```
$ docker network inspect bridge
```

When executed, this outputs a big chunk of detailed information about the network in question. This information should look as follows:

```
C:\Users\admin>docker network inspect bridge
[
    {
        "Name": "bridge",
        "Id": "3b08c1c711ada84ae859c4bed48b5af1f45b68db89356ca5045dc7ee8672e946",
        "Created": "2018-04-09T09:47:29.9424652Z",
        "Scope": "local",
        "Driver": "bridge",
        "EnableIPv6": false,
        "IPAM": {
            "Driver": "default",
            "Options": null,
            "Config": [
                {
                    "Subnet": "172.17.0.0/16",
                    "Gateway": "172.17.0.1"
                }
            ]
        },
        "Internal": false,
        "Attachable": false,
        "Ingress": false,
        "ConfigFrom": {
            "Network": ""
        },
        "ConfigOnly": false,
        "Containers": {},
        "Options": {
            "com.docker.network.bridge.default_bridge": "true",
            "com.docker.network.bridge.enable_icc": "true",
            "com.docker.network.bridge.enable_ip_masquerade": "true",
            "com.docker.network.bridge.host_binding_ipv4": "0.0.0.0",
            "com.docker.network.bridge.name": "docker0",
            "com.docker.network.driver.mtu": "1500"
        },
        "Labels": {}
    }
]
```

Output generated when inspecting the Docker bridge network

We saw the ID, Name, Driver, and Scope values when we listed all the networks, so that is nothing new. But let's have a look at the **IP address management** (**IPAM**) block. IPAM is a piece of software that is used to track IP addresses that are used on a computer. The important part of the IPAM block is the Config node with its values for Subnet and Gateway. The subnet for the bridge network is defined by default as 172.17.0.0/16. This means that all containers attached to this network will get an IP address assigned by Docker that is taken from the given range, which is 172.17.0.2 to 172.17.255.255. The 172.17.0.1 address is reserved for the router of this network whose role in this type of network is taken by the Linux bridge. We can expect that the very first container that will be attached to this network by Docker will get the 172.17.0.2 address. All subsequent containers will get a higher number; the following diagram illustrates this fact:

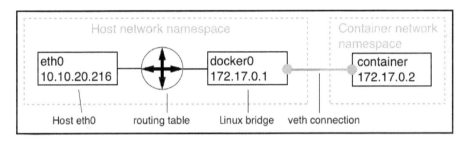

The bridge network

In the preceding diagram, we can see the network namespace of the host, which includes the host's **eth0** endpoint, which is typically a NIC if the Docker host runs on bare metal or a virtual NIC if the Docker host is a VM. All traffic to the host comes through **eth0**. The **Linux bridge** is responsible for routing the network traffic between the host's network and the subnet of the bridge network.

By default, only egress traffic is allowed, and all ingress is blocked. What this means is that while containerized applications can reach the internet, they cannot be reached by any outside traffic. Each container attached to the network gets its own **virtual ethernet (veth)** connection with the bridge. This is illustrated in the following diagram:

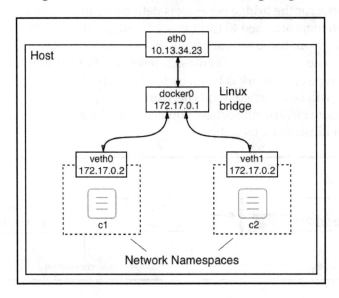

Details of the bridge network

The preceding diagram shows us the world from the perspective of the **Host**. We will explore what this situation looks like from within a container later on in this section.

We are not limited to just the bridge network, as Docker allows us to define our own custom bridge networks. This is not just a feature that is nice to have, but it is a recommended best practice to not run all containers on the same network. Instead, we should use additional bridge networks to further isolate containers that have no need to communicate with each other. To create a custom bridge network called `sample-net`, use the following command:

```
$ docker network create --driver bridge sample-net
```

If we do this, we can then inspect what subnet Docker has created for this new custom network, as follows:

```
$ docker network inspect sample-net | grep Subnet
```

This returns the following value:

```
"Subnet": "172.18.0.0/16",
```

Evidently, Docker has just assigned the next free block of IP addresses to our new custom bridge network. If, for some reason, we want to specify our own subnet range when creating a network, we can do so by using the `--subnet` parameter:

```
$ docker network create --driver bridge --subnet "10.1.0.0/16" test-net
```

 To avoid conflicts due to duplicate IP addresses, make sure you avoid creating networks with overlapping subnets.

Now that we have discussed what a bridge network is and how we can create a custom bridge network, we want to understand how we can attach containers to these networks. First, let's interactively run an Alpine container without specifying the network to be attached:

```
$ docker container run --name c1 -it --rm alpine:latest /bin/sh
```

In another Terminal window, let's inspect the c1 container:

```
$ docker container inspect c1
```

In the vast output, let's concentrate for a moment on the part that provides network-related information. This can be found under the `NetworkSettings` node. I have it listed in the following output:

```
    },
"NetworkSettings": {
    "Bridge": "",
    "SandboxID": "ae53496fba49de3d0a4727105cc0799b7fbd30746d76700238cb47c611f3eb68",
    "HairpinMode": false,
    "LinkLocalIPv6Address": "",
    "LinkLocalIPv6PrefixLen": 0,
    "Ports": {},
    "SandboxKey": "/var/run/docker/netns/ae53496fba49",
    "SecondaryIPAddresses": null,
    "SecondaryIPv6Addresses": null,
    "EndpointID": "c063a725d1f66e867b5769a80d1477cc88d07618860655fa3033a97478e55713",
    "Gateway": "172.17.0.1",
    "GlobalIPv6Address": "",
    "GlobalIPv6PrefixLen": 0,
    "IPAddress": "172.17.0.4",
    "IPPrefixLen": 16,
    "IPv6Gateway": "",
    "MacAddress": "02:42:ac:11:00:04",
    "Networks": {
        "bridge": {
            "IPAMConfig": null,
            "Links": null,
            "Aliases": null,
            "NetworkID": "026e653c2504e464748b4ce9b25cce69d29bc82a52105a25920f2b796663e635",
            "EndpointID": "c063a725d1f66e867b5769a80d1477cc88d07618860655fa3033a97478e55713",
            "Gateway": "172.17.0.1",
            "IPAddress": "172.17.0.4",
            "IPPrefixLen": 16,
            "IPv6Gateway": "",
            "GlobalIPv6Address": "",
            "GlobalIPv6PrefixLen": 0,
            "MacAddress": "02:42:ac:11:00:04",
            "DriverOpts": null
        }
    }
}
```

The NetworkSettings section of the container metadata

In the preceding output, we can see that the container is indeed attached to the `bridge` network since `NetworkID` is equal to `026e65...`, which we can see from the preceding code is the ID of the `bridge` network. We can also see that the container got the IP address of `172.17.0.4` assigned as expected and that the gateway is at `172.17.0.1`. Please note that the container also had a `MacAddress` associated with it. This is important as the Linux bridge uses the `MacAddress` for routing.

So far, we have approached this from the outside of the container's network namespace. Now, let's see what the situation looks like when we're not only inside the container but inside the containers' network namespace. Inside the `c1` container, let's use the `ip` tool to inspect what's going on. Run the `ip addr` command and observe the output that is generated, as follows:

```
/ # ip addr
1: lo: <LOOPBACK,UP,LOWER_UP> mtu 65536 qdisc noqueue state UNKNOWN qlen 1
    link/loopback 00:00:00:00:00:00 brd 00:00:00:00:00:00
    inet 127.0.0.1/8 scope host lo
        valid_lft forever preferred_lft forever
2: tunl0@NONE: <NOARP> mtu 1480 qdisc noop state DOWN qlen 1
    link/ipip 0.0.0.0 brd 0.0.0.0
3: ip6tnl0@NONE: <NOARP> mtu 1452 qdisc noop state DOWN qlen 1
    link/tunnel6 00:00:00:00:00:00:00:00:00:00:00:00:00:00:00:00 brd 00:00:00:00:00:00:00:00:00:00:00:00:00:00:00:00
19: eth0@if20: <BROADCAST,MULTICAST,UP,LOWER_UP,M-DOWN> mtu 1500 qdisc noqueue state UP
    link/ether 02:42:ac:11:00:04 brd ff:ff:ff:ff:ff:ff
    inet 172.17.0.4/16 brd 172.17.255.255 scope global eth0
        valid_lft forever preferred_lft forever
/ #
```

Container namespace, as seen by the IP tool

The interesting part of the preceding output is number `19`, that is, the `eth0` endpoint. The `veth0` endpoint that the Linux bridge created outside of the container namespace is mapped to `eth0` inside the container. Docker always maps the first endpoint of a container network namespace to `eth0`, as seen from inside the namespace. If the network namespace is attached to an additional network, then that endpoint will be mapped to `eth1`, and so on.

Since at this point we're not really interested in any endpoint other than `eth0`, we could have used a more specific variant of the command, which would have given us the following:

```
/ # ip addr show eth0
195: eth0@if196: <BROADCAST,MULTICAST,UP,LOWER_UP,M-DOWN> mtu 1500 qdisc
noqueue state UP
    link/ether 02:42:ac:11:00:02 brd ff:ff:ff:ff:ff:ff
    inet 172.17.0.2/16 brd 172.17.255.255 scope global eth0
        valid_lft forever preferred_lft forever
```

In the output, we can also see what MAC address (`02:42:ac:11:00:02`) and what IP (`172.17.0.2`) have been associated with this container network namespace by Docker.

We can also get some information about how requests are routed by using the `ip route` command:

```
/ # ip route
default via 172.17.0.1 dev eth0
172.17.0.0/16 dev eth0 scope link src 172.17.0.2
```

This output tells us that all the traffic to the gateway at `172.17.0.1` is routed through the `eth0` device.

Now, let's run another container called `c2` on the same network:

```
$ docker container run --name c2 -d alpine:latest ping 127.0.0.1
```

The `c2` container will also be attached to the `bridge` network since we have not specified any other network. Its IP address will be the next free one from the subnet, which is `172.17.0.3`, as we can readily test:

```
$ docker container inspect --format "{{.NetworkSettings.IPAddress}}" c2
172.17.0.3
```

Now, we have two containers attached to the `bridge` network. We can try to inspect this network once again to find a list of all containers attached to it in the output:

```
$ docker network inspect bridge
```

This information can be found under the `Containers` node:

```
"ConfigOnly": false,
"Containers": {
    "27b96de70b58cd918d35c235a7c180f56f71df58cf4cec50b8f0103dd529b95f": {
        "Name": "c2",
        "EndpointID": "8883649774c5c4c53063da02598c8d09fe7ee427145b348b1d1703f31213e9ca",
        "MacAddress": "02:42:ac:11:00:03",
        "IPv4Address": "172.17.0.3/16",
        "IPv6Address": ""
    },
    "35b8dd512acb985647833e1cc52625e129c15e903fd8a0c0ab247932bc910166": {
        "Name": "c1",
        "EndpointID": "28269a9cc630135ab287052fa69c72f28c57a10bd5e7523c451bf2d0976fd1b5",
        "MacAddress": "02:42:ac:11:00:02",
        "IPv4Address": "172.17.0.2/16",
        "IPv6Address": ""
    }
},
"Options": {
```

The Containers section of the output of the Docker network inspect bridge

Once again, we have shortened the output to the relevant part for readability.

Now, let's create two additional containers, c3 and c4, and attach them to `test-net`. For this, we'll use the `--network` parameter:

```
$ docker container run --name c3 -d --network test-net \
    alpine:latest ping 127.0.0.1
$ docker container run --name c4 -d --network test-net \
    alpine:latest ping 127.0.0.1
```

Let's inspect `network test-net` and confirm that containers c3 and c4 are indeed attached to it:

```
$ docker network inspect test-net
```

This will give us the following output for the `Containers` section:

```
"Containers": {
    "134295caa6012df5dc7d541436954af1a5264c6f69d5b8012e88f9c12faf40f1": {
        "Name": "c3",
        "EndpointID": "5693cd9329437a9ecec1d27f439887bb0258837b9342a1c32204fa4571298457",
        "MacAddress": "02:42:0a:01:00:02",
        "IPv4Address": "10.1.0.2/16",
        "IPv6Address": ""
    },
    "4a277d33ebfb74f00d31be272d2d74cbfec4b17666e44d88e26cfe83b0a790cc": {
        "Name": "c4",
        "EndpointID": "a1e9ecafebdcf816261883c171434273d9973832d43255b5aa224b081853ed0f",
        "MacAddress": "02:42:0a:01:00:03",
        "IPv4Address": "10.1.0.3/16",
        "IPv6Address": ""
    }
}
```

Containers section of the docker network inspect test-net command

The next question we're going to ask ourselves is whether the c3 and c4 containers can freely communicate with each other. To demonstrate that this is indeed the case, we can `exec` into the c3 container:

```
$ docker container exec -it c3 /bin/sh
```

Once inside the container, we can try to ping container c4 by name and by IP address:

```
/ # ping c4
PING c4 (10.1.0.3): 56 data bytes
64 bytes from 10.1.0.3: seq=0 ttl=64 time=0.192 ms
64 bytes from 10.1.0.3: seq=1 ttl=64 time=0.148 ms
...
```

The following is the result of the ping using the IP address of `c4`:

```
/ # ping 10.1.0.3
PING 10.1.0.3 (10.1.0.3): 56 data bytes
64 bytes from 10.1.0.3: seq=0 ttl=64 time=0.200 ms
64 bytes from 10.1.0.3: seq=1 ttl=64 time=0.172 ms
...
```

The answer in both cases confirms to us that the communication between containers attached to the same network is working as expected. The fact that we can even use the name of the container we want to connect to shows us that the name resolution provided by the Docker DNS service works inside this network.

Now, we want to make sure that the `bridge` and the `test-net` networks are firewalled from each other. To demonstrate this, we can try to ping the `c2` container from the `c3` container, either by its name or by its IP address:

```
/ # ping c2
ping: bad address 'c2'
```

The following is the result of the ping using the IP address of the `c2` container instead:

```
/ # ping 172.17.0.3
PING 172.17.0.3 (172.17.0.3): 56 data bytes
^C
--- 172.17.0.3 ping statistics ---
43 packets transmitted, 0 packets received, 100% packet loss
```

The preceding command remained hanging and I had to terminate the command with *Ctrl+C*. From the output of pinging `c2`, we can also see that the name resolution does not work across networks. This is the expected behavior. Networks provide an extra layer of isolation, and thus security, to containers.

Earlier, we learned that a container can be attached to multiple networks. Let's attach the `c5` container to the `sample-net` and `test-net` networks at the same time:

```
$ docker container run --name c5 -d \
    --network sample-net \
    --network test-net \
    alpine:latest ping 127.0.0.1
```

Now, we can test that `c5` is reachable from the `c2` container, similar to when we tested the same for the `c4` and `c2` containers. The result will show that the connection indeed works.

If we want to remove an existing network, we can use the `docker network rm` command, but note that we cannot accidentally delete a network that has containers attached to it:

```
$ docker network rm test-net
Error response from daemon: network test-net id 863192... has active
endpoints
```

Before we continue, let's clean up and remove all the containers:

```
$ docker container rm -f $(docker container ls -aq)
```

Now, we can remove the two custom networks that we created:

```
$ docker network rm sample-net
$ docker network rm test-net
```

Alternatively, we could remove all the networks that no container is attached to with the `prune` command:

```
$ docker network prune --force
```

I used the `--force` (or `-f`) argument here to prevent Docker from reconfirming that I really want to remove all unused networks.

The host and null network

In this section, we are going to look at two predefined and somewhat unique types of networks, the `host` and the `null` networks. Let's start with the former.

The host network

There are occasions where we want to run a container in the network namespace of the host. This can be necessary when we need to run some software in a container that is used to analyze or debug the host networks' traffic. But keep in mind that these are very specific scenarios. When running business software in containers, there is no good reason to ever run the respective containers attached to the host's network. For security reasons, it is strongly recommended that you do not run any such container attached to the `host` network on a production or production-like environment.

That said, *how can we run a container inside the network namespace of the host?* Simply by attaching the container to the `host` network:

```
$ docker container run --rm -it --network host alpine:latest /bin/sh
```

If we use the `ip` tool to analyze the network namespace from within the container, we will see that we get exactly the same picture as we would if we were running the `ip` tool directly on the host. For example, if I inspect the `eth0` device on my host, I get this:

```
/ # ip addr show eth0
2: eth0: <BROADCAST,MULTICAST,UP,LOWER_UP> mtu 1500 qdisc pfifo_fast state
UP qlen 1000
    link/ether 02:50:00:00:00:01 brd ff:ff:ff:ff:ff:ff
    inet 192.168.65.3/24 brd 192.168.65.255 scope global eth0
       valid_lft forever preferred_lft forever
    inet6 fe80::c90b:4219:ddbd:92bf/64 scope link
       valid_lft forever preferred_lft forever
```

Here, I can see that `192.168.65.3` is the IP address that the host has been assigned and that the MAC address shown here also corresponds to that of the host.

We can also inspect the routes to get the following (shortened):

```
/ # ip route
default via 192.168.65.1 dev eth0 src 192.168.65.3 metric 202
10.1.0.0/16 dev cni0 scope link src 10.1.0.1
127.0.0.0/8 dev lo scope host
172.17.0.0/16 dev docker0 scope link src 172.17.0.1
...
192.168.65.0/24 dev eth0 scope link src 192.168.65.3 metric 202
```

Before I let you go on to the next section of this chapter, I want to once more point out that the use of the `host` network is dangerous and needs to be avoided if possible.

The null network

Sometimes, we need to run a few application services or jobs that do not need any network connection at all to execute the task at hand. It is strongly advised that you run those applications in a container that is attached to the `none` network. This container will be completely isolated, and is thus safe from any outside access. Let's run such a container:

```
$ docker container run --rm -it --network none alpine:latest /bin/sh
```

Once inside the container, we can verify that there is no `eth0` network endpoint available:

```
/ # ip addr show eth0
ip: can't find device 'eth0'
```

There is also no routing information available, as we can demonstrate by using the following command:

```
/ # ip route
```

This returns nothing.

Running in an existing network namespace

Normally, Docker creates a new network namespace for each container we run. The network namespace of the container corresponds to the sandbox of the container network model we described earlier on. As we attach the container to a network, we define an endpoint that connects the container network namespace with the actual network. This way, we have one container per network namespace.

Docker provides an additional way for us to define the network namespace that a container runs in. When creating a new container, we can specify that it should be attached to (or maybe we should say included) in the network namespace of an existing container. With this technique, we can run multiple containers in a single network namespace:

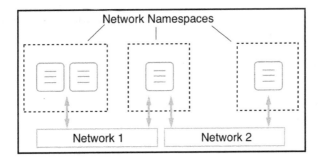

Multiple containers running in a single network namespace

In the preceding diagram, we can see that in the leftmost **Network Namespace**, we have two containers. The two containers, since they share the same namespace, can communicate on localhost with each other. The network namespace (and not the individual containers) is then attached to **Network 1**.

This is useful when we want to debug the network of an existing container without running additional processes inside that container. We can just attach a special utility container to the network namespace of the container to inspect. This feature is also used by Kubernetes when it creates a pod. We will learn more about Kubernetes and pods in `Chapter 15`, *Introduction to Kubernetes* of this book.

Now, let's demonstrate how this works:

1. First, we create a new bridge network:

   ```
   $ docker network create --driver bridge test-net
   ```

2. Next, we run a container attached to this network:

   ```
   $ docker container run --name web -d \
     --network test-net nginx:alpine
   ```

3. Finally, we run another container and attach it to the network of
   our web container:

   ```
   $ docker container run -it --rm --network container:web \
   alpine:latest /bin/sh
   ```

   Specifically, note how we define the network: `--network container:web`. This
   tells Docker that our new container shall use the same network namespace as the
   container called `web`.

4. Since the new container is in the same network namespace as the web container
   running nginx, we're now able to access nginx on localhost! We can prove this
   by using the `wget` tool, which is part of the Alpine container, to connect to nginx.
   We should see the following:

   ```
   / # wget -qO - localhost
   <!DOCTYPE html>
   <html>
   <head>
   <title>Welcome to nginx!</title>
   ...
   </html>
   ```

   Note that we have shortened the output for readability. Please also note that there
   is an important difference between running two containers attached to the same
   network and two containers running in the same network namespace. In both
   cases, the containers can freely communicate with each other, but in the latter
   case, the communication happens over localhost.

5. To clean up the container and network, we can use the following command:

   ```
   $ docker container rm --force web
   $ docker network rm test-net
   ```

In the next section, we are going to learn how to expose container ports on the container host.

Managing container ports

Now that we know how we can isolate firewall containers from each other by placing them on different networks, and that we can have a container attached to more than one network, we have one problem that remains unsolved. *How can we expose an application service to the outside world?* Imagine a container running a web server hosting our webAPI from before. We want customers from the internet to be able to access this API. We have designed it to be a publicly accessible API. To achieve this, we have to, figuratively speaking, open a gate in our firewall through which we can funnel external traffic to our API. For security reasons, we don't just want to open the doors wide; we want to have a single controlled gate that traffic flows through.

We can create such a gate by mapping a container port to an available port on the host. We're also calling this opening a gate to the container port to publish a port. Remember that the container has its own virtual network stack, as does the host. Therefore, container ports and host ports exist completely independently and by default have nothing in common at all. But we can now wire a container port with a free host port and funnel external traffic through this link, as illustrated in the following diagram:

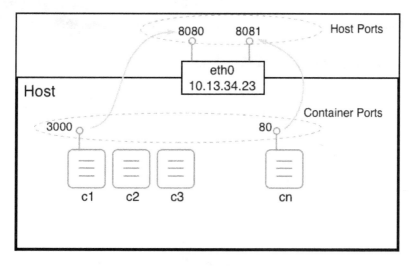

Mapping container ports to host ports

But now, it is time to demonstrate how we can actually map a container port to a host port. This is done when creating a container. We have different ways of doing so:

1. First, we can let Docker decide which host port our container port shall be mapped to. Docker will then select one of the free host ports in the range of 32xxx. This automatic mapping is done by using the -P parameter:

   ```
   $ docker container run --name web -P -d nginx:alpine
   ```

   The preceding command runs an nginx server in a container. nginx is listening at port 80 inside the container. With the -P parameter, we're telling Docker to map all the exposed container ports to a free port in the 32xxx range. We can find out which host port Docker is using by using the `docker container port` command:

   ```
   $ docker container port web
   80/tcp -> 0.0.0.0:32768
   ```

   The nginx container only exposes port 80, and we can see that it has been mapped to the host port 32768. If we open a new browser window and navigate to `localhost:32768`, we should see the following screen:

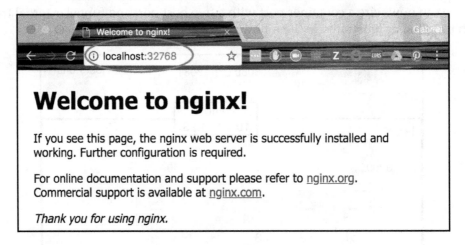

The welcome page of nginx

2. An alternative way to find out which host port Docker is using for our container is to inspect it. The host port is part of the `NetworkSettings` node:

   ```
   $ docker container inspect web | grep HostPort
   32768
   ```

3. Finally, the third way of getting this information is to list the container:

```
$ docker container ls
CONTAINER ID    IMAGE         ...    PORTS                  NAMES
56e46a14b6f7    nginx:alpine  ...    0.0.0.0:32768->80/tcp  web
```

Please note that in the preceding output, the /tcp part tells us that the port has been opened for communication with the TCP protocol, but not for the UDP protocol. TCP is the default, and if we want to specify that we want to open the port for UDP, then we have to specify this explicitly. 0.0.0.0 in the mapping tells us that traffic from any host IP address can now reach container port 80 of the web container.

Sometimes, we want to map a container port to a very specific host port. We can do this by using the -p parameter (or --publish). Let's look at how this is done with the following command:

```
$ docker container run --name web2 -p 8080:80 -d nginx:alpine
```

The value of the -p parameter is in the form of <host port>:<container port>. Therefore, in the preceding case, we map container port 80 to host port 8080. Once the web2 container runs, we can test it in the browser by navigating to localhost:8080, and we should be greeted by the same nginx welcome page that we saw in the previous example that dealt with automatic port mapping.

When using the UDP protocol for communication over a certain port, the publish parameter will look like -p 3000:4321/udp. Note that if we want to allow communication with both TCP and UDP protocols over the same port, then we have to map each protocol separately.

HTTP-level routing using a reverse proxy

Imagine you have been tasked with containerizing a monolithic application. The application has organically evolved over the years into an unmaintainable monster. Changing even a minor feature in the source code may break other features due to the tight coupling existing in the code base. Releases are rare due to their complexity and require the whole team to be on deck. The application has to be taken down during the release window, which costs the company a lot of money due to lost opportunities, not to mention their loss of reputation.

Management has decided to put an end to that vicious cycle and improve the situation by containerizing the monolith. This alone will lead to a massively decreased time between releases as witnessed by the industry. In a later step, the company wants to break out every piece of functionality from the monolith and implement them as microservices. This process will continue until the monolith has been completely starved.

But it is this second point that leads to some head-scratching in the team involved. How will we break down the monolith into loosely coupled microservices without affecting all the many clients of the monolith out there? The public API of the monolith, though very complex, has a well-structured design. Public URIs had been carefully crafted and should not be changed at all costs. For example, there is a product catalog function implemented in the app that can be accessed via `https://acme.com/catalog?category=bicycles` so that we can access a list of bicycles offered by the company.

On the other hand, there is a URL called `https://acme.com/checkout` that we can use to initiate the checkout of a customers' shopping cart, and so on. I hope it is clear where we are going with this.

Containerizing the monolith

Let's start with the monolith. I have prepared a simple code base that has been implemented in Python 2.7 and uses Flask to implement the public REST API. The sample app is not really a full-blown application but just complex enough to allow for some redesign. The sample code can be found in the `ch10/e-shop` folder. Inside this folder is a subfolder called `monolith` containing the Python application. Follow these steps:

1. In a new Terminal window, navigate to that folder, install the required dependencies, and run the application:

```
$ cd ~/fod/ch10/e-shop/monolith
$ pip install -r requirements.txt
$ export FLASK_APP=main.py
$ flask run
```

The application will be starting and listening on `localhost` on port `5000`:

```
$ flask run
 * Serving Flask app "main.py"
 * Environment: production
   WARNING: This is a development server. Do not use it in a production deployment.
   Use a production WSGI server instead.
 * Debug mode: off
 * Running on http://127.0.0.1:5000/ (Press CTRL+C to quit)
```

Running the Python monolith

2. We can use `curl` to test the app. Use the following command to retrieve a list of all the bicycles the company offers:

   ```
   $ curl localhost:5000/catalog?category=bicycles
   ```

   ```
   [{"id": 1, "name": "Mountanbike Driftwood 24\"", "unitPrice": 199},
   {"id": 2, "name": "Tribal 100 Flat Bar Cycle Touring Road Bike",
   "unitPrice": 300}, {"id": 3, "name": "Siech Cycles Bike (58 cm)",
   "unitPrice": 459}]
   ```

   You should see a JSON formatted list of three types of bicycles. OK – so far, so good.

3. Now, let's change the `hosts` file, add an entry for `acme.com`, and map it to `127.0.0.1`, the loop-back address. This way, we can simulate a real client accessing the app with the URL `http://acme.cnoteom/catalog?category=bicycles` instead of using `localhost`. You need to use sudo to edit the hosts file on a macOS or on Linux. You should add a line to the `hosts` file that looks like this:

   ```
   127.0.0.1 acme.com
   ```

4. Save your changes and assert that it works by pinging `acme.com`:

   ```
   $ ping acme.com

   Ping wird ausgeführt für acme.com [127.0.0.1] mit 32 Bytes Daten:
   Antwort von 127.0.0.1: Bytes=32 Zeit<1ms TTL=128
   Antwort von 127.0.0.1: Bytes=32 Zeit<1ms TTL=128
   Antwort von 127.0.0.1: Bytes=32 Zeit<1ms TTL=128
   ```

Mapping acme.com to the loop-back address via the hosts file

TIP

On Windows, you can edit the file by, for example, running Notepad as an administrator, opening the `c:\Windows\System32\Drivers\etc\hosts` file, and modifying it.

After all this, it is time to containerize the application. The only change we need to make in the application is ensuring that we have the application web server listening on `0.0.0.0` instead of `localhost`.

5. We can do this easily by modifying the application and adding the following start logic at the end of `main.py`:

```
if __name__ == '__main__':
    app.run(host='0.0.0.0', port=5000)
```

Then, we can start the application with `python main.py`.

6. Now, add a `Dockerfile` to the `monolith` folder with the following content:

```
FROM python:3.7-alpine
WORKDIR /app
COPY requirements.txt ./
RUN pip install -r requirements.txt
COPY . .
EXPOSE 5000
CMD python main.py
```

7. In your Terminal window, from within the monolith folder, execute the following command to build a Docker image for the application:

```
$ docker image build -t acme/eshop:1.0 .
```

8. After the image has been built, try to run the application:

```
$ docker container run --rm -it \
    --name eshop \
    -p 5000:5000 \
    acme/eshop:1.0
```

Notice that the output from the app now running inside a container is indistinguishable from what we got when running the application directly on the host. We can now test if the application still works as before by using the two `curl` commands to access the catalog and the checkout logic:

```
$ curl http://acme.com:5000/catalog?type=bicycles
[{"id": 1, "name": "Mountanbike Driftwood 24\"", "unitPrice": 199}, {"id": 2, "name": "Tribal 100 Flat Bar Cycle Touring Road Bike", "u
nitPrice": 300}, {"id": 3, "name": "Siech Cycles Bike (58 cm)", "unitPrice": 459}]$
$
$ curl http://acme.com:5000/checkout
Starting checkout of your shopping cart...$
$ ▊
```

Testing the monolith while running in a container

Evidently, the monolith still works exactly the same way as before, even when using the correct URL, that is, `http://acme.com`. Great! Now, let's break out part of the monolith's functionality into a Node.js microservice, which will be deployed separately.

Extracting the first microservice

The team, after some brainstorming, has decided that the product `catalog` is a good candidate for the first piece of functionality that is cohesive yet self-contained enough to be extracted from the monolith. They decide to implement the product catalog as a microservice implemented in Node.js.

You can find the code they came up with and the `Dockerfile` in the `catalog` subfolder of the project folder, that is, `e-shop`. It is a simple Express.js application that replicates the functionality that was previously available in the monolith. Let's get started:

1. In your Terminal window, from within the `catalog` folder, build the Docker image for this new microservice:

   ```
   $ docker image build -t acme/catalog:1.0 .
   ```

2. Then, run a container from the new image you just built:

   ```
   $ docker run --rm -it --name catalog -p 3000:3000 acme/catalog:1.0
   ```

3. From a different Terminal window, try to access the microservice and validate that it returns the same data as the monolith:

   ```
   $ curl http://acme.com:3000/catalog?type=bicycle
   ```

Please notice the differences in the URL compared to when accessing the same functionality in the monolith. Here, we are accessing the microservice on port `3000` (instead of `5000`). But we said that we didn't want to have to change the clients that access our e-shop application. What can we do? Luckily, there are solutions to problems like this. We need to reroute incoming requests. We'll show you how to do this in the next section.

Using Traefik to reroute traffic

In the previous section, we realized that we will have to reroute incoming traffic with a target URL starting with `http://acme.com:5000/catalog` to an alternative URL such as `product-catalog:3000/catalog`. We will be using Traefik to do exactly that.

Traefik is a cloud-native edge router and it is open source, which is great for our specific case. It even has a nice web UI that you can use to manage and monitor your routes. Traefik can be combined with Docker in a very straightforward way, as we will see in a moment.

To integrate well with Docker, Traefik relies on metadata found on each container or service. This metadata can be applied in the form of labels that contain the routing information.

First, let's look at how to run the catalog service:

1. Here is the Docker `run` command:

```
$ docker container run --rm -d \
    --name catalog \
    --label traefik.enable=true \
    --label traefik.port=3000 \
    --label traefik.priority=10 \
    --label traefik.http.routers.catalog.rule="Host(\"acme.com\")
&& PathPrefix(\"/catalog\")" \
    acme/catalog:1.0
```

2. Let's quickly look at the four labels we define:

   - `traefik.enable=true`: This tells Traefik that this particular container should be included in the routing (the default is `false`).

   - `traefik.port=3000`: The router should forward the call to port 3000 (which is the port that the Express.js app is listening on).

   - `traefik.priority=10`: Give this route high priority. We will see why in a second.

   - `traefik.http.routers.catalog.rule="Host(\"acme.com\") && PathPrefix(\"/catalog\")"`: The route must include the hostname, `acme.com`, and the path must start with `/catalog` in order to be rerouted to this service. As an example, `acme.com/catalog?type=bicycles` would qualify for this rule.

Please note the special form of the fourth label. Its general form is
`traefik.http.routers.<service name>.rule`.

3. Now, let's look at how we can run the `eshop` container:

```
$ docker container run --rm -d \
    --name eshop \
    --label traefik.enable=true \
    --label traefik.port=5000 \
    --label traefik.priority=1 \
    --label traefik.http.routers.eshop.rule="Host(\"acme.com\")" \
    acme/eshop:1.0
```

Here, we forward any matching calls to port `5000`, which corresponds to the port where the `eshop` application is listening. Pay attention to the priority, which is set to `1` (low). This, in combination with the high priority of the `catalog` service, allows us to have all URLs starting with `/catalog` being filtered out and redirected to the `catalog` service, while all other URLs will go to the `eshop` service.

4. Now, we can finally run Traefik as the edge router that will serve as a reverse proxy in front of our application. This is how we start it:

```
$ docker run -d \
    --name traefik \
    -p 8080:8080 \
    -p 80:80 \
    -v /var/run/docker.sock:/var/run/docker.sock \
    traefik:v2.0 --api.insecure=true --providers.docker
```

Note how we mount the Docker socket into the container so that Traefik can interact with the Docker engine. We will be able to send web traffic to port `80` of Traefik, from where it will be rerouted according to our rules in the routing definitions found in the metadata of the participating container. Furthermore, we can access the web UI of Traefik via port `8080`.

Now that everything is running, that is, the monolith, the first microservice called `catalog`, and Traefik, we can test if all works as expected. Use `curl` once again to do so:

```
$ curl http://acme.com/catalog?type=bicycles
$ curl http://acme.com/checkout
```

As we mentioned earlier, we are now sending all traffic to port 80, which is what Traefik is listening on. This proxy will then reroute the traffic to the correct destination.

Before proceeding, stop all containers:

```
$ docker container rm -f traefik eshop catalog
```

That's it for this chapter.

Summary

In this chapter, we have learned about how containers running on a single host can communicate with each other. First, we looked at the CNM, which defines the requirements of a container network, and then we investigated several implementations of the CNM, such as the bridge network. We then looked at how the bridge network functions in detail and also what kind of information Docker provides us with about the networks and the containers attached to those networks. We also learned about adopting two different perspectives, from both outside and inside the container. Last but not least we introduced Traefik as a means to provide application level routing to our applications.

In the next chapter, we're going to introduce Docker Compose. We will learn about creating an application that consists of multiple services, each running in a container, and how Docker Compose allows us to easily build, run, and scale such an application using a declarative approach.

Questions

To assess the skills that you have gained from this chapter, please try to answer the following questions:

1. Name the three core elements of the **container network model** (**CNM**).
2. How do you create a custom bridge network called, for example, `frontend`?
3. How do you run two `nginx:alpine` containers attached to the `frontend` network?
4. For the `frontend` network, get the following:
   - The IPs of all the attached containers
   - The subnet associated with the network
5. What is the purpose of the `host` network?

6. Name one or two scenarios where the use of the `host` network is appropriate.
7. What is the purpose of the `none` network?
8. In what scenarios should the `none` network be used?
9. Why would we use a reverse proxy such as Traefik together with our containerized application?

Further reading

Here are some articles that describe the topics that were presented in this chapter in more detail:

- Docker networking overview: `http://dockr.ly/2sXGzQn`
- Container networking: `http://dockr.ly/2HJfQKn`
- What is a bridge?: `https://bit.ly/2HyC3Od`
- Using bridge networks: `http://dockr.ly/2BNxjRr`
- Using Macvlan networks: `http://dockr.ly/2ETjy2x`
- Networking using the host network: `http://dockr.ly/2F4aI59`

11
Docker Compose

In the previous chapter, we learned a lot about how container networking works on a single Docker host. We introduced the **Container Network Model** (**CNM**), which forms the basis of all networking between Docker containers, and then we dove deep into different implementations of the CNM, specifically the bridge network. Finally, we introduced Traefik, a reverse proxy, to enable sophisticated HTTP application-level routing between containers.

This chapter introduces the concept of an application consisting of multiple services, each running in a container, and how Docker Compose allows us to easily build, run, and scale such an application using a declarative approach.

This chapter covers the following topics:

- Demystifying declarative versus imperative
- Running a multi-service application
- Scaling a service
- Building and pushing an application
- Using Docker Compose overrides

After completing this chapter, the reader will be able to do the following:

- Explain in a few short sentences the main differences between an imperative and declarative approach for defining and running an application
- Describe in their own words the difference between a container and a Docker Compose service
- Author a Docker Compose YAML file for a simple multi-service application
- Build, push, deploy, and tear down a simple multi-service application using Docker Compose
- Use Docker Compose to scale an application service up and down
- Define environment-specific Docker Compose files using overrides

Technical requirements

The code accompanying this chapter can be found at `https://github.com/PacktPublishing/Learn-Docker---Fundamentals-of-Docker-19.x-Second-Edition/tree/master/ch11`.

You need to have `docker-compose` installed on your system. This is automatically the case if you have installed Docker for Desktop or Docker Toolbox on your Windows or macOS computer. Otherwise, you can find detailed installation instructions here: `https://docs.docker.com/compose/install/`

Demystifying declarative versus imperative

Docker Compose is a tool provided by Docker that is mainly used where you need to run and orchestrate containers running on a single Docker host. This includes, but is not limited to, development, **continuous integration (CI)**, automated testing, manual QA, or demos.

Docker Compose uses files formatted in YAML as input. By default, Docker Compose expects these files to be called `docker-compose.yml`, but other names are possible. The content of a `docker-compose.yml` is said to be a *declarative* way of describing and running a containerized application potentially consisting of more than a single container.

So, *what is the meaning of declarative?*

First of all, *declarative* is the antonym of *imperative*. Well, that doesn't help much. Now that I have introduced another definition, I need to explain both of them:

- **Imperative:** This is a way in which we can solve problems by specifying the exact procedure that has to be followed by the system.

  If I tell a system such as the Docker daemon imperatively how to run an application, then that means that I have to describe step by step what the system has to do and how it has to react if some unexpected situation occurs. I have to be very explicit and precise in my instructions. I need to cover all edge cases and how they need to be treated.

- **Declarative:** This is a way in which we can solve problems without requiring the programmer to specify an exact procedure to be followed.

A declarative approach means that I tell the Docker engine what my desired state for an application is and it has to figure out on its own how to achieve this desired state and how to reconcile it if the system deviates from it.

Docker clearly recommends the declarative approach when dealing with containerized applications. Consequently, the Docker Compose tool uses this approach.

Running a multi-service app

In most cases, applications do not consist of only one monolithic block, but rather of several application services that work together. When using Docker containers, each application service runs in its own container. When we want to run such a multi-service application, we can, of course, start all the participating containers with the well-known `docker container run` command, and we have done this in previous chapters. But this is inefficient at best. With the Docker Compose tool, we are given a way to define the application in a declarative way in a file that uses the YAML format.

Let's have a look at the content of a simple `docker-compose.yml` file:

```
version: "2.4"
services:
  web:
    image: fundamentalsofdocker/ch11-web:2.0
    build: web
    ports:
    - 80:3000
  db:
    image: fundamentalsofdocker/ch11-db:2.0
    build: db
    volumes:
    - pets-data:/var/lib/postgresql/data

volumes:
  pets-data:
```

The lines in the file are explained as follows:

- `version`: In this line, we specify the version of the Docker Compose format we want to use. At the time of writing, this is version 2.4.
- `services`: In this section, we specify the services that make up our application in the `services` block. In our sample, we have two application services and we call them `web` and `db`:

- web: The web service is using an image called `fundamentalsofdocker/ch11-web:2.0`, which, if not already in the image cache, is built from the `Dockerfile` found in the web folder . The service is also publishing container port `3000` to the host port `80`.
- db: The db service, on the other hand, is using the image name `fundamentalsofdocker/ch11-db:2.0`, which is a customized PostgreSQL database. Once again, if the image is not already in the cache, it is built from the `Dockerfile` found in the db folder . We are mounting a volume called `pets-data` into the container of the db service.

- `volumes`: The volumes used by any of the services have to be declared in this section. In our sample, this is the last section of the file. The first time the application is run, a volume called `pets-data` will be created by Docker and then, in subsequent runs, if the volume is still there, it will be reused. This could be important when the application, for some reason, crashes and has to be restarted. Then, the previous data is still around and ready to be used by the restarted database service.

 Note that we are using version 2.x of the Docker Compose file syntax. This is the one targeted toward deployments on a single Docker host. There exists also a version 3.x of the Docker Compose file syntax. This version is used when you want to define an application that is targeted either at Docker Swarm or Kubernetes. We will discuss this in more detail starting with `Chapter 12`, *Orchestrators*.

Building images with Docker Compose

Navigate to the `ch11` subfolder of the `fods` folder and then build the images:

```
$ cd ~/fod/ch11
$ docker-compose build
```

If we enter the preceding command, then the tool will assume that there must be a file in the current directory called `docker-compose.yml` and it will use that one to run. In our case, this is indeed the case and the tool will build the images.

In your Terminal window, you should see an output similar to this:

```
$ docker-compose build
Building web
Step 1/7 : FROM node:12.12-alpine
12.12-alpine: Pulling from library/node
e7c96db7181b: Pull complete
96ed4fdcea75: Pull complete
c1504b6f0fcb: Pull complete
16d47b051efb: Pull complete
Digest: sha256:3d8c2e124f20861de12d72ce29685ca73e0ebe57f232800ae1c4cadbb5e63c36
Status: Downloaded newer image for node:12.12-alpine
 ---> 0fcfd7e52b09
Step 2/7 : WORKDIR /app
 ---> Running in fb6284297648
Removing intermediate container fb6284297648
 ---> cda3a345e8c4
Step 3/7 : COPY package.json /app/
 ---> 4384dbe02fcd
Step 4/7 : RUN npm install
 ---> Running in beef36cc6c97
npm notice created a lockfile as package-lock.json. You should commit this file.
npm WARN pets@2.0.0 No repository field.

added 71 packages from 55 contributors and audited 147 packages in 3.343s
found 0 vulnerabilities

Removing intermediate container beef36cc6c97
 ---> d2c2e538a621
Step 5/7 : COPY ./src /app/src
 ---> f11a333bbe0c
Step 6/7 : EXPOSE 3000
 ---> Running in b309697fb93b
Removing intermediate container b309697fb93b
 ---> 5df5cec904e9
Step 7/7 : CMD npm start
 ---> Running in 885a71e9b006
Removing intermediate container 885a71e9b006
 ---> 639bfb80b96a

Successfully built 639bfb80b96a
Successfully tagged fundamentalsofdocker/ch11-web:2.0
```

Building the Docker image for the web service

In the preceding screenshot, you can see that `docker-compose` first downloads the base image `node:12.12-alpine`, for the web image we're building from Docker Hub. Subsequently, it uses the `Dockerfile` found in the `web` folder to build the image and names it `fundamentalsofdocker/ch11-web:2.0`. But this is only the first part; the second part of the output should look similar to this:

```
Building db
Step 1/5 : FROM postgres:12.0-alpine
12.0-alpine: Pulling from library/postgres
9d48c3bd43c5: Pull complete
f112202a5fec: Pull complete
e2827e7bbe4a: Pull complete
5ce43a1630c4: Pull complete
13772e4e58b6: Pull complete
a9c3c1abc664: Pull complete
b8495f782617: Pull complete
8ba4145edc35: Pull complete
Digest: sha256:fe9a6bf89c50fb3c6755c0c2d67cb09dc8e90ac468b3212167700b155c902a5d
Status: Downloaded newer image for postgres:12.0-alpine
 ---> cef3c8b4bfa5
Step 2/5 : COPY init-db.sql /docker-entrypoint-initdb.d/
 ---> 1332ed0660c4
Step 3/5 : ENV POSTGRES_USER dockeruser
 ---> Running in daf9af0488f5
Removing intermediate container daf9af0488f5
 ---> 600702032c3c
Step 4/5 : ENV POSTGRES_PASSWORD dockerpass
 ---> Running in 445f8befc1d3
Removing intermediate container 445f8befc1d3
 ---> d78418ece041
Step 5/5 : ENV POSTGRES_DB pets
 ---> Running in abac2c36a4db
Removing intermediate container abac2c36a4db
 ---> 1c7fc1935863

Successfully built 1c7fc1935863
Successfully tagged fundamentalsofdocker/ch11-db:2.0
```

Building the Docker image for the db service

Here, once again, `docker-compose` pulls the base image, `postgres:12.0-alpine`, from Docker Hub and then uses the `Dockerfile` found in the `db` folder to build the image we call `fundamentalsofdocker/ch11-db:2.0`.

Running an application with Docker Compose

Once we have built our images, we can start the application using Docker Compose:

```
$ docker-compose up
```

The output will show us the application starting. We should see the following:

```
$ docker-compose up
Creating network "ch11_default" with the default driver
Creating volume "ch11_pets-data" with default driver
Creating ch11_web_1 ... done
Creating ch11_db_1  ... done
Attaching to ch11_db_1, ch11_web_1
db_1    | The files belonging to this database system will be owned by user "postgres".
db_1    | This user must also own the server process.
db_1    |
db_1    | The database cluster will be initialized with locale "en_US.utf8".
db_1    | The default database encoding has accordingly been set to "UTF8".
db_1    | The default text search configuration will be set to "english".
db_1    |
db_1    | Data page checksums are disabled.
db_1    |
db_1    | fixing permissions on existing directory /var/lib/postgresql/data ... ok
db_1    | creating subdirectories ... ok
db_1    | selecting dynamic shared memory implementation ... posix
db_1    | selecting default max_connections ... 100
db_1    | selecting default shared_buffers ... 128MB
db_1    | selecting default time zone ... UTC
db_1    | creating configuration files ... ok
db_1    | running bootstrap script ... ok
db_1    | performing post-bootstrap initialization ... sh: locale: not found
db_1    | 2019-10-19 09:41:15.324 UTC [26] WARNING:  no usable system locales were found
web_1   |
web_1   | > pets@2.0.0 start /app
web_1   | > node src/server.js
web_1   |
web_1   | Listening at 0.0.0.0:3000
db_1    | ok
db_1    | syncing data to disk ... ok
db_1    |
```

Running the sample application, part 1

In this first part of the output, we see how Docker Compose does the following:

- Creates a bridge network called `ch11_default`
- Creates a volume called `ch11_pets-data`
- Creates the two services, `ch11_web_1` and `ch11_db_1`, and attaches them to the network

Docker Compose then also shows log output generated by the database (blue) and by the web service (yellow) that are both stating up. The third last line in the output shows us that the web service is ready and listens at port 3000. Remember though that this is the container port and not the host port. We have mapped container port 3000 to host port 80, and that is the port we will be accessing later on.

Now let's look at the second part of the output:

```
db_1  |    done
db_1  |  server started
db_1  |  CREATE DATABASE
db_1  |
db_1  |
db_1  |  /usr/local/bin/docker-entrypoint.sh: running /docker-entrypoint-initdb.d/init-db.sql
db_1  |  CREATE TABLE
db_1  |  ALTER TABLE
db_1  |  ALTER ROLE
db_1  |  INSERT 0 1
db_1  |  INSERT 0 1
db_1  |  INSERT 0 1
db_1  |  INSERT 0 1
db_1  |  INSERT 0 1
db_1  |  INSERT 0 1
db_1  |  INSERT 0 1
db_1  |  INSERT 0 1
db_1  |  INSERT 0 1
db_1  |  INSERT 0 1
db_1  |  INSERT 0 1
db_1  |
db_1  |
db_1  |  2019-10-19 09:41:16.026 UTC [30] LOG:   received fast shutdown request
db_1  |  waiting for server to shut down....2019-10-19 09:41:16.028 UTC [30] LOG:   aborting any active transac
db_1  |  2019-10-19 09:41:16.029 UTC [30] LOG:   background worker "logical replication launcher" (PID 37) exit
db_1  |  2019-10-19 09:41:16.029 UTC [32] LOG:   shutting down
db_1  |  2019-10-19 09:41:16.050 UTC [30] LOG:   database system is shut down
db_1  |    done
db_1  |  server stopped
db_1  |
db_1  |  PostgreSQL init process complete; ready for start up.
db_1  |
db_1  |  2019-10-19 09:41:16.132 UTC [1] LOG:   starting PostgreSQL 12.0 on x86_64-pc-linux-musl, compiled by g
db_1  |  2019-10-19 09:41:16.133 UTC [1] LOG:   listening on IPv4 address "0.0.0.0", port 5432
db_1  |  2019-10-19 09:41:16.133 UTC [1] LOG:   listening on IPv6 address "::", port 5432
db_1  |  2019-10-19 09:41:16.136 UTC [1] LOG:   listening on Unix socket "/var/run/postgresql/.s.PGSQL.5432"
db_1  |  2019-10-19 09:41:16.147 UTC [43] LOG:   database system was shut down at 2019-10-19 09:41:16 UTC
db_1  |  2019-10-19 09:41:16.151 UTC [1] LOG:   database system is ready to accept connections
```

Running the sample application, part 2

We have shortened the second part of the output a bit. It shows us how the database finalizes its initialization. We can specifically see how our initialization script, init-db.sql, is applied, which defines a database and seeds it with some data.

We can now open a browser tab and navigate to `localhost/animal`. We should be greeted by a wild animal whose picture I took at the Masai Mara national park in Kenya:

The sample application in the browser

Refresh the browser a few times to see other cat images. The application selects the current image randomly from a set of 12 images whose URLs are stored in the database.

As the application is running in interactive mode and, thus, the Terminal where we ran Docker Compose is blocked, we can cancel the application by pressing *Ctrl + C*. If we do so, we will see the following:

```
^CGracefully stopping... (press Ctrl+C again to force)
Stopping ch11_web_1 ... done
Stopping ch11_db_1 ... done
```

We will notice that the database and the web services stop immediately. Sometimes, though, some services will take about 10 seconds to do so. The reason for this is that the database and the web service listen to, and react to, the SIGTERM signal sent by Docker while other services might not, and so Docker kills them after a predefined timeout interval of 10 seconds.

If we run the application again with docker-compose up, the output will be much shorter:

```
Starting ch11_db_1   ... done
Starting ch11_web_1 ... done
Attaching to ch11_db_1, ch11_web_1
db_1    | 2019-10-19 10:40:06.611 UTC [1] LOG:   starting PostgreSQL 12.0 on x86_64-pc-linux-musl, compiled by gcc
db_1    | 2019-10-19 10:40:06.611 UTC [1] LOG:   listening on IPv4 address "0.0.0.0", port 5432
db_1    | 2019-10-19 10:40:06.611 UTC [1] LOG:   listening on IPv6 address "::", port 5432
db_1    | 2019-10-19 10:40:06.616 UTC [1] LOG:   listening on Unix socket "/var/run/postgresql/.s.PGSQL.5432"
db_1    | 2019-10-19 10:40:06.628 UTC [18] LOG:   database system was shut down at 2019-10-19 10:39:32 UTC
db_1    | 2019-10-19 10:40:06.631 UTC [1] LOG:   database system is ready to accept connections
web_1   |
web_1   | > pets@2.0.0 start /app
web_1   | > node src/server.js
web_1   |
web_1   | Listening at 0.0.0.0:3000
```

Output of docker-compose up

This time, we didn't have to download the images and the database didn't have to initialize from scratch, but it was just reusing the data that was already present in the pets-data volume from the previous run.

We can also run the application in the background. All containers will run as daemons. For this, we just need to use the -d parameter, as shown in the following code:

```
$ docker-compose up -d
```

Docker Compose offers us many more commands than just up. We can use the tool to list all services that are part of the application:

```
$ docker-compose ps
    Name              Command              State          Ports
-----------------------------------------------------------------------------
ch11_db_1    docker-entrypoint.sh postgres    Up      5432/tcp
ch11_web_1   docker-entrypoint.sh /bin/ ...   Up      0.0.0.0:80->3000/tcp
```

Output of docker-compose ps

This command is similar to docker container ls, with the only difference being that docker-compose only lists containers or services that are part of the application.

To stop and clean up the application, we use the `docker-compose down` command:

```
$ docker-compose down
Stopping ch11_web_1 ... done
Stopping ch11_db_1 ... done
Removing ch11_web_1 ... done
Removing ch11_db_1 ... done
Removing network ch11_default
```

If we also want to remove the volume for the database, then we can use the following command:

```
$ docker volume rm ch11_pets-data
```

Alternatively, instead of using the two commands, `docker-compose down` and `docker volume rm <volume name>`, we can combine them into a single command:

```
$ docker-compose down -v
```

Here, the argument `-v` (or `--volumes`) removes named volumes declared in the `volumes` section of the `compose` file and anonymous volumes attached to containers.

Why is there a `ch11` prefix in the name of the volume? In the `docker-compose.yml` file, we have called the volume to use `pets-data`. But, as we have already mentioned, Docker Compose prefixes all names with the name of the parent folder of the `docker-compose.yml` file plus an underscore. In this case, the parent folder is called `ch11`. If you don't like this approach, you can define a project name explicitly, for example, as follows:

```
$ docker-compose -p my-app up
```

which uses a project name my-app for the application to run under.

Scaling a service

Now, let's, for a moment, assume that our sample application has been live on the web and become very successful. Loads of people want to see our cute animal images. So now we're facing a problem, since our application has started to slow down. To counteract this problem, we want to run multiple instances of the web service. With Docker Compose, this is readily done.

Running more instances is also called scaling up. We can use this tool to scale our web service up to, say, three instances:

```
$ docker-compose up --scale web=3
```

If we do this, we are in for a surprise. The output will look similar to the following screenshot:

```
$ docker-compose up --scale web=3
ch11_db_1 is up-to-date
WARNING: The "web" service specifies a port on the host. If multiple containers for this service are created on a single host, the port will c
lash.
Starting ch11_web_1 ... done
Creating ch11_web_2 ... error
Creating ch11_web_3 ... error

ERROR: for ch11_web_3  Cannot start service web: driver failed programming external connectivity on endpoint ch11_web_3 (b71b482cd511c1d610204
8a91188faf8102a2a6766016f2be0fb7a7fd081aa7c): Bind for 0.0.0.0:80 failed: port is already allocated

ERROR: for ch11_web_2  Cannot start service web: driver failed programming external connectivity on endpoint ch11_web_2 (a96198908fe8eeeb16f2a
e7f69266da08c755fa42244c064cc6d93f4ca960ea9): Bind for 0.0.0.0:80 failed: port is already allocated

ERROR: for web  Cannot start service web: driver failed programming external connectivity on endpoint ch11_web_3 (b71b482cd511c1d6102048a91188
faf8102a2a6766016f2be0fb7a7fd081aa7c): Bind for 0.0.0.0:80 failed: port is already allocated
ERROR: Encountered errors while bringing up the project.
```

Output of docker-compose --scale

The second and third instances of the web service fail to start. The error message tells us why: we cannot use the same host port 80 more than once. When instances 2 and 3 try to start, Docker realizes that port 80 is already taken by the first instance. *What can we do?* Well, we can just let Docker decide which host port to use for each instance.

If, in the `ports` section of the `compose` file, we only specify the container port and leave out the host port, then Docker automatically selects an ephemeral port. Let's do exactly this:

1. First, let's tear down the application:

    $ docker-compose down

2. Then, we modify the `docker-compose.yml` file to look as follows:

    ```
    version: "2.4"
    services:
      web:
        image: fundamentalsofdocker/ch11-web:2.0
        build: web
        ports:
          - 3000
      db:
        image: fundamentalsofdocker/ch11-db:2.0
        build: db
        volumes:
          - pets-data:/var/lib/postgresql/data

    volumes:
      pets-data:
    ```

3. Now, we can start the application again and scale it up immediately after that:

```
$ docker-compose up -d
$ docker-compose up -d --scale web=3
Starting ch11_web_1 ... done
Creating ch11_web_2 ... done
Creating ch11_web_3 ... done
```

4. If we now do `docker-compose ps`, we should see the following screenshot:

```
$ docker-compose ps
    Name              Command              State            Ports
----------------------------------------------------------------------------
ch11_db_1     docker-entrypoint.sh postgres    Up      5432/tcp
ch11_web_1    docker-entrypoint.sh /bin/ ...   Up      0.0.0.0:32771->3000/tcp
ch11_web_2    docker-entrypoint.sh /bin/ ...   Up      0.0.0.0:32773->3000/tcp
ch11_web_3    docker-entrypoint.sh /bin/ ...   Up      0.0.0.0:32772->3000/tcp
```

Output of docker-compose ps

5. As we can see, each service has been associated to a different host port. We can try to see whether they work, for example, using `curl`. Let's test the third instance, `ch11_web_3`:

```
$ curl -4 localhost:32772
Pets Demo Application
```

The answer, `Pets Demo Application`, tells us that, indeed, our application is still working as expected. Try it out for the other two instances to be sure.

Building and pushing an application

We have seen earlier that we can also use the `docker-compose build` command to just build the images of an application defined in the underlying `docker-compose` file. But to make this work, we'll have to add the build information to the `docker-compose` file. In the folder, we have a file, `docker-compose.dev.yml`, which has those instructions already added. It is basically a copy of the `docker-compose.yml` file we have used so far:

```
version: "2.4"
services:
  web:
    build: web
    image: fundamentalsofdocker/ch11-web:2.0
    ports:
      - 80:3000
```

```
  db:
    build: db
    image: fundamentalsofdocker/ch1-db:2.0
    volumes:
      - pets-data:/var/lib/postgresql/data

volumes:
  pets-data:
```

Please note the `build` key for each service. The value of that key indicates the context or folder where Docker is expecting to find the `Dockerfile` to build the corresponding image. If we wanted to use a `Dockerfile` that is named differently, say `Dockerfile-dev`, for the `web` service, then the `build` block in the `docker-compose` file would look like this:

```
build:
    context: web
    dockerfile: Dockerfile-dev
```

Let's use that alternative `docker-compose-dev.yml` file now:

```
$ docker-compose -f docker-compose.dev.yml build
```

The `-f` parameter will tell the Docker Compose application which `compose` file to use.

To push all images to Docker Hub, we can use `docker-compose push`. We need to be logged in to Docker Hub so that this succeeds, otherwise we get an authentication error while pushing. Thus, in my case, I do the following:

```
$ docker login -u fundamentalsofdocker -p <password>
```

Assuming the login succeeds, I can then push the following code:

```
$ docker-compose -f docker-compose.dev.yml push
```

This may take a while, depending on the bandwidth of your internet connection. While pushing, your screen may look similar to this:

Pushing images with docker-compose to Docker Hub

The preceding command pushes the two images to the
fundamentalsofdocker account on Docker Hub. You can find these two images at the
following URL: https://hub.docker.com/u/fundamentalsofdocker/

Using Docker Compose overrides

Sometimes, we want to run our applications in different environments that need specific
configuration settings. Docker Compose provides a handy capability to address exactly this
issue.

Let's make a specific sample. We can define a base Docker Compose file and then define
environment-specific overrides. Let's assume we have a file called docker-
compose.base.yml with the following content:

```
version: "2.4"
services:
  web:
    image: fundamentalsofdocker/ch11-web:2.0
  db:
    image: fundamentalsofdocker/ch11-db:2.0
    volumes:
      - pets-data:/var/lib/postgresql/data

volumes:
  pets-data:
```

This only defines the part that should be the same in all environments. All specific settings
have been taken out.

Let's assume for a moment that we want to run our sample application on a CI system, but
there we want to use different settings for the database. The Dockerfile we used to create
the database image looked like this:

```
FROM postgres:12.0-alpine
COPY init-db.sql /docker-entrypoint-initdb.d/
ENV POSTGRES_USER dockeruser
ENV POSTGRES_PASSWORD dockerpass
ENV POSTGRES_DB pets
```

Notice the three environment variables we define on lines 3 through 5. The `Dockerfile` of the `web` service has similar definitions. Let's say that on the CI system, we want to do the following:

- Build the images from code
- Define `POSTGRES_PASSWORD` as `ci-pass`
- Map container port `3000` of the web service to host port `5000`

Then, the corresponding override file would look like this:

```
version: "2.4"
services:
  web:
    build: web
    ports:
      - 5000:3000
    environment:
      POSTGRES_PASSWORD: ci-pass
  db:
    build: db
    environment:
      POSTGRES_PASSWORD: ci-pass
```

And we can run this application with the following command:

```
$ docker-compose -f docker-compose.yml -f docker-compose-ci.yml up -d --build
```

Note that with the first `-f` parameter, we provide the base Docker Compose file, and with the second one, we provide the override. The `--build` parameter is used to force `docker-compose` to rebuild the images.

When using environment variables, note the following precedence:

- Declaring them in the Docker file defines a default value
- Declaring the same variable in the Docker Compose file overrides the value from the Dockerfile

Had we followed the standard naming convention and called the base file just `docker-compose.yml` and the override file `docker-compose.override.yml` instead, then we could have started the application with `docker-compose up -d` without explicitly naming the compose files.

Summary

In this chapter, we introduced the `docker-compose` tool. This tool is mostly used to run and scale multi-service applications on a single Docker host. Typically, developers and CI servers work with single hosts and those two are the main users of Docker Compose. The tool is using YAML files as input that contain the description of the application in a declarative way.

The tool can also be used to build and push images, among many other helpful tasks. The code accompanying this chapter can be found in `fod/ch11`.

In the next chapter, we are going to introduce **orchestrators**. An orchestrator is an infrastructure software that is used to run and manage containerized applications in a cluster while making sure that these applications are in their desired state at all times.

Questions

To assess your learning progress, please answer the following questions:

1. How will you use `docker-compose` to run an application in daemon mode?
2. How will you use `docker-compose` to display the details of the running service?
3. How will you scale up a particular web service to, say, three instances?

Further reading

The following links provide additional information on the topics discussed in this chapter:

- The official YAML website: `http://www.yaml.org/`
- Docker Compose documentation: `http://dockr.ly/1FL2VQ6`
- Compose file version 2 reference: `http://dohttps://docs.docker.com/compose/compose-file/compose-file-v2/`
- Share Compose configurations between files and projects: `https://docs.docker.com/compose/extends/`

12
Orchestrators

In the previous chapter, we introduced Docker Compose, a tool that allows us to work with multi-service applications that are defined in a declarative way on a single Docker host.

This chapter introduces the concept of orchestrators. It teaches us why orchestrators are needed, and how they work conceptually. This chapter will also provide an overview of the most popular orchestrators and list a few of their pros and cons.

In this chapter, we will cover the following topics:

- What are orchestrators and why do we need them?
- The tasks of an orchestrator
- Overview of popular orchestrators

After finishing this chapter, you will be able to do the following:

- Name three to four tasks for which an orchestrator is responsible
- List two to three of the most popular orchestrators
- Explain to an interested layman, in your own words, and with appropriate analogies, why we need container orchestrators

What are orchestrators and why do we need them?

In Chapter 9, *Distributed Application Architecture*, we learned which patterns and best practices are commonly used to successfully build, ship, and run a highly distributed application. Now, if our distributed application is containerized, then we're facing the exact same problems or challenges that a non-containerized distributed application faces. Some of these challenges are those that were discussed in Chapter 9, *Distributed Application Architecture*—service discovery, load balancing, scaling, and so on.

Similar to what Docker did with containers—standardizing the packaging and shipping of software with the introduction of those containers—we would like to have some tool or infrastructure software that handles all or most of the challenges mentioned. This software turns out to be what we call container orchestrators or, as we also call them, orchestration engines.

If what I just said doesn't make much sense to you yet, then let's look at it from a different angle. Take an artist who plays an instrument. They can play wonderful music to an audience all on their own—just the artist and their instrument. But now take an orchestra of musicians. Put them all in a room, give them the notes of a symphony, ask them to play it, and leave the room. Without any director, this group of very talented musicians would not be able to play this piece in harmony; it would more or less sound like a cacophony. Only if the orchestra has a conductor, who orchestrates the group of musicians, will the resulting music of the orchestra be enjoyable to our ears:

A container orchestrator is like the conductor of an orchestra

Source: https://it.wikipedia.org/wiki/Giuseppe_Lanzetta#/media/File:UMB_5945.JPG

License: https://creativecommons.org/licenses/by-sa/3.0/deed.en

Instead of musicians, we now have containers, and instead of different instruments, we have containers that have different requirements to the container hosts to run. And instead of the music being played at varying tempi, we have containers that communicate with each other in particular ways, and have to scale up and scale down. In this regard, a container orchestrator has very much the same role as a conductor in an orchestra. It makes sure that the containers and other resources in a cluster play together in harmony.

I hope that you can now see more clearly what a container orchestrator is, and why we need one. Assuming that you confirm this question, we can now ask ourselves how the orchestrator is going to achieve the expected outcome, namely, to make sure that all the containers in the cluster play with each other in harmony. Well, the answer is, the orchestrator has to execute very specific tasks, similar to the way in which the conductor of an orchestra also has a set of tasks that they execute in order to tame and, at the same time, elevate the orchestra.

The tasks of an orchestrator

So, what are the tasks that we expect an orchestrator worth its money to execute for us? Let's look at them in detail. The following list shows the most important tasks that, at the time of writing, enterprise users typically expect from their orchestrator.

Reconciling the desired state

When using an orchestrator, you tell it, in a declarative way, how you want it to run a given application or application service. We learned what declarative versus imperative means in `Chapter 11`, *Docker Compose*. Part of this declarative way of describing the application service that we want to run includes elements such as which container image to use, how many instances of this service to run, which ports to open, and more. This declaration of the properties of our application service is what we call the *desired state*.

So, when we now tell the orchestrator for the first time to create such a new application service based on the declaration, then the orchestrator makes sure to schedule as many containers in the cluster as requested. If the container image is not yet available on the target nodes of the cluster where the containers are supposed to run, then the scheduler makes sure that they're first downloaded from the image registry. Next, the containers are started with all the settings, such as networks to which to attach, or ports to expose. The orchestrator works as hard as it can to exactly match, in reality, the cluster to the declaration.

Once our service is up and running as requested, that is, it is running in the desired state, then the orchestrator continues to monitor it. Each time the orchestrator discovers a discrepancy between the actual state of the service and its desired state, it again tries its best to reconcile the desired state.

What could such a discrepancy between the actual and desired states of an application service be? Well, let's say one of the replicas of the service, that is, one of the containers, crashes due to, say, a bug, then the orchestrator will discover that the actual state differs from the desired state in the number of replicas: there is one replica missing. The orchestrator will immediately schedule a new instance to another cluster node, which replaces the crashed instance. Another discrepancy could be that there are too many instances of the application service running, if the service has been scaled down. In this case, the orchestrator will just randomly kill as many instances as needed in order to achieve parity between the actual and the desired number of instances. Yet another discrepancy could be when the orchestrator discovers that there is an instance of the application service running a wrong (maybe old) version of the underlying container image. By now, you should get the picture, right?

Thus, instead of us actively monitoring our application's services that are running in the cluster and correcting any deviation from the desired state, we delegate this tedious task to the orchestrator. This works very well provided we use a declarative and not an imperative way of describing the desired state of our application services.

Replicated and global services

There are two quite different types of services that we might want to run in a cluster that is managed by an orchestrator. They are *replicated* and *global* services. A replicated service is a service that is required to run in a specific number of instances, say 10. A global service, in turn, is a service that is required to have exactly one instance running on every single worker node of the cluster. I have used the term *worker node* here. In a cluster that is managed by an orchestrator, we typically have two types of nodes, *managers* and *workers*. A manager node is usually exclusively used by the orchestrator to manage the cluster and does not run any other workload. Worker nodes, in turn, run the actual applications.

So, the orchestrator makes sure that, for a global service, an instance of it is running on every single worker node, no matter how many there are. We do not need to care about the number of instances, but only that on each node, it is guaranteed to run a single instance of the service.

Once again, we can fully rely on the orchestrator to handle this. In a replicated service, we will always be guaranteed to find the exact desired number of instances, while for a global service, we can be assured that on every worker node, there will always run exactly one instance of the service. The orchestrator will always work as hard as it can to guarantee this desired state.

 In Kubernetes, a global service is also called a **DaemonSet**.

Service discovery

When we describe an application service in a declarative way, we are never supposed to tell the orchestrator on which cluster nodes the different instances of the service have to run. We leave it up to the orchestrator to decide which nodes best fit this task.

It is, of course, technically possible to instruct the orchestrator to use very deterministic placement rules, but this would be an anti-pattern, and is not recommended at all, other than in very special edge cases.

So, if we now assume that the orchestration engine has complete and free will as to where to place individual instances of the application service and, furthermore, that instances can crash and be rescheduled by the orchestrator to different nodes, then we will realize that it is a futile task for us to keep track of where the individual instances are running at any given time. Even better, we shouldn't even try to know this, since it is not important.

OK, you might say, but what about if I have two services, A and B, and Service A relies on Service B; *shouldn't any given instance of Service A know where it can find an instance of Service B?*

Here, I have to say loudly and clearly—no, it shouldn't. This kind of knowledge is not desirable in a highly distributed and scalable application. Rather, we should rely on the orchestrator to provide us with the information that we need in order to reach the other service instances that we depend on. It is a bit like in the old days of telephony, when we could not directly call our friends, but had to call the phone company's central office, where some operator would then route us to the correct destination. In our case, the orchestrator plays the role of the operator, routing a request coming from an instance of Service A to an available instance of Service B. This whole process is called **service discovery**.

Routing

We have learned so far that in a distributed application, we have many interacting services. When Service A interacts with Service B, it happens through the exchange of data packets. These data packets need to somehow be funneled from Service A to Service B. This process of funneling the data packets from a source to a destination is also called **routing**. As authors or operators of an application, we do expect the orchestrator to take over this task of routing. As we will see in later chapters, routing can happen on different levels. It is like in real life. Suppose you're working in a big company in one of their office buildings. Now, you have a document that needs to be forwarded to another employee of the company. The internal post service will pick up the document from your outbox, and take it to the post office located in the same building. If the target person works in the same building, the document can then be directly forwarded to that person. If, on the other hand, the person works in another building of the same block, the document will be forwarded to the post office in that target building, from where it is then distributed to the receiver through the internal post service. Thirdly, if the document is targeted at an employee working in another branch of the company that is located in a different city or even country, then the document is forwarded to an external postal service such as UPS, which will transport it to the target location, from where, once again, the internal post service takes over and delivers it to the recipient.

Similar things happen when routing data packets between application services that are running in containers. The source and target containers can be located on the same cluster node, which corresponds to the situation where both employees work in the same building. The target container can be running on a different cluster node, which corresponds to the situation where the two employees work in different buildings of the same block. Finally, the third situation is when a data packet comes from outside of the cluster and has to be routed to the target container that is running inside the cluster.

All these situations, and more, have to be handled by the orchestrator.

Load balancing

In a highly available distributed application, all components have to be redundant. That means that every application service has to be run in multiple instances, so that if one instance fails, the service as a whole is still operational.

To make sure that all instances of a service are actually doing work and are not just sitting around idle, you have to make sure that the requests for service are distributed equally to all the instances. This process of distributing workload among service instances is called **load balancing**. Various algorithms exist for how the workload can be distributed. Usually, a load balancer works using the so-called round robin algorithm, which makes sure that the workload is distributed equally to the instances using a cyclic algorithm.

Once again, we expect the orchestrator to take care of the load balancing requests from one service to another, or from external sources to internal services.

Scaling

When running our containerized, distributed application in a cluster that is managed by an orchestrator, we additionally want an easy way to handle expected or unexpected increases in workload. To handle an increased workload, we usually just schedule additional instances of a service that is experiencing this increased load. Load balancers will then automatically be configured to distribute the workload over more available target instances.

But in real-life scenarios, the workload varies over time. If we look at a shopping site such as Amazon, it might have a high load during peak hours in the evening, when everyone is at home and shopping online; it may experience extreme loads during special days such as Black Friday; and it may experience very little traffic early in the morning. Thus, services need to not just be able to scale up, but also to scale down when the workload goes down.

We also expect orchestrators to distribute the instances of a service in a meaningful way when scaling up or down. It would not be wise to schedule all instances of the service on the same cluster node, since, if that node goes down, the whole service goes down. The scheduler of the orchestrator, which is responsible for the placement of the containers, needs to also consider not placing all instances into the same rack of computers, since, if the power supply of the rack fails, again, the whole service is affected. Furthermore, service instances of critical services should even be distributed across data centers in order to avoid outages. All these decisions, and many more, are the responsibility of the orchestrator.

In the cloud, instead of computer racks, the term '**availability zones**' is often used.

Self-healing

These days, orchestrators are very sophisticated and can do a lot for us to maintain a healthy system. Orchestrators monitor all containers that are running in the cluster, and they automatically replace crashed or unresponsive ones with new instances. Orchestrators monitor the health of cluster nodes, and take them out of the scheduler loop if a node becomes unhealthy or is down. A workload that was located on those nodes is automatically rescheduled to different available nodes.

All these activities, where the orchestrator monitors the current state and automatically repairs the damage or reconciles the desired state, lead to a so-called **self-healing** system. We do not, in most cases, have to actively engage and repair damage. The orchestrator will do this for us automatically.

However, there are a few situations that the orchestrator cannot handle without our help. Imagine a situation where we have a service instance running in a container. The container is up and running and, from the outside, looks perfectly healthy. But, the application running inside it is in an unhealthy state. The application did not crash, it just is not able to work as it was originally designed anymore. *How could the orchestrator possibly know about this without us giving it a hint?* It can't! Being in an unhealthy or invalid state means something completely different for each application service. In other words, the health status is service dependent. Only the authors of the service, or its operators, know what health means in the context of a service.

Now, orchestrators define seams or probes, over which an application service can communicate to the orchestrator about what state it is in. Two fundamental types of probe exist:

- The service can tell the orchestrator that it is healthy or not
- The service can tell the orchestrator that it is ready or temporarily unavailable

How the service determines either of the preceding answers is totally up to the service. The orchestrator only defines how it is going to ask, for example, through an `HTTP GET` request, or what type of answers it is expecting, for example, `OK` or `NOT OK`.

If our services implement logic in order to answer the preceding health or availability questions, then we have a truly self-healing system, since the orchestrator can kill unhealthy service instances and replace them with new healthy ones, and it can take service instances that are temporarily unavailable out of the load balancer's round robin.

Zero downtime deployments

These days, it gets harder and harder to justify a complete downtime for a mission-critical application that needs to be updated. Not only does that mean missed opportunities, but it can also result in a damaged reputation for the company. Customers using the application are no longer prepared to accept such an inconvenience, and will turn away quickly. Furthermore, our release cycles get shorter and shorter. Where, in the past, we would have one or two new releases per year, these days, a lot of companies update their applications multiple times a week, or even multiple times per day.

The solution to that problem is to come up with a zero downtime application update strategy. The orchestrator needs to be able to update individual application services, batch-wise. This is also called **rolling updates**. At any given time, only one or a few of the total number of instances of a given service are taken down and replaced by the new version of the service. Only if the new instances are operational, and do not produce any unexpected errors or show any misbehavior, will the next batch of instances be updated. This is repeated until all instances are replaced with their new version. If, for some reason, the update fails, then we expect the orchestrator to automatically roll the updated instances back to their previous version.

Other possible zero downtime deployments are blue–green deployments and canary releases. In both cases, the new version of a service is installed in parallel with the current, active version. But initially, the new version is only accessible internally. Operations can then run smoke tests against the new version, and when the new version seems to be running just fine, then, in the case of a blue–green deployment, the router is switched from the current blue version, to the new green version. For some time, the new green version of the service is closely monitored and, if everything is fine, the old blue version can be decommissioned. If, on the other hand, the new green version does not work as expected, then it is only a matter of setting the router back to the old blue version in order to achieve a complete rollback.

In the case of a canary release, the router is configured in such a way that it funnels a tiny percentage, say 1%, of the overall traffic through the new version of the service, while 99% of the traffic is still routed through the old version. The behavior of the new version is closely monitored and compared to the behavior of the old version. If everything looks good, then the percentage of the traffic that is funneled through the new service is slightly increased. This process is repeated until 100% of the traffic is routed through the new service. If the new service has run for a while and everything looks good, then the old service can be decommissioned.

Most orchestrators support at least the rolling update type of zero downtime deployment out of the box. Blue–green deployments and canary releases are often quite easy to implement.

Affinity and location awareness

Sometimes, certain application services require the availability of dedicated hardware on the nodes on which they run. For example, I/O-bound services require cluster nodes with an attached high-performance **solid-state drive (SSD)**, or some services that are used for machine learning, or similar, require an **Accelerated Processing Unit (APU)**. Orchestrators allow us to define node affinities per application service. The orchestrator will then make sure that its scheduler only schedules containers on cluster nodes that fulfill the required criteria.

Defining an affinity to a particular node should be avoided; this would introduce a single point of failure and thus compromise high availability. Always define a set of multiple cluster nodes as the target for an application service.

Some orchestration engines also support what is called **location awareness** or **geo awareness**. What this means is that you can ask the orchestrator to equally distribute instances of a service over a set of different locations. You could, for example, define a `datacenter` label, with the possible `west`, `center`, and `east` values, and apply the label to all of the cluster nodes with the value that corresponds to the geographical region in which the respective node is located. Then, you instruct the orchestrator to use this label for the geo awareness of a certain application service. In this case, if you request nine replicas of the service, then the orchestrator would make sure that three instances are deployed to the nodes in each of the three data centers—west, center, and east.

Geo awareness can even be defined hierarchically; for example, you can have a data center as the top-level discriminator, followed by the availability zone.

Geo awareness, or location awareness, is used to decrease the probability of outages due to power supply failures or data center outages. If the application instances are distributed across nodes, availability zones, or even data centers, it is extremely unlikely that everything will go down at once. One region will always be available.

Security

These days, security in IT is a very hot topic. Cyber warfare is at an all-time high. Most high-profile companies have been victims of hacker attacks, with very costly consequences. One of the worst nightmares of each **chief information officer (CIO)** or **chief technology officer (CTO)** is to wake up in the morning and hear in the news that their company has become a victim of a hacker attack, and that sensitive information has been stolen or compromised.

To counter most of these security threats, we need to establish a secure software supply chain, and enforce security defense in depth. Let's look at some of the tasks that you can expect from an enterprise-grade orchestrator.

Secure communication and cryptographic node identity

First and foremost, we want to make sure that our cluster that is managed by the orchestrator is secure. Only trusted nodes can join the cluster. Each node that joins the cluster gets a cryptographic node identity, and all communication between the nodes must be encrypted. For this, nodes can use **Mutual Transport Layer Security (MTLS)**. In order to authenticate nodes of the cluster with each other, certificates are used. These certificates are automatically rotated periodically, or on request, to protect the system in case a certificate is leaked.

The communication that happens in a cluster can be separated into three types. You talk about communication planes—management, control, and data planes:

- The management plane is used by the cluster managers, or masters, to, for example, schedule service instances, execute health checks, or create and modify any other resources in the cluster, such as data volumes, secrets, or networks.
- The control plane is used to exchange important state information between all nodes of the cluster. This kind of information is, for example, used to update the local IP tables on clusters, which are used for routing purposes.
- The data plane is where the actual application services communicate with each other and exchange data.

Normally, orchestrators mainly care about securing the management and control plane. Securing the data plane is left to the user, although the orchestrator may facilitate this task.

Secure networks and network policies

When running application services, not every service needs to communicate with every other service in the cluster. Thus, we want the ability to sandbox services from each other, and only run those services in the same networking sandbox that absolutely need to communicate with each other. All other services and all network traffic coming from outside of the cluster should have no possibility of accessing the sandboxed services.

There are at least two ways in which this network-based sandboxing can happen. We can either use a **software-defined network** (**SDN**) to group application services, or we can have one flat network, and use network policies to control who does and does not have access to a particular service or group of services.

Role-based access control (RBAC)

One of the most important tasks (next to security) that an orchestrator must fulfill in order to make it enterprise-ready is to provide role-based access to the cluster and its resources. RBAC defines how subjects, users, or groups of users of the system, organized into teams, and so on, can access and manipulate the system. It makes sure that unauthorized personnel cannot do any harm to the system, nor can they see any of the available resources in the system that they're not supposed to know of or see.

A typical enterprise might have user groups such as Development, QA, and Prod, and each of those groups can have one or many users associated with it. John Doe, the developer, is a member of the Development group and, as such, can access resources that are dedicated to the development team, but he cannot access, for example, the resources of the Prod team, of which Ann Harbor is a member. She, in turn, cannot interfere with the Development team's resources.

One way of implementing RBAC is through the definition of **grants**. A grant is an association between a subject, a role, and a resource collection. Here, a role is comprised of a set of access permissions to a resource. Such permissions can be to create, stop, remove, list, or view containers; to deploy a new application service; to list cluster nodes or view the details of a cluster node; and many more.

A resource collection is a group of logically related resources of the cluster, such as application services, secrets, data volumes, or containers.

Secrets

In our daily life, we have loads of secrets. Secrets are information that is not meant to be publicly known, such as the username and password combination that you use to access your online bank account, or the code to your cell phone or your locker at the gym.

When writing software, we often need to use secrets, too. For example, we need a certificate to authenticate our application service with the external service that we want to access, or we need a token to authenticate and authorize our service when accessing some other API. In the past, developers, for convenience, have just hardcoded those values, or put them in clear text in some external configuration files. There, this very sensitive information has been accessible to a broad audience, which, in reality, should never have had the opportunity to see those secrets.

Luckily, these days, orchestrators offer what's called secrets to deal with such sensitive information in a highly secure way. Secrets can be created by authorized or trusted personnel. The values of those secrets are then encrypted and stored in the highly available cluster state database. The secrets, since they are encrypted, are now secure at rest. Once a secret is requested by an authorized application service, the secret is only forwarded to the cluster nodes that actually run an instance of that particular service, and the secret value is never stored on the node but mounted into the container in a `tmpfs` RAM-based volume. Only inside the respective container is the secret value available in clear text.

We already mentioned that the secrets are secure at rest. Once they are requested by a service, the cluster manager, or master, decrypts the secret and sends it over the wire to the target nodes. *So, what about the secrets being secure in transit?* Well, we learned earlier that the cluster nodes use MTLS for their communication, and so the secret, although transmitted in clear text, is still secure, since data packets will be encrypted by MTLS. Thus, secrets are secure both at rest and in transit. Only services that are authorized to use secrets will ever have access to those secret values.

Content trust

For added security, we want to make sure that only trusted images run in our production cluster. Some orchestrators allow us to configure a cluster so that it can only ever run signed images. Content trust and signing images is all about making sure that the authors of the image are the ones that we expect them to be, namely, our trusted developers or, even better, our trusted CI server. Furthermore, with content trust, we want to guarantee that the image that we get is fresh, and is not an old and maybe vulnerable image. And finally, we want to make sure that the image cannot be compromised by malicious hackers in transit. The latter is often called a **man-in-the-middle** (**MITM**) attack.

By signing images at the source, and validating the signature at the target, we can guarantee that the images that we want to run are not compromised.

Reverse uptime

The last point I want to discuss in the context of security is reverse uptime. *What do we mean by that?* Imagine that you have configured and secured a production cluster. On this cluster, you're running a few mission-critical applications of your company. Now, a hacker has managed to find a security hole in one of your software stacks, and has gained root access to one of your cluster nodes. That alone is already bad enough but, even worse, this hacker could now mask their presence on this node, on which they have root access, after all, and then use it as a base to attack other nodes in your cluster.

 Root access in Linux or any Unix-type operating system means that you can do anything on this system. It is the highest level of access that someone can have. In Windows, the equivalent role is that of an administrator.

But *what if we leverage the fact that containers are ephemeral and cluster nodes are quickly provisioned, usually in a matter of minutes if fully automated?* We just kill each cluster node after a certain uptime of, say, 1 day. The orchestrator is instructed to drain the node and then exclude it from the cluster. Once the node is out of the cluster, it is torn down and replaced by a freshly provisioned node.

That way, the hacker has lost their base and the problem has been eliminated. This concept is not yet broadly available, though, but to me it seems to be a huge step toward increased security and, as far as I have discussed it with engineers who are working in this area, it is not difficult to implement.

Introspection

So far, we have discussed a lot of tasks for which the orchestrator is responsible, and that it can execute in a completely autonomous way. But there is also the need for human operators to be able to see and analyze what's currently running on the cluster, and in what state or health the individual applications are. For all this, we need the possibility of introspection. The orchestrator needs to surface crucial information in a way that is easily consumable and understandable.

The orchestrator should collect system metrics from all the cluster nodes and make them accessible to the operators. Metrics include CPU, memory and disk usage, network bandwidth consumption, and more. The information should be easily available on a node-per-node basis, as well as in an aggregated form.

We also want the orchestrator to give us access to logs that are produced by service instances or containers. Even more, the orchestrator should provide us with `exec` access to each and every container if we have the correct authorization to do so. With `exec` access to containers, you can then debug misbehaving containers.

In highly distributed applications, where each request to the application goes through numerous services until it is completely handled, tracing requests is a really important task. Ideally, the orchestrator supports us in implementing a tracing strategy, or gives us some good guidelines to follow.

Finally, human operators can best monitor a system when working with a graphical representation of all the collected metrics and logging and tracing information. Here, we are speaking about dashboards. Every decent orchestrator should offer at least some basic dashboard with a graphical representation of the most critical system parameters.

However, human operators are not the only ones concerned about introspection. We also need to be able to connect external systems with the orchestrator in order to consume this information. There needs to be an API available, over which external systems can access data such as cluster state, metrics, and logs, and use this information to make automated decisions, such as creating pager or phone alerts, sending out emails, or triggering an alarm siren if some thresholds are exceeded by the system.

Overview of popular orchestrators

At the time of writing, there are many orchestration engines out there and in use, but there are a few clear winners. The number one spot is clearly held by Kubernetes, which reigns supreme. A distant second is Docker's own SwarmKit, followed by others such as Apache Mesos, AWS **Elastic Container Service (ECS)**, or Microsoft **Azure Container Service (ACS)**.

Kubernetes

Kubernetes was originally designed by Google and later donated to the **Cloud Native Computing Foundation (CNCF)**. Kubernetes was modeled after Google's proprietary Borg system, which has been running containers on a super massive scale for years. Kubernetes was Google's attempt to go back to the drawing board, and completely start over and design a system that incorporates all the lessons that were learned with Borg.

Contrary to Borg, which is proprietary technology, Kubernetes was open sourced early on. This was a very wise choice by Google, since it attracted a huge number of contributors from outside of the company and, over only a couple of years, an even more massive ecosystem evolved around Kubernetes. You can rightfully say that Kubernetes is the darling of the community in the container orchestration space. No other orchestrator has been able to produce so much hype and attract so many talented people who are willing to contribute in a meaningful way to the success of the project as a contributor or an early adopter.

In that regard, Kubernetes in the container orchestration space looks to me very much like what Linux has become in the server operating system space. Linux has become the *de facto* standard of server operating systems. All relevant companies, such as Microsoft, IBM, Amazon, Red Hat, and even Docker, have embraced Kubernetes.

And there is one thing that cannot be denied: Kubernetes was designed from the very beginning for massive scalability. After all, it was designed with Google Borg in mind.

One negative aspect that you could be voiced against Kubernetes is that it is still complex to set up and manage, at least at the time of writing. There is a significant hurdle to overcome for newcomers. The first step is steep, but once you have worked with this orchestrator for a while, it all makes sense. The overall design is carefully thought through and executed very well.

In release 1.10 of Kubernetes, whose **general availability (GA)** was in March 2018, most of the initial shortcomings compared to other orchestrators such as Docker Swarm have been eliminated. For example, security and confidentiality is now not only an afterthought, but an integral part of the system.

New features are implemented at a tremendous speed. New releases are happening every 3 months or so, more precisely, about every 100 days. Most of the new features are demand-driven, that is, companies using Kubernetes to orchestrate their mission-critical applications can voice their needs. This makes Kubernetes enterprise-ready. It would be wrong to assume that this orchestrator is only for start-ups and not for risk-averse enterprises. The contrary is the case. *On what do I base this claim?* Well, my claim is justified by the fact that companies such as Microsoft, Docker, and Red Hat, whose clients are mostly big enterprises, have fully embraced Kubernetes, and provide enterprise-grade support for it if it is used and integrated into their enterprise offerings.

Kubernetes supports both Linux and Windows containers.

Docker Swarm

It is well known that Docker popularized and commoditized software containers. Docker did not invent containers, but standardized them and made them broadly available, not least by offering the free image registry—Docker Hub. Initially, Docker focused mainly on the developer and the development life cycle. However, companies that started to use and love containers soon also wanted to use them not just during the development or testing of new applications, but also to run those applications in production.

Initially, Docker had nothing to offer in that space, so other companies jumped into that vacuum and offered help to the users. But it didn't take long, and Docker recognized that there was a huge demand for a simple yet powerful orchestrator. Docker's first attempt was a product called classic swarm. It was a standalone product that enabled users to create a cluster of Docker host machines that could be used to run and scale their containerized applications in a highly available and self-healing way.

The setup of a classic Docker swarm, though, was hard. A lot of complicated manual steps were involved. Customers loved the product, but struggled with its complexity. So, Docker decided it could do better. It went back to the drawing board and came up with SwarmKit. SwarmKit was introduced at DockerCon 2016 in Seattle, and was an integral part of the newest version of the Docker engine. Yes, you got that right; SwarmKit was, and still is to this day, an integral part of the Docker engine. Thus, if you install a Docker host, you automatically have SwarmKit available with it.

SwarmKit was designed with simplicity and security in mind. The mantra was, and still is, that it has to be almost trivial to set up a swarm, and that the swarm has to be highly secure out of the box. Docker Swarm operates on the assumption of least privilege.

Installing a complete, highly available Docker swarm is literally as simple as starting with `docker swarm init` on the first node in the cluster, which becomes the so-called leader, and then `docker swarm join <join-token>` on all other nodes. `join-token` is generated by the leader during initialization. The whole process takes fewer that 5 minutes on a swarm with up to 10 nodes. If it is automated, it takes even less time.

As I already mentioned, security was top on the list of must-haves when Docker designed and developed SwarmKit. Containers provide security by relying on Linux kernel namespaces and cgroups, as well as Linux syscall whitelisting (seccomp), and the support of Linux capabilities and the **Linux security module** (**LSM**). Now, on top of that, SwarmKit adds MTLS and secrets that are encrypted at rest and in transit. Furthermore, Swarm defines the so-called **container network model** (**CNM**), which allows for SDNs that provide sandboxing for application services that are running on the swarm.

Docker SwarmKit supports both Linux and Windows containers.

Apache Mesos and Marathon

Apache Mesos is an open source project, and was originally designed to make a cluster of servers or nodes look like one single big server from the outside. Mesos is software that makes the management of computer clusters simple. Users of Mesos should not have to care about individual servers, but just assume they have a gigantic pool of resources at their disposal, which corresponds to the aggregate of all the resources of all the nodes in the cluster.

Mesos, in IT terms, is already pretty old, at least compared to the other orchestrators. It was first publicly presented in 2009, but at that time, of course, it wasn't designed to run containers, since Docker didn't even exist yet. Similar to what Docker does with containers, Mesos uses Linux cgroups to isolate resources such as CPU, memory, or disk I/O for individual applications or services.

Mesos is really the underlying infrastructure for other interesting services built on top of it. From the perspective of containers specifically, Marathon is important. Marathon is a container orchestrator that runs on top of Mesos, which is able to scale to thousands of nodes.

Marathon supports multiple container runtimes, such as Docker or its own Mesos containers. It supports not only stateless, but also stateful, application services, for example, databases such as PostgreSQL or MongoDB. Similar to Kubernetes and Docker SwarmKit, it supports many of the features that were described earlier in this chapter, such as high availability, health checks, service discovery, load balancing, and location awareness, to name but a few of the most important ones.

Although Mesos and, to a certain extent, Marathon, are rather mature projects, their reach is relatively limited. It seems to be most popular in the area of big data, that is, to run data-crunching services such as Spark or Hadoop.

Amazon ECS

If you are looking for a simple orchestrator and have already heavily bought into the AWS ecosystem, then Amazon's ECS might be the right choice for you. It is important to point out one very important limitation of ECS: if you buy into this container orchestrator, then you lock yourself into AWS. You will not be able to easily port an application that is running on ECS to another platform or cloud.

Amazon promotes its ECS service as a highly scalable, fast container management service that makes it easy to run, stop, and manage Docker containers on a cluster. Next to running containers, ECS gives direct access to many other AWS services from the application services that run inside the containers. This tight and seamless integration with many popular AWS services is what makes ECS compelling for users who are looking for an easy way to get their containerized applications up and running in a robust and highly scalable environment. Amazon also provides its own private image registry.

With AWS ECS, you can use Fargate to have it fully manage the underlying infrastructure, allowing you to concentrate exclusively on deploying containerized applications, and you do not have to care about how to create and manage a cluster of nodes. ECS supports both Linux and Windows containers.

In summary, ECS is simple to use, highly scalable, and well integrated with other popular AWS services; but it is not as powerful as, say, Kubernetes or Docker SwarmKit, and it is only available on Amazon AWS.

Microsoft ACS

Similar to what we said about ECS, we can claim the same for Microsoft's ACS. It is a simple container orchestration service that makes sense if you are already heavily invested in the Azure ecosystem. I should say the same as I have pointed out for Amazon ECS: if you buy into ACS, then you lock yourself in to the offerings of Microsoft. It will not be easy to move your containerized applications from ACS to any other platform or cloud.

ACS is Microsoft's container service, which supports multiple orchestrators such as Kubernetes, Docker Swarm, and Mesos DC/OS. With Kubernetes becoming more and more popular, the focus of Microsoft has clearly shifted to that orchestrator. Microsoft has even rebranded its service and called it **Azure Kubernetes Service (AKS)** in order to put the focus on Kubernetes.

AKS manages, for you, a hosted Kubernetes or Docker Swarm or DC/OS environment in Azure, so that you can concentrate on the applications that you want to deploy, and you don't have to care about configuring the infrastructure. Microsoft, in its own words, claims the following:

> *"AKS makes it quick and easy to deploy and manage containerized applications without container orchestration expertise. It also eliminates the burden of ongoing operations and maintenance by provisioning, upgrading, and scaling resources on demand, without taking your applications offline."*

Summary

This chapter demonstrated why orchestrators are needed in the first place, and how they conceptually work. It pointed out which orchestrators are the most prominent ones at the time of writing, and discussed the main commonalities and differences between the various orchestrators.

The next chapter will introduce Docker's native orchestrator, SwarmKit. It will elaborate on all the concepts and objects that SwarmKit uses to deploy and run a distributed, resilient, robust, and highly available application in a cluster—on-premises or in the cloud.

Questions

Answer the following questions to assess your learning progress:

1. Why do we need an orchestrator? Provide two or three reasons.
2. Name three to four typical responsibilities of an orchestrator.
3. Name at least two container orchestrators, as well as the main sponsors behind them.

Further reading

The following links provide some deeper insight into orchestration-related topics:

- Kubernetes—production-grade orchestration: `https://kubernetes.io/`.
- An overview of Docker Swarm mode: `https://docs.docker.com/engine/swarm/`.
- Marathon, A container orchestration platform for Mesos and DC/OS: `https://mesosphere.github.io/marathon/`
- Containers and orchestration are explained: `http://bit.ly/2DFoQgx`.

Introduction to Docker Swarm

13

In the last chapter, we introduced orchestrators. Like a conductor in an orchestra, an orchestrator makes sure that all of our containerized application services play together nicely and contribute harmoniously to a common goal. Such orchestrators have quite a few responsibilities, which we discussed in detail. Finally, we provided a short overview of the most important container orchestrators on the market.

This chapter introduces Docker's native orchestrator, SwarmKit. It elaborates on all of the concepts and objects SwarmKit uses to deploy and run distributed, resilient, robust, and highly available applications in a cluster on premises or in the cloud. This chapter also introduces how SwarmKit ensures secure applications by using a **Software-Defined Network** (**SDN**) to isolate containers. Additionally, this chapter demonstrates how to install a highly available Docker Swarm in the cloud. It introduces the routing mesh, which provides layer-4 routing and load balancing. Finally, it demonstrates how to deploy a first application consisting of multiple services onto the swarm.

These are the topics we are going to discuss in this chapter:

- The Docker Swarm architecture
- Swarm nodes
- Stacks, services, and tasks
- Multi-host networking
- Creating a Docker Swarm
- Deploying a first application
- The Swarm routing mesh

After completing this chapter, you will be able to do the following:

- Sketch the essential parts of a highly available Docker Swarm on a whiteboard
- Explain in two or three simple sentences to an interested layman what a (swarm) service is

- Create a highly available Docker Swarm in AWS, Azure, or GCP consisting of three manager and two worker nodes
- Successfully deploy a replicated service such as Nginx on a Docker Swarm
- Scale a running Docker Swarm service up and down
- Retrieve the aggregated log of a replicated Docker Swarm service
- Write a simple stack file for a sample application consisting of at least two interacting services
- Deploy a stack into a Docker Swarm

The Docker Swarm architecture

The architecture of a Docker Swarm from a 30,000-foot view consists of two main parts—a raft consensus group of an odd number of manager nodes, and a group of worker nodes that communicate with each other over a gossip network, also called the control plane. The following diagram illustrates this architecture:

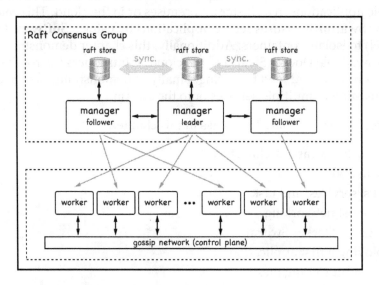

High-level architecture of a Docker Swarm

The **manager** nodes manage the swarm while the **worker** nodes execute the applications deployed into the swarm. Each **manager** has a complete copy of the full state of the Swarm in its local raft store. Managers synchronously communicate with each other and their raft stores are always in sync.

The **workers**, on the other hand, communicate with each other asynchronously for scalability reasons. There can be hundreds if not thousands of **worker** nodes in a Swarm. Now that we have a high-level overview of what a Docker Swarm is, let's describe all of the individual elements of a Docker Swarm in more detail.

Swarm nodes

A Swarm is a collection of nodes. We can classify a node as a physical computer or **Virtual Machine** (**VM**). Physical computers these days are often referred to as *bare metal*. People say *we're running on bare metal* to distinguish from running on a VM.

When we install Docker on such a node, we call this node a Docker host. The following diagram illustrates a bit better what a node and what a Docker host is:

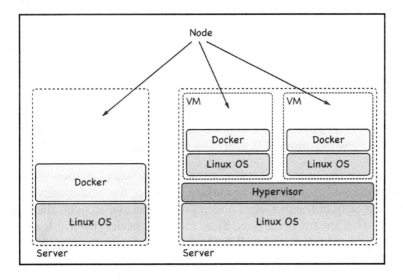

Bare metal and VM types of Docker Swarm nodes

To become a member of a Docker Swarm, a node must be a Docker host. A node in a Docker Swarm can have one of two roles. It can be a manager or it can be a worker. Manager nodes do what their name implies; they manage the Swarm. The worker nodes, in turn, execute the application workload.

Technically, a manager node can also be a worker node and hence run application workload—although that is not recommended, especially if the Swarm is a production system running mission-critical applications.

Swarm managers

Each Docker Swarm needs to include at least one manager node. For high availability reasons, we should have more than one manager node in a Swarm. This is especially true for production or production-like environments. If we have more than one manager node, then these nodes work together using the Raft consensus protocol. The Raft consensus protocol is a standard protocol that is often used when multiple entities need to work together and always need to agree with each other as to which activity to execute next.

To work well, the Raft consensus protocol asks for an odd number of members in what is called the consensus group. Hence, we should always have 1, 3, 5, 7, and so on manager nodes. In such a consensus group, there is always a leader. In the case of Docker Swarm, the first node that starts the Swarm initially becomes the leader. If the leader goes away then the remaining manager nodes elect a new leader. The other nodes in the consensus group are called followers.

Now, let's assume that we shut down the current leader node for maintenance reasons. The remaining manager nodes will elect a new leader. When the previous leader node comes back online, it will now become a follower. The new leader remains the leader.

All of the members of the consensus group communicate synchronously with each other. Whenever the consensus group needs to make a decision, the leader asks all followers for agreement. If a majority of the manager nodes give a positive answer, then the leader executes the task. That means if we have three manager nodes, then at least one of the followers has to agree with the leader. If we have five manager nodes, then at least two followers have to agree.

Since all manager follower nodes have to communicate synchronously with the leader node to make a decision in the cluster, the decision-making process gets slower and slower the more manager nodes we have forming the consensus group. The recommendation of Docker is to use one manager for development, demo, or test environments. Use three managers nodes in small to medium size Swarms, and use five managers in large to extra large Swarms. To use more than five managers in a Swarm is hardly ever justified.

The manager nodes are not only responsible for managing the Swarm but also for maintaining the state of the Swarm. *What do we mean by that?* When we talk about the state of the Swarm we mean all of the information about it—for example, *how many nodes are in the Swarm and what are the properties of each node, such as name or IP address.* We also mean what containers are running on which node in the Swarm and more. What, on the other hand, is not included in the state of the Swarm is data produced by the application services running in containers on the Swarm. This is called application data and is definitely not part of the state that is managed by the manager nodes:

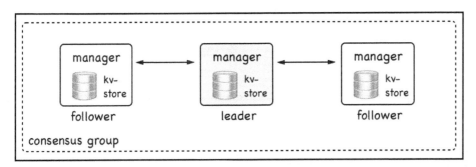

A Swarm manager consensus group

All of the Swarm states are stored in a high-performance key-value store (**kv-store**) on each **manager** node. That's right, each **manager** node stores a complete replica of the whole Swarm state. This redundancy makes the Swarm highly available. If a **manager** node goes down, the remaining **managers** all have the complete state at hand.

If a new **manager** joins the consensus group, then it synchronizes the Swarm state with the existing members of the group until it has a complete replica. This replication is usually pretty fast in typical Swarms but can take a while if the Swarm is big and many applications are running on it.

Swarm workers

As we mentioned earlier, a Swarm worker node is meant to host and run containers that contain the actual application services we're interested in running on our cluster. They are the workhorses of the Swarm. In theory, a manager node can also be a worker. But, as we already said, this is not recommended on a production system. On a production system, we should let managers be managers.

Worker nodes communicate with each other over the so-called control plane. They use the gossip protocol for their communication. This communication is asynchronous, which means that, at any given time, it is likely that not all worker nodes are in perfect sync.

Now, you might ask—*what information do worker nodes exchange?* It is mostly information that is needed for service discovery and routing, that is, information about which containers are running on with nodes and more:

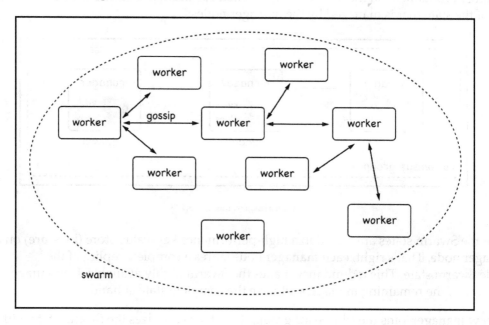

Worker nodes communicating with each other

In the preceding diagram, you can see how workers communicate with each other. To make sure the gossiping scales well in a large Swarm, each **worker** node only synchronizes its own state with three random neighbors. For those who are familiar with Big O notation, that means that the synchronization of the **worker** nodes using the gossip protocol scales with O(0).

Worker nodes are kind of passive. They never actively do something other than run the workloads that they get assigned by the manager nodes. The **worker** makes sure, though, that it runs these workloads to the best of its capabilities. Later on in this chapter, we will get to know more about exactly what workloads the worker nodes are assigned by the manager nodes.

Stacks, services, and tasks

When using a Docker Swarm versus a single Docker host, there is a paradigm change. Instead of talking of individual containers that run processes, we are abstracting away to services that represent a set of replicas of each process, and, in this way, become highly available. We also do not speak anymore of individual Docker hosts with well-known names and IP addresses to which we deploy containers; we'll now be referring to clusters of hosts to which we deploy services. We don't care about an individual host or node anymore. We don't give it a meaningful name; each node rather becomes a number to us. We also don't care about individual containers and where they are deployed any longer—we just care about having a desired state defined through a service. We can try to depict that as shown in the following diagram:

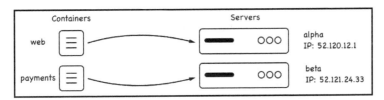

Containers are deployed to well-known servers

Instead of deploying individual containers to well-known servers like in the preceding diagram, where we deploy the **web** container to the **alpha** server with the IP address 52.120.12.1, and the **payments** container to the **beta** server with the IP 52.121.24.33, we switch to this new paradigm of services and Swarms (or, more generally, clusters):

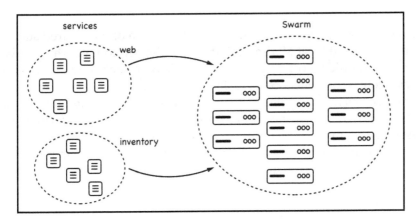

Services are deployed to Swarms

In the preceding diagram, we see that a **web** service and an **inventory** service are both deployed to a **Swarm** that consists of many nodes. Each of the services has a certain number of replicas: six for **web** and five for **inventory**. We don't really care on which node the replicas will run; we only care that the requested number of replicas is always running on whatever nodes the **Swarm** scheduler decides to put them on.

Services

A Swarm service is an abstract thing. It is a description of the desired state of an application or application service that we want to run in a Swarm. The Swarm service is like a manifest describing such things as the following:

- Name of the service
- Image from which to create the containers
- Number of replicas to run
- Network(s) that the containers of the service are attached to
- Ports that should be mapped

Having this service manifest, the Swarm manager then makes sure that the described desired state is always reconciled if ever the actual state should deviate from it. So, if for example, one instance of the service crashes, then the scheduler on the Swarm manager schedules a new instance of this particular service on a node with free resources so that the desired state is reestablished.

Task

We have learned that a service corresponds to a description of the desired state in which an application service should be at all times. Part of that description was the number of replicas the service should be running. Each replica is represented by a task. In this regard, a Swarm service contains a collection of tasks. On Docker Swarm, a task is the atomic unit of deployment. Each task of a service is deployed by the Swarm scheduler to a worker node. The task contains all of the necessary information that the worker node needs to run a container based on the image, which is part of the service description. Between a task and a container, there is a one-to-one relation. The container is the instance that runs on the worker node, while the task is the description of this container as a part of a Swarm service.

Stack

Now that we have a good idea about what a Swarm service is and what tasks are, we can introduce the stack. A stack is used to describe a collection of Swarm services that are related, most probably because they are part of the same application. In that sense, we could also say that a stack describes an application that consists of one to many services that we want to run on the Swarm.

Typically, we describe a stack declaratively in a text file that is formatted using the YAML format and that uses the same syntax as the already-known Docker Compose file. This leads to a situation where people sometimes say that a stack is described by a docker-compose file. A better wording would be: a stack is described in a stack file that uses similar syntax to a docker-compose file.

Let's try to illustrate the relationship between the stack, services, and tasks in the following diagram and connect it with the typical content of a stack file:

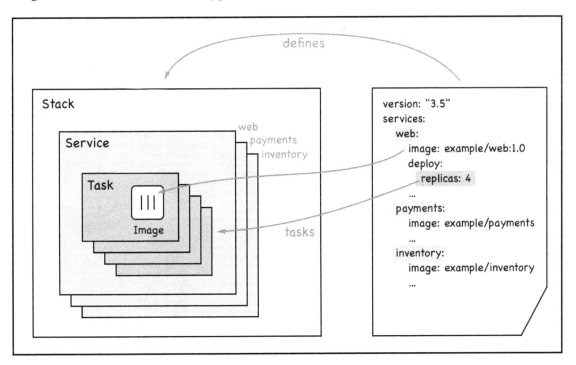

Diagram showing the relationship between stack, services, and tasks

In the preceding diagram, we see on the right-hand side a declarative description of a sample **Stack**. The **Stack** consists of three services called **web**, **payments**, and **inventory**. We also see that the **web** service uses the **example/web:1.0** image and has four replicas.

On the left-hand side of the diagram, we see that the **Stack** embraces the three services mentioned. Each service, in turn, contains a collection of **Tasks**, as many as there are replicas. In the case of the **web** service, we have a collection of four **Tasks**. Each **Task** contains the name of the **Image** from which it will instantiate a container once the **Task** is scheduled on a Swarm node.

Multi-host networking

In `Chapter 10`, *Single-Host Networking*, we discussed how containers communicate on a single Docker host. Now, we have a Swarm that consists of a cluster of nodes or Docker hosts. Containers that are located on different nodes need to be able to communicate with each other. Many techniques can help us to achieve this goal. Docker has chosen to implement an **overlay network** driver for Docker Swarm. This **overlay network** allows containers attached to the same **overlay network** to discover each other and freely communicate with each other. The following is a schema for how an **overlay network** works:

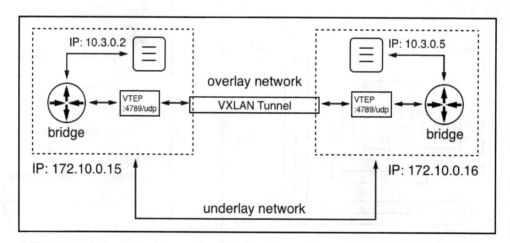

Overlay network

We have two nodes or Docker hosts with the IP
addresses `172.10.0.15` and `172.10.0.16`. The values we have chosen for the IP
addresses are not important; what is important is that both hosts have a distinct IP address
and are connected by a physical network (a network cable), which is called the **underlay
network**.

On the node on the left-hand side we have a container running with the IP
address `10.3.0.2`, and on the node on the right-hand side another container with the IP
address `10.3.0.5`. Now, the former container wants to communicate with the latter. *How
can this happen?* In `Chapter 10`, *Single-Host Networking*, we saw how this works when both
containers are located on the same node—by using a Linux bridge. But Linux bridges only
operate locally and cannot span across nodes. So, we need another mechanism. Linux
VXLAN comes to the rescue. VXLAN has been available on Linux since way before
containers were a thing.

When the left-hand container sends a data packet, the **bridge** realizes that the target of the
packet is not on this host. Now, each node participating in an overlay network gets a so-
called **VXLAN Tunnel Endpoint (VTEP)** object, which intercepts the packet (the packet at
that moment is an OSI layer 2 data packet), wraps it with a header containing the target IP
address of the host that runs the destination container (this makes it now an OSI layer 3
data packet), and sends it over the **VXLAN tunnel**. The **VTEP** on the other side of the
tunnel unpacks the data packet and forwards it to the local bridge, which in turn forwards
it to the destination container.

The overlay driver is included in SwarmKit and is in most cases the recommended network
driver for Docker Swarm. There are other multi-node-capable network drivers available
from third parties that can be installed as plugins to each participating Docker host.
Certified network plugins are available from the Docker store.

Creating a Docker Swarm

Creating a Docker Swarm is almost trivial. It is so easy that it seems unreal if you know
what an orchestrator is all about. But it is true, Docker has done a fantastic job in making
Swarms simple and elegant to use. At the same time, Docker Swarm has been proven in use
by large enterprises to be very robust and scalable.

Creating a local single node swarm

So, enough imagining — let's demonstrate how we can create a Swarm. In its most simple form, a fully functioning Docker Swarm consists only of a single node. If you're using Docker for Mac or Windows, or even if you're using Docker Toolbox, then your personal computer or laptop is such a node. Hence, we can start right there and demonstrate some of the most important features of a Swarm.

Let's initialize a Swarm. On the command line, just enter the following command:

```
$ docker swarm init
```

And after an incredibly short time, you should see something like the following screenshot:

```
$ docker swarm init
Swarm initialized: current node (mc07c43kp8v8d4ofnl5i9skb2) is now a manager.

To add a worker to this swarm, run the following command:

    docker swarm join --token SWMTKN-1-1ynzcy7z2tze0zhrbw7h85Sbiywspmg9mjewknn5hwg6g10b5m-7h98rot6dfi5723ftkitsb1vt 192.168.65.3:2377

To add a manager to this swarm, run 'docker swarm join-token manager' and follow the instructions.
```

Output of the Docker Swarm init command

Our computer is now a Swarm node. Its role is that of a manager and it is the leader (of the managers, which makes sense since there is only one manager at this time). Although it took only a very short time to finish `docker swarm init`, the command did a lot of things during that time. Some of them are as follows:

- It created a root **Certificate Authority** (**CA**).
- It created a key-value store that is used to store the state of the whole Swarm.

Now, in the preceding output, we can see a command that can be used to join other nodes to the Swarm that we just created. The command is as follows:

```
$ docker swarm join --token <join-token> <IP address>:2377
```

Here, we have the following:

- `<join-token>` is a token generated by the Swarm leader at the time the Swarm was initialized.
- `<IP address>` is the IP address of the leader.

Although our cluster remains simple, as it consists of only one member, we can still ask the Docker CLI to list all of the nodes of the Swarm. This will look similar to the following screenshot:

```
$ docker node ls
ID                            HOSTNAME          STATUS    AVAILABILITY    MANAGER STATUS    ENGINE VERSION
s5hjreg5z3cqk4jmsslqx6auc *   docker-desktop    Ready     Active          Leader            19.03.4
```

Listing the nodes of the Docker Swarm

In this output, we first see ID that was given to the node. The star (*) that follows ID indicates that this is the node on which `docker node ls` was executed—basically saying that this is the active node. Then, we have the (human-readable) name of the node, its status, availability, and manager status. As mentioned earlier, this very first node of the Swarm automatically became the leader, which is indicated in the preceding screenshot. Lastly, we see which version of the Docker engine we're using.

To get even more information about a node, we can use the `docker node inspect` command, as shown in the following screenshot:

```
$ docker node inspect s5hjreg5z3cqk4jmsslqx6auc
[
    {
        "ID": "s5hjreg5z3cqk4jmsslqx6auc",
        "Version": {
            "Index": 9
        },
        "CreatedAt": "2019-11-03T18:18:54.4662205Z",
        "UpdatedAt": "2019-11-03T18:18:54.9865568Z",
        "Spec": {
            "Labels": {},
            "Role": "manager",
            "Availability": "active"
        },
        "Description": {
            "Hostname": "docker-desktop",
            "Platform": {
                "Architecture": "x86_64",
                "OS": "linux"
            },
            "Resources": {
                "NanoCPUs": 2000000000,
                "MemoryBytes": 2076631040
            },
            "Engine": {
                "EngineVersion": "19.03.4",
                "Plugins": [
                    {
                        "Type": "Log",
                        "Name": "awslogs"
                    },
```

Truncated output of the docker node inspect command

There is a lot of information generated by this command, so we only present a truncated version of the output. This output can be useful, for example, when you need to troubleshoot a misbehaving cluster node.

Creating a local Swarm in VirtualBox or Hyper-V

Sometimes, a single node Swarm is not enough, but we don't have or don't want to use an account to create a Swarm in the cloud. In this case, we can create a local Swarm in either VirtualBox or Hyper-V. Creating the Swarm in VirtualBox is slightly easier than creating it in Hyper-V, but if you're using Windows 10 and have Docker for Windows running, then you cannot use VirtualBox at the same time. The two hypervisors are mutually exclusive.

Let's assume we have VirtualBox and `docker-machine` installed on our laptop. We can then use `docker-machine` to list all Docker hosts that are currently defined and may be running in VirtualBox:

```
$ docker-machine ls
NAME ACTIVE DRIVER STATE URL SWARM DOCKER ERRORS
default - virtualbox Stopped Unknown
```

In my case, I have one VM called `default` defined, which is currently stopped. I can easily start the VM by issuing the `docker-machine start default` command. This command takes a while and will result in the following (shortened) output:

```
$ docker-machine start default
Starting "default"...
(default) Check network to re-create if needed...
(default) Waiting for an IP...
Machine "default" was started.
Waiting for SSH to be available...
Detecting the provisioner...
Started machines may have new IP addresses. You may need to re-run the
`docker-machine env` command.
```

Now, if I list my VMs again, I should see the following screenshot:

```
$ docker-machine ls
NAME      ACTIVE   DRIVER   STATE     URL                        SWARM   DOCKER    ERRORS
default    -       hyperv   Running   tcp://192.168.8.104:2376           v19.03.4
```

List of all VMs running in Hyper-V

If we do not have a VM called `default` yet, we can easily create one using the `create` command:

```
docker-machine create --driver virtualbox default
```

This results in the following output:

```
$ docker-machine create --driver virtualbox default
Running pre-create checks...
Creating machine...
(default) Copying /Users/gabriel/.docker/machine/cache/boot2docker.iso to /Users/gabriel/.docker/n
(default) Creating VirtualBox VM...
(default) Creating SSH key...
(default) Starting the VM...
(default) Check network to re-create if needed...
(default) Waiting for an IP...
Waiting for machine to be running, this may take a few minutes...
Detecting operating system of created instance...
Waiting for SSH to be available...
Detecting the provisioner...
Provisioning with boot2docker...
Copying certs to the local machine directory...
Copying certs to the remote machine...
Setting Docker configuration on the remote daemon...
Checking connection to Docker...
Docker is up and running!
To see how to connect your Docker Client to the Docker Engine running on this virtual machine, rur
$
```

Output of docker-machine create

We can see in the preceding output how `docker-machine` creates the VM from an ISO image, defines SSH keys and certificates, and copies them to the VM and to the local `~/.docker/machine` directory, where we will use it later when we want to remotely access this VM through the Docker CLI. It also provisions an IP address for the new VM.

We're using the `docker-machine create` command with the `--driver virtualbox` parameter. The docker-machine can also work with other drivers such as Hyper-V, AWS, Azure, DigitalOcean, and many more. Please see the documentation of `docker-machine` for more information. By default, a new VM gets 1 GB of memory associated, which is enough to use this VM as a node for a development or test Swarm.

If you're on Windows 10 with Docker for Desktop, use the
`hyperv` driver instead. To be successful though, you need to run as
Administrator. Furthermore, you need to have an external virtual switch
defined on Hyper-V first. You can use the Hyper-V Manager to do so. The
output of the command will look very similar to the one for
the `virtualbox` driver.

Now, let's create five VMs for a five-node Swarm. We can use a bit of scripting to reduce
the manual work:

```
$ for NODE in `seq 1 5`; do
   docker-machine create --driver virtualbox "node-${NODE}"
done
```

The `docker-machine` will now create five VMs with the names `node-1` to `node-5`. This
might take a few moments, so this is a good time to get yourself a hot cup of tea. After the
VMs are created, we can list them:

```
$ docker-machine ls
NAME       ACTIVE   DRIVER       STATE     URL                            SWARM   DOCKER        ERRORS
default    -        virtualbox   Running   tcp://192.168.99.100:2376              v17.12.1-ce
node-1     -        virtualbox   Running   tcp://192.168.99.101:2376              v17.12.1-ce
node-2     -        virtualbox   Running   tcp://192.168.99.102:2376              v17.12.1-ce
node-3     -        virtualbox   Running   tcp://192.168.99.103:2376              v17.12.1-ce
node-4     -        virtualbox   Running   tcp://192.168.99.104:2376              v17.12.1-ce
node-5     -        virtualbox   Running   tcp://192.168.99.105:2376              v17.12.1-ce
$
```

List of all the VMs we need for the Swarm

Now, we're ready to build a Swarm. Technically, we could SSH into the first
VM `node-1` and initialize a Swarm and then SSH into all the other VMs and join them to
the Swarm leader. But this is not efficient. Let's again use a script that does all of the hard
work:

```
# get IP of Swarm leader
$ export IP=$(docker-machine ip node-1)
# init the Swarm
$ docker-machine ssh node-1 docker swarm init --advertise-addr $IP
# Get the Swarm join-token
$ export JOIN_TOKEN=$(docker-machine ssh node-1 \
    docker swarm join-token worker -q)
```

Now that we have the join token and the IP address of the Swarm leader, we can ask the other nodes to join the Swarm as follows:

```
$ for NODE in `seq 2 5`; do
    NODE_NAME="node-${NODE}"
    docker-machine ssh $NODE_NAME docker swarm join \
        --token $JOIN_TOKEN $IP:2377
done
```

To make the Swarm highly available, we can now promote, for example, node-2 and node-3 to become managers:

```
$ docker-machine ssh node-1 docker node promote node-2 node-3
Node node-2 promoted to a manager in the swarm.
Node node-3 promoted to a manager in the swarm.
```

Finally, we can list all of the nodes of the Swarm:

```
$ docker-machine ssh node-1 docker node ls
```

We should see the following:

List of all of the nodes of the Docker Swarm on VirtualBox

This is proof that we have just created a highly available Docker Swarm locally on our laptop or workstation. Let's pull all of our code snippets together and make the whole thing a bit more robust. The script will look as follows:

```
alias dm="docker-machine"
for NODE in `seq 1 5`; do
  NODE_NAME=node-${NODE}
  dm rm --force $NODE_NAME
  dm create --driver virtualbox $NODE_NAME
done
alias dms="docker-machine ssh"
export IP=$(docker-machine ip node-1)
dms node-1 docker swarm init --advertise-addr $IP;
export JOIN_TOKEN=$(dms node-1 docker swarm join-token worker -q);
```

```
for NODE in `seq 2 5`; do
  NODE_NAME="node-${NODE}"
  dms $NODE_NAME docker swarm join --token $JOIN_TOKEN $IP:2377
done;
dms node-1 docker node promote node-2 node-3
```

The preceding script first deletes (if present) and then recreates five VMs called `node-1` to `node-5`, and then initializes a Swarm on `node-1`. After that, the remaining four VMs are added to the Swarm, and finally, `node-2` and `node-3` are promoted to manager status to make the Swarm highly available. The whole script will take less than 5 minutes to execute and can be repeated as many times as desired. The complete script can be found in the repository, in the `docker-swarm` subfolder; it is called `create-swarm.sh`.

It is a highly recommended best practice to always script and hence automate operations.

Using Play with Docker to generate a Swarm

To experiment with Docker Swarm without having to install or configure anything locally on our computer, we can use **Play with Docker** (**PWD**). PWD is a website that can be accessed with a browser and that offers us the ability to create a Docker Swarm consisting of up to five nodes. It is definitely a playground, as the name implies, and the time for which we can use it is limited to four hours per session. We can open as many sessions as we want, but each session automatically ends after four hours. Other than that, it is a fully functional Docker environment that is ideal for tinkering with Docker or to demonstrate some features.

Let's access the site now. In your browser, navigate to the website `https://labs.play-with-docker.com`. You will be presented with a welcome and login screen. Use your Docker ID to log in. After successfully going so, you will be presented with a screen that looks like the following screenshot:

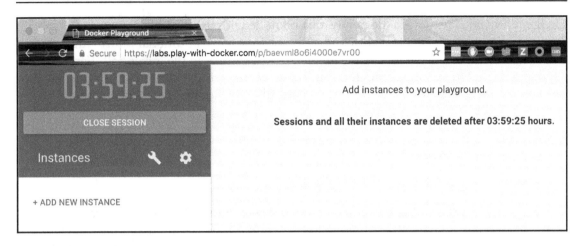

Play with Docker window

As we can see immediately, there is a big timer counting down from four hours. That's how much time we have left to play in this session. Furthermore, we see a **+ ADD NEW INSTANCE** link. Click it to create a new Docker host. When you do that, your screen should look like the following screenshot:

PWD with one new node

On the left-hand side, we see the newly created node with its IP address (`192.168.0.48`) and its name (`node1`). On the right-hand side, we have some additional information about this new node in the upper half of the screen and a Terminal in the lower half. Yes, this Terminal is used to execute commands on this node that we just created. This node has the Docker CLI installed, and hence we can execute all of the familiar Docker commands on it such as `docker version`. Try it out.

But now we want to create a Docker Swarm. Execute the following command in the Terminal in your browser:

```
$ docker swarm init --advertise-addr=eth0
```

The output generated by the preceding command corresponds to what we already know from our previous trials with the one-node cluster on our workstation and the local cluster using VirtualBox or Hyper-V. The important information, once again, is the `join` command that we want to use to join additional nodes to the cluster we just created.

You might have noted that this time we specified the `--advertise-addr` parameter in the Swarm `init` command. *Why is that necessary here?* The reason is that the nodes generated by PWD have more than one IP address associated with them. We can easily verify that by executing the `ip a` command on the node. This command will show us that there are indeed two endpoints, `eth0` and `eth1`, present. We hence have to specify explicitly to the new to-be swarm manager which one we want to use. In our case, it is `eth0`.

Create four additional nodes in PWD by clicking four times on the **+ ADD NEW INSTANCE** link. The new nodes will be called `node2`, `node3`, `node4`, and `node5` and will all be listed on the left-hand side. If you click on one of the nodes on the left-hand side, then the right-hand side shows the details of the respective node and a Terminal window for that node.

Select each node (2 to 5) and execute the `docker swarm join` command that you have copied from the leader node (`node1`) in the respective Terminal:

Joining a node to the Swarm in PWD

Once you have joined all four nodes to the Swarm, switch back to `node1` and list all nodes, which, unsurprisingly, results in this:

List of all of the nodes of the swarm in PWD

Still on `node1`, we can now promote, say, `node2` and `node3`, to make the Swarm highly available:

```
$ docker node promote node2 node3
Node node2 promoted to a manager in the swarm.
Node node3 promoted to a manager in the swarm.
```

With this, our Swarm on PWD is ready to accept a workload. We have created a highly available Docker Swarm with three manager nodes that form a Raft consensus group and two worker nodes.

Creating a Docker Swarm in the cloud

All of the Docker Swarms we have created so far are wonderful to use in development or to experiment or to use for demonstration purposes. If we want to create a Swarm that can be used as a production environment where we run our mission-critical applications, though, then we need to create a—I'm tempted to say—real Swarm in the cloud or on premises. In this book, we are going to demonstrate how to create a Docker Swarm in AWS.

One way to create a Swarm is by using **docker-machine** (**DM**). DM has a driver for AWS. If we have an account on AWS, we need the AWS access key ID and the AWS secret access key. We can add those two values to a file called `~/.aws/configuration`. It should look like the following:

```
[default]
aws_access_key_id = AKID1234567890
aws_secret_access_key = MY-SECRET-KEY
```

Every time we run `docker-machine create`, DM will look up those values in that file. For more in-depth information on how to get an AWS account and how to obtain the two secret keys, please consult this link: `http://dockr.ly/2FFelyT`.

Once we have an AWS account in place and have stored the access keys in the configuration file, we can start building our Swarm. The necessary code looks exactly the same as the one we used to create a Swarm on our local machine in VirtualBox. Let's start with the first node:

```
$ docker-machine create --driver amazonec2 \
    --amazonec2-region us-east-1 aws-node-1
```

This will create an EC2 instance called `aws-node-1` in the requested region (`us-east-1` in my case). The output of the preceding command looks like the following screenshot:

```
▶ ~ docker-machine create --driver amazonec2 aws-node-1
Running pre-create checks...
Creating machine...
(aws-node-1) Launching instance...
Waiting for machine to be running, this may take a few minutes...
Detecting operating system of created instance...
Waiting for SSH to be available...
Detecting the provisioner...
Provisioning with ubuntu(systemd)...
Installing Docker...
Copying certs to the local machine directory...
Copying certs to the remote machine...
Setting Docker configuration on the remote daemon...
Checking connection to Docker...
Docker is up and running!
To see how to connect your Docker Client to the Docker Engine running on this virtual machine, run: docker-machine env aws-node-1
▶ ~ █
```

Creating a swarm node on AWS with DM

It looks very similar to the output we already know from working with VirtualBox. We can now configure our Terminal for remote access to that EC2 instance:

```
$ eval $(docker-machine env aws-node-1)
```

This will configure the environment variables used by the Docker CLI accordingly:

```
▶ ~ export | grep DOCKER
DOCKER_CERT_PATH=/Users/gabriel/.docker/machine/machines/aws-node-1
DOCKER_HOST=tcp://35.172.240.127:2376
DOCKER_MACHINE_NAME=aws-node-1
DOCKER_TLS_VERIFY=1
▶ ~ █
```

Environment variables used by Docker to enable remote access to the AWS EC2 node

For security reasons, **Transport Layer Security (TLS)** is used for the communication between our CLI and the remote node. The certificates necessary for that were copied by DM to the path we assigned to the environment variable DOCKER_CERT_PATH.

All Docker commands that we now execute in our Terminal will be remotely executed in AWS on our EC2 instance. Let's try to run Nginx on this node:

```
$ docker container run -d -p 8000:80 nginx:alpine
```

We can use docker container ls to verify that the container is running. If so, then let's test it using curl:

```
$ curl -4 <IP address>:8000
```

Here, `<IP address>` is the public IP address of the AWS node; in my case, it would be `35.172.240.127`. Sadly, this doesn't work; the preceding command times out:

```
➤ ~ curl -4 35.172.240.127:8000
curl: (7) Failed to connect to 35.172.240.127 port 8000: Operation timed out
➤ ~
```

Accessing Nginx on the AWS node times out

The reason for this is that our node is part of an AWS **Security Group** (**SG**). By default, access to objects inside this SG is denied. Hence, we have to find out to which SG our instance belongs and configure access explicitly. For this, we typically use the AWS console. Go to the **EC2 Dashboard** and select **Instances** on the left-hand side. Locate the EC2 instance called `aws-node-1` and select it. In the details view, under **Security groups,** click on the **docker-machine** link, as shown in the following screenshot:

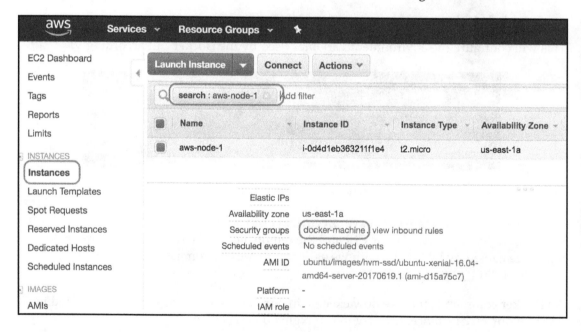

Locating the SG to which our Swarm node belongs

This will lead us to the SG page with the `docker-machine` SG pre-selected. In the details section under the **Inbound** tab, add a new rule for your IP address (the IP address of workstation):

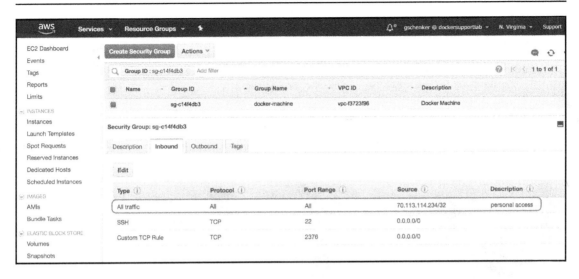

Open access to SG for our computer

In the preceding screenshot, the IP address `70.113.114.234` happens to be the one assigned to my personal workstation. I have enabled all inbound traffic coming from this IP address to the `docker-machine` SG. Note that in a production system you should be very careful about which ports of the SG to open to the public. Usually, it is ports `80` and `443` for HTTP and HTTPS access. Everything else is a potential invitation to hackers.

You can get your own IP address through a service such as `https://www.whatismyip.com/`. Now, if we execute the `curl` command again, the greeting page of Nginx is returned.

Before we leave the SG, we should add another rule to it. The Swarm nodes need to be able to freely communicate on ports `7946` and `4789` through TCP and UDP and on port `2377` through TCP. We could now add five rules with these requirements where the source is the SG itself, or we just define a crude rule that allows all inbound traffic inside the SG (`sg-c14f4db3` in my case):

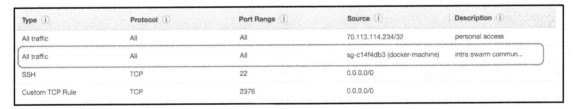

SG rule to enable intra-Swarm communication

Now, let's continue with the creation of the remaining four nodes. Once again, we can use a script to ease the process:

```
$ for NODE in `seq 2 5`; do
    docker-machine create --driver amazonec2 \
        --amazonec2-region us-east-1 aws-node-${NODE}
done
```

After the provisioning of the nodes is done, we can list all nodes with DM. In my case, I see this:

```
⟼ ~ docker-machine ls
NAME        ACTIVE   DRIVER       STATE     URL                          SWARM   DOCKER       ERRORS
aws-node-1  *        amazonec2    Running   tcp://35.172.240.127:2376            v18.02.0-ce
aws-node-2  -        amazonec2    Running   tcp://54.236.40.1:2376               v18.02.0-ce
aws-node-3  -        amazonec2    Running   tcp://34.205.171.56:2376             v18.02.0-ce
aws-node-4  -        amazonec2    Running   tcp://34.239.93.22:2376              v18.02.0-ce
aws-node-5  -        amazonec2    Running   tcp://52.205.26.218:2376             v18.02.0-ce
node-1      -        virtualbox   Running   tcp://192.168.99.100:2376            v17.12.1-ce
node-2      -        virtualbox   Running   tcp://192.168.99.101:2376            v17.12.1-ce
node-3      -        virtualbox   Running   tcp://192.168.99.102:2376            v17.12.1-ce
node-4      -        virtualbox   Running   tcp://192.168.99.103:2376            v17.12.1-ce
node-5      -        virtualbox   Running   tcp://192.168.99.104:2376            v17.12.1-ce
⟼ ~
```

List of all the nodes created by DM

In the preceding screenshot, we can see the five nodes that we originally created in VirtualBox and the five new nodes that we created in AWS. Apparently, the nodes on AWS are using a new version of Docker; here, the version is 18.02.0-ce. The IP addresses we see in the URL column are the public IP addresses of my EC2 instances.

Because our CLI is still configured for remote access to the aws-node-1 node, we can just run the swarm init command as follows:

```
$ docker swarm init
```

To get the join token do the following:

```
$ export JOIN_TOKEN=$(docker swarm join-token -q worker)
```

To get the IP address of the leader use the following command:

```
$ export LEADER_ADDR=$(docker node inspect \
    --format "{{.ManagerStatus.Addr}}" self)
```

With this information, we can now join the other four nodes to the Swarm leader:

```
$ for NODE in `seq 2 5`; do
    docker-machine ssh aws-node-${NODE} \
       sudo docker swarm join --token ${JOIN_TOKEN} ${LEADER_ADDR}
done
```

An alternative way to achieve the same without needing to SSH into the individual nodes would be to reconfigure our client CLI every time we want to access a different node:

```
$ for NODE in `seq 2 5`; do
    eval $(docker-machine env aws-node-${NODE})
    docker swarm join --token ${JOIN_TOKEN} ${LEADER_ADDR}
done
```

As a last step, we want to promote nodes 2 and 3 to manager:

```
$ eval $(docker-machine env node-1)
$ docker node promote aws-node-2 aws-node-3
```

We can then list all of the Swarm nodes, as shown in the following screenshot:

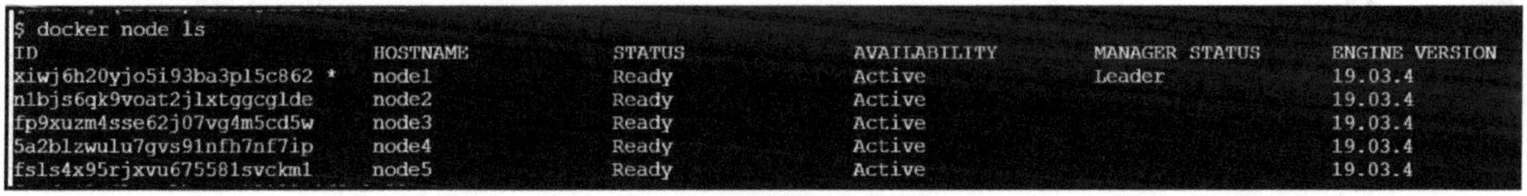

List of all nodes of our swarm in the cloud

And hence we have a highly available Docker Swarm running in the cloud. To clean up the Swarm in the cloud and avoid incurring unnecessary costs, we can use the following command:

```
$ for NODE in `seq 1 5`; do
    docker-machine rm -f aws-node-${NODE}
done
```

Deploying a first application

We have created a few Docker Swarms on various platforms. Once created, a Swarm behaves the same way on any platform. The way we deploy and update applications on a Swarm is not platform-dependent. It has been one of Docker's main goals to avoid vendor lock-in when using a Swarm. Swarm-ready applications can be effortlessly migrated from, say, a Swarm running on premises to a cloud-based Swarm. It is even technically possible to run part of a Swarm on premises and another part in the cloud. It works, yet we have, of course, to consider possible side effects due to the higher latency between nodes in geographically distant areas.

Now that we have a highly available Docker Swarm up and running, it is time to run some workloads on it. I'm using a local Swarm created with docker-machine. We'll start by first creating a single service. For this, we need to SSH into one of the manager nodes. I select `node-1`:

```
$ docker-machine ssh node-1
```

Creating a service

A service can be either created as part of a stack or directly using the Docker CLI. Let's first look at a sample stack file that defines a single service:

```
version: "3.7"
services:
  whoami:
    image: training/whoami:latest
    networks:
      - test-net
    ports:
      - 81:8000
    deploy:
      replicas: 6
      update_config:
        parallelism: 2
        delay: 10s
      labels:
        app: sample-app
        environment: prod-south

networks:
  test-net:
    driver: overlay
```

In the preceding example, we see what the desired state of a service called `whoami` is:

- It is based on the `training/whoami:latest` image.
- Containers of the service are attached to the `test-net` network.
- The container port `8000` is published to port `81`.
- It is running with six replicas (or tasks)
- During a rolling update, the individual tasks are updated in batches of two, with a delay of 10 seconds between each successful batch.
- The service (and its tasks and containers) is assigned the two labels `app` and `environment` with the values `sample-app` and `prod-south`, respectively

There are many more settings that we could define for a service, but the preceding ones are some of the more important ones. Most settings have meaningful default values. If, for example, we do not specify the number of replicas, then Docker defaults it to `1`. The name and image of a service are, of course, mandatory. Note that the name of the service must be unique in the Swarm.

To create the preceding service, we use the `docker stack deploy` command. Assuming that the file in which the preceding content is stored is called `stack.yaml`, we have the following:

```
$ docker stack deploy -c stack.yaml sample-stack
```

Here, we have created a stack called `sample-stack` that consists of one service, `whoami`. We can list all stacks on our Swarm, whereupon we should get this:

```
$ docker stack ls
NAME               SERVICES
sample-stack       1
```

If we list the services defined in our Swarm, we get the following output:

List of all services running in the Swarm

In the output, we can see that currently, we have only one service running, which was to be expected. The service has an ID. The format of ID, contrary to what you have used so far for containers, networks, or volumes, is alphanumeric (in the latter cases it was always sha256). We can also see that NAME of the service is a combination of the service name we defined in the stack file and the name of the stack, which is used as a prefix. This makes sense since we want to be able to deploy multiple stacks (with different names) using the same stack file into our Swarm. To make sure that service names are unique, Docker decided to combine service name and stack name.

In the third column, we see the mode, which is replicated. The number of REPLICAS is shown as 6/6. This tells us that six out of the six requested REPLICAS are running. This corresponds to the desired state. In the output, we also see the image that the service uses and the port mappings of the service.

Inspecting the service and its tasks

In the preceding output, we cannot see the details of the 6 replicas that have been created. To get some deeper insight into that, we can use the docker service ps command. If we execute this command for our service, we will get the following output:

```
docker@node-1:~$ docker service ps sample-stack_whoami
ID              NAME                    IMAGE                   NODE      DESIRED STATE   CURRENT STATE           ERROR     PORTS
mtvvunqieacg    sample-stack_whoami.1   training/whoami:latest  node-5    Running         Running 26 seconds ago
n21e7ktyvo4b    sample-stack_whoami.2   training/whoami:latest  node-1    Running         Running 26 seconds ago
lozzitfydlad    sample-stack_whoami.3   training/whoami:latest  node-2    Running         Running 27 seconds ago
xyml0hw68639    sample-stack_whoami.4   training/whoami:latest  node-2    Running         Running 27 seconds ago
yn8418fc83el    sample-stack_whoami.5   training/whoami:latest  node-3    Running         Running 28 seconds ago
3hvu4qul0dzs    sample-stack_whoami.6   training/whoami:latest  node-4    Running         Running 27 seconds ago
docker@node-1:~$
```

Details of the whoami service

In the preceding output, we can see the list of six tasks that correspond to the requested six replicas of our whoami service. In the NODE column, we can also see the node to which each task has been deployed. The name of each task is a combination of the service name plus an increasing index. Also note that, similar to the service itself, each task gets an alphanumeric ID assigned.

In my case, apparently task 2, with the name `sample-stack_whoami.2`, has been deployed to `node-1`, which is the leader of our Swarm. Hence, I should find a container running on this node. Let's see what we get if we list all containers running on `node-1`:

List of containers on node-1

As expected, we find a container running from the `training/whoami:latest` image with a name that is a combination of its parent task name and ID. We can try to visualize the whole hierarchy of objects that we generated when deploying our sample stack:

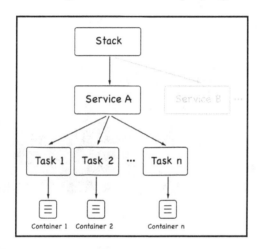

Object hierarchy of a Docker Swarm stack

A **stack** can consist of one to many services. Each service has a collection of tasks. Each task has a one-to-one association with a container. Stacks and services are created and stored on the Swarm manager nodes. Tasks are then scheduled to Swarm worker nodes, where the worker node creates the corresponding container. We can also get some more information about our service by inspecting it. Execute the following command:

```
$ docker service inspect sample-stack_whoami
```

This provides a wealth of information about all of the relevant settings of the service. This includes those we have explicitly defined in our `stack.yaml` file, but also those that we didn't specify and that therefore got their default values assigned. We're not going to list the whole output here, as it is too long, but I encourage the reader to inspect it on their own machine. We will discuss part of the information in more detail in the *The swarm routing mesh* section.

Logs of a service

In an earlier chapter, we worked with the logs produced by a container. Here, we're concentrating on a service. Remember that, ultimately, a service with many replicas has many containers running. Hence, we would expect that, if we ask the service for its logs, Docker returns an aggregate of all logs of those containers belonging to the service. And indeed, that's what we get if we use the `docker service logs` command:

```
docker@node-1:~$ docker service logs sample-stack_whoami
sample-stack_whoami.2.n21e7ktyvo4b@node-1    | Listening on :8000
sample-stack_whoami.1.mtvvunqieacg@node-5    | Listening on :8000
sample-stack_whoami.6.3hvu4qul0dzs@node-4    | Listening on :8000
sample-stack_whoami.4.xymlohw68639@node-2    | Listening on :8000
sample-stack_whoami.3.lozzitfydlad@node-2    | Listening on :8000
sample-stack_whoami.5.yn84l8fc83el@node-3    | Listening on :8000
docker@node-1:~$
```

Logs of the whoami service

There is not much information in the logs at this point, but it is enough to discuss what we get. The first part of each line in the log always contains the name of the container combined with the node name from which the log entry originates. Then, separated by the vertical bar (|), we get the actual log entry. So, if we would, say, ask for the logs of the first container in the list directly, we would only get a single entry, and the value we would see in this case would be `Listening on :8000`.

The aggregated logs that we get with the `docker service logs` command are not sorted in any particular way. So, if the correlation of events is happening in different containers, you should add information to your log output that makes this correlation possible. Typically, this is a timestamp for each log entry. But this has to be done at the source; for example, the application that produces a log entry needs to also make sure a timestamp is added.

We can as well query the logs of an individual task of the service by providing the task ID instead of the service ID or name. So, querying the logs from task 2 gives us the following output:

```
docker@node-1:~$ docker service logs n21e7ktyvo4b
sample-stack_whoami.2.n21e7ktyvo4b@node-1    | Listening on :8000
docker@node-1:~$
```

Logs of an individual task of the whoami service

Reconciling the desired state

We have learned that a Swarm service is a description or manifest of the desired state that we want an application or application service to run in. Now, let's see how Docker Swarm reconciles this desired state if we do something that causes the actual state of the service to be different from the desired state. The easiest way to do this is to forcibly kill one of the tasks or containers of the service.

Let's do this with the container that has been scheduled on `node-1`:

```
$ docker container rm -f sample-stack_whoami.2.n21e7ktyvo4b2sufalk0aibzy
```

If we do that and then do `docker service ps` right afterward, we will see the following output:

Docker Swarm reconciling the desired state after one task failed

We see that task 2 failed with exit code `137` and that the Swarm immediately reconciled the desired state by rescheduling the failed task on a node with free resources. In this case, the scheduler selected the same node as the failed tasks, but this is not always the case. So, without us intervening, the Swarm completely fixed the problem, and since the service is running in multiple replicas, at no time was the service down.

Let's try another failure scenario. This time we're going to shut down an entire node and are going to see how the Swarm reacts. Let's take `node-2` for this, as it has two tasks (tasks 3 and 4) running on it. For this, we need to open a new Terminal window and use `docker-machine` to stop `node-2`:

```
$ docker-machine stop node-2
```

Back on `node-1`, we can now again run `docker service ps` to see what happened:

Swarm reschedules all tasks of a failed node

In the preceding screenshot, we can see that immediately task 3 was rescheduled on `node-1` while task 4 was rescheduled on `node-3`. Even this more radical failure is handled gracefully by Docker Swarm.

It is important to note though that if `node-2` ever comes back online in the Swarm, the tasks that had previously been running on it will not automatically be transferred back to it. But the node is now ready for a new workload.

Deleting a service or a stack

If we want to remove a particular service from the Swarm, we can use the `docker service rm` command. If, on the other hand, we want to remove a stack from the Swarm, we analogously use the `docker stack rm` command. This command removes all services that are part of the stack definition. In the case of the `whoami` service, it was created by using a stack file and hence we're going to use the latter command:

```
docker@node-1:~$ docker stack rm sample-stack
Removing service sample-stack_whoami
Removing network sample-stack_test-net
docker@node-1:~$
```

Removing a stack

The preceding command will make sure that all tasks of each service of the stack are terminated, and the corresponding containers are stopped by first sending SIGTERM, and then, if not successful, SIGKILL after 10 seconds of timeout.

It is important to note that the stopped containers are not removed from the Docker host. Hence, it is advised to purge containers from time to time on worker nodes to reclaim unused resources. Use docker container purge -f for this purpose.

 Question: Why does it make sense to leave stopped or crashed containers on the worker node and not automatically remove them?

Deploying a multi-service stack

In Chapter 11, *Docker Compose*, we used an application consisting of two services that were declaratively described in a Docker compose file. We can use this compose file as a template to create a stack file that allows us to deploy the same application into a Swarm. The content of our stack file, called pet-stack.yaml, looks like this:

```
version: "3.7"
services:
  web:
    image: fundamentalsofdocker/ch11-web:2.0
    networks:
    - pets-net
    ports:
    - 3000:3000
    deploy:
      replicas: 3
  db:
    image: fundamentalsofdocker/ch11-db:2.0
    networks:
    - pets-net
    volumes:
    - pets-data:/var/lib/postgresql/data

volumes:
  pets-data:

networks:
  pets-net:
  driver: overlay
```

We request that the `web` service has three replicas, and both services are attached to the overlay network, `pets-net`. We can deploy this application using the `docker stack deploy` command:

```
docker@node-1:~$ docker stack deploy -c pet-stack.yaml pets
Creating network pets_pets-net
Creating service pets_db
Creating service pets_web
docker@node-1:~$ 4
```

Deploy the pets stack

Docker creates the `pets_pets-net` overlay network and then the two services `pets_web` and `pets_db`. We can then list all of the tasks in the `pets` stack:

```
$ docker stack ps pets
ID             NAME         IMAGE                                NODE     DESIRED STATE    CURRENT STATE           ERRO
h9z90us6qy6i   pets db.1    fundamentalsofdocker/ch11-db:2.0     node4    Running          Running 5 seconds ago
u14wevitw9mq   pets web.1   fundamentalsofdocker/ch11-web:2.0    node2    Running          Running 4 seconds ago
qsf7wbqwwr9g   pets web.2   fundamentalsofdocker/ch11-web:2.0    node3    Running          Running 4 seconds ago
umza51f7beqs   pets web.3   fundamentalsofdocker/ch11-web:2.0    node1    Running          Running 4 seconds ago
```

List of all of the tasks in the pets stack

Finally, let's test the application using `curl`. And, indeed, the application works as expected:

```
$ curl localhost:3000/pet
<html>
<head>
    <link rel="stylesheet" href="css/main.css">
</head>
<body>
    <div class="container">
        <h4>Animal of the day</h4>
        <img src="images&#x2F;male-lion.png"" />
        <p><small>Photo taken at <a href="https://www.maasaimara.com/">Massai Mara National Park</a></small></p>
        <p>Delivered to you by container 8b906b509a7e<p>
    </div>
</body>
</html>[node1] (local) root@192.168.0.33 ~
```

Testing the pets application using curl

The container ID is in the output, where it says `Delivered to you by container 8b906b509a7e`. If you run the `curl` command multiple times, the ID should cycle between three different values. These are the IDs of the three containers (or replicas) that we have requested for the `web` service.

Once we're done, we can remove the stack with `docker stack rm pets`.

The swarm routing mesh

If you have been paying attention, then you might have noticed something interesting in the last section. We had the `pets` application deployed and it resulted in the fact that an instance of the `web` service was installed on the three nodes, `node-1`, `node-2`, and `node-3`. Yet, we were able to access the `web` service on `node-1` with `localhost` and we reached each container from there. *How is that possible?* Well, this is due to the so-called Swarm routing mesh. The routing mesh makes sure that when we publish a port of a service; that port is then published on all nodes of the Swarm. Hence, network traffic that hits any node of the Swarm and requests to use a specific port will be forwarded to one of the service containers by the routing mesh. Let's look at the following diagram to see how that works:

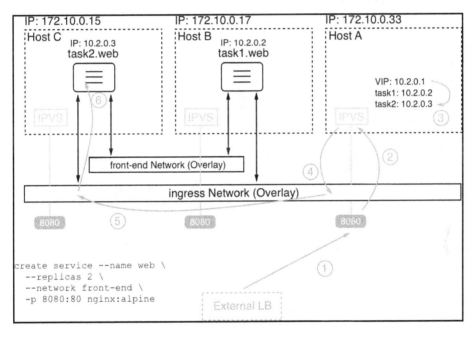

Docker Swarm routing mesh

In this situation, we have three nodes, called **Host A** to **Host C**, with the IP addresses `172.10.0.15`, `172.10.0.17`, and `172.10.0.33`. In the lower-left corner of the diagram, we see the command that created a **web** service with two replicas. The corresponding tasks have been scheduled on **Host B** and **Host C**. Task 1 landed on **Host B** while task 2 landed on **Host C**.

When a service is created on Docker Swarm, it automatically gets a **Virtual IP** (**VIP**) address assigned. This IP address is stable and reserved during the whole life cycle of the service. Let's assume that in our case the VIP is 10.2.0.1.

If now a request for port 8080 coming from an external **Load Balancer** (**LB**) is targeted at one of the nodes of our Swarm, then this request is handled by the Linux **IP Virtual Server** (**IPVS**) service on that node. This service makes a lookup with the given port 8080 in the IP table and will find that this corresponds to the VIP of the **web** service. Now, since the VIP is not a real target, the IPVS service will load balance the IP addresses of the tasks that are associated with this service. In our case, it picked task 2, with the IP address, 10.2.0.3. Finally, the **ingress Network** (**Overlay**) is used to forward the request to the target container on **Host C**.

It is important to note that it doesn't matter which Swarm node the external request is forwarded to by the **External LB**. The routing mesh will always handle the request correctly and forward it to one of the tasks of the targeted service.

Summary

In this chapter, we introduced Docker Swarm, which, next to Kubernetes, is the second most popular orchestrator for containers. We have looked into the architecture of a Swarm, discussed all of the types of resources running in a Swarm, such as services, tasks, and more, and we have created services in the Swarm and deployed an application that consists of multiple related services.

In the next chapter, we are going to explore how to deploy services or applications onto a Docker Swarm with zero downtime and automatic rollback capabilities. We are also going to introduce secrets as a means to protect sensitive information.

Questions

To assess your learning progress, please answer the following questions:

1. How do you initialize a new Docker Swarm?
   A. `docker init swarm`
   B. `docker swarm init --advertise-addr <IP address>`
   C. `docker swarm join --token <join token>`

2. You want to remove a worker node from a Docker Swarm. What steps are necessary?

3. How do you create an overlay network called `front-tier`? Make the network attachable.

4. How would you create a service called `web` from the `nginx:alpine` image with five replicas, which exposes port `3000` on the ingress network and is attached to the `front-tier` network?

5. How would you scale the web service down to three instances?

Further reading

Please consult the following link for more in-depth information about selected topics:

- AWS EC2 example at `http://dockr.ly/2FFelyT`
- The Raft Consensus Algorithm at `https://raft.github.io/`
- The Gossip Protocol at `https://en.wikipedia.org/wiki/Gossip_protocol`
- VXLAN and Linux at `https://vincent.bernat.ch/en/blog/2017-vxlan-linux`

14
Zero-Downtime Deployments and Secrets

In the previous chapter, we explored Docker Swarm and its resources in detail. We learned how to build a highly available swarm locally and in the cloud. Then, we discussed Swarm services and stacks in depth. Finally, we created services and stacks in the swarm.

In this chapter, we will show you how we can update services and stacks running in Docker Swarm without interrupting their availability. This is called zero-downtime deployment. We are also going to introduce swarm secrets as a means to securely provide sensitive information to containers of a service using those secrets.

In this chapter, we will cover the following topics:

- Zero-downtime deployment
- Storing configuration data in the swarm
- Protecting sensitive data with Docker Secrets

After finishing this chapter, you will be able to do the following:

- List two to three different deployment strategies commonly used to update a service without downtime.
- Update a service in batches without causing a service interruption.
- Define a rollback strategy for a service that is used if an update fails.
- Store non-sensitive configuration data using Docker configs.
- Use a Docker secret with a service.
- Update the value of a secret without causing downtime.

Technical requirements

The code files for this chapter can be found on GitHub at `https://github.com/
PacktPublishing/Learn-Docker---Fundamentals-of-Docker-19.x-Second-Edition`. If
you have checked out the repository as indicated in `Chapter 2`, *Setting up a Working
Environment*, then you'll find the code at `~/fod-solution/ch14`.

Zero-downtime deployment

One of the most important aspects of a mission-critical application that needs frequent
updates is the ability to do updates in a fashion that requires no outage at all. We call this a
zero-downtime deployment. At all times, the application that is updated must be fully
operational.

Popular deployment strategies

There are various ways to achieve this. Some of them are as follows:

- Rolling updates
- Blue-green deployments
- Canary releases

Docker Swarm supports rolling updates out of the box. The other two types of deployments
can be achieved with some extra effort from our side.

Rolling updates

In a mission-critical application, each application service has to run in multiple replicas.
Depending on the load, that can be as few as two to three instances and as many as dozens,
hundreds, or thousands of instances. At any given time, we want to have a clear majority
when it comes to all the service instances running. So, if we have three replicas, we want to
have at least two of them up and running at all times. If we have 100 replicas, we can be
content with a minimum of, say, 90 replicas, being available. By doing this, we can define a
batch size of replicas that we may take down to upgrade. In the first case, the batch size
would be 1 and in the second case, it would be 10.

When we take replicas down, Docker Swarm will automatically take those instances out of the load balancing pool and all traffic will be load balanced across the remaining active instances. Those remaining instances will thus experience a slight increase in traffic. In the following diagram, prior to the start of the rolling update, if **Task A3** wanted to access **Service B**, it could have been load balanced to any of the three tasks of **Service B** by SwarmKit. Once the rolling update started, SwarmKit took down **Task B1** for updates. Automatically, this task is then taken out of the pool of targets. So, if **Task A3** now requests to connect to **Service B**, load balancing will only select from the remaining tasks, that is, **B2** and **B3**. Thus, those two tasks might experience a higher load temporarily:

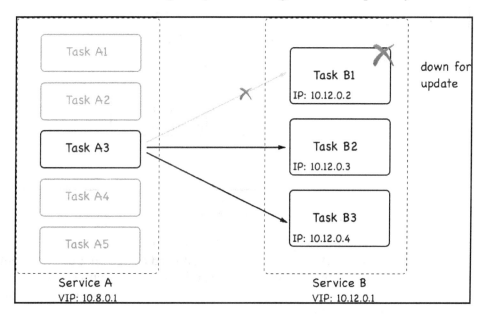

Task B1 is taken down to be updated

The stopped instances are then replaced by an equivalent number of new instances of the new version of the application service. Once the new instances are up and running, we can have the Swarm observe them for a given period of time and make sure they're healthy. If all is well, then we can continue by taking down the next batch of instances and replacing them with instances of the new version. This process is repeated until all the instances of the application service have been replaced.

In the following diagram, we can see that **Task B1** of **Service B** has been updated to version 2. The container of **Task B1** was assigned a new **IP** address, and it was deployed to another worker node with free resources:

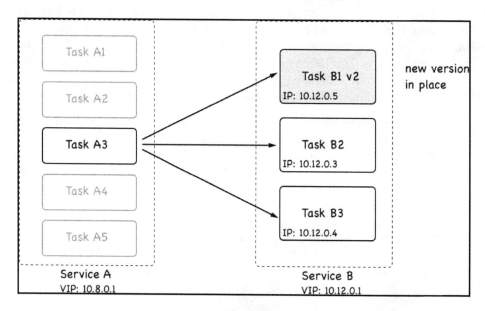

The first batch being updated in a rolling update

It is important to understand that when the task of a service is updated, in most cases, it gets deployed to a different worker node than the one it used to live on. But that should be fine as long as the corresponding service is stateless. If we have a stateful service that is location- or node-aware and we'd like to update it, then we have to adjust our approach, but this is outside of the scope of this book.

Now, let's look at how we can actually instruct the Swarm to perform a rolling update of an application service. When we declare a service in a stack file, we can define multiple options that are relevant in this context. Let's look at a snippet of a typical stack file:

```
version: "3.5"
services:
  web:
    image: nginx:alpine
    deploy:
      replicas: 10
      update_config:
        parallelism: 2
        delay: 10s
...
```

In this snippet, we can see a section, `update_config`, with the `parallelism` and `delay` properties. `parallelism` defines the batch size of how many replicas are going to be updated at a time during a rolling update. `delay` defines how long Docker Swarm is going to wait between updating individual batches. In the preceding case, we have `10` replicas that are being updated in two instances at a time and, between each successful update, Docker Swarm waits for `10` seconds.

Let's test such a rolling update. Navigate to the `ch14` subfolder of our `labs` folder and use the `stack.yaml` file to create a web service that's been configured for a rolling update. The service uses an Alpine-based Nginx image whose version is `1.12-alpine`. We will update the service to a newer version, that is, `1.13-alpine`.

To start, we will deploy this service to our swarm that we created locally in VirtualBox. Let's take a look:

1. First, we need to make sure that we have our Terminal window configured so that we can access one of the master nodes of our cluster. Let's take the leader, that is, `node-1`:

   ```
   $ eval $(docker-machine env node-1)
   ```

2. Now, we can deploy the service using the stack file:

   ```
   $ docker stack deploy -c stack.yaml web
   ```

   The output of the preceding command looks like this:

   ```
   $ docker stack deploy -c stack.yaml web
   Creating network web_default
   Creating service web_web
   $
   ```

   Deployment of the web stack

3. Once the service has been deployed, we can monitor it using the following command:

   ```
   $ watch docker stack ps web
   ```

We will see the following output:

```
Every 2.0s: docker stack ps web

ID                NAME          IMAGE              NODE      DESIRED STATE    CURRENT STATE            ERROR        PORTS
ze29yvu4jyyc      web_web.1     nginx:1.12-alpine  node-2    Running          Running 3 minutes ago
i1cy5v4o91d3      web_web.2     nginx:1.12-alpine  node-2    Running          Running 3 minutes ago
kzqylcub4a49      web_web.3     nginx:1.12-alpine  node-1    Running          Running 3 minutes ago
ynt8n4ke8yld      web_web.4     nginx:1.12-alpine  node-3    Running          Running 3 minutes ago
qai8xv1u9v1d      web_web.5     nginx:1.12-alpine  node-3    Running          Running 3 minutes ago
5inv9mkxlpkv      web_web.6     nginx:1.12-alpine  node-4    Running          Running 3 minutes ago
iyjntpgy6cwe      web_web.7     nginx:1.12-alpine  node-1    Running          Running 3 minutes ago
q230vi6rlwrv      web_web.8     nginx:1.12-alpine  node-5    Running          Running 3 minutes ago
nh6jm2fyzwre      web_web.9     nginx:1.12-alpine  node-3    Running          Running 3 minutes ago
iuu56iot6dxm      web_web.10    nginx:1.12-alpine  node-4    Running          Running 3 minutes ago
```

Service web of the web stack running in Swarm with 10 replicas

 If you're working on a macOS machine, you need to make sure your watch tool is installed. Use the `brew install watch` command to do so.

The previous command will continuously update the output and provide us with a good overview of what happens during the rolling update.

Now, we need to open a second Terminal and configure it for remote access for the manager node of our swarm. Once we have done that, we can execute the `docker` command, which will update the image of the `web` service of the stack, also called `web`:

```
$ docker service update --image nginx:1.13-alpine web_web
```

The preceding command leads to the following output, indicating the progress of the rolling update:

```
overall progress: 4 out of 10 tasks
1/10: running   [==================================================>]
2/10: running   [==================================================>]
3/10: running   [==================================================>]
4/10: running   [==================================================>]
5/10: preparing [=============================>                       ]
6/10: preparing [=============================>                       ]
7/10:
8/10:
9/10:
10/10:
```

Screen showing the progress of the rolling update

The preceding output indicates that the first two batches, each with two tasks, have been successful and that the third batch is preparing.

In the first Terminal window, where we're watching the stack, we should now see how Docker Swarm updates the service batch by batch with an interval of 10 seconds. After the first batch, it should look like the following screenshot:

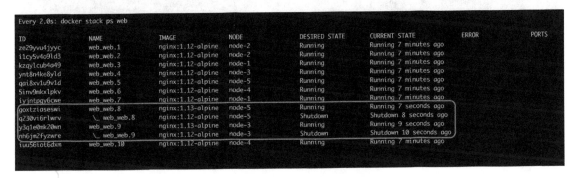

Rolling update for a service in Docker Swarm

In the preceding screenshot, we can see that the first batch of the two tasks, 8 and 9, has been updated. Docker Swarm is waiting for 10 seconds to proceed with the next batch.

It is interesting to note that in this particular case, SwarmKit deploys the new version of the task to the same node as the previous version. This is accidental since we have five nodes and two tasks on each node. SwarmKit always tries to balance the workload evenly across the nodes. So, when SwarmKit takes down a task, the corresponding node has a smaller workload than all the others, so the new instance is scheduled to it. Normally, you cannot expect to find the new instance of a task on the same node. Just try it out yourself by deleting the stack with docker stack rm web and changing the number of replicas to say, seven, and then redeploy and update it.

Once all the tasks have been updated, the output of our `docker stack ps web` command will look similar to the following screenshot:

```
Every 2.0s: docker stack ps web

ID              NAME            IMAGE               NODE      DESIRED STATE    CURRENT STATE                  ERROR       PORTS
v99yet3urtyf    web_web.1       nginx:1.13-alpine   node-2    Running          Running 2 minutes ago
ze29yvu4jyyc     \_ web_web.1   nginx:1.12-alpine   node-2    Shutdown         Shutdown 2 minutes ago
s6was0b36hoa    web_web.2       nginx:1.13-alpine   node-2    Running          Running 2 minutes ago
i1cy5v4o9ld3     \_ web_web.2   nginx:1.12-alpine   node-2    Shutdown         Shutdown 2 minutes ago
m2fvxq7yxfqc    web_web.3       nginx:1.13-alpine   node-1    Running          Running 2 minutes ago
kzqylcub4o49     \_ web_web.3   nginx:1.12-alpine   node-1    Shutdown         Shutdown 2 minutes ago
xsjjudndb7jm    web_web.4       nginx:1.13-alpine   node-3    Running          Running 2 minutes ago
ynt8n4ke8yld     \_ web_web.4   nginx:1.12-alpine   node-3    Shutdown         Shutdown 2 minutes ago
fuk4xpb5g5un    web_web.5       nginx:1.13-alpine   node-5    Running          Running about a minute ago
qai8xv1u9v1d     \_ web_web.5   nginx:1.12-alpine   node-5    Shutdown         Shutdown about a minute ago
ipa1sc5hee7d    web_web.6       nginx:1.13-alpine   node-4    Running          Running about a minute ago
5inv9mkxlpkv     \_ web_web.6   nginx:1.12-alpine   node-4    Shutdown         Shutdown about a minute ago
feyu3l2ufjgr    web_web.7       nginx:1.13-alpine   node-1    Running          Running 2 minutes ago
iyjntpgy6cwe     \_ web_web.7   nginx:1.12-alpine   node-1    Shutdown         Shutdown 2 minutes ago
goxtziaseswi    web_web.8       nginx:1.13-alpine   node-5    Running          Running 2 minutes ago
q230vi6rlwrv     \_ web_web.8   nginx:1.12-alpine   node-5    Shutdown         Shutdown 2 minutes ago
y3q1e0mk20wn    web_web.9       nginx:1.13-alpine   node-3    Running          Running 2 minutes ago
nh6jm2fyzwre     \_ web_web.9   nginx:1.12-alpine   node-3    Shutdown         Shutdown 2 minutes ago
7r93m02hhizg    web_web.10      nginx:1.13-alpine   node-4    Running          Running 2 minutes ago
iuu56iot6dxm     \_ web_web.10  nginx:1.12-alpine   node-4    Shutdown         Shutdown 2 minutes ago
```

All tasks have been updated successfully

Please note that SwarmKit does not immediately remove the containers of the previous versions of the tasks from the corresponding nodes. This makes sense as we might want to, for example, retrieve the logs from those containers for debugging purposes, or we might want to retrieve their metadata using `docker container inspect`. SwarmKit keeps the four latest terminated task instances around before it purges older ones so that it doesn't clog the system with unused resources.

> We can use the `--update-order` parameter to instruct Docker to start the new container replica before stopping the old one. This can improve application availability. Valid values are `"start-first"` and `"stop-first"`. The latter is the default.

Once we're done, we can tear down the stack using the following command:

```
$ docker stack rm web
```

Although using stack files to define and deploy applications is the recommended best practice, we can also define the update behavior in a service `create` statement. If we just want to deploy a single service, this might be the preferred way of doing things. Let's look at such a `create` command:

```
$ docker service create --name web \
    --replicas 10 \
    --update-parallelism 2 \
    --update-delay 10s \
    nginx:alpine
```

This command defines the same desired state as the preceding stack file. We want the service to run with `10` replicas and we want a rolling update to happen in batches of two tasks at a time, with a 10-second interval between consecutive batches.

Health checks

To make informed decisions, for example, during a rolling update of a Swarm service regarding whether or not the just-installed batch of new service instances is running OK or if a rollback is needed, the SwarmKit needs a way to know about the overall health of the system. On its own, SwarmKit (and Docker) can collect quite a bit of information. But there is a limit. Imagine a container containing an application. The container, as seen from the outside, can look absolutely healthy and carry on just fine. But that doesn't necessarily mean that the application running inside the container is also doing well. The application could, for example, be in an infinite loop or be in a corrupt state, yet still running. However, as long as the application runs, the container runs and from outside, everything looks perfect.

Thus, SwarmKit provides a seam where we can provide it with some help. We, the authors of the application services running inside the containers in the swarm, know best as to whether or not our service is in a healthy state. SwarmKit gives us the opportunity to define a command that is executed against our application service to test its health. What exactly this command does is not important to Swarm; the command just needs to return OK, NOT OK, or `time out`. The latter two situations, namely NOT OK or `timeout`, will tell SwarmKit that the task it is investigating is potentially unhealthy.

Here, I am writing potentially on purpose and later, we will see why:

```
FROM alpine:3.6
...
HEALTHCHECK --interval=30s \
    --timeout=10s
    --retries=3
    --start-period=60s
    CMD curl -f http://localhost:3000/health || exit 1
...
```

In the preceding snippet from a `Dockerfile`, we can see the keyword HEALTHCHECK. It has a few options or parameters and an actual command, that is, CMD. Let's discuss the options:

- `--interval`: Defines the wait time between health checks. Thus, in our case, the orchestrator executes a check every 30 seconds.

- `--timeout`: This parameter defines how long Docker should wait if the health check does not respond until it times out with an error. In our sample, this is 10 seconds. Now, if one health check fails, SwarmKit retries a couple of times until it gives up and declares the corresponding task as unhealthy and opens the door for Docker to kill this task and replace it with a new instance.

- The number of retries is defined with the `--retries` parameter. In the preceding code, we want to have three retries.

- Next, we have the start period. Some containers take some time to start up (not that this is a recommended pattern, but sometimes it is inevitable). During this startup time, the service instance might not be able to respond to health checks. With the start period, we can define how long SwarmKit should wait before it executes the very first health check and thus give the application time to initialize. To define the startup time, we use the `--start-period` parameter. In our case, we do the first check after 60 seconds. How long this start period needs to be depends on the application and its startup behavior. The recommendation is to start with a relatively low value and if you have a lot of false positives and tasks that are restarted many times, you might want to increase the time interval.

- Finally, we define the actual probing command on the last line with the CMD keyword. In our case, we are defining a request to the `/health` endpoint of `localhost` at port 3000 as a probing command. This call is expected to have three possible outcomes:
  - The command succeeds.
  - The command fails.
  - The command times out.

The latter two are treated the same way by SwarmKit. This is the orchestrator telling us that the corresponding task might be unhealthy. I did say *might* with intent since SwarmKit does not immediately assume the worst-case scenario but assumes that this might just be a temporary fluke of the task and that it will recover from it. This is the reason why we have a `--retries` parameter. There, we can define how many times SwarmKit should retry before it can assume that the task is indeed unhealthy, and consequently kill it and reschedule another instance of this task on another free node to reconcile the desired state of the service.

Why can we use localhost in our probing command? This is a very good question, and the reason is because SwarmKit, when probing a container running in the Swarm, executes this `probing` command inside the container (that is, it does something like `docker container exec <containerID> <probing command>`). Thus, the command executes in the same network namespace as the application running inside the container. In the following diagram, we can see the life cycle of a service task from its beginning:

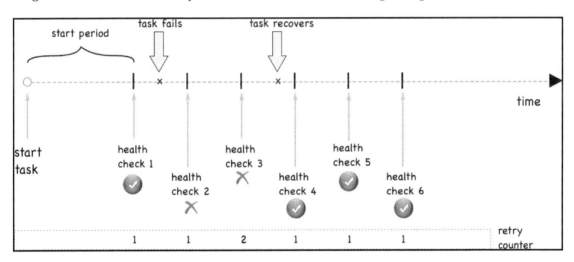

Service task with transient health failure

First, SwarmKit waits to probe until the start period is over. Then, we have our first health check. Shortly thereafter, the task fails when probed. It fails two consecutive times but then it recovers. Thus, **health check 4** is successful and SwarmKit leaves the task running.

Here, we can see a task that is permanently failing:

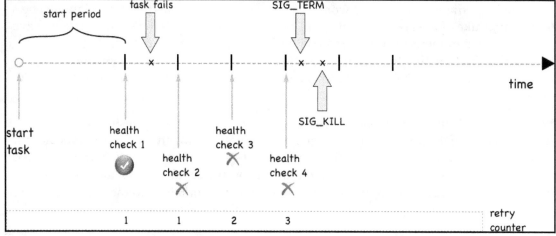

Permanent failure of a task

We have just learned how we can define a health check for a service in the `Dockerfile` of its image. But this is not the only way we can do this. We can also define the health check in the stack file that we use to deploy our application into Docker Swarm. Here is a short snippet of what such a stack file would look like:

```
version: "3.5"
services:
  web:
    image: example/web:1.0
    healthcheck:
      test: ["CMD", "curl", "-f", "http://localhost:3000/health"]
      interval: 30s
      timeout: 10s
      retries: 3
      start_period: 60s
  ...
```

In the preceding snippet, we can see how the health check-related information is defined in the stack file. First and foremost, it is important to realize that we have to define a health check for every service individually. There is no health check at an application or global level.

Similar to what we defined previously in the `Dockerfile`, the command that is used to execute the health check by SwarmKit is `curl -f http://localhost:3000/health`. We also have definitions for `interval`, `timeout`, `retries`, and `start_period`. These four key-value pairs have the same meaning as the corresponding parameters we used in the `Dockerfile`. If there are health check-related settings defined in the image, then the ones defined in the stack file override the ones from the `Dockerfile`.

Now, let's try to use a service that has a health check defined. In our `lab` folder, we have a file called `stack-health.yaml` with the following content:

```
version: "3.5"
services:
  web:
    image: nginx:alpine
    healthcheck:
      test: ["CMD", "wget", "-qO", "-", "http://localhost"]
      interval: 5s
      timeout: 2s
      retries: 3
      start_period: 15s
```

Let's deploy this:

```
$ docker stack deploy -c stack-health.yaml myapp
```

We can find out where the single task was deployed to using `docker stack ps myapp`. On that particular node, we can list all the containers to find one of our stacks. In my example, the task had been deployed to `node-3`:

Displaying the health status of a running task instance

The interesting thing in this screenshot is the `STATUS` column. Docker, or more precisely, SwarmKit, has recognized that the service has a health check function defined and is using it to determine the health of each task of the service.

Rollback

Sometimes, things don't go as expected. A last-minute fix in an application release may have inadvertently introduced a new bug, or the new version significantly decreases the throughput of the component, and so on. In such cases, we need to have a plan B, which in most cases means the ability to roll back the update to the previous good version.

As with the update, the rollback has to happen in such a way that it does not cause any outages in terms of the application; it needs to cause zero-downtime. In that sense, a rollback can be looked at as a reverse update. We are installing a new version, yet this new version is actually the previous version.

As with the update behavior, we can declare, either in our stack files or in the Docker service `create` command, how the system should behave in case it needs to execute a rollback. Here, we have the stack file that we used previously, but this time with some rollback-relevant attributes:

```
version: "3.5"
services:
  web:
    image: nginx:1.12-alpine
    ports:
      - 80:80
    deploy:
      replicas: 10
      update_config:
        parallelism: 2
        delay: 10s

        failure_action: rollback
        monitor: 10s

    healthcheck:
      test: ["CMD", "wget", "-qO", "-", "http://localhost"]
      interval: 2s
      timeout: 2s
      retries: 3
      start_period: 2s
```

In this stack file, which is available in our lab as `stack-rollback.yaml`, we defined the details about the rolling update, the health checks, and the behavior during rollback. The health check is defined so that after an initial wait time of 2 seconds, the orchestrator starts to poll the service on `http://localhost` every 2 seconds and it retries 3 times before it considers a task as unhealthy.

If we do the math, then it takes at least 8 seconds until a task will be stopped if it is unhealthy due to a bug. So, now under deploy, we have a new entry called `monitor`. This entry defines how long newly deployed tasks should be monitored for health and whether or not to continue with the next batch in the rolling update. Here, in this sample, we have given it `10` seconds. This is slightly more than the 8 seconds we calculated it takes to discover that a defective service has been deployed, so this is good.

We also have a new entry, `failure_action`, which defines what the orchestrator will do if it encounters a failure during the rolling update, such as that the service is unhealthy. By default, the action is just to stop the whole update process and leave the system in an intermediate state. The system is not down since it is a rolling update and at least some healthy instances of the service are still operational, but an operations engineer would be better at taking a look and fixing the problem.

In our case, we have defined the action to be a `rollback`. Thus, in case of failure, SwarmKit will automatically revert all tasks that have been updated back to their previous version.

Blue–green deployments

In `Chapter 9`, *Distributed Application Architecture*, we discussed what blue-green deployments are, in an abstract way. It turns out that, on Docker Swarm, we cannot really implement blue-green deployments for arbitrary services. The service discovery and load balancing between two services running in Docker Swarm are part of the Swarm routing mesh and cannot be (easily) customized.

If **Service A** wants to call **Service B**, then Docker does this implicitly. Docker, given the name of the target service, will use the Docker **DNS** service to resolve this name to a **virtual IP** (**VIP**) address. When the request is then targeted at the **VIP**, the Linux **IPVS** service will do another lookup in the Linux kernel IP tables with the **VIP** and load balance the request to one of the physical IP addresses of the tasks of the service represented by the **VIP**, as shown in the following diagram:

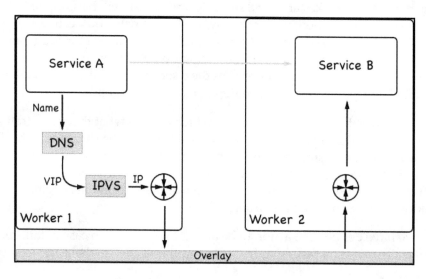

How service discovery and load balancing work in Docker Swarm

Unfortunately, there is no easy way to intercept this mechanism and replace it with a custom behavior. But this would be needed to allow for a true blue-green deployment of **Service B**, which is the target service in our example. As we will see in `Chapter 16,` *Deploying, Updating, and Securing an Application with Kubernetes,* Kubernetes is more flexible in this area.

That being said, we can always deploy the public-facing services in a blue-green fashion. We can use interlock 2 and its layer 7 routing mechanism to allow for a true blue-green deployment.

Canary releases

Technically speaking, rolling updates are a kind of canary release. But due to their lack of seams, where you could plug customized logic into the system, rolling updates are only a very limited version of canary releases.

True canary releases require us to have more fine-grained control over the update process. Also, true canary releases do not take down the old version of the service until 100% of the traffic has been funneled through the new version. In that regard, they are treated like blue-green deployments.

In a canary release scenario, we don't just want to use things such as health checks as deciding factors regarding whether or not to funnel more and more traffic through the new version of the service; we also want to consider external input in the decision-making process, such as metrics that are collected and aggregated by a log aggregator or tracing information. An example that could be used as a decision-maker includes conformance to **service-level agreements** (**SLAs**), namely if the new version of the service shows response times that are outside of the tolerance band. This can happen if we add new functionality to an existing service, yet this new functionality degrades the response time.

Storing configuration data in the swarm

If we want to store non-sensitive data such as configuration files in Docker Swarm, then we can use Docker configs. Docker configs are very similar to Docker secrets, which we will discuss in the next section. The main difference is that config values are not encrypted at rest, while secrets are. Docker configs can only be used in Docker Swarm, that is, they cannot be used in your non-Swarm development environment. Docker configs are mounted directly into the container's filesystem. Configuration values can either be strings or binary values up to a size of 500 KB.

With the use of Docker configs, you can separate the configuration from Docker images and containers. This way, your services can easily be configured with environment-specific values. The production swarm environment has different configuration values than the staging swarm, which in turn has different config values than the development or integration environment.

We can add configs to services and also remove them from running services. Configs can even be shared among different services running in the swarm.

Now, let's create some Docker configs:

1. First, we start with a simple string value:

```
$ echo "Hello world" | docker config create hello-config -
rrin36epd63pu6w3gqcmlpbz0
```

The preceding command creates the `Hello world` configuration value and uses it as input to the config named `hello-config`. The output of this command is the unique `ID` of this new config that's being stored in the swarm.

2. Let's see what we got and use the list command to do so:

```
$ docker config ls
ID                          NAME            CREATED
UPDATED
rrin36epd63pu6w3gqcmlpbz0   hello-config    About a minute ago
About a minute ago
```

The output of the list command shows the `ID` and the `NAME` of the config we just created, as well as its `CREATED` and (last) updated time. But since configs are non-confidential, we can do more and even output the content of a config, like so:

```
$ docker config docker config inspect hello-config
[
    {
        "ID": "rrin36epd63pu6w3gqcmlpbz0",
        "Version": {
            "Index": 11
        },
        "CreatedAt": "2019-11-30T07:59:20.6340015Z",
        "UpdatedAt": "2019-11-30T07:59:20.6340015Z",
        "Spec": {
            "Name": "hello-config",
            "Labels": {},
            "Data": "SGVsbG8gd29ybGQK"
        }
    }
]
```

Hmmm, interesting. In the `Spec` subnode of the preceding JSON-formatted output, we have the `Data` key with a value of `SGVsbG8gd29ybGQK`. Didn't we just say that the config data is not encrypted at rest? It turns out that the value is just our string encoded as `base64`, as we can easily verify:

```
$ echo 'SGVsbG8gd29ybGQK' | base64 -d
Hello world
```

So far, so good.

Now, let's define a somewhat more complicated Docker config. Let's assume we are developing a Java application. Java's preferred way of passing configuration data to the application is the use of so-called `properties` files. A `properties` file is just a text file containing a list of key-value pairs. Let's take a look:

1. Let's create a file called `my-app.properties` and add the following content to it:

```
username=pguser
database=products
port=5432
dbhost=postgres.acme.com
```

2. Save the file and create a Docker config called `app.properties` from it:

```
$ docker config create app.properties ./my-app.properties
2yzl73cg4cwny95hyft7fj80u
```

Now, we can use this (somewhat contrived) command to get the clear text value of the config we just created:

```
$ docker config inspect app.properties | jq .[].Spec.Data | xargs
echo | base64 -d
username=pguser
database=products
port=5432
dbhost=postgres.acme.com
```

This is exactly what we expected.

3. Now, let's create a Docker service that uses the preceding config. For simplicity, we will be using the nginx image to do so:

```
$ docker service create \
    --name nginx \
    --config source=app.properties,target=/etc/my-
app/conf/app.properties,mode=0440 \
    nginx:1.13-alpine

p3f686vinibdhlnrllnspqpr0
overall progress: 1 out of 1 tasks
1/1: running [==================================================>]
verify: Service converged
```

The interesting part in the preceding service `create` command is the line that contains `--config`. With this line, we're telling Docker to use the config named `app.properties` and mount it as a file at `/etc/my-app/conf/app.properties` inside the container. Furthermore, we want that file to have the mode `0440` assigned to it.

Let's see what we got:

```
$ docker service ps nginx
ID              NAME      IMAGE              NODE DESIRED    STATE
CURRENT STATE ...
b8lzzwl3eg6y  nginx.1   nginx:1.13-alpine  node-1  Running  Running
2 minutes ago
```

In the preceding output, we can see that the only instance of the service is running on node `node-1`. On this node, I can now list the containers to get the `ID` of the nginx instance:

```
$ docker container ls
CONTAINER ID    IMAGE                COMMAND                     CREATED
STATUS          PORTS ...
bde33d92cca7    nginx:1.13-alpine    "nginx -g 'daemon of..."    5
minutes ago     Up 5 minutes    80/tcp ...
```

Finally, we can `exec` into that container and output the value of the `/etc/my-app/conf/app.properties` file:

```
$ docker exec bde33 cat /etc/my-app/conf/app.properties
username=pguser
database=products
port=5432
dbhost=postgres.acme.com
```

No surprise here; this is exactly what we expected.

Docker configs can, of course, also be removed from the swarm, but only if they are not being used. If we try to remove the config we were just using previously, without first stopping and removing the service, we would get the following output:

```
$ docker config rm app.properties
Error response from daemon: rpc error: code = InvalidArgument desc
= config 'app.properties' is in use by the following service: nginx
```

We get an error message in which Docker is nice enough to tell us that the config is being used by our service called `nginx`. This behavior is somewhat similar to what we are used to when working with Docker volumes.

Thus, first, we need to remove the service and then we can remove the config:

```
$ docker service rm nginx
nginx
$ docker config rm app.properties
app.properties
```

 It is important to note once more that Docker configs should never be used to store confidential data such as secrets, passwords, or access keys and key secrets.

In the next section, we will discuss how to handle confidential data.

Protecting sensitive data with Docker secrets

Secrets are used to work with confidential data in a secure way. Swarm secrets are secure at rest and in transit. That is, when a new secret is created on a manager node, and it can only be created on a manager node, its value is encrypted and stored in the raft consensus storage. This is why it is secure at rest. If a service gets a secret assigned to it, then the manager reads the secret from storage, decrypts it, and forwards it to all the containers who are instances of the swarm service that requested the secret. Since node-to-node communication in Docker Swarm uses mutual **transport layer security** (**TLS**), the secret value, although decrypted, is still secure in transit. The manager forwards the secret only to the worker nodes that a service instance is running on. Secrets are then mounted as files into the target container. Each secret corresponds to a file. The name of the secret will be the name of the file inside the container, and the value of the secret is the content of the respective file. Secrets are never stored on the filesystem of a worker node and are instead mounted using `tmpFS` into the container. By default, secrets are mounted into the container at `/run/secrets`, but you can change that to any custom folder.

It is important to note that secrets will not be encrypted on Windows nodes since there is no concept similar to `tmpfs`. To achieve the same level of security that you would get on a Linux node, the administrator should encrypt the disk of the respective Windows node.

Creating secrets

First, let's see how we can actually create a secret:

```
$ echo "sample secret value" | docker secret create sample-secret -
```

This command creates a secret called `sample-secret` with the `sample secret value` value. Please note the hyphen at the end of the `docker secret create` command. This means that Docker expects the value of the secret from standard input. This is exactly what we're doing by piping the `sample secret value` value into the `create` command.

Alternatively, we can use a file as the source for the secret value:

```
$ docker secret create other-secret ~/my-secrets/secret-value.txt
```

Here, the value of the secret with the name `other-secret` is read from a file called `~/my-secrets/secret-value.txt`. Once a secret has been created, there is no way to access the value of it. We can, for example, list all our secrets to get the following output:

```
$ docker secret ls
ID                          NAME            DRIVER      CREATED           UPDATED
axykb7msipit1g5so63ef02it   other-secret                28 seconds ago    28 seconds ago
puns1op5wr5hi21st5h3wjd64   sample-secret               3 minutes ago     3 minutes ago
$
```

List of all secrets

In this list, we can only see the ID and NAME of the secret, plus some other metadata, but the actual value of the secret is not visible. We can also use `inspect` on a secret, for example, to get more information about `other-secret`:

```
$ docker secret inspect other-secret
[
    {
        "ID": "axykb7msipit1g5so63ef02it",
        "Version": {
            "Index": 135
        },
        "CreatedAt": "2018-03-16T01:29:14.3678729931Z",
        "UpdatedAt": "2018-03-16T01:29:14.3678729931Z",
        "Spec": {
            "Name": "other-secret",
            "Labels": {}
        }
    }
]
$
```

Inspecting a swarm secret

Even here, we do not get the value of the secret back. This is, of course, intentional: a secret is a secret and thus needs to remain confidential. We can assign labels to secrets if we want and we can even use a different driver to encrypt and decrypt the secret if we're not happy with what Docker delivers out of the box.

Using a secret

Secrets are used by services that run in the swarm. Usually, secrets are assigned to a service at creation time. Thus, if we want to run a service called `web` and assign it a secret, say, `api-secret-key`, the syntax would look as follows:

```
$ docker service create --name web \
    --secret api-secret-key \
    --publish 8000:8000 \
    fundamentalsofdocker/whoami:latest
```

This command creates a service called `web` based on the `fundamentalsofdocker/whoami:latest` image, publishes the container port `8000` to port `8000` on all swarm nodes, and assigns it the secret called `api-secret-key`.

This will only work if the secret called `api-secret-key` is defined in the swarm; otherwise, an error will be generated with the text `secret not found: api-secret-key`. Thus, let's create this secret now:

```
$ echo "my secret key" | docker secret create api-secret-key -
```

Now, if we rerun the service `create` command, it will succeed:

```
$ docker service create --name web \
>     --secret api-secret-key \
>     --publish 8000:8000 \
>     fundamentalsofdocker/whoami:latest
dzxxme8kmo0bglr2ufwrhcztm
overall progress: 1 out of 1 tasks
1/1: running   [==================================================>]
verify: Service converged
$
```

Creating a service with a secret

Now, we can use `docker service ps web` to find out on which node the sole service instance has been deployed, and then `exec` into this container. In my case, the instance has been deployed to `node-3`, so I need to SSH into that node:

```
$ docker-machine ssh node-3
```

Then, I list all my containers on that node to find the one instance belonging to my service and copy its `container ID`. We can then run the following command to make sure that the secret is indeed available inside the container under the expected filename containing the secret value in clear text:

```
$ docker exec -it <container ID> cat /run/secrets/api-secret-key
```

Once again, in my case, this looks like this:

```
docker@node-1:~$ docker container exec -it d5133b0e3eb3 cat /run/secrets/api-secret-key
my secret key
docker@node-1:~$
```

A secret as a container sees it

If, for some reason, the default location where Docker mounts the secrets inside the container is not acceptable to you, you can define a custom location. In the following command, we mount the secret to `/app/my-secrets`:

```
$ docker service create --name web \
    --name web \
    -p 8000:8000 \
    --secret source=api-secret-key,target=/run/my-secrets/api-secret-key \
    fundamentalsofdocker/whoami:latest
```

In this command, we are using the extended syntax to define a secret that includes the destination folder.

Simulating secrets in a development environment

When working in development, we usually don't have a local swarm on our machine. But secrets only work in a swarm. So, *what can we do*? Well, luckily, this answer is really simple. Due to the fact that secrets are treated as files, we can easily mount a volume that contains the secrets into the container to the expected location, which by default is at `/run/secrets`.

Let's assume that we have a folder called `./dev-secrets` on our local workstation. For each secret, we have a file named the same as the secret name and with the unencrypted value of the secret as the content of the file. For example, we can simulate a secret called `demo-secret` with a secret value of `demo secret value` by executing the following command on our workstation:

```
$ echo "demo secret value" > ./dev-secrets/sample-secret
```

Then, we can create a container that mounts this folder, like this:

```
$ docker container run -d --name whoami \
    -p 8000:8000 \
    -v $(pwd)/dev-secrets:/run/secrets \
    fundamentalsofdocker/whoami:latest
```

The process running inside the container will be unable to distinguish these mounted files from the ones originating from a secret. So, for example, demo-secret is available as a file called /run/secrets/demo-secret inside the container and has the expected value demo secret value. Let's take a look at this in more detail in the following steps:

1. To test this, we can exec a shell inside the preceding container:

```
$ docker container exec -it whoami /bin/bash
```

2. Now, we can navigate to the /run/secrets folder and display the content of the demo-secret file:

```
/# cd /run/secrets
/# cat demo-secret
demo secret value
```

Next, we will be looking at secrets and legacy applications.

Secrets and legacy applications

Sometimes, we want to containerize a legacy application that we cannot easily, or do not want to, change. This legacy application might expect a secret value to be available as an environment variable. *How are we going to deal with this now?* Docker presents us with the secrets as files but the application is expecting them in the form of environment variables.

In this situation, it is helpful to define a script that runs when the container is started (a so-called entry point or startup script). This script will read the secret value from the respective file and define an environment variable with the same name as the file, assigning the new variable the value read from the file. In the case of a secret called demo-secret whose value should be available in an environment variable called DEMO_SECRET, the necessary code snippet in this startup script could look like this:

```
export DEMO_SECRET=$(cat /run/secrets/demo-secret)
```

Similarly, let's say we have a legacy application that expects the secret values to be present as an entry in, say, a YAML configuration file located in the /app/bin folder and called app.config, whose relevant part looks like this:

```
. . .

secrets:
  demo-secret: "<<demo-secret-value>>"
  other-secret: "<<other-secret-value>>"
  yet-another-secret: "<<yet-another-secret-value>>"
. . .
```

Our initialization script now needs to read the secret value from the secret file and replace the corresponding placeholder in the config file with the secret value. For demo-secret, this could look like this:

```
file=/app/bin/app.conf
demo_secret=$(cat /run/secret/demo-secret)
sed -i "s/<<demo-secret-value>>/$demo_secret/g" "$file"
```

In the preceding snippet, we're using the sed tool to replace a placeholder with a value in place. We can use the same technique for the other two secrets in the config file.

We put all the initialization logic into a file called entrypoint.sh, make this file executable and, for example, add it to the root of the container's filesystem. Then, we define this file as ENTRYPOINT in the Dockerfile, or we can override the existing ENTRYPOINT of an image in the docker container run command.

Let's make a sample. Let's assume that we have a legacy application running inside a container defined by the fundamentalsofdocker/whoami:latest image that expects a secret called db_password to be defined in a file, whoami.conf, in the application folder. Let's take a look at these steps:

1. We can define a file, whoami.conf, on our local machine that contains the following content:

```
database:
  name: demo
  db_password: "<<db_password_value>>"
others:
  val1=123
  val2="hello world"
```

The important part is line 3 of this snippet. It defines where the secret value has to be put by the startup script.

2. Let's add a file called `entrypoint.sh` to the local folder that contains the following content:

```
file=/app/whoami.conf
db_pwd=$(cat /run/secret/db-password)
sed -i "s/<<db_password_value>>/$db_pwd/g" "$file"

/app/http
```

The last line in the preceding script stems from the fact that this is the start command that was used in the original `Dockerfile`.

3. Now, change the mode of this file to an executable:

```
$ sudo chmod +x ./entrypoint.sh
```

Now, we define a `Dockerfile` that inherits from the `fundamentalsofdocker/whoami:latest` image.

4. Add a file called `Dockerfile` to the current folder that contains the following content:

```
FROM fundamentalsofdocker/whoami:latest
COPY ./whoami.conf /app/
COPY ./entrypoint.sh /
CMD ["/entrypoint.sh"]
```

5. Let's build the image from this `Dockerfile`:

```
$ docker image build -t secrets-demo:1.0 .
```

6. Once the image has been built, we can run a service from it. But before we can do that, we need to define the secret in Swarm:

```
$ echo "passw0rD123" | docker secret create demo-secret -
```

7. Now, we can create a service that uses the following secret:

```
$ docker service create --name demo \
    --secret demo-secret \
    secrets-demo:1.0
```

Updating secrets

At times, we need to update a secret in a running service since secrets could be leaked out to the public or be stolen by malicious people, such as hackers. In this case, we need to change our confidential data since the moment it is leaked to a non-trusted entity, it has to be considered as insecure.

Updating secrets, like any other update, has to happen in a way that requires zero-downtime. Docker SwarmKit supports us in this regard.

First, we create a new secret in the swarm. It is recommended to use a versioning strategy when doing so. In our example, we use a version as a postfix of the secret name. We originally started with the secret named `db-password` and now the new version of this secret is called `db-password-v2`:

```
$ echo "newPassw0rD" | docker secret create db-password-v2 -
```

Let's assume that the original service that used the secret had been created like this:

```
$ docker service create --name web \
    --publish 80:80
    --secret db-password
    nginx:alpine
```

The application running inside the container was able to access the secret at `/run/secrets/db-password`. Now, SwarmKit does not allow us to update an existing secret in a running service, so we have to remove the now obsolete version of the secret and then add the new one. Let's start with removal with the following command:

```
$ docker service update --secret-rm db-password web
```

Now, we can add the new secret with the following command:

```
$ docker service update \
    --secret-add source=db-password-v2,target=db-password \
    web
```

Please note the extended syntax of `--secret-add` with the `source` and `target` parameters.

Summary

In this chapter, we learned how SwarmKit allows us to update services without requiring downtime. We also discussed the current limits of SwarmKit in regard to zero-downtime deployments. In the second part of this chapter, we introduced secrets as a means to provide confidential data to services in a highly secure way.

In the next chapter, we will introduce the currently most popular container orchestrator, Kubernetes. We'll discuss the objects that are used to define and run a distributed, resilient, robust, and highly available application in a Kubernetes cluster. Furthermore, this chapter will familiarize us with MiniKube, a tool that's used to locally deploy a Kubernetes application, and also demonstrate the integration of Kubernetes with Docker for macOS and Docker for Windows.

Questions

To assess your understanding of the topics that were discussed in this chapter, please answer the following questions:

6. In a few simple sentences, explain to an interested layman what zero-downtime deployment means.
7. How does SwarmKit achieve zero-downtime deployments?
8. Contrary to traditional (non-containerized) systems, why does a rollback in Docker Swarm just work? Explain this in a few short sentences.
9. Describe two to three characteristics of a Docker secret.
10. You need to roll out a new version of the `inventory` service. What does your command look like? Here is some more information:
    - The new image is called `acme/inventory:2.1`.
    - We want to use a rolling update strategy with a batch size of two tasks.
    - We want the system to wait for one minute after each batch.
11. You need to update an existing service named `inventory` with a new password that is provided through a Docker secret. The new secret is called `MYSQL_PASSWORD_V2`. The code in the service expects the secret to be called `MYSQL_PASSWORD`. What does the update command look like? (Note that we do not want the code of the service to be changed!)

Further reading

Here are some links to external sources:

- Apply rolling updates to a service, at `https://dockr.ly/2HfGjlD`
- Managing sensitive data with Docker secrets, at `https://dockr.ly/2vUNbuH`
- Introducing Docker secrets management, at `https://dockr.ly/2k7zwzE`
- From env variables to Docker secrets, at `https://bit.ly/2GY3UUB`

Section 4: Docker, Kubernetes, and the Cloud

In this section, you will successfully deploy, run, monitor, and troubleshoot your highly distributed applications in Kubernetes, either on-premises or in the cloud.

This section comprises the following chapters:

- Chapter 15, *Introduction to Kubernetes*
- Chapter 16, *Deploying, Updating, and Securing an Application with Kubernetes*
- Chapter 17, *Monitoring and Troubleshooting an App Running in Production*
- Chapter 18, *Running a Containerized App in the Cloud*

15
Introduction to Kubernetes

In the previous chapter, we learned how SwarmKit uses rolling updates to achieve zero downtime deployments. We were also introduced to Docker configs, which are used to store nonsensitive data in clusters and use this to configure application services, as well as Docker secrets, which are used to share confidential data with an application service running in a Docker Swarm.

In this chapter, we're going to introduce Kubernetes. Kubernetes is currently the clear leader in the container orchestration space. We will start with a high-level overview of the architecture of a Kubernetes cluster and then discuss the main objects used in Kubernetes to define and run containerized applications.

This chapter covers the following topics:

- Kubernetes architecture
- Kubernetes master nodes
- Cluster nodes
- Introduction to MiniKube
- Kubernetes support in Docker for Desktop
- Introduction to pods
- Kubernetes ReplicaSet
- Kubernetes deployment
- Kubernetes service
- Context-based routing
- Comparing SwarmKit with Kubernetes

After finishing this chapter, you will be able to do the following:

- Draft the high-level architecture of a Kubernetes cluster on a napkin
- Explain three to four main characteristics of a Kubernetes pod
- Describe the role of Kubernetes ReplicaSets in two to three short sentences

- Explain two or three main responsibilities of a Kubernetes service
- Create a pod in Minikube
- Configure Docker for Desktop in order to use Kubernetes as an orchestrator
- Create a deployment in Docker for Desktop
- Create a Kubernetes service to expose an application service internally (or externally) to the cluster

Technical requirements

The code files for this chapter can be found on GitHub at `https://github.com/PacktPublishing/Learn-Docker---Fundamentals-of-Docker-19.x-Second-Edition`. Alternatively, if you cloned the GitHub repository that accompanies this book to your computer, as described in `Chapter 2`, *Setting Up a Working Environment*, then you can find the code at `~/fod-solution/ch15`.

Kubernetes architecture

A Kubernetes cluster consists of a set of servers. These servers can be VMs or physical servers. The latter are also called *bare metal*. Each member of the cluster can have one of two roles. It is either a Kubernetes master or a (worker) node. The former is used to manage the cluster, while the latter will run an application workload. I have put the worker in parentheses since, in Kubernetes parlance, you only talk about a node when you're talking about a server that runs application workloads. But in Docker parlance and in Swarm, the equivalent is a *worker node*. I think that the notion of a worker node better describes the role of the server than a simple *node*.

In a cluster, you have a small and odd number of masters and as many worker nodes as needed. Small clusters might only have a few worker nodes, while more realistic clusters might have dozens or even hundreds of worker nodes. Technically, there is no limit to how many worker nodes a cluster can have; in reality, though, you might experience a significant slowdown in some management operations when dealing with thousands of nodes. All members of the cluster need to be connected by a physical network, the so-called **underlay network**.

Kubernetes defines one flat network for the whole cluster. Kubernetes does not provide any networking implementation out of the box; instead, it relies on plugins from third parties. Kubernetes just defines the **Container Network Interface (CNI)** and leaves the implementation to others. The CNI is pretty simple. It basically states that each pod running in the cluster must be able to reach any other pod also running in the cluster without any **Network Address Translation (NAT)** happening in-between. The same must be true between cluster nodes and pods, that is, applications or daemons running directly on a cluster node must be able to reach each pod in the cluster and vice versa.

The following diagram illustrates the high-level architecture of a Kubernetes cluster:

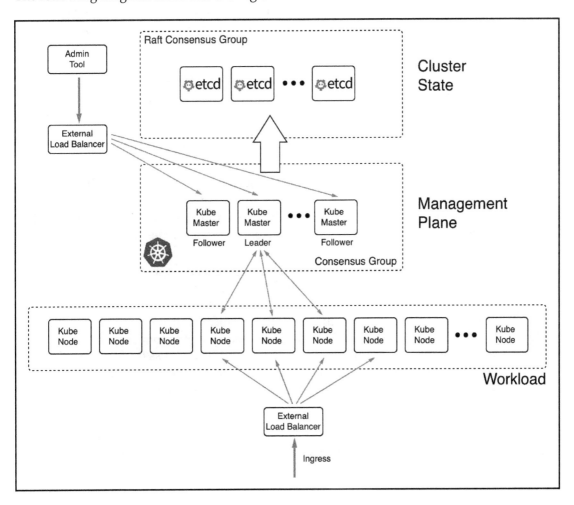

High-level architecture diagram of Kubernetes

The preceding diagram is explained as follows:

- On the top, in the middle, we have a cluster of **etcd** nodes. **etcd** is a distributed key-value store that, in a Kubernetes cluster, is used to store all the state of the cluster. The number of **etcd** nodes has to be odd, as mandated by the Raft consensus protocol, which states which nodes are used to coordinate among themselves. When we talk about the **Cluster State**, we do not include data that is produced or consumed by applications running in the cluster; instead, we're talking about all the information on the topology of the cluster, what services are running, network settings, secrets used, and more. That said, this **etcd** cluster is really mission-critical to the overall cluster and thus, we should never run only a single **etcd** server in a production environment or any environment that needs to be highly available.

- Then, we have a cluster of Kubernetes **master** nodes, which also form a **Consensus Group** among themselves, similar to the **etcd** nodes. The number of master nodes also has to be odd. We can run cluster with a single master but we should never do that in a production or mission-critical system. There, we should always have at least three master nodes. Since the master nodes are used to manage the whole cluster, we are also talking about the management plane. Master nodes use the **etcd** cluster as their backing store. It is good practice to put a **load balancer (LB)** in front of master nodes with a well-known **Fully Qualified Domain Name (FQDN)**, such as `https://admin.example.com`. All tools that are used to manage the Kubernetes cluster should access it through this LB rather than using the public IP address of one of the master nodes. This is shown on the left upper side of the preceding diagram.

- Toward the bottom of the diagram, we have a cluster of **worker** nodes. The number of nodes can be as low as one and does not have an upper limit. Kubernetes master and worker nodes communicate with each other. It is a bidirectional form of communication that is different from the one we know from Docker Swarm. In Docker Swarm, only manager nodes communicate with worker nodes and never the other way around. All ingress traffic accessing applications running in the cluster should go through another **load balancer**. This is the application **load balancer** or reverse proxy. We never want external traffic to directly access any of the worker nodes.

Now that we have an idea about the high-level architecture of a Kubernetes cluster, let's delve a bit more deeply and look at the Kubernetes master and worker nodes.

Kubernetes master nodes

Kubernetes master nodes are used to manage a Kubernetes cluster. The following is a high-level diagram of such a master:

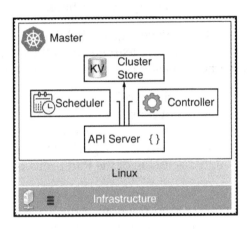

Kubernetes master

At the bottom of the preceding diagram, we have the **Infrastructure**, which can be a VM on-premise or in the cloud or a server (often called bare metal) on-premise or in the cloud. Currently, Kubernetes masters only run on **Linux**. The most popular Linux distributions, such as RHEL, CentOS, and Ubuntu, are supported. On this Linux machine, we have at least the following four Kubernetes services running:

- **API server**: This is the gateway to Kubernetes. All requests to list, create, modify, or delete any resources in the cluster must go through this service. It exposes a REST interface that tools such as `kubectl` use to manage the cluster and applications in the cluster.
- **Controller**: The controller, or more precisely the controller manager, is a control loop that observes the state of the cluster through the API server and makes changes, attempting to move the current or effective state toward the desired state if they differ.
- **Scheduler**: The scheduler is a service that tries its best to schedule pods on worker nodes while considering various boundary conditions, such as resource requirements, policies, quality of service requirements, and more.
- **Cluster Store**: This is an instance of etcd that is used to store all information about the state of the cluster.

To be more precise, etcd, which is used as a cluster store, does not necessarily have to be installed on the same node as the other Kubernetes services. Sometimes, Kubernetes clusters are configured to use standalone clusters of etcd servers, as shown in the architecture diagram in the previous section. But which variant to use is an advanced management decision and is outside the scope of this book.

We need at least one master, but to achieve high availability, we need three or more master nodes. This is very similar to what we have learned about the manager nodes of a Docker Swarm. In this regard, a Kubernetes master is equivalent to a Swarm manager node.

Kubernetes masters never run application workloads. Their sole purpose is to manage the cluster. Kubernetes masters build a Raft consensus group. The Raft protocol is a standard protocol used in situations where a group of members needs to make decisions. It is used in many well-known software products such as MongoDB, Docker SwarmKit, and Kubernetes. For a more thorough discussion of the Raft protocol, see the link in the *Further reading* section.

As we mentioned in the previous section, the state of the Kubernetes cluster is stored in etcd. If the Kubernetes cluster is supposed to be highly available, then etcd must also be configured in HA mode, which normally means that we have at least three etcd instances running on different nodes.

Let's state once again that the whole cluster state is stored in etcd. This includes all the information about all the cluster nodes, all the replica sets, deployments, secrets, network policies, routing information, and so on. It is, therefore, crucial that we have a robust backup strategy in place for this key-value store.

Now, let's look at the nodes that will be running the actual workload of the cluster.

Cluster nodes

Cluster nodes are the nodes with which Kubernetes schedules application workloads. They are the workhorses of the cluster. A Kubernetes cluster can have a few, dozens, hundreds, or even thousands of cluster nodes. Kubernetes has been built from the ground up for high scalability. Don't forget that Kubernetes was modeled after Google Borg, which has been running tens of thousands of containers for years:

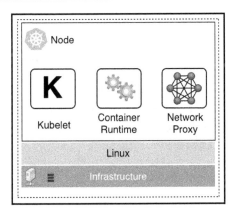

Kubernetes worker node

A worker node can run on a VM, bare metal, on-premise, or in the cloud. Originally, worker nodes could only be configured on Linux. But since version 1.10 of Kubernetes, worker nodes can also run on Windows Server. It is perfectly fine to have a mixed cluster with Linux and Windows worker nodes.

On each node, we have three services that need to run, as follows:

- **Kubelet**: This is the first and foremost service. Kubelet is the primary node agent. The kubelet service uses pod specifications to make sure all of the containers of the corresponding pods are running and healthy. Pod specifications are files written in YAML or JSON format and they declaratively describe a pod. We will get to know what pods are in the next section. PodSpecs are provided to kubelet primarily through the API server.
- **Container runtime**: The second service that needs to be present on each worker node is a container runtime. Kubernetes, by default, has used `containerd` since version 1.9 as its container runtime. Prior to that, it used the Docker daemon. Other container runtimes, such as rkt or CRI-O, can be used. The container runtime is responsible for managing and running the individual containers of a pod.
- **kube-proxy**: Finally, there is the kube-proxy. It runs as a daemon and is a simple network proxy and load balancer for all application services running on that particular node.

Now that we have learned about the architecture of Kubernetes and the master and worker nodes, it is time to introduce the tooling that we can use to develop applications targeted at Kubernetes.

Introduction to Minikube

Minikube is a tool that creates a single-node Kubernetes cluster in VirtualBox or Hyper-V (other hypervisors are supported too) ready to be used during the development of a containerized application. In Chapter 2, *Setting Up a Working Environment,* we learned how Minikube and kubectl can be installed on our macOS or Windows laptop. As stated there, Minikube is a single-node Kubernetes cluster and thus the node is, at the same time, a Kubernetes master as well as a worker node.

Let's make sure that Minikube is running with the following command:

```
$ minikube start
```

Once Minikube is ready, we can access its single node cluster using kubectl. We should see something similar to the following:

```
$ kubectl get nodes
NAME       STATUS   ROLES    AGE    VERSION
minikube   Ready    master   2m2s   v1.16.2
```

Listing all nodes in Minikube

As we mentioned previously, we have a single-node cluster with a node called minikube. The version of Kubernetes that Minikube is using is v1.16.2 in my case.

Now, let's try to deploy a pod to this cluster. Don't worry about what a pod is for now; we will delve into all the details about it later in this chapter. For the moment, just take it as-is.

We can use the sample-pod.yaml file in the ch15 subfolder of our labs folder to create such a pod. It has the following content:

```
apiVersion: v1
kind: Pod
metadata:
  name: nginx
spec:
  containers:
  - name: nginx
    image: nginx:alpine
    ports:
    - containerPort: 80
    - containerPort: 443
```

Use the following steps to run the pod:

1. First, navigate to the correct folder:

   ```
   $ cd ~/fod/ch15
   ```

2. Now, let's use the Kubernetes CLI called kubectl to deploy this pod:

   ```
   $ kubectl create -f sample-pod.yaml
   pod/nginx created
   ```

   If we now list all of the pods, we should see the following:

   ```
   $ kubectl get pods
   NAME    READY   STATUS    RESTARTS   AGE
   nginx   1/1     Running   0          51s
   ```

3. To be able to access this pod, we need to create a service. Let's use the sample-service.yaml file, which has the following content:

   ```
   apiVersion: v1
   kind: Service
   metadata:
     name: nginx-service
   spec:
     type: LoadBalancer
     ports:
     - port: 8080
       targetPort: 80
       protocol: TCP
     selector:
       app: nginx
   ```

4. Again, don't worry about what exactly a service is at this time. We'll explain this later. Let's just create this service:

   ```
   $ kubectl create -f sample-service.yaml
   ```

5. Now, we can use curl to access the service:

   ```
   $ curl -4 http://localhost
   ```

   We should receive the Nginx welcome page as an answer.

6. Before you continue, please remove the two objects you just created:

   ```
   $ kubectl delete po/nginx
   $ kubectl delete svc/nginx-service
   ```

Kubernetes support in Docker for Desktop

Starting from version 18.01-ce, Docker for macOS and Docker for Windows have started to support Kubernetes out of the box. Developers who want to deploy their containerized applications to Kubernetes can use this orchestrator instead of SwarmKit. Kubernetes support is turned off by default and has to be enabled in the settings. The first time Kubernetes is enabled, Docker for macOS or Windows will need a moment to download all the components that are needed to create a single-node Kubernetes cluster. Contrary to Minikube, which is also a single-node cluster, the version provided by the Docker tools uses containerized versions of all Kubernetes components:

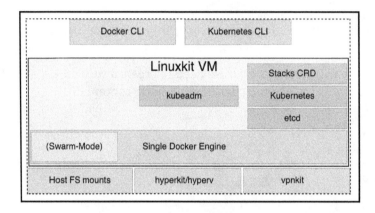

Kubernetes support in Docker for macOS and Windows

The preceding diagram gives us a rough overview of how Kubernetes support has been added to Docker for macOS and Windows. Docker for macOS uses hyperkit to run a LinuxKit-based VM. Docker for Windows uses Hyper-V to achieve the result. Inside the VM, the Docker engine is installed. Part of the engine is SwarmKit, which enables **Swarm-Mode**. Docker for macOS or Windows uses the **kubeadm** tool to set up and configure Kubernetes in that VM. The following three facts are worth mentioning: Kubernetes stores its cluster state in **etcd**, thus we have **etcd** running on this VM. Then, we have all the services that make up Kubernetes and, finally, some services that support the deployment of Docker stacks from the **Docker CLI** into Kubernetes. This service is not part of the official Kubernetes distribution, but it is Docker-specific.

All Kubernetes components run in containers in the **LinuxKit VM**. These containers can be hidden through a setting in Docker for macOS or Windows. Later in this section, we'll provide a complete list of Kubernetes system containers that will be running on your laptop, if you have Kubernetes support enabled. To avoid repetition, from now on, I will only talk about Docker for Desktop instead of Docker for macOS and Docker for Windows. Everything that I will be saying equally applies to both editions.

One big advantage of Docker for Desktop with Kubernetes enabled over Minikube is that the former allows developers to use a single tool to build, test, and run a containerized application targeted at Kubernetes. It is even possible to deploy a multi-service application into Kubernetes using a Docker Compose file.

Now, let's get our hands dirty:

1. First, we have to enable Kubernetes. On macOS, click on the Docker icon in the menu bar; or, on Windows, go to the command tray and select **Preferences**. In the dialog box that opens, select **Kubernetes**, as shown in the following screenshot:

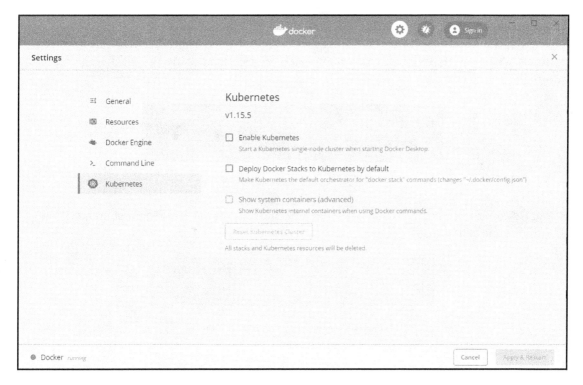

Enabling Kubernetes in Docker for Desktop

2. Then, tick the **Enable Kubernetes** checkbox. Also, tick the **Deploy Docker Stacks to Kubernetes by default** and **Show system containers (advanced)** checkboxes. Then, click the **Apply & Restart** button. Installing and configuring of Kubernetes takes a few minutes. Now, it's time to take a break and enjoy a nice cup of tea.

3. Once the installation is finished (which Docker notifies us of by showing a green status icon in the **Settings** dialog), we can test it. Since we now have two Kubernetes clusters running on our laptop, that is, Minikube and Docker for Desktop, we need to configure `kubectl` to access the latter.

First, let's list all the contexts that we have:

List of contexts for kubectl

Here, we can see that, on my laptop, I have the two contexts we mentioned previously. Currently, the Minikube context is still active, flagged by the asterisk in the CURRENT column. We can switch to the `docker-for-desktop` context using the following command:

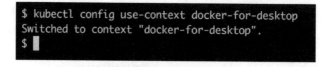

Changing the context for the Kubernetes CLI

Now, we can use `kubectl` to access the cluster that Docker for Desktop just created. We should see the following:

The single-node Kubernetes cluster created by Docker for Desktop

OK, this looks very familiar. It is pretty much the same as what we saw when working with Minikube. The version of Kubernetes that my Docker for Desktop is using is 1.15.5. We can also see that the node is a master node.

If we list all the containers that are currently running on our Docker for Desktop, we get the list shown in the following screenshot (note that I use the `--format` argument to output the `Container ID` and `Names` of the containers):

```
$ docker container ls --format "table {{.ID}}\t{{.Names}}"
CONTAINER ID        NAMES
29703c62234c        k8s_compose_compose-7b7c5cbbcc-b1mq2_docker_15818891-db82-40cb-889c-e5b9fa1cb9a9_0
45e112a9e861        k8s_compose_compose-api-dbbf7c5db-d4vmt_docker_36a7d59e-d87f-4a3b-b4e4-a0a764d9b0d4_0
f155297794da        k8s_POD_compose-7b7c5cbbcc-b1mq2_docker_15818891-db82-40cb-889c-e5b9fa1cb9a9_0
923022934d6f        k8s_POD_compose-api-dbbf7c5db-d4vmt_docker_36a7d59e-d87f-4a3b-b4e4-a0a764d9b0d4_0
481bb29b5e03        k8s_coredns_coredns-5c98db65d4-jh2nm_kube-system_69575ab5-0844-4e25-9eb3-659bee0f393f_0
225b9e9d6fe3        k8s_coredns_coredns-5c98db65d4-xnzgx_kube-system_77a9a4b1-4deb-4a70-b52b-294f2a81ac30_0
5347452ad6a1        k8s_POD_coredns-5c98db65d4-xnzgx_kube-system_77a9a4b1-4deb-4a70-b52b-294f2a81ac30_0
e0eb2c4a801e        k8s_POD_coredns-5c98db65d4-jh2nm_kube-system_69575ab5-0844-4e25-9eb3-659bee0f393f_0
67a719547cf8        k8s_kube-proxy_kube-proxy-29ddv_kube-system_bc4255b1-bc51-48f6-be64-4d10b86c3dd2_0
8767002b6df6        k8s_POD_kube-proxy-29ddv_kube-system_bc4255b1-bc51-48f6-be64-4d10b86c3dd2_0
0748011e43ac        k8s_kube-scheduler_kube-scheduler-docker-desktop_kube-system_131c3f63daec7c0750818f64a2f75d20_0
76c60b2d2319        k8s_kube-apiserver_kube-apiserver-docker-desktop_kube-system_556b996466155d7ad37d896897208f67_0
f445f90a286b        k8s_etcd_etcd-docker-desktop_kube-system_f132e1c85abd4953a304d1c65d9d74f9_0
93da22c08ab9        k8s_kube-controller-manager_kube-controller-manager-docker-desktop_kube-system_1197f92998203f9630beada45e56954f_0
bae7c1399278        k8s_POD_kube-scheduler-docker-desktop_kube-system_131c3f63daec7c0750818f64a2f75d20_0
4c69c69aa4e8        k8s_POD_kube-controller-manager-docker-desktop_kube-system_1197f92998203f9630beada45e56954f_0
081a8411ae7a        k8s_POD_kube-apiserver-docker-desktop_kube-system_556b996466155d7ad37d896897208f67_0
c6a8d74b2af3        k8s_POD_etcd-docker-desktop_kube-system_f132e1c85abd4953a304d1c65d9d74f9_0
```

Kubernetes system containers

In the preceding list, we can identify all the now-familiar components that make up Kubernetes, as follows:

- API server
- etcd
- Kube proxy
- DNS service
- Kube controller
- Kube scheduler

There are also containers that have the word `compose` in them. These are Docker-specific services and allow us to deploy Docker Compose applications onto Kubernetes. Docker translates the Docker Compose syntax and implicitly creates the necessary Kubernetes objects, such as deployments, pods, and services.

Normally, we don't want to clutter our list of containers with these system containers. Therefore, we can uncheck the **Show system containers (advanced)** checkbox in the settings for Kubernetes.

Now, let's try to deploy a Docker Compose application to Kubernetes. Navigate to the `ch15` subfolder of our `~/fod` folder. We deploy the app as a stack using the `docker-compose.yml` file:

```
$ docker stack deploy -c docker-compose.yml app
```

We should see the following:

```
$ docker stack deploy -c docker-compose.yml app
Stack app was created
Waiting for the stack to be stable and running...
 - Service db has one container running
 - Service web has one container running
Stack app is stable and running
```

Deploying the stack to Kubernetes

We can test the application, for example, using `curl`, and we will see that it is running as expected:

```
$ curl localhost:3000/pet
  % Total    % Received % Xferd  Average Speed   Time    Time     Time  Current
                                 Dload  Upload   Total   Spent    Left  Speed
100   395  100   395    0     0   7900      0 --:--:-- --:--:-- --:--:--  7900<html>
<head>
    <link rel="stylesheet" href="css/main.css">
</head>
<body>
    <div class="container">
        <h4>Animal of the day</h4>
        <img src="images&#x2F;buffalo.png"" />
        <p><small>Photo taken at <a href="https://www.maasaimara.com/">Massai Mara National Park</a></small></p>
        <p>Delivered to you by container e535c40a3e6b<p>
    </div>
</body>
</html>
```

Pets application running in Kubernetes on Docker for Desktop

Now, let's see exactly what Docker did when we executed the `docker stack deploy` command. We can use `kubectl` to find out:

```
$ kubectl get all
NAME            DESIRED    CURRENT   UP-TO-DATE   AVAILABLE   AGE
deploy/web  1              1         1            1           9m

NAME                    DESIRED    CURRENT   READY    AGE
rs/web-5c5964c9b8   1              1         1        9m

NAME            DESIRED    CURRENT   UP-TO-DATE   AVAILABLE   AGE
deploy/web  1              1         1            1           9m

NAME                    DESIRED    CURRENT   READY    AGE
rs/web-5c5964c9b8   1              1         1        9m

NAME                DESIRED    CURRENT   AGE
statefulsets/db  1             1         9m

NAME                          READY    STATUS    RESTARTS   AGE
po/db-0                       1/1      Running   0          9m
po/web-5c5964c9b8-b5jq9       1/1      Running   0          9m

NAME                    TYPE           CLUSTER-IP       EXTERNAL-IP   PORT(S)        AGE
svc/db              ClusterIP      None             <none>        55555/TCP      9m
svc/kubernetes      ClusterIP      10.96.0.1        <none>        443/TCP        45m
svc/web             ClusterIP      None             <none>        55555/TCP      9m
svc/web-published   LoadBalancer   10.111.43.147    localhost     3000:32590/TCP 9m
$
```

Listing all Kubernetes objects created by docker stack deploy

Docker created a deployment for the web service and a stateful set for the db service. It also automatically created Kubernetes services for web and db so that they can be accessed inside the cluster. It also created the Kubernetes svc/web-published service, which is used for external access.

This is pretty cool, to say the least, and tremendously decreases friction in the development process for teams targeting Kubernetes as their orchestration platform

Before you continue, please remove the stack from the cluster:

```
$ docker stack rm app
```

Also, make sure you reset the context for kubectl back to Minikube, as we will be using Minikube for all our samples in this chapter:

```
$ kubectl config use-context minikube
```

Now that we have had an introduction to the tools we can use to develop applications that will eventually run in a Kubernetes cluster, it is time to learn about all the important Kubernetes objects that are used to define and manage such an application. We will start with pods.

Introduction to pods

Contrary to what is possible in Docker Swarm, you cannot run containers directly in a Kubernetes cluster. In a Kubernetes cluster, you can only run pods. Pods are the atomic units of deployment in Kubernetes. A pod is an abstraction of one or many co-located containers that share the same Kernel namespaces, such as the network namespace. No equivalent exists in Docker SwarmKit. The fact that more than one container can be co-located and share the same network namespace is a very powerful concept. The following diagram illustrates two pods:

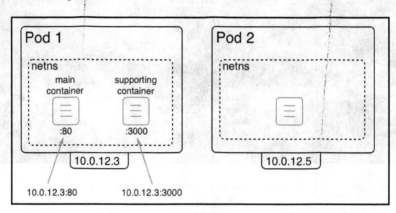

Kubernetes pods

In the preceding diagram, we have two pods, **Pod 1** and **Pod 2**. The first pod contains two containers, while the second one only contains a single container. Each pod gets an IP address assigned by Kubernetes that is unique in the whole Kubernetes cluster. In our case, these are the following IP addresses: `10.0.12.3` and `10.0.12.5`. Both are part of a private subnet managed by the Kubernetes network driver.

A pod can contain one to many containers. All those containers share the same Linux kernel namespaces, and in particular, they share the network namespace. This is indicated by the dashed rectangle surrounding the containers. Since all containers running in the same pod share the network namespace, each container needs to make sure to use their own port since duplicate ports are not allowed in a single network namespace. In this case, in **Pod 1**, the **main container** is using port `80` while the **supporting container** is using port `3000`.

Requests from other pods or nodes can use the pod's IP address combined with the corresponding port number to access the individual containers. For example, you could access the application running in the main container of **Pod 1** through `10.0.12.3:80`.

Comparing Docker container and Kubernetes pod networking

Now, let's compare Docker's container networking and Kubernetes pod networking. In the following diagram, we have the former on the left-hand side and the latter on the right-hand side:

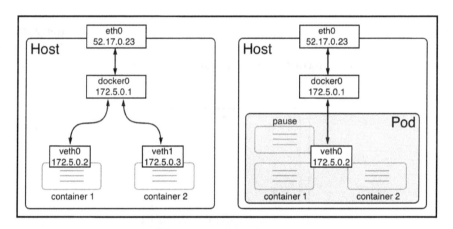

Containers in a pod sharing the same network namespace

When a Docker container is created and no specific network is specified, then the Docker engine creates a **virtual ethernet (veth)** endpoint. The first container gets **veth0**, the next one gets **veth1**, and so on. These virtual ethernet endpoints are connected to the Linux bridge, **docker0**, that Docker automatically creates upon installation. Traffic is routed from the **docker0** bridge to every connected **veth** endpoint. Every container has its own network namespace. No two containers use the same namespace. This is on purpose, to isolate applications running inside the containers from each other.

For a Kubernetes pod, the situation is different. When creating a new pod, Kubernetes first creates a so-called **pause** container whose only purpose is to create and manage the namespaces that the pod will share with all containers. Other than that, it does nothing useful; it is just sleeping. The **pause** container is connected to the **docker0** bridge through **veth0**. Any subsequent container that will be part of the pod uses a special feature of the Docker engine that allows it to reuse an existing network namespace. The syntax to do so looks like this:

```
$ docker container create --net container:pause ...
```

The important part is the `--net` argument, which uses `container:<container name>`as a value. If we create a new container this way, then Docker does not create a new veth endpoint; the container uses the same one as the `pause` container.

Another important consequence of multiple containers sharing the same network namespace is the way they communicate with each other. Let's consider the following situation: a pod containing two containers, one listening at port `80` and the other at port `3000`:

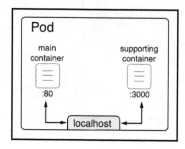

Containers in pods communicating via localhost

When two containers use the same Linux kernel network namespace, they can communicate with each other through localhost, similarly to how, when two processes are running on the same host, they can communicate with each other through localhost too. This is illustrated in the preceding diagram. From the main container, the containerized application inside it can reach out to the service running inside the supporting container through `http://localhost:3000`.

Sharing the network namespace

After all this theory, you might be wondering how a pod is actually created by Kubernetes. Kubernetes only uses what Docker provides. So, *how does this network namespace share work?* First, Kubernetes creates the so-called `pause` container, as mentioned previously. This container has no other function than to reserve the kernel namespaces for that pod and keep them alive, even if no other container inside the pod is running. Let's simulate the creation of a pod, then. We start by creating the `pause` container and use Nginx for this purpose:

```
$ docker container run -d --name pause nginx:alpine
```

Now, we add a second container called `main`, attaching it to the same network namespace as the `pause` container:

```
$ docker container run --name main -dit \
    --net container:pause \
    alpine:latest /bin/sh
```

Since `pause` and the sample container are both parts of the same network namespace, they can reach each other through `localhost`. To show this, we have to `exec` into the main container:

```
$ docker exec -it main /bin/sh
```

Now, we can test the connection to Nginx running in the `pause` container and listening on port `80`. The following what we get if we use the `wget` utility to do so:

```
/ # wget -q0 - localhost
<!DOCTYPE html>
<html>
<head>
<title>Welcome to nginx!</title>
<style>
    body {
        width: 35em;
        margin: 0 auto;
        font-family: Tahoma, Verdana, Arial, sans-serif;
    }
</style>
</head>
<body>
<h1>Welcome to nginx!</h1>
<p>If you see this page, the nginx web server is successfully installed and
working. Further configuration is required.</p>

<p>For online documentation and support please refer to
<a href="http://nginx.org/">nginx.org</a>.<br/>
Commercial support is available at
<a href="http://nginx.com/">nginx.com</a>.</p>

<p><em>Thank you for using nginx.</em></p>
</body>
</html>
/ #
```

Two containers sharing the same network namespace

The output shows that we can indeed access Nginx on `localhost`. This is proof that the two containers share the same namespace. If that is not enough, we can use the `ip` tool to show `eth0` inside both containers and we will get the exact same result, specifically, the same IP address, which is one of the characteristics of a pod where all its containers share the same IP address:

```
/ # ip a show eth0
11: eth0@if12: <BROADCAST,MULTICAST,UP,LOWER_UP,M-DOWN> mtu 1500 qdisc noqueue state UP
    link/ether 02:42:ac:11:00:02 brd ff:ff:ff:ff:ff:ff
    inet 172.17.0.2/16 brd 172.17.255.255 scope global eth0
       valid_lft forever preferred_lft forever
/ #
```

Displaying the properties of eth0 with the ip tool

If we inspect the `bridge` network, we can see that only the `pause` container is listed. The other container didn't get an entry in the `Containers` list since it is reusing the `pause` container's endpoint:

```
$ docker network inspect bridge
[
    {
        "Name": "bridge",
        "Id": "41909c08794041cabc3a9d2e034426f2344f5310bd1cbfcbae65c5f25a05f541",
        "Created": "2018-03-26T22:16:44.790966007Z",
        "Scope": "local",
        "Driver": "bridge",
        "EnableIPv6": false,
        "IPAM": {
            "Driver": "default",
            "Options": null,
            "Config": [
                {
                    "Subnet": "172.17.0.0/16",
                    "Gateway": "172.17.0.1"
                }
            ]
        },
        "Internal": false,
        "Attachable": false,
        "Ingress": false,
        "ConfigFrom": {
            "Network": ""
        },
        "ConfigOnly": false,
        "Containers": {
            "8965ec65ca4a1de1f1d9c987b68e888c1115cf64f44ba3842953d29a2b9a0ea8": {
                "Name": "pause",
                "EndpointID": "890fc0527f7cb6484d24b7886772db23bb5a0502fe34269fc306277ea7a6f95e",
                "MacAddress": "02:42:ac:11:00:02",
                "IPv4Address": "172.17.0.2/16",
                "IPv6Address": ""
            }
        },
        "Options": {
            "com.docker.network.bridge.default_bridge": "true",
            "com.docker.network.bridge.enable_icc": "true",
            "com.docker.network.bridge.enable_ip_masquerade": "true",
            "com.docker.network.bridge.host_binding_ipv4": "0.0.0.0",
            "com.docker.network.bridge.name": "docker0",
            "com.docker.network.driver.mtu": "1500"
        },
        "Labels": {}
    }
]
$
```

Inspecting the Docker default bridge network

Next, we will be looking at the pod life cycle.

Pod life cycle

Earlier in this book, we learned that containers have a life cycle. A container is initialized, run, and ultimately exited. When a container exits, it can do this gracefully with an exit code zero or it can terminate with an error, which is equivalent to a nonzero exit code.

Similarly, a pod has a life cycle. Due to the fact that a pod can contain more than one container, this life cycle is slightly more complicated than that of a single container. The life cycle of a pod can be seen in the following diagram:

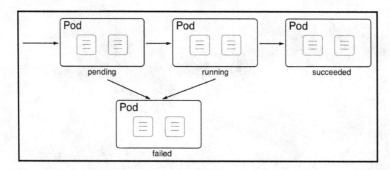

The life cycle of Kubernetes pods

When a **Pod** is created on a cluster node, it first enters into the **pending** status. Once all the containers of the pod are up and running, the pod enters into the **running** status. The pod only enters into this state if all its containers run successfully. If the pod is asked to terminate, it will request all its containers to terminate. If all containers terminate with exit code zero, then the pod enters into the **succeeded** status. This is the happy path.

Now, let's look at some scenarios that lead to the pod being in the **failed** state. There are three possible scenarios:

- If, during the startup of the pod, at least one container is not able to run and fails (that is, it exits with a nonzero exit code), the pod goes from the **pending** state into the **failed** state.
- If the pod is in the running status and one of the containers suddenly crashes or exits with a nonzero exit code, then the pod transitions from the **running** state into the **failed** state.
- If the pod is asked to terminate and, during the shutdown at least one of the containers, exits with a nonzero exit code, then the pod also enters into the **failed** state.

Now, let's look at the specifications for a pod.

Pod specifications

When creating a pod in a Kubernetes cluster, we can use either an imperative or a declarative approach. We discussed the difference between the two approaches earlier in this book but, to rephrase the most important aspect, using a declarative approach signifies that we write a manifest that describes the end state we want to achieve. We'll leave out the details of the orchestrator. The end state that we want to achieve is also called the **desired state**. In general, the declarative approach is strongly preferred in all established orchestrators, and Kubernetes is no exception.

Thus, in this chapter, we will exclusively concentrate on the declarative approach. Manifests or specifications for a pod can be written using either the YAML or JSON formats. In this chapter, we will concentrate on YAML since it is easier to read for us humans. Let's look at a sample specification. Here is the content of the pod.yaml file, which can be found in the ch12 subfolder of our labs folder:

```
apiVersion: v1
kind: Pod
metadata:
  name: web-pod
spec:
  containers:
  - name: web
    image: nginx:alpine
    ports:
    - containerPort: 80
```

Each specification in Kubernetes starts with the version information. Pods have been around for quite some time and thus the API version is v1. The second line specifies the type of Kubernetes object or resource we want to define. Obviously, in this case, we want to specify a Pod. Next follows a block containing metadata. At a bare minimum, we need to give the pod a name. Here, we call it web-pod. The next block that follows is the spec block, which contains the specification of the pod. The most important part (and the only one in this simple sample) is a list of all containers that are part of this pod. We only have one container here, but multiple containers are possible. The name we choose for our container is web and the container image is nginx:alpine. Finally, we define a list of ports the container is exposing.

Once we have authored such a specification, we can apply it to the cluster using the Kubernetes CLI, kubectl. In a Terminal, navigate to the ch15 subfolder and execute the following command:

```
$ kubectl create -f pod.yaml
```

This will respond with `pod "web-pod" created`. We can then list all the pods in the cluster with `kubectl get pods`:

```
$ kubectl get pods
NAME      READY  STATUS    RESTARTS  AGE
web-pod   1/1    Running   0         2m
```

As expected, we have one of one pods in the running status. The pod is called `web-pod`, as defined. We can get more detailed information about the running pod by using the `describe` command:

```
$ kubectl describe pod/web-pod
Name:          web-pod
Namespace:     default
Node:          minikube/192.168.99.105
Start Time:    Sun, 25 Mar 2018 22:47:49 -0500
Labels:        <none>
Annotations:   <none>
Status:        Running
IP:            172.17.0.3
Containers:
  web:
    Container ID:  docker://e8784dfc2e3fcf1de4bfb9ab1508176799b6024b96d9447126e1db5dd5e2201f
    Image:         nginx:alpine
    Image ID:      docker-pullable://nginx@sha256:17c4704e19a11cd47545fa3c17e6903fc88672021f7f907f212d6663baf6ab57
    Port:          80/TCP
    State:         Running
      Started:     Sun, 25 Mar 2018 22:47:50 -0500
    Ready:         True
    Restart Count: 0
    Environment:   <none>
    Mounts:
      /var/run/secrets/kubernetes.io/serviceaccount from default-token-fhdsm (ro)
Conditions:
  Type           Status
  Initialized    True
  Ready          True
  PodScheduled   True
Volumes:
  default-token-fhdsm:
    Type:        Secret (a volume populated by a Secret)
    SecretName:  default-token-fhdsm
    Optional:    false
QoS Class:       BestEffort
Node-Selectors:  <none>
Tolerations:     <none>
Events:
  Type    Reason               Age   From               Message
  ----    ------               ----  ----               -------
  Normal  Scheduled            5m    default-scheduler  Successfully assigned web-pod to minikube
  Normal  SuccessfulMountVolume 5m   kubelet, minikube  MountVolume.SetUp succeeded for volume "default-token-fhdsm"
  Normal  Pulled               5m    kubelet, minikube  Container image "nginx:alpine" already present on machine
  Normal  Created              5m    kubelet, minikube  Created container
  Normal  Started              5m    kubelet, minikube  Started container
$
```

Describing a pod running in the cluster

Please note the `pod/web-pod` notation in the previous `describe` command. Other variants are possible; for example, `pods/web-pod`, `po/web-pod`. `pod` and `po` are aliases of `pods`. The `kubectl` tool defines many aliases to make our lives a bit easier.

The `describe` command gives us a plethora of valuable information about the pod, not the least of which is a list of events that happened and affected this pod. The list is shown at the end of the output.

The information in the `Containers` section is very similar to what we find in a `docker container inspect` output.

We can also see a `Volumes` section with an entry of the `Secret` type. We will discuss Kubernetes secrets in the next chapter. Volumes, on the other hand, will be discussed next.

Pods and volumes

In `Chapter 5`, *Data Volumes and Configuration*, we learned about volumes and their purpose: accessing and storing persistent data. Since containers can mount volumes, pods can do so as well. In reality, it is really the containers inside the pod that mount the volumes, but that is just a semantic detail. First, let's see how we can define a volume in Kubernetes. Kubernetes supports a plethora of volume types, so we won't delve into too much detail about this. Let's just create a local volume implicitly by defining a `PersistentVolumeClaim` called `my-data-claim`:

```
apiVersion: v1
kind: PersistentVolumeClaim
metadata:
  name: my-data-claim
spec:
  accessModes:
    - ReadWriteOnce
  resources:
    requests:
      storage: 2Gi
```

We have defined a claim that requests 2 GB of data. Let's create this claim:

```
$ kubectl create -f volume-claim.yaml
```

We can list the claim using `kubectl` (pvc is a shortcut for `PersistentVolumeClaim`):

```
$ kubectl get pvc
NAME            STATUS   VOLUME                                        CAPACITY   ACCESS MODES   STORAGECLASS   AGE
my-data-claim   Bound    pvc-aac3bb2c-3224-11e8-a07f-080027c10823      2Gi        RWO            standard       14m
$
```

List of PersistentStorageClaim objects in the cluster

In the output, we can see that the claim has implicitly created a volume called `pvc-<ID>`. We are now ready to use the volume created by the claim in a pod. Let's use a modified version of the pod specification that we used previously. We can find this updated specification in the `pod-with-vol.yaml` file in the `ch12` folder. Let's look at this specification in detail:

```
apiVersion: v1
kind: Pod
metadata:
  name: web-pod
spec:
  containers:
  - name: web
    image: nginx:alpine
    ports:
    - containerPort: 80
    volumeMounts:
    - name: my-data
      mountPath: /data
  volumes:
  - name: my-data
    persistentVolumeClaim:
      claimName: my-data-claim
```

In the last four lines, in the `volumes` block, we define a list of volumes we want to use for this pod. The volumes that we list here can be used by any of the containers of the pod. In our particular case, we only have one volume. We specify that we have a volume called `my-data`, which is a persistent volume claim whose claim name is the one we just created. Then, in the container specification, we have the `volumeMounts` block, which is where we define the volume we want to use and the (absolute) path inside the container where the volume will be mounted. In our case, we mount the volume to the `/data` folder of the container filesystem. Let's create this pod:

```
$ kubectl create -f pod-with-vol.yaml
```

Then, we can `exec` into the container to double-check that the volume has mounted by navigating to the `/data` folder, creating a file there, and exiting the container:

```
$ kubectl exec -it web-pod -- /bin/sh
/ # cd /data
/data # echo "Hello world!" > sample.txt
/data # exit
```

If we are right, then the data in this container must persist beyond the life cycle of the pod. Thus, let's delete the pod and then recreate it and exec into it to make sure the data is still there. This is the result:

```
$ kubectl delete po/web-pod
pod "web-pod" deleted
$ kubectl create -f pod-with-vol.yaml
pod "web-pod" created
$ kubectl exec -it web-pod -- /bin/sh
/ # cat /data/sample.txt
Hello world!
/ #
```

Data stored in volume survives pod recreation

Now that we have a good understanding of pods, let's look into how those pods are managed with the help of ReplicaSets.

Kubernetes ReplicaSet

A single pod in an environment with high availability requirements is insufficient. *What if the pod crashes? What if we need to update the application running inside the pod but cannot afford any service interruption?* These questions and more indicate that pods alone are not enough and we need a higher-level concept that can manage multiple instances of the same pod. In Kubernetes, the **ReplicaSet** is used to define and manage such a collection of identical pods that are running on different cluster nodes. Among other things, a ReplicaSet defines which container images are used by the containers running inside a pod and how many instances of the pod will run in the cluster. These properties and many others are called the desired state.

The ReplicaSet is responsible for reconciling the desired state at all times, if the actual state ever deviates from it. Here is a Kubernetes ReplicaSet:

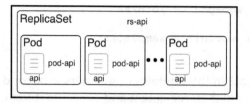

Kubernetes ReplicaSet

In the preceding diagram, we can see a **ReplicaSet** called **rs-api,** which governs a number of pods. The pods are called **pod-api**. The **ReplicaSet** is responsible for making sure that, at any given time, there are always the desired number of pods running. If one of the pods crashes for whatever reason, the **ReplicaSet** schedules a new pod on a node with free resources instead. If there are more pods than the desired number, then the **ReplicaSet** kills superfluous pods. With this, we can say that the **ReplicaSet** guarantees a self-healing and scalable set of pods. There is no limit to how many pods a **ReplicaSet** can hold.

ReplicaSet specification

Similar to what we have learned about pods, Kubernetes also allows us to either imperatively or declaratively define and create a ReplicaSet. Since the declarative approach is by far the most recommended one in most cases, we're going to concentrate on this approach. Here is a sample specification for a Kubernetes ReplicaSet:

```
apiVersion: apps/v1
kind: ReplicaSet
metadata:
  name: rs-web
spec:
  selector:
    matchLabels:
      app: web
  replicas: 3
  template:
    metadata:
      labels:
        app: web
    spec:
      containers:
      - name: nginx
        image: nginx:alpine
```

```
    ports:
    - containerPort: 80
```

This looks an awful lot like the pod specification we introduced earlier. Let's concentrate on the differences, then. First, on line 2, we have the `kind`, which was `Pod` and is now `ReplicaSet`. Then, on lines 6–8, we have a selector, which determines the pods that will be part of the `ReplicaSet`. In this case, it is all the pods that have `app` as a label with the value `web`. Then, on line 9, we define how many replicas of the pod we want to run; three, in this case. Finally, we have the `template` section, which first defines the `metadata` and then the `spec`, which defines the containers that run inside the pod. In our case, we have a single container using the `nginx:alpine` image and exporting port `80`.

The really important elements are the number of replicas and the selector, which specifies the set of pods governed by the `ReplicaSet`.

In our `ch15` folder, we have a file called `replicaset.yaml` that contains the preceding specification. Let's use this file to create the `ReplicaSet`:

```
$ kubectl create -f replicaset.yaml
replicaset "rs-web" created
```

If we list all the ReplicaSets in the cluster, we get the following (`rs` is a shortcut for `replicaset`):

```
$ kubectl get rs
NAME      DESIRED    CURRENT    READY    AGE
rs-web    3          3          3        51s
```

In the preceding output, we can see that we have a single ReplicaSet called `rs-web` whose desired state is three (pods). The current state also shows three pods and tell us that all three pods are ready. We can also list all the pods in the system. This results in the following output:

```
$ kubectl get pods
NAME            READY    STATUS     RESTARTS    AGE
rs-web-6qzld    1/1      Running    0           4m
rs-web-frj2m    1/1      Running    0           4m
rs-web-zd2kt    1/1      Running    0           4m
```

Here, we can see our three expected pods. The names of the pods use the name of the ReplicaSet with a unique ID appended for each pod. In the READY column, we can see how many containers have been defined in the pod and how many of them are ready. In our case, we only have a single container per pod and, in each case, it is ready. Thus, the overall status of the pod is `Running`. We can also see how many times each pod had to be restarted. In our case, we don't have any restarts.

Self-healing

Now, let's test the magic powers of the self-healing `ReplicaSet` by randomly killing one of its pods and observing what happens. Let's delete the first pod from the previous list:

```
$ kubectl delete po/rs-web-6qzld
pod "rs-web-6qzld" deleted
```

Now, let's list all the pods again. We expect to see only two pods, *right*? Wrong:

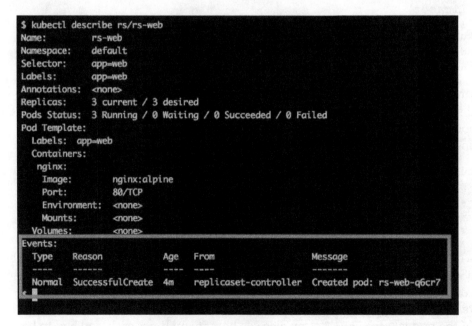

```
$ kubectl get pods
NAME           READY    STATUS     RESTARTS    AGE
rs-web-frj2m   1/1      Running    0           22h
rs-web-q6cr7   1/1      Running    0           41s
rs-web-zd2kt   1/1      Running    0           22h
$
```

List of pods after killing a pod of the ReplicaSet

OK; evidently, the second pod in the list has been recreated, as we can see from the AGE column. This is auto-healing in action. Let's see what we discover if we describe the ReplicaSet:

```
$ kubectl describe rs/rs-web
Name:           rs-web
Namespace:      default
Selector:       app=web
Labels:         app=web
Annotations:    <none>
Replicas:       3 current / 3 desired
Pods Status:    3 Running / 0 Waiting / 0 Succeeded / 0 Failed
Pod Template:
  Labels: app=web
  Containers:
   nginx:
    Image:          nginx:alpine
    Port:           80/TCP
    Environment:    <none>
    Mounts:         <none>
  Volumes:          <none>
Events:
  Type     Reason            Age    From                   Message
  ----     ------            ----   ----                   -------
  Normal   SuccessfulCreate  4m     replicaset-controller  Created pod: rs-web-q6cr7
```

Describe the ReplicaSet

And indeed, we find an entry under `Events` that tells us that the `ReplicaSet` created the new pod called `rs-web-q6cr7`.

Kubernetes deployment

Kubernetes takes the single-responsibility principle very seriously. All Kubernetes objects are designed to do one thing and one thing only, and they are designed to do this one thing very well. In this regard, we have to understand Kubernetes **ReplicaSets** and **Deployments**. A **ReplicaSet**, as we have learned, is responsible for achieving and reconciling the desired state of an application service. This means that the **ReplicaSet** manages a set of pods.

Deployment augments a **ReplicaSet** by providing rolling updates and rollback functionality on top of it. In Docker Swarm, the Swarm service incorporates the functionality of both **ReplicaSet** and **Deployment**. In this regard, SwarmKit is much more monolithic than Kubernetes. The following diagram shows the relationship of a **Deployment** to a **ReplicaSet**:

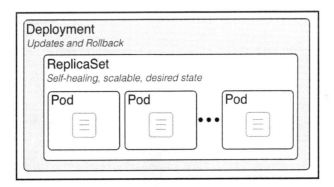

Kubernetes deployment

In the preceding diagram, the **ReplicaSet** is defining and governing a set of identical pods. The main characteristics of the **ReplicaSet** are that it is **self-healing**, **scalable**, and always does its best to reconcile the **desired state**. Kubernetes Deployment, in turn, adds rolling updates and rollback functionality to this. In this regard, a deployment is really a wrapper object to a ReplicaSet.

We will learn more about rolling updates and rollbacks in the Chapter 16, *Deploying, Updating, and Securing an Application with Kubernetes*.

In the next section, we will learn more about Kubernetes services and how they enable service discovery and routing.

Kubernetes service

The moment we start to work with applications consisting of more than one application service, we need service discovery. The following diagram illustrates this problem:

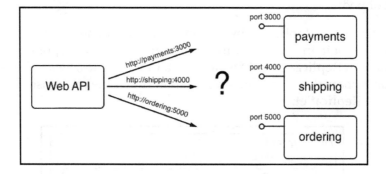

Service discovery

In the preceding diagram, we have a **Web API** service that needs access to three other services: **payments**, **shipping**, and **ordering**. The **Web API** should never have to care about how and where to find those three services. In the API code, we just want to use the name of the service we want to reach and its port number. A sample would be the following URL http://payments:3000, which is used to access an instance of the payments service.

In Kubernetes, the payments application service is represented by a ReplicaSet of pods. Due to the nature of highly distributed systems, we cannot assume that pods have stable endpoints. A pod can come and go on a whim. But that's a problem if we need to access the corresponding application service from an internal or external client. If we cannot rely on pod endpoints being stable, *what else can we do?*

This is where Kubernetes services come into play. They are meant to provide stable endpoints to ReplicaSets or Deployments, as follows:

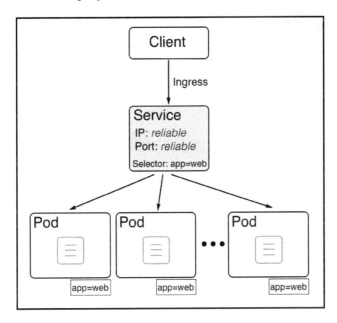

Kubernetes service providing stable endpoints to clients

In the preceding diagram, in the center, we can see such a Kubernetes **Service**. It provides a **reliable** cluster-wide **IP** address, also called a **virtual IP (VIP)**, as well as a **reliable Port** that's unique in the whole cluster. The pods that the Kubernetes service is proxying are determined by the **Selector** defined in the service specification. Selectors are always based on labels. Every Kubernetes object can have zero to many labels assigned to it. In our case, the **Selector** is **app=web**; that is, all pods that have a label called app with a value of web are proxied.

In the next section, we will learn more about context-based routing and how Kubernetes alleviates this task.

Context-based routing

Often, we want to configure context-based routing for our Kubernetes cluster. Kubernetes offers us various ways to do this. The preferred and most scalable way at this time is to use an **IngressController**. The following diagram tries to illustrate how this ingress controller works:

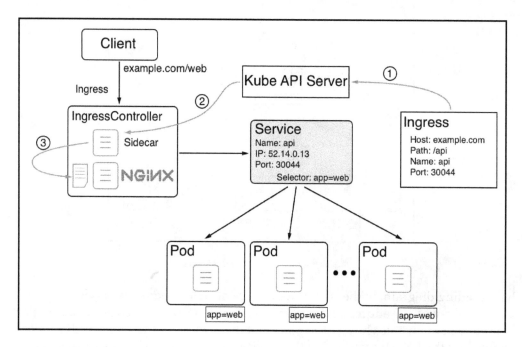

Context-based routing using a Kubernetes ingress controller

In the preceding diagram, we can see how context-based (or layer 7) routing works when using an **IngressController**, such as Nginx. Here, we have the deployment of an application service called **web**. All the pods of this application service have the following label: **app=web**. Then, we have a Kubernetes service called **web** that provides a stable endpoint to those pods. The service has a (virtual) **IP** of 52.14.0.13 and exposes port 30044. That is, if a request comes to any node of the Kubernetes cluster for the name **web** and port 30044, then it is forwarded to this service. The service then load-balances the request to one of the pods.

So far, so good, *but how is an ingress request from a client to the* `http[s]://example.com/web` *URL routed to our web service?* First, we have to define routing from a context-based request to a corresponding `<service name>/<port> request`. This is done through an **Ingress** object:

1. In the **Ingress** object, we define the **Host** and **Path** as the source and the (service) name, and the port as the target. When this Ingress object is created by the Kubernetes API server, then a process that runs as a sidecar in `IngressController` picks this change up.

2. The process modifies the configuration the configuration file of the Nginx reverse proxy.

3. By adding the new route, Nginx is then asked to reload its configuration and thus will be able to correctly route any incoming requests to `http[s]://example.com/web`.

In the next section, we are going to compare Docker SwarmKit with Kubernetes by contrasting some of the main resources of each orchestration engine.

Comparing SwarmKit with Kubernetes

Now that we have learned a lot of details about the most important resources in Kubernetes, it is helpful to compare the two orchestrators, SwarmKit and Kubernetes, by matching important resources. Let's take a look:

SwarmKit	Kubernetes	Description
Swarm	Cluster	Set of servers/nodes managed by the respective orchestrator.
Node	Cluster member	Single host (physical or virtual) that's a member of the Swarm/cluster.
Manager node	Master	Node managing the Swarm/cluster. This is the control plane.
Worker node	Node	Member of the Swarm/cluster running application workload.
Container	Container**	An instance of a container image running on a node. **Note: In a Kubernetes cluster, we cannot run a container directly.
Task	Pod	An instance of a service (Swarm) or ReplicaSet (Kubernetes) running on a node. A task manages a single container while a Pod contains one to many containers that all share the same network namespace.

Service	ReplicaSet	Defines and reconciles the desired state of an application service consisting of multiple instances.
Service	Deployment	A deployment is a ReplicaSet augmented with rolling updates and rollback capabilities.
Routing Mesh	Service	The Swarm Routing Mesh provides L4 routing and load balancing using IPVS. A Kubernetes service is an abstraction that defines a logical set of pods and a policy that can be used to access them. It is a stable endpoint for a set of pods.
Stack	Stack **	The definition of an application consisting of multiple (Swarm) services. **Note: While stacks are not native to Kubernetes, Docker's tool, Docker for Desktop, will translate them for deployment onto a Kubernetes cluster.
Network	Network policy	Swarm **software-defined networks (SDNs)** are used to firewall containers. Kubernetes only defines a single flat network. Every pod can reach every other pod and/or node, unless network policies are explicitly defined to constrain inter-pod communication.

Summary

In this chapter, we learned about the basics of Kubernetes. We took an overview of its architecture and introduced the main resources that are used to define and run applications in a Kubernetes cluster. We also introduced Minikube and Kubernetes support in Docker for Desktop.

In the next chapter, we're going to deploy an application into a Kubernetes cluster. Then, we're going to be updating one of the services of this application using a zero downtime strategy. Finally, we're going to instrument application services running in Kubernetes with sensitive data using secrets. Stay tuned!

Questions

Please answer the following questions to assess your learning progress:

1. Explain in a few short sentences what the role of a Kubernetes master is.
2. List the elements that need to be present on each Kubernetes (worker) node.

3. We cannot run individual containers in a Kubernetes cluster.

   A. Yes
   B. No

4. Explain the reason why the containers in a pod can use `localhost` to communicate with each other.

5. What is the purpose of the so-called pause container in a pod?

6. Bob tells you "Our application consists of three Docker images: `web`, `inventory`, and `db`. Since we can run multiple containers in a Kubernetes pod, we are going to deploy all the services of our application in a single pod." List three to four reasons why this is a bad idea.

7. Explain in your own words why we need Kubernetes ReplicaSets.

8. Under which circumstances do we need Kubernetes deployments?

9. List at least three types of Kubernetes service and explain their purposes and their differences.

Further reading

Here is a list of articles that contain more detailed information about the various topics that we discussed in this chapter:

- The Raft Consensus Algorithm: `https://raft.github.io/`
- Docker Compose and Kubernetes with Docker for Desktop: `https://dockr.ly/2G8Iqb9`
- Kubernetes Documentation: `https://kubernetes.io/docs/home/`

16
Deploying, Updating, and Securing an Application with Kubernetes

In the previous chapter, we learned about the basics of the container orchestrator, Kubernetes. We got a high-level overview of the architecture of Kubernetes and learned a lot about the important objects used by Kubernetes to define and manage a containerized application.

In this chapter, we will learn how to deploy, update, and scale applications into a Kubernetes cluster. We will also explain how zero downtime deployments are achieved to enable disruption-free updates and rollbacks of mission-critical applications. Finally, we will introduce Kubernetes secrets as a means to configure services and protect sensitive data.

This chapter covers the following topics:

- Deploying a first application
- Defining liveness and readiness
- Zero downtime deployments
- Kubernetes secrets

After working through this chapter, you will be able to do the following:

- Deploy a multi-service application into a Kubernetes cluster
- Define a liveness and readiness probe for your Kubernetes application service
- Update an application service running in Kubernetes without causing downtime
- Define secrets in a Kubernetes cluster
- Configure an application service to use Kubernetes secrets

Technical requirements

In this chapter, we're going to use Minikube on our local computer. Please refer to Chapter 2, *Setting Up a Working Environment*, for more information on how to install and use Minikube.

The code for this chapter can be found here: https://github.com/PacktPublishing/ Learn-Docker---Fundamentals-of-Docker-19.x-Second-Edition/tree/master/ch16/ probes.

Please make sure you have cloned this book's GitHub repository, as described in Chapter 2, *Setting Up a Working Environment*.

In your Terminal, navigate to the ~/fod/ch16 folder.

Deploying a first application

We will take our pets application, which we first introduced in Chapter 11, *Docker Compose*, and deploy it into a Kubernetes cluster. Our cluster will be Minikube, which, as you know, is a single-node cluster. However, from the perspective of a deployment, it doesn't really matter how big the cluster is and where the cluster is located in the cloud, in your company's data center, or on your personal workstation.

Deploying the web component

Just as a reminder, our application consists of two application services: the Node-based web component and the backing PostgreSQL database. In the previous chapter, we learned that we need to define a Kubernetes Deployment object for each application service we want to deploy. Let's do this first for the web component. As always in this book, we will choose the declarative way of defining our objects. Here is the YAML defining a Deployment object for the web component:

```
! web-deployment.yaml ×

ch16 > ! web-deployment.yaml
    1    apiVersion: apps/v1
    2    kind: Deployment
    3    metadata:
    4      name: web
    5    spec:
    6      replicas: 1
    7      selector:
    8        matchLabels:
    9          app: pets
   10          service: web
   11      template:
   12        metadata:
   13          labels:
   14            app: pets
   15            service: web
   16        spec:
   17          containers:
   18          - image: fundamentalsofdocker/ch11-web:2.0
   19            name: web
   20            ports:
   21            - containerPort: 3000
   22              protocol: TCP
   23    |
```

Kubernetes deployment definition for the web component

The preceding deployment definition can be found in the `web-deployment.yaml` file in the `~/fod/ch16` folder. The lines of code are as follows:

- On line 4: We define the name for our `Deployment` object as `web`.
- On line 6: We declare that we want to have one instance of the `web` component running.
- From line 8 to 10: We define which pods will be part of our deployment, namely those that have the `app` and `service` labels with values of `pets` and `web`, respectively.
- On line 11: In the template for the pods starting at line 11, we define that each pod will have the `app` and `service` labels applied to them.
- From line 17: We define the single container that will be running in the pod. The image for the container is our well-known `fundamentalsofdocker/ch11-web:2.0` image and the name of the container will be `web`.
- `ports`: Finally, we declare that the container exposes port 3000 for TCP-type traffic.

Please make sure that you have set the context of kubectl to Minikube. See `Chapter 2, Setting Up a Working Environment,` for details on how to do that.

We can deploy this Deployment object using kubectl:

```
$ kubectl create -f web-deployment.yaml
```

We can double-check that the deployment has been created again using our Kubernetes CLI. We should see the following output:

```
$ kubectl get all
NAME                           READY    STATUS     RESTARTS    AGE
pod/web-5989d6fc88-52mbf       1/1      Running    0           8s

NAME                   TYPE         CLUSTER-IP    EXTERNAL-IP    PORT(S)    AGE
service/kubernetes     ClusterIP    10.96.0.1     <none>         443/TCP    126m

NAME                     READY    UP-TO-DATE    AVAILABLE    AGE
deployment.apps/web      1/1      1             1            9s

NAME                               DESIRED    CURRENT    READY    AGE
replicaset.apps/web-5989d6fc88     1          1          1        9s
```

Listing all resources running in Minikube

In the preceding output, we can see that Kubernetes created three objects – the deployment, a pertaining ReplicaSet, and a single pod (remember that we specified that we want one replica only). The current state corresponds to the desired state for all three objects, so we are fine so far.

Now, the web service needs to be exposed to the public. For this, we need to define a Kubernetes Service object of the `NodePort` type. Here is the definition, which can be found in the `web-service.yaml` file in the `~/fod/ch16` folder:

```
! web-service.yaml  ×
1   apiVersion: v1
2   kind: Service
3   metadata:
4     name: web
5   spec:
6     type: NodePort
7     ports:
8     - port: 3000
9       protocol: TCP
10    selector:
11      app: pets
12      service: web
```

Definition of the Service object for our web component

The preceding lines of codes are as follows:

- On line 4: We set the `name` of this Service object to `web`.
- On line 6: We define the `type` of Service object we're using. Since the web component has to be accessible from outside of the cluster, this cannot be a Service object of the `ClusterIP` type and must be either of the `NodePort` or `LoadBalancer` type. We discussed the various types of Kubernetes services in the previous chapter, so will not go into further detail about this. In our sample, we're using a `NodePort` type of service.
- On lines 8 and 9: We specify that we want to expose port `3000` for access through the `TCP` protocol. Kubernetes will map container port `3000` automatically to a free host port in the range of 30,000 to 32,768. Which port Kubernetes effectively chooses can be determined using the `kubectl get service` or `kubectl describe` command for the service after it has been created.
- From line 10 to 12: We define the filter criteria for the pods that this service will be a stable endpoint for. In this case, it is all the pods that have the `app` and `service` labels with the `pets` and `web` values, respectively.

Now that we have this specification for a Service object, we can create it using `kubectl`:

```
$ kubectl create -f web-service.yaml
```

We can list all the services to see the result of the preceding command:

```
$ kubectl get services
NAME         TYPE        CLUSTER-IP     EXTERNAL-IP   PORT(S)          AGE
kubernetes   ClusterIP   10.96.0.1      <none>        443/TCP          131m
web          NodePort    10.99.99.133   <none>        3000:31331/TCP   12s
```

The Service object created for the web component

In the preceding output, we can see that a service called `web` has been created. A unique clusterIP of `10.99.99.133` has been assigned to this service, and the container port `3000` has been published on port `31331` on all cluster nodes.

If we want to test this deployment, we need to find out what IP address Minikube has, and then use this IP address to access our web service. The following is the command that we can use to do this:

```
$ IP=$(minikube ip)
$ curl -4 $IP:31331/
Pets Demo Application
```

OK, the response is `Pets Demo Application`, which is what we expected. The web service is up and running in the Kubernetes cluster. Next, we want to deploy the database.

Deploying the database

A database is a stateful component and has to be treated differently to stateless components, such as our web component. We discussed the difference between stateful and stateless components in a distributed application architecture in detail in `Chapter 9`, *Distributed Application Architecture*, and `Chapter 12`, *Orchestrators*.

Kubernetes has defined a special type of `ReplicaSet` object for stateful components. The object is called a `StatefulSet`. Let's use this kind of object to deploy our database. The definition can be found in the `~fod/ch16/db-stateful-set.yaml` file. The details are as follows:

```yaml
! db-stateful-set.yaml ×
1   apiVersion: apps/v1
2   kind: StatefulSet
3   metadata:
4     name: db
5   spec:
6     selector:
7       matchLabels:
8         app: pets
9         service: db
10    serviceName: db
11    template:
12      metadata:
13        labels:
14          app: pets
15          service: db
16      spec:
17        containers:
18          - image: fundamentalsofdocker/ch08-db:1.0
19            name: db
20            ports:
21              - containerPort: 5432
22            volumeMounts:
23              - mountPath: /var/lib/postgresql/data
24                name: pets-data
25    volumeClaimTemplates:
26      - metadata:
27          name: pets-data
28        spec:
29          accessModes:
30            - ReadWriteOnce
31          resources:
32            requests:
33              storage: 100Mi
34
```

A StatefulSet for the DB component

OK, this looks a bit scary, but it isn't. It is a bit longer than the definition of the deployment for the `web` component due to the fact that we also need to define a volume where the PostgreSQL database can store the data. The volume claim definition is on lines 25 to 33. We want to create a volume with the name `pets-data` that has a maximum size equal to 100 MB. On lines 22 to 24, we use this volume and mount it into the container at `/var/lib/postgresql/data`, where PostgreSQL expects it. On line 21, we also declare that PostgreSQL is listening at port 5432.

As always, we use kubectl to deploy the `StatefulSet`:

```
$ kubectl create -f db-stateful-set.yaml
```

Now, if we list all the resources in the cluster, we will be able to see the additional objects that were created:

```
$ kubectl get all
NAME                        READY    STATUS     RESTARTS    AGE
pod/db-0                    1/1      Running    0           6s
pod/web-5989d6fc88-52mbf    1/1      Running    0           13m


NAME                  TYPE        CLUSTER-IP      EXTERNAL-IP    PORT(S)           AGE
service/kubernetes    ClusterIP   10.96.0.1       <none>         443/TCP           140m
service/web           NodePort    10.99.99.133    <none>         3000:31331/TCP    9m9s


NAME                    READY    UP-TO-DATE    AVAILABLE    AGE
deployment.apps/web     1/1      1             1            13m


NAME                                 DESIRED    CURRENT    READY    AGE
replicaset.apps/web-5989d6fc88       1          1          1        13m


NAME                      READY    AGE
statefulset.apps/db       1/1      6s
```

The StatefulSet and its pod

Here, we can see that a `StatefulSet` and a pod have been created. For both, the current state corresponds to the desired state and thus the system is healthy. But that doesn't mean that the web component can access the database at this time. Service discovery won't work so far. Remember that the web component wants to access the `db` service under the name `db`.

To make service discovery work inside the cluster, we have to define a
Kubernetes Service object for the database component too. Since the database should only
ever be accessible from within the cluster, the type of Service object we need is `ClusterIP`.
Here is the specification, which can be found in the `~/fod/ch16/db-service.yaml` file:

```
! db-service.yaml  ×
       Gabriel Schenker, 2 days ago | 1
  1    apiVersion: v1
  2    kind: Service
  3    metadata:
  4      name: db
  5    spec:
  6      type: ClusterIP
  7      ports:
  8      - port: 5432
  9        protocol: TCP
 10      selector:
 11        app: pets
 12        service: db
```

Definition of the Kubernetes Service object for the database

The database component will be represented by this Service object and it can be reached by
the name `db`, which is the name of the service, as defined on line 4. The database
component does not have to be publicly accessible, so we decided to use a Service object of
the `ClusterIP` type. The selector on lines 10 to 12 defines that this service represents a
stable endpoint for all the pods that have the according labels defined, that is, `app:`
`pets` and `service: db`.

Let's deploy this service with the following command:

```
$ kubectl create -f db-service.yaml
```

Now, we should be ready to test the application. We can use the browser this time to enjoy
the beautiful animal images:

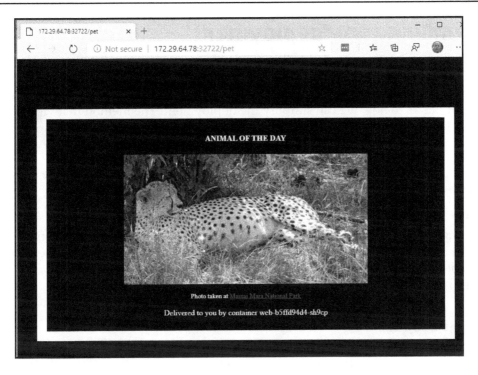

ANIMAL OF THE DAY

Photo taken at Massai Mara National Park

Delivered to you by container web-b5ffd94d4-sh9cp

Testing the pets application running in Kubernetes

`172.29.64.78` is the IP address of my Minikube. Verify your address using the `minikube ip` command. Port number `32722` is the number that Kubernetes automatically selected for my `web` Service object. Replace this number with the port that Kubernetes assigned to your service. You can get the number by using the `kubectl get services` command.

Now, we have successfully deployed the pets application to Minikube, which is a single-node Kubernetes cluster. We had to define four artifacts to do so, which are as follows:

- A Deployment and a Service object for the web component
- A StatefulSet and a Service object for the database component

To remove the application from the cluster, we can use the following small script:

```
kubectl delete svc/web
kubectl delete deploy/web
kubectl delete svc/db
kubectl delete statefulset/db
```

Next, we will be streamlining the deployment.

Streamlining the deployment

So far, we have created four artifacts that needed to be deployed to the cluster. This is only a very simple application, consisting of two components. Imagine having a much more complex application. It would quickly become a maintenance nightmare. Luckily, we have several options as to how we can simplify the deployment. The method that we are going to discuss here is the possibility of defining all the components that make up an application in Kubernetes in a single file.

Other solutions that lie outside of the scope of this book would include the use of a package manager, such as Helm.

If we have an application consisting of many Kubernetes objects such as `Deployment` and `Service` objects, then we can keep them all in one single file and separate the individual object definitions by three dashes. For example, if we wanted to have the `Deployment` and the `Service` definition for the `web` component in a single file, this would look as follows:

```
apiVersion: extensions/v1beta1
kind: Deployment
metadata:
  name: web
spec:
  replicas: 1
  selector:
    matchLabels:
      app: pets
      service: web
  template:
    metadata:
      labels:
        app: pets
        service: web
    spec:
      containers:
      - image: fundamentalsofdocker/ch11-web:2.0
        name: web
        ports:
        - containerPort: 3000
          protocol: TCP
---
apiVersion: v1
kind: Service
metadata:
  name: web
spec:
```

```
type: NodePort
ports:
- port: 3000
  protocol: TCP
selector:
  app: pets
  service: web
```

Here, we have collected all four object definitions for the `pets` application in the `~/fod/ch16/pets.yaml` file, and we can deploy the application in one go:

```
$ kubectl create -f pets.yaml
deployment "web" created
service "web" created
statefulset "db" created
service "db" created
$
```

Using a single script to deploy the pets application

Similarly, we have created a script called `~/fod/ch16/remove-pets.sh` to remove all the artifacts of the pets application from the Kubernetes cluster:

```
$ ./remove-pets.sh
deployment "web" deleted
service "web" deleted
statefulset "db" deleted
service "db" deleted
$
```

Removing pets from the Kubernetes cluster

With this, we have taken our pets application we introduced in `Chapter 11`, *Docker Compose*, and defined all the Kubernetes objects that are necessary to deploy this application into a Kubernetes cluster. In each step, we have made sure that we got the expected result, and once all the artifacts existed in the cluster, we showed the running application.

Defining liveness and readiness

Container orchestration systems such as Kubernetes and Docker swarm make it significantly easier to deploy, run, and update highly distributed, mission-critical applications. The orchestration engine automates many of the cumbersome tasks such as scaling up or down, asserting that the desired state is maintained at all times, and more.

But, the orchestration engine cannot just do everything automagically. Sometimes, we developers need to support the engine with some information that only we can know about. So, what do I mean by that?

Let's look at a single application service. Let's assume it is a microservice and let's call it **service A**. If we run service A containerized on a Kubernetes cluster, then Kubernetes can make sure that we have the five instances that we require in the service definition running at all times. If one instance crashes, Kubernetes can quickly launch a new instance and thus maintain the desired state. But, what if an instance of the service does not crash, but is unhealthy or just not ready yet to serve requests? It is evident that Kubernetes should know about both situations. But it can't, since healthy or not from an application service perspective is outside of the knowledge of the orchestration engine. Only we application developers can know when our service is healthy and when it is not.

The application service could, for example, be running, but its internal state could have been corrupted due to some bug, it could be in an endless loop, or in a deadlock situation. Similarly, only we application developers know if our service is ready to work, or if it is still initializing. Although it is highly recommended to keep the initialization phase of a microservice as short as possible, it often cannot be avoided if there is a significant time span needed by a particular service so that it's ready to operate. Being in this state of initialization is not the same thing as being unhealthy, though. The initialization phase is an expected part of the life cycle of a microservice or any other application service.

Thus, Kubernetes should not try to kill our microservice if it is in the initialization phase. If our microservice is unhealthy, though, Kubernetes should kill it as quickly as possible and replace it with a fresh instance.

Kubernetes has a concept of probes to provide the seam between the orchestration engine and the application developer. Kubernetes uses these probes to find out more about the inner state of the application service at hand. Probes are executed locally, inside each container. There is a probe for the health – also called liveness – of the service, a startup probe, and a probe for the readiness of the service. Let's look at them in turn.

Kubernetes liveness probe

Kubernetes uses the liveness probe to decide when a container needs to be killed and when another instance should be launched instead. Since Kubernetes operates at a pod level, the respective pod is killed if at least one of its containers reports as being unhealthy. Alternatively, we can say it the other way around: only if all the containers of a pod report to be healthy, is the pod considered to be healthy.

We can define the liveness probe in the specification for a pod as follows:

```
apiVersion: v1
kind: Pod
metadata:
  ...
spec:
 containers:
 - name: liveness-demo
 image: postgres:12.10
 ...
 livenessProbe:
   exec:
    command: nc localhost 5432 || exit -1
   initialDelaySeconds: 10
   periodSeconds: 5
```

The relevant part is in the `livenessProbe` section. First, we define a command that Kubernetes will execute as a probe inside the container. In our case, we have a PostresSQL container and use the `netcat` Linux tool to probe port `5432` over TCP. The `nc localhost 5432` command is successful once Postgres listens at it.

The other two settings, `initialDelaySeconds` and `periodSeconds`, define how long Kubernetes should wait after starting the container until it first executes the probe and how frequently the probe should be executed thereafter. In our case, Kubernetes waits for 10 seconds prior to executing the first probe and then executes a probe every 5 seconds.

It is also possible to probe an HTTP endpoint instead of using a command. Let's assume we're running a microservice from an image, `acme.com/my-api:1.0`, with an API that has an endpoint called `/api/health` that returns status `200` `(OK)` if the microservice is healthy, and `50x` `(Error)` if it is unhealthy. Here, we can define the liveness probe as follows:

```
apiVersion: v1
kind: Pod
metadata:
  ...
```

```
spec:
  containers:
  - name: liveness
    image: acme.com/my-api:1.0
    ...
    livenessProbe:
      httpGet:
        path: /api/health
        port: 3000
      initialDelaySeconds: 5
      periodSeconds: 3
```

In the preceding snippet, I have defined the liveness probe so that it uses the HTTP protocol and executed a GET request to the /api/health endpoint on port 5000 of localhost. Remember, the probe is executed inside the container, which means I can use localhost.

We can also directly use the TCP protocol to probe a port on the container. But wait a second – didn't we just do that in our first sample, where we used the generic liveness probe based on an arbitrary command? Yes, you're right, we did. But we had to rely on the presence of the netcat tool in the container to do so. We cannot assume that this tool is always there. Thus, it is favorable to rely on Kubernetes to do the TCP-based probing for us out of the box. The modified pod spec looks like this:

```
apiVersion: v1
kind: Pod
metadata:
  ...
spec:
  containers:
  - name: liveness-demo
    image: postgres:12.10
    ...
    livenessProbe:
      tcpSocket:
        port: 5432
      initialDelaySeconds: 10
      periodSeconds: 5
```

This looks very similar. The only change is that the type of probe has been changed from exec to tcpSocket and that, instead of providing a command, we provide the port to probe.

Let's try this out:

1. Navigate to the `~/fod/ch16/probes` folder and build the Docker image with the following command:

    ```
    $ docker image build -t fundamentalsofdocker/probes-demo:2.0 .
    ```

2. Use `kubectl` to deploy the sample pod that's defined in `probes-demo.yaml`:

    ```
    $ kubectl apply -f probes-demo.yaml
    ```

3. Describe the pod and specifically analyze the log part of the output:

    ```
    $ kubectl describe pods/probes-demo
    ```

    During the first half minute or so, you should get the following output:

```
Events:
  Type    Reason     Age   From                   Message
  ----    ------     ----  ----                   -------
  Normal  Scheduled  26s   default-scheduler      Successfully assigned default/probes-demo to docker-desktop
  Normal  Pulled     25s   kubelet, docker-desktop  Container image "fundamentalsofdocker/probes-demo:2.0" already present on machine
  Normal  Created    25s   kubelet, docker-desktop  Created container probes-demo
  Normal  Started    25s   kubelet, docker-desktop  Started container probes-demo
```

Log output of the healthy pod

4. Wait at least 30 seconds and then describe the pod again. This time, you should see the following output:

```
Events:
  Type     Reason     Age             From                   Message
  ----     ------     ----            ----                   -------
  Normal   Scheduled  72s             default-scheduler      Successfully assigned default/probes-demo to docker-desktop
  Normal   Pulled     71s             kubelet, docker-desktop  Container image "fundamentalsofdocker/probes-demo:2.0" already present on machine
  Normal   Created    71s             kubelet, docker-desktop  Created container probes-demo
  Normal   Started    71s             kubelet, docker-desktop  Started container probes-demo
  Warning  Unhealthy  30s (x3 over 40s) kubelet, docker-desktop  Liveness probe failed: cat: /app/healthy: No such file or directory
  Normal   Killing    30s             kubelet, docker-desktop  Container probes-demo failed liveness probe, will be restarted
```

Log output of the pod after it has changed its state to `Unhealthy`

The last two lines are indicating the failure of the probe and the fact that the pod is going to be restarted.

If you get the list of pods, you will see that the pod has been restarted a number of times:

```
$ kubectl get pods
NAME          READY   STATUS    RESTARTS   AGE
probes-demo   1/1     Running   5          7m22s
```

When you're done with the sample, delete the pod with the following command:

```
$ kubectl delete pods/probes-demo
```

Next, we will have a look at the Kubernetes readiness probe.

Kubernetes readiness probe

Kubernetes uses a readiness probe to decide when a service instance, that is, a container, is ready to accept traffic. Now, we all know that Kubernetes deploys and runs pods and not containers, so it only makes sense to talk about the readiness of a pod. Only if all containers in a pod report to be ready is the pod considered to be ready itself. If a pod reports not to be ready, then Kubernetes removes it from the service load balancers.

Readiness probes are defined exactly the same way as liveness probes: just switch the livenessProbe key in the pod spec to readinessProbe. Here is an example using our prior pod spec:

```
    ...
  spec:
   containers:
   - name: liveness-demo
     image: postgres:12.10
     ...
     livenessProbe:
       tcpSocket:
         port: 5432
       failureThreshold: 2
       periodSeconds: 5
     readinessProbe:
       tcpSocket:
         port: 5432
       initialDelaySeconds: 10
       periodSeconds: 5
```

Note that, in this example, we don't really need an initial delay for the liveness probe anymore since we now have a readiness probe. Thus, I have replaced the initial delay entry for the liveness probe with an entry called failureThreshold, which is indicating how many times Kubernetes should repeat probing in case of a failure until it assumes that the container is unhealthy.

Kubernetes startup probe

It is often helpful for Kubernetes to know when a service instance has started. If we define a startup probe for a container, then Kubernetes does not execute the liveness or readiness probes, as long as the container's startup probe does not succeed. Once again, Kubernetes looks at pods and starts executing liveness and readiness probes on its containers if the startup probes of all the pod's containers succeed.

When would we use a startup probe, given the fact that we already have the liveness and readiness probes? There might be situations where we have to account for exceptionally long startup and initialization times, such as when containerizing a legacy application. We could technically configure the readiness or the liveness probes to account for this fact, but that would defeat the purpose of these probes. The latter probes are meant to provide quick feedback to Kubernetes on the health and availability of the container. If we configure for long initial delays or periods, then this would counter the desired outcome.

Unsurprisingly, the startup probe is defined exactly the same way as the readiness and liveness probes. Here is an example:

```
spec:
  containers:
    ..
    startupProbe:
      tcpSocket:
        port: 3000
      failureThreshold: 30
      periodSeconds: 5
  ...
```

Make sure that you define the `failureThreshold` * `periodSeconds` product so that it's big enough to account for the worst startup time.

 In our example, the max startup time should not exceed 150 seconds.

Zero downtime deployments

In a mission-critical environment, it is important that the application is always up and running. These days, we cannot afford any downtime anymore. Kubernetes gives us various means of achieving this. Performing an update on an application in the cluster that causes no downtime is called a zero downtime deployment. In this section, we will present two ways of achieving this. These are as follows:

- Rolling updates
- Blue-green deployments

Let's start by discussing rolling updates.

Rolling updates

In the previous chapter, we learned that the Kubernetes Deployment object distinguishes itself from the ReplicaSet object in that it adds rolling updates and rollbacks on top of the latter's functionality. Let's use our web component to demonstrate this. Evidently, we will have to modify the manifest or description of the deployment for the web component.

We will use the same deployment definition as in the previous section, with one important difference – we will have five replicas of the web component running. The following definition can also be found in the `~/fod/ch16/web-deploy-rolling-v1.yaml` file:

```
apiVersion: apps/v1
kind: Deployment
metadata:
  name: web
spec:
  replicas: 5
  selector:
    matchLabels:
      app: pets
      service: web
  template:
    metadata:
      labels:
        app: pets
        service: web
    spec:
      containers:
      - image: fundamentalsofdocker/ch11-web:2.0
        name: web
        ports:
```

```
    - containerPort: 3000
      protocol: TCP
```

Now, we can create this deployment as usual and also, at the same time, the service that makes our component accessible:

```
$ kubectl create -f web-deploy-rolling-v1.yaml
$ kubectl create -f web-service.yaml
```

Once we have deployed the pods and the service, we can test our web component with the following command:

```
$ PORT=$(kubectl get svc/web -o yaml | grep nodePort | cut -d' ' -f5)
$ IP=$(minikube ip)
$ curl -4 ${IP}:${PORT}/
Pets Demo Application
```

As we can see, the application is up and running and returns the expected message, `Pets Demo Application`.

Now. our developers have created a new version, 2.1, of the web component. The code of the new version of the web component can be found in the `~/fod/ch16/web` folder, and the only change is located on line 12 of the `server.js` file:

```
 9    app.set('views', __dirname);
10
11    app.get('/',function(req,res){
12        res.status(200).send('Pets Demo Application v2\n');
13    });
14
```

Code change for version 2.0 of the web component

The developers have built the new image as follows:

```
$ docker image build -t fundamentalsofdocker/ch16-web:2.1 web
```

Subsequently, they pushed the image to Docker Hub, as follows:

```
$ docker image push fundamentalsofdocker/ch16-web:2.1
```

Now, we want to update the image that's used by our pods that are part of the web Deployment object. We can do this by using the `set image` command of `kubectl`:

```
$ kubectl set image deployment/web \
    web=fundamentalsofdocker/ch16-web:2.1
```

If we test the application again, we'll get a confirmation that the update has indeed happened:

```
$ curl -4 ${IP}:${PORT}/
Pets Demo Application v2
```

Now, how do we know that there hasn't been any downtime during this update? Did the update really happen in a rolling fashion? What does rolling update mean at all? Let's investigate. First, we can get a confirmation from Kubernetes that the deployment has indeed happened and was successful by using the `rollout status` command:

```
$ kubectl rollout status deploy/web
deployment "web" successfully rolled out
```

If we describe the deployment web with `kubectl describe deploy/web`, we get the following list of events at the end of the output:

```
Events:
  Type    Reason             Age           From                    Message
  ----    ------             ----          ----                    -------
  Normal  ScalingReplicaSet  12m           deployment-controller   Scaled up replica set web-769b88f67 to 5
  Normal  ScalingReplicaSet  3m            deployment-controller   Scaled up replica set web-55cdf67cd to 1
  Normal  ScalingReplicaSet  3m            deployment-controller   Scaled down replica set web-769b88f67 to 4
  Normal  ScalingReplicaSet  3m            deployment-controller   Scaled up replica set web-55cdf67cd to 2
  Normal  ScalingReplicaSet  3m            deployment-controller   Scaled down replica set web-769b88f67 to 3
  Normal  ScalingReplicaSet  3m            deployment-controller   Scaled up replica set web-55cdf67cd to 3
  Normal  ScalingReplicaSet  3m            deployment-controller   Scaled down replica set web-769b88f67 to 2
  Normal  ScalingReplicaSet  3m            deployment-controller   Scaled up replica set web-55cdf67cd to 4
  Normal  ScalingReplicaSet  3m            deployment-controller   Scaled down replica set web-769b88f67 to 1
  Normal  ScalingReplicaSet  3m (x2 over 3m) deployment-controller (combined from similar events): Scaled down replica
set web-769b88f67 to 0
$
```

List of events found in the output of the deployment description of the web component

The first event tells us that, when we created the deployment, a ReplicaSet called `web-769b88f67` with five replicas was created. Then, we executed the update command. The second event in the list tells us that this meant creating a new ReplicaSet called `web-55cdf67cd` with, initially, one replica only. Thus, at that particular moment, six pods existed on the system: the five initial pods and one pod with the new version. But, since the desired state of the Deployment object states that we want five replicas only, Kubernetes now scales down the old ReplicaSet to four instances, which we can see in the third event.

Then, again, the new ReplicaSet is scaled up to two instances and, subsequently, the old ReplicaSet scaled was down to three instances, and so on, until we had five new instances and all the old instances were decommissioned. Although we cannot see any precise time (other than 3 minutes) when that happened, the order of the events tells us that the whole update happened in a rolling fashion.

During a short time period, some of the calls to the web service would have had an answer from the old version of the component, and some calls would have received an answer from the new version of the component, but, at no time would the service have been down.

We can also list the ReplicaSet objects in the cluster and will get confirmation of what I said in the preceding section:

Listing all the ReplicaSet objects in the cluster

Here, we can see that the new ReplicaSet has five instances running and that the old one has been scaled down to zero instances. The reason that the old ReplicaSet object is still lingering is that Kubernetes provides us with the possibility of rolling back the update and, in that case, will reuse that ReplicaSet.

To roll back the update of the image in case some undetected bug sneaked into the new code, we can use the `rollout undo` command:

```
$ kubectl rollout undo deploy/web
deployment "web"
$ curl -4 ${IP}:${PORT}/
Pets Demo Application
```

I have also listed the test command using `curl` in the preceding snippet to verify that the rollback indeed happened. If we list the ReplicaSets, we will see the following output:

Listing ReplicaSet objects after rollback

This confirms that the old ReplicaSet (`web-769b88f67`) object has been reused and that the new one has been scaled down to zero instances.

Sometimes, though, we cannot, or do not want to, tolerate the mixed state of an old version coexisting with the new version. We want an *all-or-nothing* strategy. This is where blue-green deployments come into play, which we will discuss next.

Blue-green deployment

If we want to do a blue-green style deployment for our component web of the pets application, then we can do so by using labels creatively. First, let's remind ourselves how blue-green deployments work. Here is a rough step-by-step instruction:

1. Deploy the first version of the web component as `blue`. We will label the pods with a label of `color: blue` to do so.
2. Deploy the Kubernetes service for these pods with the `color: blue` label in the selector section.
3. Now, we can deploy version 2 of the web component, but, this time, the pods have a label of `color: green`.
4. We can test the green version of the service to check that it works as expected.
5. Now, we flip traffic from blue to green by updating the Kubernetes service for the web component. We modify the selector so that it uses the `color: green` label.

Let's define a Deployment object for version 1, blue:

```yaml
! web-deploy-blue.yaml ×
ch16 > ! web-deploy-blue.yaml
1    apiVersion: extensions/v1beta1
2    kind: Deployment
3    metadata:
4      name: web-blue
5    spec:
6      replicas: 1
7      selector:
8        matchLabels:
9          app: pets
10         service: web
11         color: blue
12     template:
13       metadata:
14         labels:
15           app: pets
16           service: web
17           color: blue
18       spec:
19         containers:
20           - image: fundamentalsofdocker/ch11-web:2.0
21             name: web
22             ports:
23               - containerPort: 3000
24                 protocol: TCP
25
```

Specification of the blue deployment for the web component

The preceding definition can be found in the ~/fod/ch16/web-deploy-blue.yaml file. Please take note of line 4, where we define the name of the deployment as web-blue to distinguish it from the upcoming deployment, web-green. Also, note that we have added the label color: blue on lines 11 and 17. Everything else remains the same as before.

Now, we can define the Service object for the web component. It will be the same as the one we used before but with a minor change, as shown in the following screenshot:

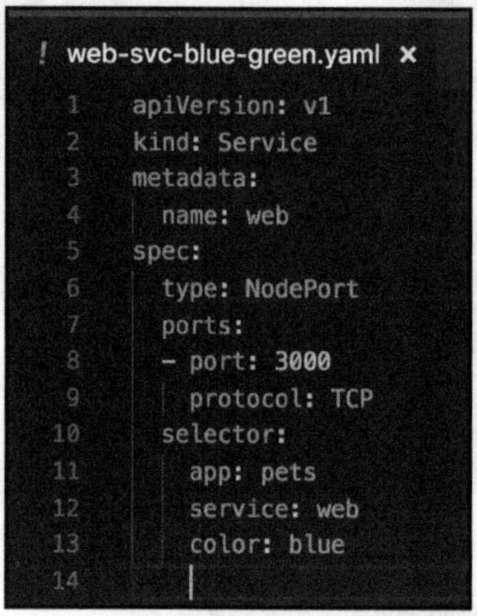

```
! web-svc-blue-green.yaml  ×
1    apiVersion: v1
2    kind: Service
3    metadata:
4      name: web
5    spec:
6      type: NodePort
7      ports:
8      - port: 3000
9        protocol: TCP
10     selector:
11       app: pets
12       service: web
13       color: blue
14       |
```

Kubernetes service for the web component supporting blue-green deployments

The only difference regarding the definition of the service we used earlier in this chapter is line 13, which adds the `color: blue` label to the selector. We can find the preceding definition in the `~/fod/ch16/web-svc-blue-green.yaml` file.

Then, we can deploy the blue version of the web component with the following command:

```
$ kubectl create -f web-deploy-blue.yaml
$ kubectl create -f web-svc-blue-green.yaml
```

Once the service is up and running, we can determine its IP address and port number and test it:

```
$ PORT=$(kubectl get svc/web -o yaml | grep nodePort | cut -d' ' -f5)
$ IP=$(minikube ip)
$ curl -4 ${IP}:${PORT}/
Pets Demo Application
```

As expected, we get the response `Pets Demo Application`. Now, we can deploy the green version of the web component. The definition of its Deployment object can be found in the `~/fod/ch16/web-deploy-green.yaml` file and looks as follows:

```
! web-deploy-green.yaml ×

ch16 >  ! web-deploy-green.yaml
    1   apiVersion: extensions/v1beta1
    2   kind: Deployment
    3   metadata:
    4     name: web-green
    5   spec:
    6     replicas: 1
    7     selector:
    8       matchLabels:
    9         app: pets
   10         service: web
   11         color: green
   12     template:
   13       metadata:
   14         labels:
   15           app: pets
   16           service: web
   17           color: green
   18       spec:
   19         containers:
   20         - image: fundamentalsofdocker/ch16-web:2.1
   21           name: web
   22           ports:
   23           - containerPort: 3000
   24             protocol: TCP
```

Specification of the deployment green for the web component

The interesting lines are as follows:

- Line 4: Named `web-green` to distinguish it from `web-blue` and allow for parallel installation
- Lines 11 and 17: Have the color `green`
- Line 20: Now using version 2.1 of the image

Now, we're ready to deploy this green version of the service. It should run separately from the blue service:

```
$ kubectl create -f web-deploy-green.yaml
```

We can make sure that both deployments coexist like so:

```
$ kubectl get deploy
NAME         DESIRED    CURRENT    UP-TO-DATE    AVAILABLE    AGE
web-blue     1          1          1             1            23h
web-green    1          1          1             1            3s
$
```

Displaying the list of Deployment objects running in the cluster

As expected, we have both blue and green running. We can verify that blue is still the active service:

```
$ curl -4 ${IP}:${PORT}/
Pets Demo Application
```

Now comes the interesting part. We can flip traffic from blue to green by editing the existing service for the web component. To do so, execute the following command:

```
$ kubectl edit svc/web
```

Change the value of the label color from blue to green. Then, save and quit the editor. The Kubernetes CLI will automatically update the service. When we now query the web service again, we get this:

```
$ curl -4 ${IP}:${PORT}/
Pets Demo Application v2
```

This confirms that the traffic has indeed switched to the green version of the web component (note the v2 at the end of the response to the curl command).

If we realize that something went wrong with our green deployment and the new version has a defect, we can easily switch back to the blue version by editing the service web again and replacing the value of the label color with blue. This rollback is instantaneous and should always work. Then, we can remove the buggy green deployment and fix the component. When we have corrected the problem, we can deploy the green version once again.

Once the green version of the component is running as expected and performing well, we can decommission the blue version:

```
$ kubectl delete deploy/web-blue
```

When we're ready to deploy a new version, 3.0, this one becomes the blue version. We update the `~/fod/ch16/web-deploy-blue.yaml` file accordingly and deploy it. Then, we flip the service web from `green` to `blue`, and so on.

We have successfully demonstrated, with our component web of the pets application, how blue-green deployment can be achieved in a Kubernetes cluster.

Kubernetes secrets

Sometimes, services that we want to run in the Kubernetes cluster have to use confidential data such as passwords, secret API keys, or certificates, to name just a few. We want to make sure that this sensitive information can only ever be seen by the authorized or dedicated service. All other services running in the cluster should not have any access to this data.

For this reason, Kubernetes secrets have been introduced. A secret is a key-value pair where the key is the unique name of the secret and the value is the actual sensitive data. Secrets are stored in etcd. Kubernetes can be configured so that secrets are encrypted at rest, that is, in etcd, and in transit, that is, when the secrets are going over the wire from a master node to the worker nodes that the pods of the service using this secret are running on.

Manually defining secrets

We can create a secret declaratively the same way as we can create any other object in Kubernetes. Here is the YAML for such a secret:

```
apiVersion: v1
kind: Secret
metadata:
  name: pets-secret
type: Opaque
data:
  username: am9obi5kb2UK
  password: cOVjcmV0LXBhc1N3MHJECg==
```

The preceding definition can be found in the `~/fod/ch16/pets-secret.yaml` file. Now, you might be wondering what the values are. Are these the real (unencrypted) values? No, they are not. And they are also not really encrypted values, but just base64-encoded values. Thus, they are not really secure, since base64-encoded values can be easily reverted to clear text values. How did I get these values? That's easy: follow these steps:

1. Use the `base64` tool as follows to encode the values:

```
$ echo "john.doe" | base64
am9obi5kb2UK
$ echo "sEcret-pasSw0rD" | base64
c0VjcmV0LXBhc1N3MHJECg==
$
```

Creating base64-encoded values for the secret

2. Using the preceding values, we can create the secret and describe it:

```
$ kubectl create -f pets-secret.yaml
secret "pets-secret" created
$ kubectl describe secrets/pets-secret
Name:          pets-secret
Namespace:     default
Labels:        <none>
Annotations:   <none>

Type:  Opaque

Data
====
password:  16 bytes
username:  9 bytes
$
```

Creating and describing the Kubernetes secret

3. In the description of the secret, the values are hidden and only their length is given. So, maybe the secrets are safe now? No, not really. We can easily decode this secret using the `kubectl get` command:

```
$ kubectl get secrets/pets-secret -o yaml
apiVersion: v1
data:
  password: c0VjcmV0LXBhc1N3MHJECg==
  username: am9obi5kb2UK
kind: Secret
metadata:
  creationTimestamp: 2018-03-31T20:36:05Z
  name: pets-secret
  namespace: default
  resourceVersion: "154786"
  selfLink: /api/v1/namespaces/default/secrets/pets-secret
  uid: 22d818bd-3523-11e8-a3cb-080027c10823
type: Opaque
$
```

Kubernetes secret decoded

As we can see in the preceding screenshot, we have our original secret values back.

4. Decode the values you got previously:

```
$ echo "c0VjcmV0LXBhc1N3MHJECg==" | base64 --decode
sEcret-pasSw0rD
```

Thus, the consequences are that this method of creating a Kubernetes is not to be used in any environment other than development, where we deal with non-sensitive data. In all other environments, we need a better way to deal with secrets.

Creating secrets with kubectl

A much safer way to define secrets is to use kubectl. First, we create files containing the base64-encoded secret values similar to what we did in the preceding section, but, this time, we store the values in temporary files:

```
$ echo "sue-hunter" | base64 > username.txt
$ echo "123abc456def" | base64 > password.txt
```

Now, we can use `kubectl` to create a secret from those files, as follows:

```
$ kubectl create secret generic pets-secret-prod \
    --from-file=./username.txt \
    --from-file=./password.txt
secret "pets-secret-prod" created
```

The secret can then be used the same way as the manually created secret.

Why is this method more secure than the other one, you might ask? Well, first of all, there is no YAML that defines a secret and is stored in some source code version control system, such as GitHub, which many people have access to and so can see and decode the secrets. Only the admin that is authorized to know the secrets ever sees their values and uses them to directly create the secrets in the (production) cluster. The cluster itself is protected by role-based access control so that no unauthorized persons have access to it, nor can they possibly decode the secrets defined in the cluster.

Now, let's see how we can actually use the secrets that we have defined.

Using secrets in a pod

Let's say we want to create a Deployment object where the web component uses our secret, `pets-secret`, that we introduced in the preceding section. We can use the following command to create the secret in the cluster:

```
$ kubectl create -f pets-secret.yaml
```

In the `~/fod/ch16/web-deploy-secret.yaml` file, we can find the definition of the `Deployment` object. We had to add the part starting from line 23 to the original definition of the `Deployment` object:

```
! web-deploy-secret.yaml  ×

ch16 > ! web-deploy-secret.yaml
    1    apiVersion: apps/v1
    2    kind: Deployment
    3    metadata:
    4      name: web
    5    spec:
    6      replicas: 1
    7      selector:
    8        matchLabels:
    9          app: pets
   10          service: web
   11      template:
   12        metadata:
   13          labels:
   14            app: pets
   15            service: web
   16        spec:
   17          containers:
   18          - image: fundamentalsofdocker/ch11-web:2.0
   19            name: web
   20            ports:
   21            - containerPort: 3000
   22              protocol: TCP
   23            volumeMounts:
   24            - name: secrets
   25              mountPath: "/etc/secrets"
   26              readOnly: true
   27          volumes:
   28          - name: secrets
   29            secret:
   30              secretName: pets-secret
```

Deployment object for the web component with a secret

On lines 27 through 30, we define a volume called `secrets` from our secret, `pets-secret`. Then, we use this volume in the container, as described on lines 23 through 26. We mount the secrets in the container filesystem at `/etc/secrets` and we mount the volume in read-only mode. Thus, the secret values will be available to the container as files in the said folder. The names of the files will correspond to the key names, and the content of the files will be the values of the corresponding keys. The values will be provided in unencrypted form to the application running inside the container.

In our case, since we have the `username` and `password` keys in the secret, we will find two files, named `username` and `password`, in the /etc/secrets folder in the container filesystem. The `username` file should contain the value `john.doe` and the `password` file should contain the value `sEcret-pasSw0rD`. Here is the confirmation:

```
$ kubectl exec -it web-597b7f7749-87mq5 -- /bin/sh
/app # cd /etc/secrets/
/etc/secrets # ls -l
total 0
lrwxrwxrwx    1 root      root           15 Apr  2 01:26 password -> ..data/password
lrwxrwxrwx    1 root      root           15 Apr  2 01:26 username -> ..data/username
/etc/secrets # cat username && cat password
john.doe
sEcret-pasSw0rD
/etc/secrets #
```

Confirming that secrets are available inside the container

On line 1 of the preceding output, we `exec` into the container where the web component runs. Then, on lines 2 to 5, we list the files in the /etc/secrets folder, and, finally, on lines 6 to 8, we show the content of the two files, which, unsurprisingly, show the secret values in clear text.

Since any application written in any language can read simple files, this mechanism of using secrets is very backward compatible. Even an old Cobol application can read clear text files from the filesystem.

Sometimes, though, applications expect secrets to be available in environment variables. Let's look at what Kubernetes offers us in this case.

Secret values in environment variables

Let's say our web component expects the username in the environment variable, `PETS_USERNAME`, and the password in `PETS_PASSWORD`. If this is the case, we can modify our deployment YAML so that it looks as follows:

```
! web-deploy-secret-env.yaml  ×
 1    apiVersion: extensions/v1beta1
 2    kind: Deployment
 3    metadata:
 4      name: web
 5    spec:
 6      replicas: 1
 7      selector:
 8        matchLabels:
 9          app: pets
10          service: web
11      template:
12        metadata:
13          labels:
14            app: pets
15            service: web
16        spec:
17          containers:
18          - image: fundamentalsofdocker/ch08-web:1.0
19            name: web
20            ports:
21            - containerPort: 3000
22              protocol: TCP
23            env:
24            - name: PETS_USERNAME
25              valueFrom:
26                secretKeyRef:
27                  name: pets-secret
28                  key: username
29            - name: PETS_PASSWORD
30              valueFrom:
31                secretKeyRef:
32                  name: pets-secret
33                  key: password
34
```

Deployment mapping secret values to environment variables

On lines 23 through 33, we define the two environment
variables, PETS_USERNAME and PETS_PASSWORD, and map the corresponding key-value
pair of pets-secret to them.

Note that we don't need a volume anymore; instead, we directly map the individual keys of our `pets-secret` into the corresponding environment variables that are valid inside the container. The following sequence of commands shows that the secret values are indeed available inside the container in the respective environment variables:

```
$ kubectl exec -it web-694f958cd4-6zq89 -- /bin/sh
/app # echo $PETS_USERNAME && echo $PETS_PASSWORD
john.doe
sEcret-pasSw0rD
/app #
```

Secret values are mapped to environment variables

In this section, we have shown you how to define secrets in a Kubernetes cluster and how to use those secrets in containers running as part of the pods of a deployment. We have shown two variants of how secrets can be mapped inside a container, the first using files and the second using environment variables.

Summary

In this chapter, we have learned how to deploy an application into a Kubernetes cluster and how to set up application-level routing for this application. Furthermore, we have learned how to update application services running in a Kubernetes cluster without causing any downtime. Finally, we used secrets to provide sensitive information to application services running in the cluster.

In the next chapter, we are going to learn about different techniques that are used to monitor an individual service or a whole distributed application running on a Kubernetes cluster. We will also learn how we can troubleshoot an application service that is running in production without altering the cluster or the cluster nodes that the service is running on. Stay tuned.

Questions

To assess your learning progress, please answer the following questions:

1. You have an application consisting of two services, the first one being a web API and the second one being a DB, such as Mongo DB. You want to deploy this application into a Kubernetes cluster. In a few short sentences, explain how you would proceed.

2. Describe in your own words what components you need in order to establish layer 7 (or application level) routing for your application.

3. List the main steps needed to implement a blue-green deployment for a simple application service. Avoid going into too much detail.

4. Name three or four types of information that you would provide to an application service through Kubernetes secrets.

5. Name the sources that Kubernetes accepts when creating a secret.

Further reading

Here are a few links that provide additional information on the topics that were discussed in this chapter:

- Performing a rolling update: `https://bit.ly/2o2okEQ`
- Blue-green deployment: `https://bit.ly/2r2IxNJ`
- Secrets in Kubernetes: `https://bit.ly/2C6hMZF`

17
Monitoring and Troubleshooting an App Running in Production

In the previous chapter, we learned how to deploy a multi-service application into a Kubernetes cluster. We configured application-level routing for the application and updated its services using a zero-downtime strategy. Finally, we provided confidential data to the running services by using Kubernetes Secrets.

In this chapter, you will learn the different techniques used to monitor an individual service or a whole distributed application running on a Kubernetes cluster. You will also learn how you can troubleshoot an application service that is running in production, without altering the cluster or the cluster nodes on which the service is running.

The chapter covers the following topics:

- Monitoring an individual service
- Using Prometheus to monitor your distributed application
- Troubleshooting a service running in production

After working through this chapter, you will be able to do the following:

- Configure application-level monitoring for a service.
- Use Prometheus to collect and centrally aggregate relevant application metrics.
- Troubleshoot a service running in production using a special tools container.

Technical requirements

In this chapter, we're going to use Minikube on our local computer. Please refer to Chapter 2, *Setting Up a Working Environment*, for more information on how to install and use Minikube.

The code for this chapter can be found at: `https://github.com/PacktPublishing/Learn-Docker---Fundamentals-of-Docker-19.x-Second-Edition/tree/master/ch17`.

Please make sure you have cloned the GitHub repository as described in `Chapter 2`, *Setting Up a Working Environment*.

In your Terminal, navigate to the `~/fod/ch17` folder.

Monitoring an individual service

When working with a distributed mission-critical application in production or in any production-like environment, then it is of utmost importance to gain as much insight as possible into the inner workings of those applications. Have you ever had a chance to look into the cockpit of an airplane or the command center of a nuclear power plant? Both the airplane and the power plant are samples of highly complex systems that deliver mission-critical services. If a plane crashes or a power plant shuts down unexpectedly, a lot of people are negatively affected, to say the least. Thus the cockpit and the command center are full of instruments showing the current or past state of some part of the system. What you see is the visual representation of some sensors that are placed in strategic parts of the system, and constantly collect data such as the temperature or the flow rate.

Similar to the airplane or the power plant, our application needs to be instrumented with "sensors" that can feel the "temperature" of our application services or the infrastructure they run on. I put the temperature in double quotes since it is only a placeholder for things that matter in an application, such as the number of requests per second on a given RESTful endpoint, or the average latency of request to the same endpoint.

The resulting values or readings that we collect, such as the average latency of requests, are often called metrics. It should be our goal to expose as many meaningful metrics as possible of the application services we build. Metrics can be both functional and non-functional. Functional metrics are values that say something business-relevant about the application service, such as how many checkouts are performed per minute if the service is part of an e-commerce application, or which are the five most popular songs over the last 24 hours if we're talking about a streaming application.

Non-functional metrics are important values that are not specific to the kind of business the application is used for, such as what is the average latency of a particular web request or how many `4xx` status codes are returned per minute by another endpoint, or how much RAM or how many CPU cycles a given service is using.

In a distributed system where each part is exposing metrics, some overarching service should be collecting and aggregating the values periodically from each component. Alternatively, each component should forward its metrics to a central metrics server. Only if the metrics for all components of our highly distributed system are available for inspection in a central location are they of any value. Otherwise, monitoring the system becomes impossible. That's why pilots of an airplane never have to go and inspect individual and critical parts of the airplane in person during a flight; all necessary readings are collected and displayed in the cockpit.

Today one of the most popular services that is used to expose, collect, and store metrics is Prometheus. It is an open source project and has been donated to the **Cloud Native Computing Foundation (CNCF)**. Prometheus has first-class integration with Docker containers, Kubernetes, and many other systems and programming platforms. In this chapter, we will use Prometheus to demonstrate how to instrument a simple service that exposes important metrics.

Instrumenting a Node.js-based service

In this section, we want to learn how to instrument a microservice authored in Node Express.js by following these steps:

1. Create a new folder called `node` and navigate to it:

   ```
   $ mkdir node && cd node
   ```

2. Run `npm init` in this folder, and accept all defaults except the **entry point**, which you change from the `index.js` default to `server.js`.

3. We need to add `express` to our project with the following:

   ```
   $ npm install --save express
   ```

4. Now we need to install the Prometheus adapter for Node Express with the following:

   ```
   $ npm install --save prom-client
   ```

5. Add a file called `server.js` to the folder with this content:

   ```
   const app = require("express")();

   app.get('/hello', (req, res) => {
     const { name = 'World' } = req.query;
     res.json({ message: `Hello, ${name}!` });
   ```

```
});

app.listen(port=3000, () => {
  console.log(`Example api is listening on http://localhost:3000`);
});
```

This is a very simple Node Express app with a single endpoint: /hello.

6. To the preceding code, add the following snippet to initialize the Prometheus client:

```
const client = require("prom-client");
const register = client.register;
const collectDefaultMetrics = client.collectDefaultMetrics;
collectDefaultMetrics({ register });
```

7. Next, add an endpoint to expose the metrics:

```
app.get('/metrics', (req, res) => {
  res.set('Content-Type', register.contentType);
  res.end(register.metrics());
});
```

8. Now let's run this sample microservice:

$ npm start

```
> node@1.0.0 start C:\Users\Gabriel\fod\ch17\node
> node server.js

Example api is listening on http://localhost:3000
```

We can see in the preceding output that the service is listening at port 3000.

8. Let's now try to access the metrics at the /metrics endpoint, as we defined in the code:

```
$ curl localhost:3000/metrics
...
process_cpu_user_seconds_total 0.016 1577633206532

# HELP process_cpu_system_seconds_total Total system CPU time spent in
seconds.
# TYPE process_cpu_system_seconds_total counter
process_cpu_system_seconds_total 0.015 1577633206532

# HELP process_cpu_seconds_total Total user and system CPU time spent in
seconds.
```

```
# TYPE process_cpu_seconds_total counter
process_cpu_seconds_total 0.031 1577633206532
...
nodejs_version_info{version="v10.15.3",major="10",minor="15",patch="3"} 1
```

What we get as output is a pretty long list of metrics, ready for consumption by a Prometheus server.

This was pretty easy, wasn't it? By adding a node package and adding a few trivial lines of code to our application startup, we have gained access to a plethora of system metrics.

Now let's define our own custom metric. Let it be a `Counter` object:

1. Add the following code snippet to `server.js` to define a custom counter called `my_hello_counter`:

```
const helloCounter = new client.Counter({
  name: 'my_hello_counter',
  help: 'Counts the number of hello requests',
});
```

2. To our existing `/hello` endpoint, add code to increase the counter:

```
app.get('/hello', (req, res) => {
  helloCounter.inc();
  const { name = 'World' } = req.query;
  res.json({ message: `Hello, ${name}!` });
});
```

3. Rerun the application with `npm start`.
4. To test the new counter, let's access our `/hello` endpoint twice:

   $ curl localhost:3000/hello?name=Sue

5. We will get this output when accessing the `/metrics` endpoint:

   $ curl localhost:3000/metrics

   ```
   ...
   # HELP my_hello_counter Counts the number of hello requests
   # TYPE my_hello_counter counter
   my_hello_counter 2
   ```

The counter we defined in code clearly works and is output with the HELP text we added.

Now that we know how to instrument a Node Express application, let's do the same for a .NET Core-based microservice.

Instrumenting a .NET Core-based service

Let's start by creating a simple .NET Core microservice based on the Web API template.

1. Create a new `dotnet` folder, and navigate to it:

   ```
   $ mkdir dotnet && cd dotnet
   ```

2. Use the `dotnet` tool to scaffold a new microservice called `sample-api`:

   ```
   $ dotnet new webapi --output sample-api
   ```

3. We will use the Prometheus adapter for .NET, which is available to us as a NuGet package called `prometheus-net.AspNetCore`. Add this package to the `sample-api` project, with the following command:

   ```
   $ dotnet add sample-api package prometheus-net.AspNetCore
   ```

4. Open the project in your favorite code editor; for example, when using VS Code execute the following:

   ```
   $ code .
   ```

5. Locate the `Startup.cs` file, and open it. At the beginning of the file, add a `using` statement:

   ```
   using Prometheus;
   ```

6. Then in the `Configure` method add the `endpoints.MapMetrics()` statement to the mapping of the endpoints. Your code should look as follows:

   ```
   public void Configure(IApplicationBuilder app, IWebHostEnvironment
   env)
   {
       ...
       app.UseEndpoints(endpoints =>
       {
           endpoints.MapControllers();
           endpoints.MapMetrics();
       });
   }
   ```

Note that the above is valid for version 3.x of .NET Core. If you're on an earlier version, the configuration looks slightly different. Consult the following repo for more details, at `https://github.com/prometheus-net/prometheus-net`.

7. With this, the Prometheus component will start publishing the request metrics of ASP.NET Core. Let's try it. First, start the application with the following:

```
$ dotnet run --project sample-api

info: Microsoft.Hosting.Lifetime[0]
      Now listening on: https://localhost:5001
info: Microsoft.Hosting.Lifetime[0]
      Now listening on: http://localhost:5000
...
```

The preceding output tells us that the microservice is listening at `https://localhost:5001`.

8. We can now use `curl` to call the metrics endpoint of the service:

```
$ curl --insecure https://localhost:5001/metrics

# HELP process_private_memory_bytes Process private memory size
# TYPE process_private_memory_bytes gauge
process_private_memory_bytes 55619584
# HELP process_virtual_memory_bytes Virtual memory size in bytes.
# TYPE process_virtual_memory_bytes gauge
process_virtual_memory_bytes 2221930053632
# HELP process_working_set_bytes Process working set
# TYPE process_working_set_bytes gauge
process_working_set_bytes 105537536
...
dotnet_collection_count_total{generation="1"} 0
dotnet_collection_count_total{generation="0"} 0
dotnet_collection_count_total{generation="2"} 0
```

What we get is a list of system metrics for our microservice. That was easy: we only needed to add a NuGet package and a single line of code to get our service instrumented!

What if we want to add our own (functional) metrics? This is equally straightforward. Assume we want to measure the number of concurrent accesses to our `/weatherforecast` endpoint. To do this, we define a `gauge` and use it to wrap the logic in the appropriate endpoint with this gauge. We can do this by following these steps:

1. Locate the `Controllers/WeatherForecastController.cs` class.
2. Add `using Prometheus;` to the top of the file.
3. Define a private instance variable of the `Gauge` type in the `WeatherForecastController` class:

   ```
   private static readonly Gauge weatherForecastsInProgress = Metrics
       .CreateGauge("myapp_weather_forecasts_in_progress",
               "Number of weather forecast operations ongoing.");
   ```

4. Wrap the logic of the `Get` method with a `using` statement:

   ```
   [HttpGet]
   public IEnumerable<WeatherForecast> Get()
   {
       using(weatherForecastsInProgress.TrackInProgress())
       {
           ...
       }
   }
   ```

5. Restart the microservice.
6. Call the `/weatherforecast` endpoint a couple of times using `curl`:

   ```
   $ curl --insecure https://localhost:5001/weatherforecast
   ```

7. Use `curl` to get the metrics, as earlier in this section:

   ```
   $ curl --insecure https://localhost:5001/metrics

   # HELP myapp_weather_forecasts_in_progress Number of weather
   forecast operations ongoing.
   # TYPE myapp_weather_forecasts_in_progress gauge
   myapp_weather_forecasts_in_progress 0
   ...
   ```

You will notice that there is now a new metric called `myapp_weather_forecasts_in_progress` available in the list. Its value will be zero, since currently you are not running any requests against the tracked endpoint, and a `gauge` type metric is only measuring the number of ongoing requests.

Congratulations, you have just defined your first functional metric. This is only a start; many more sophisticated possibilities are readily available to you.

Node.js or .NET Core-based application services are by no means special. It is just as straightforward and easy to instrument services written in other languages, such as Java, Python, or Go.

Having learned how to instrument an application service so that it exposes important metrics, let's now have a look how we can use Prometheus to collect and aggregate those values to allow us to monitor a distributed application.

Using Prometheus to monitor a distributed application

Now that we have learned how to instrument an application service to expose Prometheus metrics, it's time to show how we can collect the metrics and forward them to a Prometheus server where all metrics will be aggregated and stored. We can then either use the (simple) web UI of Prometheus or a more sophisticated solution like Grafana to display important metrics on a dashboard.

Unlike most other tools that are used to collect metrics from application services and infrastructure components, the Prometheus server takes the load of work and periodically scrapes all the defined targets. This way applications and services don't need to worry about forwarding data. You can also describe this as pulling metrics versus pushing them. This makes Prometheus servers an excellent fit for our case.

We will now discuss how to deploy Prometheus to Kubernetes, followed by our two sample application services. Finally, we will deploy Grafana to the cluster, and use it to display our customer metrics on a dashboard.

Architecture

Let's have a quick overview of the architecture of the planned system. As mentioned before, we have our microservices, the Prometheus server, and Grafana. Furthermore, everything will be deployed to Kubernetes. The following diagram shows the relationships:

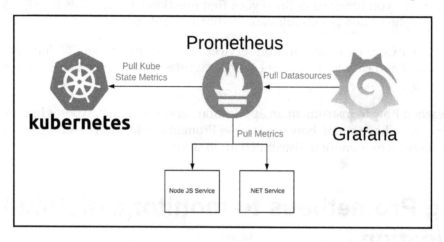

High-level overview of an application using Prometheus and Grafana for monitoring

In the top center of the diagram, we have Prometheus, which periodically scrapes metrics from Kubernetes, shown on the left. It also periodically scrapes metrics from the services, in our case from the Node.js and the .NET sample services we created and instrumented in the previous section. Finally, on the right-hand side of the diagram, we have Grafana that is pulling data periodically from Prometheus to then display it on graphical dashboards.

Deploying Prometheus to Kubernetes

As indicated, we start by deploying Prometheus to Kubernetes. Let's first define the Kubernetes YAML file that we can use to do so. First, we need to define a Kubernetes `Deployment` that will create a `ReplicaSet` of Prometheus server instances, and then we will define a Kubernetes service to expose Prometheus to us, so that we can access it from within a browser tab or that Grafana can access it. Let's do it:

1. Create a `ch17/kube` folder, and navigate to it:

```
$ mkdir -p ~/fod/ch17/kube && cd ~/fod/ch17/kube
```

2. Add a file called `prometheus.yaml` to this folder.

3. Add the following code snippet to this file; it defines `Deployment` for Prometheus:

```
apiVersion: apps/v1
kind: Deployment
metadata:
  name: prometheus-deployment
  labels:
    app: prometheus
    purpose: monitoring-demo
spec:
  replicas: 2
  selector:
    matchLabels:
      app: prometheus
      purpose: monitoring-demo
  template:
    metadata:
      labels:
        app: prometheus
        purpose: monitoring-demo
    spec:
      containers:
      - name: prometheus
        image: prom/prometheus
        volumeMounts:
          - name: config-volume
            mountPath: /etc/prometheus/prometheus.yml
            subPath: prometheus.yml
        ports:
        - containerPort: 9090
      volumes:
        - name: config-volume
          configMap:
            name: prometheus-cm
```

We are defining a replica set with two instances of Prometheus. Each instance is assigned the two labels: `app: prometheus` and `purpose: monitoring-demo` for identification purposes. The interesting part is in the `volumeMounts` of container spec. There we mount a Kubernetes `ConfigMap` object, called `prometheus-cm` containing the Prometheus configuration, into the container to the location where Prometheus expects its configuration file(s). The volume of the `ConfigMap` type is defined on the last four lines of the above code snippet.

Note that we will define the `config` map later on.

4. Now let's define the Kubernetes service for Prometheus. Append this snippet to the file:

```
---
kind: Service
apiVersion: v1
metadata:
  name: prometheus-svc
spec:
  type: NodePort
  selector:
    app: prometheus
    purpose: monitoring-demo
  ports:
  - name: promui
    protocol: TCP
    port: 9090
    targetPort: 9090
```

Please note the three dashes (---) at the beginning of the snippet are needed to separate individual object definitions in our YAML file.

We call our service `prometheus-svc` and make it a `NodePort` (and not just a service of the `ClusterIP` type) to be able to access the Prometheus web UI from the host.

5. Now we can define a simple configuration file for Prometheus. This file basically instructs the Prometheus server which services to scrape metrics from and how often to do so. First, create a `ch17/kube/config` folder:

```
$ mkdir -p ~/fod/ch17/kube/config
```

6. Please add a file called `prometheus.yml` to the last folder, and add the following content to it:

```
scrape_configs:
    - job_name: 'prometheus'
      scrape_interval: 5s
      static_configs:
        - targets: ['localhost:9090']
    - job_name: dotnet
      scrape_interval: 5s
      static_configs:
        - targets: ['dotnet-api-svc:5000']
    - job_name: node
      scrape_interval: 5s
      static_configs:
        - targets: ['node-api-svc:3000']
          labels:
             group: 'production'
```

In the preceding file, we define three jobs for Prometheus:

- The first one called `prometheus` scrapes metrics every five seconds from the Prometheus server itself. It finds those metrics the at `localhost:9090` target. Note that by default the metrics should be exposed at the `/metrics` endpoint.
- The second job called `dotnet` scrapes metrics from a service found at `dotnet-api-svc:5000`, which will be our .NET Core service that we have defined and instrumented previously.
- Finally, the third job does the same for our Node service. Note that we also have added a `group: 'production'` label to this job. This allows for further grouping of jobs or tasks.

7. Now we can define the `ConfigMap` object in our Kubernetes cluster, with the next command. From within the `ch17/kube` folder execute the following:

```
$ kubectl create configmap prometheus-cm \
  --from-file config/prometheus.yml
```

8. We can now deploy Prometheus to our Kubernetes server with the following:

```
$ kubectl apply -f prometheus.yaml
```

```
deployment.apps/prometheus-deployment created
service/prometheus-svc created
```

9. Let's double-check that the deployment succeeded:

```
$ kubectl get all
```

NAME	READY	STATUS	RESTARTS	AGE
pod/prometheus-deployment-779677977f-727hb	1/1	Running	0	24s
pod/prometheus-deployment-779677977f-f5l7k	1/1	Running	0	24s

NAME	TYPE	CLUSTER-IP	EXTERNAL-IP	PORT(S)	AGE
service/kubernetes	ClusterIP	10.96.0.1	<none>	443/TCP	28d
service/prometheus-svc	NodePort	10.110.239.245	<none>	9090:31962/TCP	24s

NAME	READY	UP-TO-DATE	AVAILABLE	AGE
deployment.apps/prometheus-deployment	2/2	2	2	24s

NAME	DESIRED	CURRENT	READY	AGE
replicaset.apps/prometheus-deployment-779677977f	2	2	2	24s

Keep a close eye on the list of pods, and make sure they are all up and running. Please also note the port mapping of the `prometheus-svc` object. In my case, the `9090` port is mapped to the `31962` host port. In your case, the latter may be different, but it will also be in the `3xxxx` range.

10. We can now access the web UI of Prometheus. Open a new browser tab, and navigate to `http://localhost:<port>/targets` where `<port>` in my case is `31962`. You should see something like this:

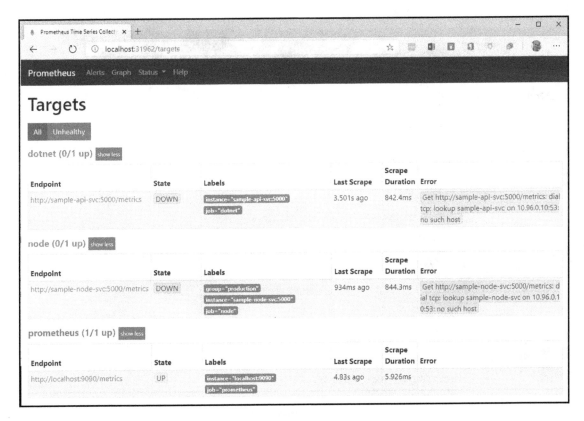

Prometheus web UI showing the configured targets

In the last screenshot, we can see that we defined three **targets** for Prometheus. Only the third one in the list is up and accessible by Prometheus. It is the endpoint we defined in the configuration file for the job that scrapes metrics from Prometheus itself. The other two services are not running at this time, and thus their state is down.

11. Now navigate to **Graph** by clicking on the respective link in the top menu of the UI.

12. Open the metrics drop-down list, and inspect all the listed metrics that Prometheus found. In this case, it is only the list of metrics defined by the Prometheus server itself:

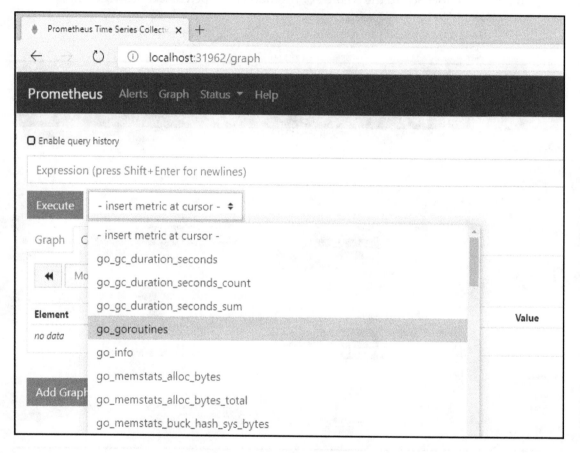

Prometheus web UI showing available metrics

With that, we are ready to deploy the .NET and the Node sample services, we created earlier, to Kubernetes.

Deploying our application services to Kubernetes

Before we can use the sample services we created earlier and deploy them to Kubernetes, we must create Docker images for them and push them to a container registry. In our case, we will just push them to Docker Hub.

Let's start with the .NET Core sample:

1. Locate the `Program.cs` file in the .NET project and open it.

2. Modify the `CreateHostBuilder` method so it looks like this:

```
Host.CreateDefaultBuilder(args)
    .ConfigureWebHostDefaults(webBuilder =>
    {
        webBuilder.UseStartup<Startup>();
        webBuilder.UseUrls("http://*:5000");
    });
```

3. Add `Dockerfile` with the following content to the `ch17/dotnet/sample-api` project folder:

```
FROM mcr.microsoft.com/dotnet/core/aspnet:3.1 AS base
WORKDIR /app
EXPOSE 5000

FROM mcr.microsoft.com/dotnet/core/sdk:3.1 AS builder
WORKDIR /src
COPY sample-api.csproj ./
RUN dotnet restore
COPY . .
RUN dotnet build -c Release -o /src/build

FROM builder AS publisher
RUN dotnet publish -c Release -o /src/publish

FROM base AS final
COPY --from=publisher /src/publish .
ENTRYPOINT ["dotnet", "sample-api.dll"]
```

4. Create a Docker image by using this command from within the `dotnet/sample-api` project folder:

```
$ docker image build -t fundamentalsofdocker/ch17-dotnet-api:2.0 .
```

Note that you may want to replace `fundamentalsofdocker` with your own Docker Hub username in the preceding and subsequent command.

5. Push the image to Docker Hub:

```
$ docker image push fundamentalsofdocker/ch17-dotnet-api:2.0
```

Now we do the same with the Node sample API:

1. Add `Dockerfile` with the following content to the `ch17/node` project folder:

```
FROM node:13.5-alpine
WORKDIR /app
COPY package.json ./
RUN npm install
COPY . .
EXPOSE 3000
CMD ["npm", "start"]
```

2. Create a Docker image by using this command from within the `ch17/node` project folder:

```
$ docker image build -t fundamentalsofdocker/ch17-node-api:2.0 .
```

 Note once again that you may want to replace `fundamentalsofdocker` with your own Docker Hub username in the preceding and subsequent command.

3. Push the image to Docker Hub:

```
$ docker image push fundamentalsofdocker/ch17-node-api:2.0
```

With this, we are ready to define the necessary Kubernetes objects for the deployment of the two services. The definition is somewhat lengthy and can be found in the `~/fod/ch17/kube/app-services.yaml` file in the repository. Please open that file and analyze its content.

Let's use this file to deploy the services:

1. Use the following command:

```
$ kubectl apply -f app-services.yaml

deployment.apps/dotnet-api-deployment created
service/dotnet-api-svc created
deployment.apps/node-api-deployment created
service/node-api-svc created
```

2. Double-check that the services are up and running using the `kubectl get all` command. Make sure all the pods of the Node and .NET sample API services are up and running.

3. List all Kubernetes services to find out the host ports for each application service:

```
$ kubectl get services
```

NAME	TYPE	CLUSTER-IP	EXTERNAL-IP	PORT(S)
AGE				
dotnet-api-svc	NodePort	10.98.137.249	<none>	
5000:30822/TCP	5m29s			
grafana-svc	NodePort	10.107.232.211	<none>	
8080:31461/TCP	33m			
kubernetes	ClusterIP	10.96.0.1	<none>	443/TCP
28d				
node-api-svc	NodePort	10.110.15.131	<none>	
5000:31713/TCP	5m29s			
prometheus-svc	NodePort	10.110.239.245	<none>	
9090:31962/TCP	77m			

In my case, the .NET API is mapped to port `30822`, and the Node API to port `31713`. Your ports may differ.

4. Use `curl` to access the `/metrics` endpoint for both services:

```
$ curl localhost:30822/metrics
# HELP process_working_set_bytes Process working set
# TYPE process_working_set_bytes gauge
process_working_set_bytes 95236096
# HELP process_private_memory_bytes Process private memory size
# TYPE process_private_memory_bytes gauge
process_private_memory_bytes 186617856
...

$ curl localhost:31713/metrics
# HELP process_cpu_user_seconds_total Total user CPU time spent in
```

```
seconds.
# TYPE process_cpu_user_seconds_total counter
process_cpu_user_seconds_total 1.0394399999999997 1578294999302
# HELP process_cpu_system_seconds_total Total system CPU time spent
in seconds.
# TYPE process_cpu_system_seconds_total counter
process_cpu_system_seconds_total 0.3370890000000001 1578294999302
...
```

5. Double-check the /targets endpoint in Prometheus to make sure the two microservices are now reachable:

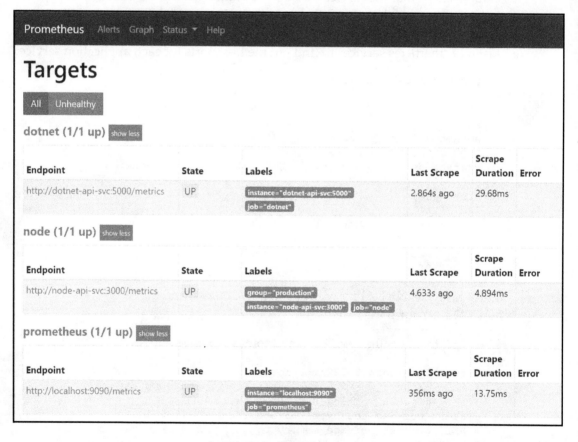

Prometheus showing all targets are up and running

6. To make sure the custom metrics we defined for our Node.js and .NET services are defined and exposed, we need to access each service at least once. Thus use `curl` to access the respective endpoints a few times:

```
# access the /weatherforecast endpoint in the .NET service
$ curl localhost:31713/weatherforecast

# and access the /hello endpoint in the Node service
$ curl localhost:30822/hello
```

The last step is to deploy Grafana to Kubernetes so that we have the ability to create sophisticated and graphically appealing dashboards displaying key metrics of our application services and/or infrastructure components.

Deploying Grafana to Kubernetes

Now let's also deploy Grafana to our Kubernetes cluster, so that we can manage this tool the same way as all the other components of our distributed application. As the tool that allows us to create dashboards for monitoring the application, Grafana can be considered mission-critical and thus warrants this treatment.

Deploying Grafana to the cluster is pretty straightforward. Let's do it as follows:

1. Add a new file called `grafana.yaml` to the `ch17/kube` folder.

2. To this file, add the definition for a Kubernetes `Deployment` for Grafana:

```yaml
apiVersion: apps/v1
kind: Deployment
metadata:
  name: grafana-deployment
  labels:
    app: grafana
    purpose: monitoring-demo
spec:
  replicas: 1
  selector:
    matchLabels:
      app: grafana
      purpose: monitoring-demo
  template:
    metadata:
      labels:
        app: grafana
        purpose: monitoring-demo
    spec:
```

```
containers:
- name: grafana
    image: grafana/grafana
```

There are no surprises in that definition. In this example, we are running a single instance of Grafana, and it uses the `app` and `purpose` labels for identification, similar to what we used for Prometheus. No special volume mapping is needed this time since we are only working with defaults.

3. We also need to expose Grafana, and thus add the following snippet to the preceding file to define a service for Grafana:

```
---
kind: Service
apiVersion: v1
metadata:
  name: grafana-svc
spec:
  type: NodePort
  selector:
    app: grafana
    purpose: monitoring-demo
  ports:
  - name: grafanaui
    protocol: TCP
    port: 3000
    targetPort: 3000
```

Once again, we are using a service of the `NodePort` type to be able to access the Grafana UI from our host.

4. We can now deploy Grafana with this command:

```
$ kubectl apply -f grafana.yaml
```

```
deployment.apps/grafana-deployment created
service/grafana-svc created
```

5. Let's find out what the port number will be, over which we can access Grafana:

```
$ kubectl get services
```

NAME AGE	TYPE	CLUSTER-IP	EXTERNAL-IP	PORT(S)
dotnet-api-svc 5000:30781/TCP	NodePort 16m	10.100.250.40	<none>	
grafana-svc	NodePort	10.102.239.176	<none>	

```
3000:32379/TCP      11m
kubernetes          ClusterIP     10.96.0.1        <none>        443/TCP
28d
node-api-svc        NodePort      10.100.76.13     <none>
3000:30731/TCP      16m
prometheus-svc      NodePort      10.104.205.217   <none>
9090:31246/TCP      16m
```

6. Open a new browser tab, and navigate to `http://localhost:<port>` where `<port>` is the port you identified in the previous step, and in my case is `32379`. You should see something like this:

Login screen of Grafana

7. Login with the default `admin` username, and the password is also `admin`. When asked to change the password click the **Skip** link for now. You will be redirected to the **Home** dashboard.

8. On the **Home** Dashboard, click on **Create your first data source**, and select **Prometheus** from the list of data sources.

9. Add `http://prometheus-svc:9090` for the URL to Prometheus, and click the green **Save & Test** button.

10. In Grafana, navigate back to the **Home** dashboard, and then select the **New** dashboard.

11. Click **Add query**, and then from the **Metrics** drop-down menu, select the custom metric we defined in the .NET sample service:

Selecting the .NET custom metric in Grafana

12. Change the value of **Relative time** from `1h` to `5m` (five minutes).

13. Change the dashboard refresh rate found in the upper-right corner of the view to `5s` (five seconds).

14. Repeat the same for the custom metric defined in the Node sample service, so that you will have two panels on your new dashboard.

15. Modify the dashboard and its panels to your liking by consulting the documentation at `https://grafana.com/docs/grafana/latest/guides/getting_started/`.

16. Use `curl` to access the two endpoints of the sample services, and observe the dashboard. It may look like this:

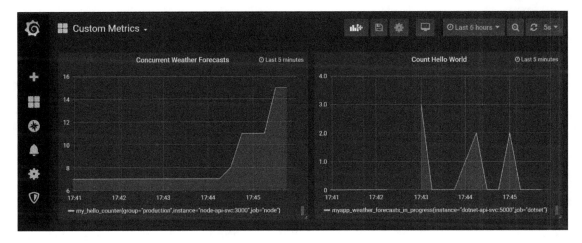

Grafana dashboard with our two custom metrics

Summarizing, we can say that Prometheus is a good fit to monitor our microservices because we just need to expose a metrics port, and thus don't need to add too much complexity or run additional services. Prometheus then is in charge of periodically scraping the configured targets, so that our services don't need to worry about emitting them.

Troubleshooting a service running in production

It is a recommended best practice to create minimal images for production that don't contain anything that is not absolutely needed. This includes common tools that are usually used to debug and troubleshoot an application, such as netcat, iostat, ip, or others. Ideally, a production system only has the container orchestration software such as Kubernetes installed on a cluster node with a minimal OS, such as Core OS. The application container in turn ideally only contains the binaries absolutely necessary to run. This minimizes the attack surface and the risk of having to deal with vulnerabilities. Furthermore, a small image has the advantage of being downloaded quickly, using less space on disk and in memory and showing faster startup times.

But this can be a problem if one of the application services running on our Kubernetes cluster shows unexpected behavior and maybe even crashes. Sometimes we are not able to find the root cause of the problem just from the logs generated and collected, so we might need to troubleshoot the component on the cluster node itself.

We may be tempted to SSH into the given cluster node and run some diagnostic tools. But this is not possible since the cluster node only runs a minimal Linux distro with no such tools installed. As a developer, we could now just ask the cluster administrator to install all the Linux diagnostic tools we intend to use. But that is not a good idea. First of all, this would open the door for potentially vulnerable software now residing on the cluster node, endangering all the other pods that run on that node, and also open a door to the cluster itself that could be exploited by hackers. Furthermore, it is always a bad idea to give developers direct access to nodes of a production cluster, no matter how much you trust your developers. Only a limited number of cluster administrators should ever be able to do so.

A better solution is to have the cluster admin run a so-called bastion container on behalf of the developers. This bastion or troubleshoot container has all the tools installed that we need to pinpoint the root cause of the bug in the application service. It is also possible to run the bastion container in the host's network namespace; thus, it will have full access to all the network traffic of the container host.

The netshoot container

Nicola Kabar, a former Docker employee, has created a handy Docker image called `nicolaka/netshoot` that field engineers at Docker use all the time to troubleshoot applications running in production on Kubernetes or Docker Swarm. We created a copy of the image for this book, available at `fundamentalsofdocker/netshoot`. The purpose of this container in the words of the creator is as follows:

> *"Purpose: Docker and Kubernetes network troubleshooting can become complex. With proper understanding of how Docker and Kubernetes networking works and the right set of tools, you can troubleshoot and resolve these networking issues. The* `netshoot` *container has a set of powerful networking troubleshooting tools that can be used to troubleshoot Docker networking issues."*

> *- Nicola Kabar*

To use this container for debugging purposes, we can proceed as follows:

1. Spin up a throwaway bastion container for debugging on Kubernetes, using the
   following command:

```
$ kubectl run tmp-shell --generator=run-pod/v1 --rm -i --tty \
    --image fundamentalsofdocker/netshoot \
    --command -- bash

bash-5.0#
```

2. You can now use tools such as `ip` from within this container:

```
bash-5.0# ip a
```

On my machine, this results in an output similar to the following if I run the pod
on Docker for Windows:

```
1: lo: <LOOPBACK,UP,LOWER_UP> mtu 65536 qdisc noqueue state UNKNOWN
group default qlen 1000
    link/loopback 00:00:00:00:00:00 brd 00:00:00:00:00:00
    inet 127.0.0.1/8 scope host lo
       valid_lft forever preferred_lft forever
 2: sit0@NONE: <NOARP> mtu 1480 qdisc noop state DOWN group default
qlen 1000
    link/sit 0.0.0.0 brd 0.0.0.0
 4: eth0@if263: <BROADCAST,MULTICAST,UP,LOWER_UP> mtu 1500 qdisc
noqueue state UP group default
    link/ether 52:52:9d:1d:fd:cc brd ff:ff:ff:ff:ff:ff link-
netnsid 0
    inet 10.1.0.71/16 scope global eth0
       valid_lft forever preferred_lft forever
```

3. To leave this troubleshoot container, just press *Ctrl* + *D* or type `exit` and then hit
   Enter.
4. If we need to dig a bit deeper and run the container in the same network
   namespace as the Kubernetes host, then we can use this command instead:

```
$ kubectl run tmp-shell --generator=run-pod/v1 --rm -i --tty \
    --overrides='{"spec": {"hostNetwork": true}}' \
    --image fundamentalsofdocker/netshoot \
    --command -- bash
```

5. If we run `ip` again in this container, we will see everything that the container
   host sees too, for example, all the `veth` endpoints.

The `netshoot` container has all the usual tools installed that an engineer ever needs to troubleshoot network-related problems. Some of the more familiar ones are `ctop`, `curl`, `dhcping`, `drill`, `ethtool`, `iftop`, `iperf`, and `iproute2`.

Summary

In this chapter, you learned some techniques used to monitor an individual service or a whole distributed application running on a Kubernetes cluster. Furthermore, you investigated troubleshooting an application service that is running in production without having to alter the cluster or the cluster nodes on which the service is running.

In the next and final chapter of this book, you will gain an overview of some of the most popular ways of running containerized applications in the cloud. The chapter includes samples on how to self-host and use hosted solutions and discuss their pros and cons. Fully managed offerings of vendors such as Microsoft Azure and Google Cloud Engine are briefly discussed.

Questions

To assess your learning progress, please answer the following questions:

1. Why is it important to instrument your application services?
2. Can you describe to an interested layperson what Prometheus is?
3. Exporting Prometheus metrics is easy. Can you describe in simple words how you can do this for a Node.js application?
4. You need to debug a service running on Kubernetes in production. Unfortunately, the logs produced by this service alone don't give enough information to pinpoint the root cause. You decide to troubleshoot the service directly on the respective Kubernetes cluster node. How do you proceed?

Further reading

Here are a few links that provide additional information on the topics discussed in this chapter:

- Kubernetes Monitoring with Prometheus: `https://sysdig.com/blog/kubernetes-monitoring-prometheus/`

- Prometheus Client Libraries: `https://prometheus.io/docs/instrumenting/clientlibs/`

- The `netshoot` container: `https://github.com/nicolaka/netshoot`

18
Running a Containerized App in the Cloud

In the previous chapter, we learned how to deploy, monitor, and troubleshoot an application in production.

In this chapter, we will give an overview of some of the most popular ways of running containerized applications in the cloud. We will explore self-hosting and hosted solutions and discuss their pros and cons. Fully managed offerings from vendors such as Microsoft Azure and Google Cloud Engine will be briefly discussed.

Here are the topics we will be discussing in this chapter:

- Deploying and using Docker **Enterprise Edition** (EE) on **Amazon Web Services (AWS)**
- Exploring Microsoft's **Azure Kubernetes Service (AKS)**
- Understanding **Google Kubernetes Engine (GKE)**

After reading this chapter, you will be able to do the following:

- Create a Kubernetes cluster in AWS using Docker EE
- Deploy and run a simple distributed application in a Docker EE cluster in AWS
- Deploy and run a simple distributed application on Microsoft's AKS
- Deploy and run a simple distributed application on GKE

Technical requirements

We are going to use AWS, Microsoft Azure, and Google Cloud in this chapter. Therefore, it is necessary to have an account for each platform. If you do not have an existing account, you can ask for a trial account for all of these cloud providers.

We'll also use the files in the `~/fod-solution/ch18` folder of our `labs` repository from GitHub at `https://github.com/PacktPublishing/Learn-Docker---Fundamentals-of-Docker-19.x-Second-Edition/tree/master/ch18`.

Deploying and using Docker EE on AWS

In this section, we're going to install Docker **Universal Control Plane** (**UCP**) version 3.0. UCP is part of Docker's enterprise offering and supports two orchestration engines, Docker Swarm and Kubernetes. UCP can be installed in the cloud or on-premises. Even hybrid clouds are possible with UCP.

To try this, you need a valid license for Docker EE or you can claim a free test license on Docker Store.

Provisioning the infrastructure

In this first section, we are going to set up the infrastructure needed to install Docker UCP. This is relatively straightforward if you are somewhat familiar with AWS. Let's do this by following these steps:

1. Create an **Auto Scaling group** (**ASG**) in AWS using the Ubuntu 16.04 server AMI. Configure the ASG to contain three instances of size `t2.xlarge`. Here is the result of this:

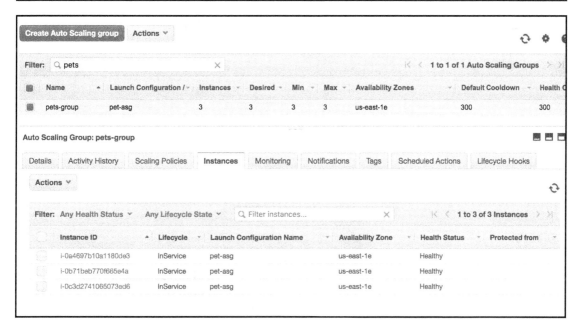

ASG on AWS ready for Docker EE

Once the ASG has been created, and before we continue, we need to open the **security group** (**SG**) a bit (which our ASG is part of) so that we can access it through SSH from our laptop and also so that the **virtual machines** (**VMs**) can communicate with each other.

2. Navigate to your SG and add two new inbound rules, which are shown here:

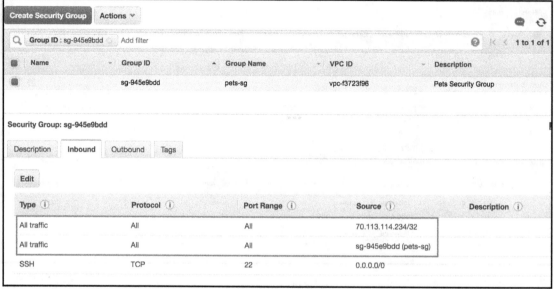

AWS SG settings

In the preceding screenshot, the first rule allows any traffic from my personal laptop (with the IP address 70.113.114.234) to access any resource in the SG. The second rule allows any traffic inside the SG itself. These settings are not meant to be used in a production-like environment as they are way too permissive. However, for this demo environment, they work well.

Next, we will show you how to install Docker on the VMs we just prepared.

Installing Docker

After having provisioned the cluster nodes, we need to install Docker on each of them. This can be easily achieved by following these steps:

1. SSH into all three instances and install Docker. Using the downloaded key, SSH into the first machine:

```
$ ssh -i pets.pem ubuntu@<IP address>
```

Here, <IP address> is the public IP address of the VM we want to SSH into.

2. Now we can install Docker. For detailed instructions, refer to `https://dockr.ly/2HiWfBc`. We have a script in the `~/fod/ch18/aws` folder called `install-docker.sh` that we can use.

3. First, we need to clone the `labs` GitHub repository to the VM:

```
$ git clone
https://github.com/PacktPublishing/Learn-Docker---Fundamentals-of-D
ocker-19.x-Second-Edition.git ~/fod
$ cd ~/fod/ch18/aws
```

4. Then, we run the script to install Docker:

```
$ ./install-docker.sh
```

5. Once the script is finished, we can verify that Docker is indeed installed using `sudo docker version`. Repeat the preceding code for the two other VMs.

 `sudo` is only necessary until the next SSH session is opened to this VM since we have added the `ubuntu` user to the `docker` group. So, we need to exit the current SSH session and connect again. This time, `sudo` should not be needed in conjunction with `docker`.

Next, we will show how to install Docker UCP on the infrastructure we just prepared.

Installing Docker UCP

We need to set a few environment variables, as follows:

```
$ export UCP_IP=<IP address>
$ export UCP_FQDN=<FQDN>
$ export UCP_VERSION=3.0.0-beta2
```

Here, `<IP address>` and `<FQDN>` are the public IP address and the public DNS name of the AWS EC2 instance we're installing in UCP.

After that, we can use the following command to download all the images that UCP needs:

```
$ docker run --rm docker/ucp:${UCP_VERSION} images --list \
   | xargs -L 1 docker pull
```

Finally, we can install UCP:

```
ubuntu@ip-172-31-8-100:~$ docker container run --rm -it --name ucp \
>     -v /var/run/docker.sock:/var/run/docker.sock \
>     docker/ucp:${UCP_VERSION} install \
>     --admin-username admin \
>     --admin-password adminadmin \
>     --san ${UCP_IP} \
>     --san ${UCP_FQDN}
INFO[0000] Verifying your system is compatible with UCP 3.0.0-beta2 (4f665c3)
INFO[0000] Your engine version 18.03.0-ce, build 0520e24 (4.4.0-1052-aws) is compatible
INFO[0000] All required images are present
INFO[0000] Initializing a new swarm at 172.31.8.100
INFO[0005] Establishing mutual Cluster Root CA with Swarm
INFO[0008] Installing UCP with host address 172.31.8.100 - If this is incorrect, please sp
INFO[0008] Generating UCP Client Root CA
INFO[0008] Deploying UCP Service
INFO[0049] Installation completed on ip-172-31-8-100 (node jatip5ocsvhighii1o55ho41v)
INFO[0049] UCP Instance ID: 803f54eedvsdlc2wvfju0iv47
INFO[0049] UCP Server SSL: SHA-256 Fingerprint=51:E8:13:FF:5F:2C:89:CC:E8:53:46:5C:D9:2F:3
INFO[0049] Login to UCP at https://172.31.8.100:443
INFO[0049] Username: admin
INFO[0049] Password: (your admin password)
ubuntu@ip-172-31-8-100:~$ 
```

Installing UCP 3.0.0-beta2 on a VM in AWS

Now, we can open a browser window and navigate to `https://<IP address>`. Log in with your username, `admin`, and password, `adminadmin`. When asked for the license, upload your license key or follow the link to procure a trial license.

Once logged in, on the left-hand side under the **Shared Resources** section, select **Nodes** and then click on the **Add Node** button:

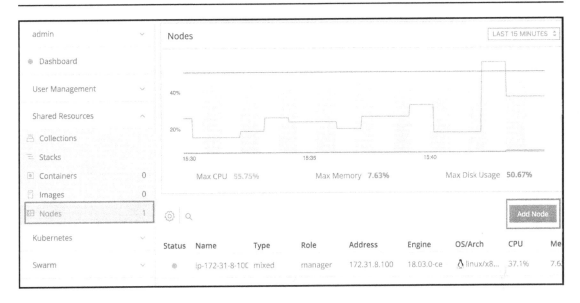

Adding a new node to UCP

In the subsequent **Add Node** dialog box, make sure that the node type is **Linux** and the **Worker** node role is selected. Then, copy the `docker swarm join` command at the bottom of the dialog box. SSH into the other two VMs you created and run this command to have the respective node join the Docker swarm as a worker node:

```
$ ssh -i pets.pem ubuntu@54.208.149.247
Welcome to Ubuntu 16.04.4 LTS (GNU/Linux 4.4.0-1052-aws x86_64)

 * Documentation:  https://help.ubuntu.com
 * Management:      https://landscape.canonical.com
 * Support:         https://ubuntu.com/advantage

   Get cloud support with Ubuntu Advantage Cloud Guest:
     http://www.ubuntu.com/business/services/cloud

30 packages can be updated.
0 updates are security updates.


*** System restart required ***
Last login: Sun Apr  8 20:58:32 2018 from 70.113.114.234
ubuntu@ip-172-31-6-57:~$ docker swarm join --token SWMTKN-1-4w858a6f37b8v4ozyxn0bxacjoxtcogizu04dmosga
c3j5ocna-983bleo9oaygu03wmyz1ekptb 172.31.8.100:2377
This node joined a swarm as a worker.
ubuntu@ip-172-31-6-57:~$
```

Joining a node as a worker to the UCP cluster

Back in the web UI of UCP, you should see that we now have three nodes ready, as shown here:

Status	Name	Type	Role	Address	Engine	OS/Arch	CPU	Memory	Disk	Details
●	ip-172-31-8-10C	mixed	manager	172.31.8.100	18.03.0-ce	⛁ linux/x8...	31.95%	7.71%	50.73%	Healthy UCP ...
●	ip-172-31-15-11	swarm	worker	172.31.15.110	18.03.0-ce	⛁ linux/x8...	3.5%	1.05%	31.36%	Healthy UCP ...
●	ip-172-31-6-57	swarm	worker	172.31.6.57	18.03.0-ce	⛁ linux/x8...	3.27%	1.07%	31.36%	Healthy UCP ...

List of nodes in the UCP cluster

By default, worker nodes are configured so that they can only run the Docker Swarm workload. This can be changed in the node details, though. In this, three settings are possible: Swarm only, Kubernetes only, or mixed workload. Let's start with Docker Swarm as the orchestration engine and deploy our pets application.

Using remote admin for the UCP cluster

To be able to manage our UCP cluster remotely from our laptop, we need to create and download a so-called **client bundle** from UCP. Proceed with the following steps:

1. In the UCP web UI, on the left-hand side under **admin**, select the **My Profile** option.
2. In the subsequent dialog, select the **New Client Bundle** option and then **Generate Client Bundle**:

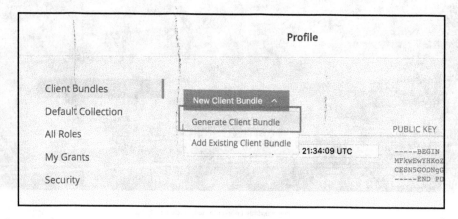

Generating and downloading a UCP client bundle

3. Locate the downloaded bundle on your disk and unzip it.
4. In a new Terminal window, navigate to that folder and source the `env.sh` file:

```
$ source env.sh
```

You should get an output similar to this:

```
Cluster "ucp_34.232.53.86:6443_admin" set.
User "ucp_34.232.53.86:6443_admin" set.
Context "ucp_34.232.53.86:6443_admin" created.
```

Now, we can verify that we can indeed remotely access the UCP cluster by, for example, listing all the nodes of the cluster:

```
$ docker node ls
ID                              HOSTNAME            STATUS    AVAILABILITY    MANAGER STATUS    ENGINE VERSION
wougljiphzk4vmmbm1tlqi2kg       ip-172-31-6-57      Ready     Active                            18.03.0-ce
jatip5ocsvhighii1o55ho41v *     ip-172-31-8-100     Ready     Active          Leader            18.03.0-ce
tlkaeww3idlte90ko5zr8xkeu       ip-172-31-15-110    Ready     Active                            18.03.0-ce
$
```

Listing all the nodes of our remote UCP cluster

In the next section, we will look at how to deploy the pets application as a stack using Docker Swarm as the orchestration engine.

Deploying to Docker Swarm

It is now time to deploy our distributed application to our cluster orchestrated by Docker Swarm. Follow these steps to do so:

1. In the Terminal, navigate to the `~/fod/ch18/ucp` folder and create the `pets` stack using the `stack.yml` file:

```
$ docker stack deploy -c stack.yml pets
Creating network pets_pets-net
Creating service pets_db
Creating service pets_web
$
```

Deploying the pets stack into the UCP cluster

2. In the UCP web UI, we can verify that the stack has been created:

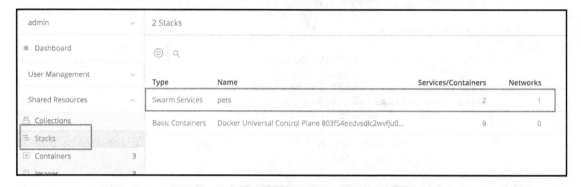

The pets stack listing in the UCP web UI

3. To test the application, we can navigate to **Services** under the main menu, **Swarm**. The list of services running in the cluster will be displayed as follows:

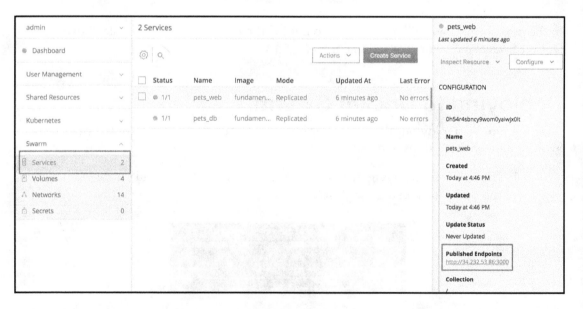

Details of the 'web' services of the pets stack

In the preceding screenshot, we see our two services, web and db, of the pets stack. If we click on the web service, its details are displayed on the right-hand side. There we find an entry, **Published Endpoints**.

4. Click on the link and our `pets` application should be displayed in the browser.

When done, remove the stack from the console with the following:

```
$ docker stack rm pets
```

Alternatively, you can try to remove that stack from within the UCP web UI.

Deploying to Kubernetes

From the same Terminal that you used to remotely access the UCP cluster to deploy the pets application as a stack using Docker Swarm as the orchestration engine, we can now try to deploy the pets application to the UCP cluster using Kubernetes as the orchestration engine.

Make sure you're still in the `~/fod/ch18/ucp` folder. Use `kubectl` to deploy the pets application. First, we need to test that we can get all the nodes of the cluster with the Kubernetes CLI:

```
$ kubectl get nodes
NAME               STATUS    ROLES     AGE    VERSION
ip-172-31-15-110   Ready     <none>    1h     v1.8.2-docker.128+56ab40b2f3e9b9
ip-172-31-6-57     Ready     <none>    1h     v1.8.2-docker.128+56ab40b2f3e9b9
ip-172-31-8-100    Ready     master    22h    v1.8.2-docker.128+56ab40b2f3e9b9
$
```

Getting all the nodes of the UCP cluster using the Kubernetes CLI

Apparently, my environment is configured correctly and `kubectl` can indeed list all the nodes in the UCP cluster. That means I can now deploy the pets application using the definitions in the `pets.yaml` file:

```
$ kubectl create -f pets.yaml
deployment "web" created
service "web" created
deployment "db" created
service "db" created
$
```

Creating the pets application in the UCP cluster using the Kubernetes CLI

We can list the objects created by using `kubectl get all`. In a browser, we can then navigate to `http://<IP address>:<port>` to access the pets application, where `<IP address>` is the public IP address of one of the UCP cluster nodes and `<port>` is the port published by the `web` Kubernetes service.

We have created a cluster of three VMs in an AWS ASG and have installed Docker and UCP 3.0 on them. We then deployed our famous pets application into the UCP cluster, once using Docker Swarm as the orchestration engine and once Kubernetes.

Docker UCP is a platform-agnostic container platform that offers a secure enterprise-grade software supply chain in any cloud and on-premises, on bare metal, or in virtualized environments. It even offers freedom of choice when it comes to orchestration engines. The user can choose between Docker Swarm and Kubernetes. It is also possible to run applications in both orchestrators in the same cluster.

Exploring Microsoft's Azure Kubernetes Service (AKS)

To experiment with Microsoft's container-related offerings in Azure, we need an account on Azure. You can create a trial account or use an existing account. You can get a free trial account here: `https://azure.microsoft.com/en-us/free/`.

Microsoft offers different container-related services on Azure. The easiest one to use is probably Azure Container Instances, which promises the fastest and simplest way to run a container in Azure, without having to provision any virtual machines and without having to adopt a higher-level service. This service is only really useful if you want to run a single container in a hosted environment. The setup is quite easy. In the Azure portal (`portal.azure.com`), you first create a new resource group and then create an Azure container instance. You only need to fill out a short form with properties such as the name of the container, the image to use, and the port to open. The container can be made available on a public or private IP address and will be automatically restarted if it crashes. There is a decent management console available, for example, to monitor resource consumption such as CPU and memory.

The second choice is **Azure Container Service** (**ACS**), which provides a way to simplify the creation, configuration, and management of a cluster of VMs that are preconfigured to run containerized applications. ACS uses Docker images and provides a choice between three orchestrators: Kubernetes, Docker Swarm, and DC/OS (powered by Apache Mesos). Microsoft claims that their service can be scaled to tens of thousands of containers. ACS is free and you are only charged for computing resources.

In this section, we will concentrate on the most popular offering, based on Kubernetes. It is called AKS and can be found here: `https://azure.microsoft.com/en-us/services/kubernetes-service/`. AKS makes it easy for you to deploy applications into the cloud and run them on Kubernetes. All the difficult and tedious management tasks are handled by Microsoft and you can concentrate fully on your applications. What that means is that you will never have to deal with tasks such as installing and managing Kubernetes, upgrading Kubernetes, or upgrading the operating system of the underlying Kubernetes nodes. All this is handled by the experts at Microsoft Azure. Furthermore, you will never have to deal with `etc` or Kubernetes master nodes. This is all hidden from you, and the only things you will interact with are the Kubernetes worker nodes that run your applications.

Preparing the Azure CLI

That said, let's start. We assume that you have created a free trial account or that you are using an existing account on Azure. There are various ways to interact with your Azure account. We will use the Azure CLI running on our local computer. We can either download and install the Azure CLI natively on our computer or run it from within a container running on our local Docker for Desktop. Since this book is all about containers, let's select the latter approach.

The latest version of the Azure CLI can be found on Docker Hub. Let's pull it:

```
$ docker image pull mcr.microsoft.com/azure-cli:latest
```

We will be running a container from this CLI and executing all subsequent commands from within the shell running inside this container. Now, there is a little problem we need to overcome. This container will not have a Docker client installed. But we will also run some Docker commands, so we have to create a custom image derived from the preceding image, which contains a Docker client. The `Dockerfile` that's needed to do so can be found in the `~/fod/ch18` folder and has this content:

```
FROM mcr.microsoft.com/azure-cli:latest
RUN apk update && apk add docker
```

On line 2, we are just using the Alpine package manager, `apk`, to install Docker. We can then use Docker Compose to build and run this custom image. The corresponding `docker-compose.yml` file looks like this:

```
version: "2.4"
services:
    az:
        image: fundamentalsofdocker/azure-cli
        build: .
```

```
command: tail -F anything
working_dir: /app
volumes:
    - /var/run/docker.sock:/var/run/docker.sock
    - .:/app
```

 Please note the command that is used to keep the container running, as well as the mounting of the Docker socket and the current folder in the `volumes` section.

 If you are running Docker for Desktop on Windows, then you need to define the `COMPOSE_CONVERT_WINDOWS_PATHS` environment variable to be able to mount the Docker socket. Use `export COMPOSE_CONVERT_WINDOWS_PATHS=1` from a Bash shell or `$Env:COMPOSE_CONVERT_WINDOWS_PATHS=1` when running PowerShell. Please refer to the following link for more details: `https://github.com/docker/compose/issues/4240`.

Now, let's build and run this container:

```
$ docker-compose up --build -d
```

Then, let's execute into the `az` container and run a Bash shell in it with the following:

```
$ docker-compose exec az /bin/bash
```

```
bash-5.0#
```

We will find ourselves running in a Bash shell inside the container. Let's first check the version of the CLI:

```
bash-5.0# az --version
```

This should result in an output similar to this (shortened):

```
azure-cli 2.0.78
...
Your CLI is up-to-date.
```

OK, we're running on version `2.0.78`. Next, we need to log in to our account. Execute this command:

```
bash-5.0# az login
```

You will be presented with the following message:

```
To sign in, use a web browser to open the page
https://microsoft.com/devicelogin and enter the code <code> to
authenticate.
```

Follow the instructions and log in through the browser. Once you have successfully authenticated your Azure account, you can go back to your Terminal and you should be logged in, as indicated by the output you'll get:

```
[
  {
    "cloudName": "AzureCloud",
    "id": "<id>",
    "isDefault": true,
    "name": "<account name>",
    "state": "Enabled",
    "tenantId": "<tenant-it>",
    "user": {
      "name": "xxx@hotmail.com",
      "type": "user"
    }
  }
]
```

Now, we are ready to first move our container images to Azure.

Creating a container registry on Azure

First, we create a new resource group named `animal-rg`. In Azure, resource groups are used to logically group a collection of associated resources. To have an optimal cloud experience and keep latency low, it is important that you select a data center located in a region near you. You can use the following command to list all regions:

```
bash-5.0# az account list-locations

[
  {
    "displayName": "East Asia",
    "id": "/subscriptions/186760ad-9152-4499-b317-
c9bff441fb9d/locations/eastasia",
    "latitude": "22.267",
    "longitude": "114.188",
    "name": "eastasia",
    "subscriptionId": null
  },
```

```
    . . .
]
```

This will give you a rather long list of all possible regions you can select from. Use the name, for example, eastasia, to identify the region of your choice. In my case, I will be selecting westeurope. Please note that not all locations listed are valid for resource groups.

The command to create a resource group is simple; we just need a name for the group and the location:

```
bash-5.0# az group create --name animals-rg --location westeurope

{
  "id": "/subscriptions/186760ad-9152-4499-b317-
c9bff441fb9d/resourceGroups/animals-rg",
  "location": "westeurope",
  "managedBy": null,
  "name": "animals-rg",
  "properties": {
    "provisioningState": "Succeeded"
  },
  "tags": null,
  "type": "Microsoft.Resources/resourceGroups"
}
```

 Make sure that your output shows "provisioningState": "Succeeded".

When running a containerized application in production, we want to make sure that we can freely download the corresponding container images from a container registry. So far, we have always downloaded our images from Docker Hub. But this is often not possible. For security reasons, the servers of a production system often have no direct access to the internet and thus are not able to reach out to Docker Hub. Let's follow this best practice and assume the same for our Kubernetes cluster that we are going to create in an instant.

So, what can we do? Well, the solution is to use a container image registry that is close to our cluster and that is in the same security context. In Azure, we can create an **Azure container registry (ACR)** and host our images there. Let's first create such a registry:

```
bash-5.0# az acr create --resource-group animals-rg --name <acr-name> --sku
Basic
```

Note that `<acr-name>` needs to be unique. In my case, I have chosen the name `fodanimalsacr`. The (shortened) output looks like this:

```
{
    "adminUserEnabled": false,
    "creationDate": "2019-12-22T10:31:14.848776+00:00",
    "id": "/subscriptions/186760ad...",
    "location": "westeurope",
    "loginServer": "fodanimalsacr.azurecr.io",
    "name": "fodanimalsacr",
    ...
    "provisioningState": "Succeeded",
```

After successfully creating the container registry, we need to log in to that registry using the following:

```
bash-5.0# az acr login --name <acr-name>

Login Succeeded
WARNING! Your password will be stored unencrypted in
/root/.docker/config.json.
Configure a credential helper to remove this warning. See
https://docs.docker.com/engine/reference/commandline/login/#credentials-sto
re
```

Once we are successfully logged in to the container registry on Azure, we need to tag our containers correctly so that we can then push them to ACR. Tagging and pushing images to ACR will be described next.

Pushing our images to ACR

Once we have successfully logged in to ACR, we can tag our images such that they can be pushed to the registry. For this, we need to get the URL of our ACR instance. We can do so with this command:

```
$ az acr list --resource-group animals-rg \
    --query "[].{acrLoginServer:loginServer}" \
    --output table

AcrLoginServer
----------------------
fodanimalsacr.azurecr.io
```

We now use the preceding URL to tag our images:

```
bash-5.0# docker image tag fundamentalsofdocker/ch11-db:2.0
fodanimalsacr.azurecr.io/ch11-db:2.0
bash-5.0# docker image tag fundamentalsofdocker/ch11-web:2.0
fodanimalsacr.azurecr.io/ch11-web:2.0
```

Then, we can push them to our ACR:

```
bash-5.0# docker image push fodanimalsacr.azurecr.io/ch11-db:2.0
bash-5.0# docker image push fodanimalsacr.azurecr.io/ch11-web:2.0
```

To double-check that our images are indeed in our ACR, we can use this command:

```
bash-5.0# az acr repository list --name <acr-name> --output table

Result
--------
ch11-db
ch11-web
```

Indeed, the two images we just pushed are listed. With that, we are ready to create our Kubernetes cluster.

Creating a Kubernetes cluster

Once again, we will be using our custom Azure CLI to create the Kubernetes cluster. We will have to make sure that the cluster can access our ACR instance, which we just created and is where our container images reside. So, the command to create a cluster named `animals-cluster` with two worker nodes looks like this:

```
bash-5.0# az aks create \
    --resource-group animals-rg \
    --name animals-cluster \
    --node-count 2 \
    --generate-ssh-keys \
    --attach-acr <acr-name>
```

This command takes a while, but after a few minutes, we should receive some JSON-formatted output with all the details about the newly created cluster.

To access the cluster, we need `kubectl`. We can easily get it installed in our Azure CLI container using this command:

```
bash-5.0# az aks install-cli
```

Having installed `kubectl`, we need the necessary credentials to use the tool to operate on our new Kubernetes cluster in Azure. We can get the necessary credentials with this:

```
bash-5.0# az aks get-credentials --resource-group animals-rg --name
animals-cluster

Merged "animals-cluster" as current context in /root/.kube/config
```

After the success of the preceding command, we can list all the nodes in our cluster:

```
bash-5.0# kubectl get nodes
```

```
NAME                                  STATUS   ROLES   AGE     VERSION
aks-nodepool1-12528297-vmss000000     Ready    agent   4m38s   v1.14.8
aks-nodepool1-12528297-vmss000001     Ready    agent   4m32s   v1.14.8
```

As expected, we have two worker nodes up and running. The version of Kubernetes that is running on those nodes is `1.14.8`.

We are now ready to deploy our application to this cluster. In the next section, we are going to learn how we can do this.

Deploying our application to the Kubernetes cluster

To deploy the application, we can use the `kubectl apply` command:

```
bash-5.0# kubectl apply -f animals.yaml
```

The output of the preceding command should look similar to this:

```
deployment.apps/web created
service/web created
deployment.apps/db created
service/db created
```

Now, we want to test the application. Remember that we had created a service of type `LoadBalancer` for the web component. This service exposes the application to the internet. This process can take a moment, as AKS, among other tasks, needs to assign a public IP address to this service. We can observe this with the following command:

```
bash-5.0# kubectl get service web --watch
```

Please note the `--watch` parameter in the preceding command. It allows us to monitor the progress of the command over time. Initially, we should see output like this:

```
NAME TYPE          CLUSTER-IP  EXTERNAL-IP  PORT(S)         AGE
web LoadBalancer  10.0.124.0  <pending>    3000:32618/TCP  5s
```

The public IP address is marked as pending. After a few minutes, that should change to this:

```
NAME TYPE          CLUSTER-IP  EXTERNAL-IP     PORT(S)         AGE
web LoadBalancer  10.0.124.0  51.105.229.192  3000:32618/TCP  63s
```

Our application is now ready at the IP address `51.105.229.192` and port number `3000`. Note that the load balancer maps the internal port `32618` to the external port `3000`; this was not evident to me the first time.

Let's check it out. In a new browser tab, navigate to `http://51.105.229.192:3000/pet` and you should see our familiar application:

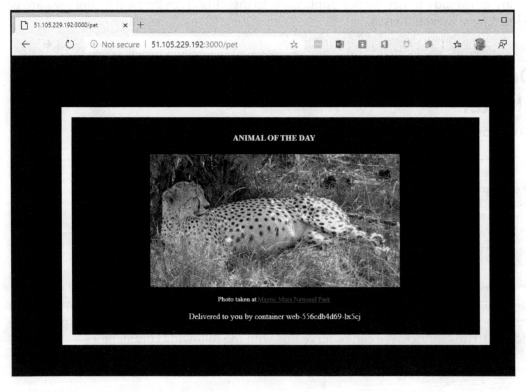

Our sample application running on AKS

With that, we have successfully deployed our distributed application to Kubernetes hosted in Azure. We did not have to worry about installing or managing Kubernetes; we could concentrate on the application itself.

Now that we are done experimenting with the application, we should not forget to delete all resources on Azure to avoid incurring unnecessary costs. We can delete all resources created by deleting the resource group as follows:

```
bash-5.0# az group delete --name animal-rg --yes --no-wait
```

Azure has a few compelling offerings regarding the container workload, and the lock-in is not as evident as it is on AWS due to the fact that Azure does mainly offer open source orchestration engines, such as Kubernetes, Docker Swarm, DC/OS, and Rancher. Technically, we remain mobile if we initially run our containerized applications in Azure and later decide to move to another cloud provider. The cost should be limited.

> It is worth noting that, when you delete your resource group, the Azure Active Directory service principal used by the AKS cluster is not removed. Refer to the online help for details on how to delete the service principal.

Next on the list is Google with their Kubernetes Engine.

Understanding GKE

Google is the inventor of Kubernetes and, to this date, the driving force behind it. You would therefore expect that Google has a compelling offering around hosted Kubernetes. Let's have a peek into it now. To continue, you need to either have an existing account with Google Cloud or create a test account here: https://console.cloud.google.com/freetrial. Proceed with the following steps:

1. In the main menu, select **Kubernetes Engine**. The first time you do that, it will take a few moments until the Kubernetes engine is initialized.
2. Next, create a new project and name it massai-mara; this may take a moment.
3. Once this is ready, we can create a cluster by clicking on **Create Cluster** in the popup.
4. Select the **Your first cluster** template on the left-hand side of the form.
5. Name the cluster animals-cluster, select the region or zone that's closest to you, leave all other settings in the **Create a Kubernetes Cluster** form with their default values, and click on **Create** at the bottom of the form.

It will again take a few moments to provision the cluster for us. Once the cluster has been created, we can open Cloud Shell by clicking on the shell icon in the upper-right corner of the view. This should look similar to the following screenshot:

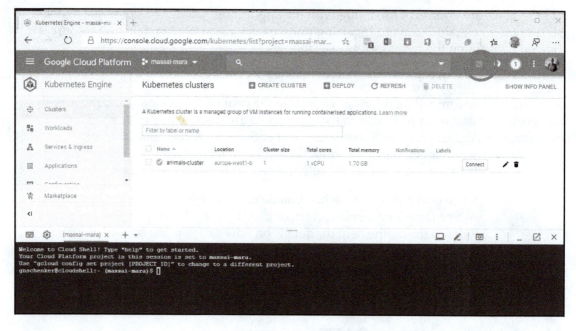

The first Kubernetes cluster ready and Cloud Shell open in GKE

We can now clone our `labs` GitHub repository to this environment with the following command:

```
$ git clone https://github.com/PacktPublishing/Learn-Docker---
Fundamentals-of-Docker-19.x-Second-Edition.git ~/fod
$ cd ~/fod/ch18/gce
```

We should now find an `animals.yaml` file in the current folder, which we can use to deploy the animals application into our Kubernetes cluster. Have a look at the file:

```
$ less animals.yaml
```

It has pretty much the same content as the same file we used in the previous chapter. The two differences are these:

- We use a service of type `LoadBalancer` (instead of `NodePort`) to publicly expose the `web` component.
- We do not use volumes for the PostgreSQL database since configuring StatefulSets correctly on GKE is a bit more involved than in Minikube. The consequence of this is that our animals application will not persist the state if the `db` pod crashes. How to use persistent volumes on GKE lies outside the scope of this book.

Also, note that we are not using Google Container Registry to host the container images but are instead directly pulling them from Docker Hub. It is very easy, and similar to what we have learned in the section about AKS, to create such a container registry in Google Cloud.

Before we can continue, we need to set up `gcloud` and `kubectl` credentials:

```
$ gcloud container clusters get-credentials animals-cluster --zone europe-
west1-b

Fetching cluster endpoint and auth data.
kubeconfig entry generated for animals-cluster.
```

Having done that, it's time to deploy the application:

```
$ kubectl create -f animals.yaml

deployment.apps/web created
service/web created
deployment.apps/db created
service/db created
```

Once the objects have been created, we can observe the `LoadBalancer` service `web` until it is assigned a public IP address:

```
$ kubectl get svc/web --watch

NAME   TYPE           CLUSTER-IP   EXTERNAL-IP     PORT(S)          AGE
web    LoadBalancer   10.0.5.222   <pending>       3000:32139/TCP   32s
web    LoadBalancer   10.0.5.222   146.148.23.70   3000:32139/TCP   39s
```

The second line in the output is showing the situation while the creation of the load balancer is still pending, and the third one gives the final state. Press *Ctrl* + *C* to quit the `watch` command. Apparently, we got the public IP address `146.148.23.70` assigned and the port is `3000`.

We can then use this IP address and navigate to `http://<IP address>:3000/pet`, and we should be greeted by the familiar animal image.

Once you are done playing with the application, delete the cluster and the project in the Google Cloud console to avoid any unnecessary costs.

We have created a hosted Kubernetes cluster in GKE. We have then used Cloud Shell, provided through the GKE portal, to first clone our `labs` GitHub repository and then the `kubectl` tool to deploy the animals application into the Kubernetes cluster.

When looking into a hosted Kubernetes solution, GKE is a compelling offering. It makes it very easy to start, and since Google is the main driving force behind Kubernetes, we can rest assured that we will always be able to leverage the full functionality of Kubernetes.

Summary

In this final chapter of the book, you first got a quick introduction to how to install and use Docker's UCP, which is part of Docker's enterprise offering on AWS. Then, you learned how to create a hosted Kubernetes cluster in AKS and run the animals application on it, followed by the same for Google's own hosted Kubernetes offering, GKE.

I am honored that you selected this book, and I want to thank you for accompanying me on this journey, where we explored Docker containers and container orchestration engines. I hope that this book has served as a valuable resource on your learning journey. I wish you all the best and much success when using containers in your current and future projects.

Questions

To assess your knowledge, please answer the following questions:

1. Give a high-level description of the tasks needed to provision and run Docker UPC on AWS.
2. List a few reasons why you would select a hosted Kubernetes offering, such as Microsoft's AKS or Google's GKE, to run your applications on Kubernetes.
3. Name two reasons when using a hosted Kubernetes solution, such as AKS or GKE, to consider hosting your container images in the container registry of the respective cloud provider.

Further reading

The following articles give you some more information related to the topics we discussed in this chapter:

- Install individual Docker EE components on Linux servers at `https://dockr.ly/2vH5dpN`
- Azure Container Service (AKS) at `https://bit.ly/2JglX9d`
- Google Kubernetes Engine at `https://bit.ly/2I8MjJx`

Assessments

Chapter 1

Here are some sample answers to the questions presented in this chapter:

1. The correct answers are **D** and **E**.
2. A Docker container is to IT what a shipping container is to the transportation industry. It defines a standard on how to package goods. In this case, goods are the application(s) developers write. The suppliers (in this case, the developers) are responsible for packaging the goods into the container and making sure everything fits as expected. Once the goods are packaged into a container, it can be shipped. Since it is a standard container, the shippers can standardize their means of transportation, such as lorries, trains, or ships. The shipper doesn't really care what's in a container. Also, the loading and unloading process from one transportation means to another (for example, train to ship) can be highly standardized. This massively increases the efficiency of transportation. Analogous to this is an operations engineer in IT, who can take a software container built by a developer and ship it to a production system and run it there in a highly standardized way, without worrying about what's in the container. It will just work.
3. Some of the reasons why containers are game changers are as follows:
    *   Containers are self-contained and thus if they run on one system, they run anywhere that a container can run.
    *   Containers run on premises and in the cloud, as well as in hybrid environments. This is important for today's typical enterprises since it allows a smooth transition from on premises to the cloud.
    *   Container images are built or packaged by the people who know best – the developers.
    *   Container images are immutable, which is important for good release management.
    *   Containers are enablers of a secure software supply chain based on encapsulation (using Linux namespaces and cgroups), secrets, content trust, and image vulnerability scanning.

4. Any given container runs anywhere where containers can run for the following reasons:

   - Containers are self-contained black boxes. They encapsulate not only an application but all its dependencies, such as libraries and frameworks, configuration data, certificates, and so on.

   - Containers are based on widely accepted standards such as OCI.

5. The answer is **B**. Containers are useful for modern applications as well as to containerize traditional applications. The benefits for an enterprise when doing the latter are huge. Cost savings in the maintenance of legacy apps of 50% or more have been reported. The time between new releases of such legacy applications could be reduced by up to 90%. These numbers have been publicly reported by real enterprise customers.

6. 50% or more.

7. Containers are based on Linux namespaces (network, process, user, and so on) and cgroups (control groups).

Chapter 2

Here are some sample answers to the questions presented in this chapter:

1. `docker-machine` can be used for the following scenarios:
   1. To create a VM on various providers such as VirtualBox, Hyper-V, AWS, MS Azure, or Google Compute Engine that will serve as a Docker Host.
   2. To start, stop, or kill a previously generated VM.
   3. To SSH into a local or remote Docker Host VM created with this tool.
   4. To re-generate certificates for the secure use of a Docker Host VM.

2. A. True. Yes, with Docker for Windows, you can develop and run Linux containers. It is also possible, but not discussed in this book, to develop and run native Windows containers with this edition of Docker for Desktop. With the macOS edition, you can only develop and run Linux containers.

3. Scripts are used to automate processes and hence avoid human errors. Building, testing, sharing, and running Docker containers are tasks that should always be automated to increase their reliability and repeatability.
4. The following Linux distros are certified to run Docker: RedHat Linux (RHEL), CentOS, Oracle Linux, Ubuntu, and more.
5. The following Windows OS are certified to run Docker: Windows 10 Pro, Windows Server 2016, and Windows Server 2019

Chapter 3

Here are some sample answers to the questions presented in this chapter:

1. The possible states of a Docker container are as follows:
     - `created`: A container that has been created but not started
     - `restarting`: A container that is in the process of being restarted
     - `running`: A currently running container
     - `paused`: A container whose processes have been paused
     - `exited`: A container that ran and completed
     - `dead`: A container that the Docker engine tried and failed to stop

2. We can use `docker container ls` (or the old, shorter version, `docker ps`) to list all containers that are currently running on our Docker host. Note that this will NOT list the stopped containers, for which you need the extra parameter--all (or -a).
3. To list all IDs of containers, running or stopped, we can use `docker container ls -a -q`, where -q stands for output ID only.

Chapter 4

Here are some sample answers to the questions presented in this chapter:

1. The `Dockerfile` could look like this:

```
FROM ubuntu:19.04
RUN apt-get update && \
    apt-get install -y iputils-ping
CMD ping 127.0.0.1
```

Note that in Ubuntu, the `ping` tool is part of the `iputils-ping` package. Build the image called `pinger`—for example— with `docker image build -t my-pinger`.

2. The `Dockerfile` could look like this:

```
FROM alpine:latest
RUN apk update && \
    apk add curl
```

Build the image with `docker image build -t my-alpine:1.0`.

3. The `Dockerfile` for a Go application could look like this:

```
FROM golang:alpine
WORKDIR /app
ADD . /app
RUN cd /app && go build -o goapp
ENTRYPOINT ./goapp
```

You can find the full solution in the `~/fod/ch04/answer03` folder.

4. A Docker image has the following characteristics:

1. It is immutable.
2. It consists of one-to-many layers.
3. It contains the files and folders needed for the packaged application to run.

5. **C.** First, you need to log in to Docker Hub; then, tag your image correctly with the username; and finally, push the image.

Chapter 5

Here are some sample answers to the questions presented in this chapter:

The easiest way to play with volumes is to use the Docker Toolbox because when directly using Docker for Desktop, the volumes are stored inside a (somewhat hidden) Linux VM that Docker for Desktop uses transparently.
Thus, we suggest the following:

```
$ docker-machine create --driver virtualbox volume-test
$ docker-machine ssh volume-test
```

And now that you're inside a Linux VM called `volume-test`, you can do the following exercise:

1. To create a named volume, run the following command:

   ```
   $ docker volume create my-products
   ```

2. Execute the following command:

   ```
   $ docker container run -it --rm \
       -v my-products:/data:ro \
       alpine /bin/sh
   ```

3. To get the path on the host for the volume, use this command:

   ```
   $ docker volume inspect my-products | grep Mountpoint
   ```

   This (if you're using `docker-machine` and VirtualBox) should result in this:

   ```
   "Mountpoint": "/mnt/sda1/var/lib/docker/volumes/myproducts/_data"
   ```

   Now execute the following command:

   ```
   $ sudo su
   $ cd /mnt/sda1/var/lib/docker/volumes/my-products/_data
   $ echo "Hello world" > sample.txt
   $ exit
   ```

4. Execute the following command:

   ```
   $ docker run -it --rm -v my-products:/data:ro alpine /bin/sh
   / # cd /data
   /data # cat sample.txt
   ```

   In another terminal, execute this command:

   ```
   $ docker run -it --rm -v my-products:/app-data alpine /bin/sh
   / # cd /app-data
   /app-data # echo "Hello other container" > hello.txt
   /app-data # exit
   ```

5. Execute a command such as this:

   ```
   $ docker container run -it --rm \
       -v $HOME/my-project:/app/data \
       alpine /bin/sh
   ```

6. Exit both containers and then, back on the host, execute this command:

```
$ docker volume prune
```

7. The answer is B. Each container is a sandbox and thus has its very own environment.

8. Collect all environment variables and their respective values in a configuration file, which you then provide to the container with the `--env-file` command-line parameter in the `docker run` command, like so:

```
$ docker container run --rm -it \
    --env-file ./development.config \
    alpine sh -c "export"
```

Chapter 6

Here are some sample answers to the questions presented in this chapter:

1. Possible answers: a) Volume mount your source code in the container; b) use a tool that automatically restarts the app running inside the container when code changes are detected; c) configure your container for remote debugging.

2. You can mount the folder containing the source code on your host in the container.

3. If you cannot cover certain scenarios easily with unit or integration tests and if the observed behavior of the application cannot be reproduced when the application runs on the host. Another scenario is a situation where you cannot run the application on the host directly due to the lack of the necessary language or framework.

4. Once the application is running in production, we cannot easily gain access to it as developers. If the application shows unexpected behavior or even crashes, logs are often the only source of information we have to help us reproduce the situation and pinpoint the root cause of the bug.

Chapter 7

Here are some sample answers to the questions presented in this chapter:

1. Pros and cons:
    - Pro: We don't need to have the particular shell, tool, or language required by the task installed on our host.
    - Pro: We can run on any Docker host, from Raspberry Pi to a mainframe computer; the only requirement is that the host can run containers.
    - Pro: After a successful run, the tool is removed without leaving any traces from the host when the container is removed.
    - Con: We need to have Docker installed on the host.
    - Con: The user needs to have a basic understanding of Docker containers.
    - Con: Use of the tool is a bit more indirect than when using it natively.

2. Running tests in a container has the following advantages:
    - They run equally well on a developer machine than on a test or CI system.
    - It is easier to start each test run with the same initial conditions.
    - All developers working with the code use the same setup, for example, versions of libraries and frameworks.

3. Here, we expect a diagram that shows a developer writing code and checking it in, for example, GitHub. We then want to see an automation server such as Jenkins or TeamCity in the picture that is either periodically polling GitHub for changes or the GitHub triggers the automation server (with an HTTP callback) to create a new build. The diagram should also show that the automation server then runs all tests against the built artifacts and, if they all succeed, deploys the application or service to an integration system where it is again tested, for example, with a few smoke tests. Once again, if those tests succeed, the automation server should either ask a human for approval to deploy to production (this equals to continuous delivery) or the automation server should automatically deploy to production (continuous deployment).

Chapter 8

Here are some sample answers to the questions presented in this chapter:

1. You could be working on a workstation with limited resources or capabilities, or your workstation could be locked down by your company so that you are not allowed to install any software that is not officially approved. Sometimes, you might need to do proof of concepts or experiments using languages or frameworks that are not yet approved by your company (but might be in the future if the proof of concept is successful).

2. Bind-mounting a Docker socket into a container is the recommended method when a containerized application needs to automate some container-related tasks. This can be an application such as an automation server such as Jenkins that you are using to build, test, and deploy Docker images.

3. Most business applications do not need root-level authorizations to do their job. From a security perspective, it is hence strongly recommended to run such applications with the least necessary access rights to their job. Any unnecessary elevated privileges could possibly be exploited by hackers in a malicious attack. By running the application as a non-root user, you make it more difficult for potential hackers to compromise your system.

4. Volumes contain data and the lifespan of data most often needs to go far beyond the life cycle of a container or an application, for that matter. Data is often mission-critical and needs to be stored safely for days, months, even years. When you delete a volume, you irreversibly delete the data associated with it. Hence, make sure you know what you're doing when deleting a volume.

Chapter 9

Here are some sample answers to the questions presented in this chapter:

1. In a distributed application architecture, every piece of the software and infrastructure needs to be redundant in a production environment, where the continuous uptime of the application is mission-critical. A highly distributed application consists of many parts and the likelihood of one of the pieces failing or misbehaving increases with the number of parts. It is guaranteed that, given enough time, every part will eventually fail. To avoid outages of the application, we need redundancy in every part, be it a server, a network switch, or a service running on a cluster node in a container.

2. In highly distributed, scalable, and fault-tolerant systems, individual services of the application can move around due to scaling needs or due to component failures. Thus, we cannot hardwire different services with each other. Service A, which needs access to Service B, should not have to know details such as the IP address of Service B. It should rely on an external provider of this information. DNS is such a provider of location information. Service A just tells it that it wants to talk to Service B and the DNS service will figure out the details.

3. A circuit breaker is a means to avoid cascading failures if a component in a distributed application is failing or misbehaving. Similar to a circuit breaker in electric wiring, a software-driven circuit breaker cuts the communication between a client and a failed service. The circuit breaker will directly report an error back to the client component if the failed service is called. This gives the system the opportunity to recover or heal from failure.

4. A monolithic application is easier to manage that a multi-service application since it consists of a single deployment package. On the other hand, a monolith is harder to scale to account for increased demand. In a distributed application, each service can be scaled individually and each service can run on optimized infrastructure, while a monolith needs to run on infrastructure that is OK for all or most of the features implemented in it. Maintaining and updating a monolith is much harder than a multi-service application, where each service can be updated and deployed independently. The monolith is often a big, complex, and tightly coupled pile of code. Minor modifications can have unexpected side effects. (Micro-) Services, on the other hand, are self-contained, simple components that behave like black boxes. Dependent services know nothing about the inner workings of the service and thus do not depend on it.

5. A blue-green deployment is a form of software deployment that allows for zero downtime deployments of new versions of an application or an application service. If, say, Service A needs to be updated with a new version, then we call the currently running version blue. The new version of the service is deployed into production, but not yet wired up with the rest of the application. This new version is called green. Once the deployment succeeds and smoke tests have shown it's ready to go, the router that funnels traffic to blue is reconfigured to switch to green. The behavior of green is observed for a while and if everything is OK, blue is decommissioned. On the other hand, if green causes difficulties, the router can simply be switched back to blue and green can be fixed and later redeployed.

Chapter 10

Here are some sample answers to the questions presented in this chapter:

1. The three core elements are **sandbox, endpoint**, and **network**.
2. Execute this command:

```
$ docker network create --driver bridge frontend
```

3. Run this command:

```
$ docker container run -d --name n1 \
    --network frontend -p 8080:80 nginx:alpine
$ docker container run -d --name n2 \
    --network frontend -p 8081:80 nginx:alpine
```

   Test that both NGINX instances are up and running:

```
$ curl -4 localhost:8080
$ curl -4 localhost:8081
```

   You should be seeing the welcome page of NGINX in both cases.

4. To get the IPs of all attached containers, run this command:

```
$ docker network inspect frontend | grep IPv4Address
```

   You should see something similar to the following:

```
"IPv4Address": "172.18.0.2/16",
"IPv4Address": "172.18.0.3/16",
```

   To get the subnet used by the network, use the following (for example):

```
$ docker network inspect frontend | grep subnet
```

   You should receive something along the lines of the following (obtained from the previous example):

```
"Subnet": "172.18.0.0/16",
```

5. The `host` network allows us to run a container in the networking namespace of the host.
6. Only use this network for debugging purposes or when building a system-level tool. Never use the `host` network for an application container running a production environment!

7. The `none` network is basically saying that the container is not attached to any network. It should be used for containers that do not need to communicate with other containers and do not need to be accessed from outside.

8. The `none` network could, for example, be used for a batch process running in a container that only needs access to local resources such as files that could be accessed via a host mounted volume.

9. Traefik can be used to provide Layer 7 or application-level routing. This is especially useful if you want to break out functionality from a monolith with a well-defined API. In this case, you have a need to reroute certain HTTP calls to the new container/service. This is just one of the possible usage scenarios, but it's also the most important one. Another one could be to use Traefik as a load balancer.

Chapter 11

Here are some sample answers to the questions presented in this chapter:

1. The following code can be used to run the application in detached or daemon mode:

```
$ docker-compose up -d
```

2. Execute the following command to display the details of the running service:

```
$ docker-compose ps
```

This should result in the following output:

```
Name                   Command               State  Ports
--------------------------------------------------------------------
mycontent_nginx_1   nginx -g daemon off;   Up
0.0.0.0:3000->80/tcp
```

3. The following command can be used to scale up the web service:

```
$ docker-compose up --scale web=3
```

Chapter 12

Here are some sample answers to the questions presented in this chapter:

1. A mission-critical, highly available application that is implemented as a highly distributed system of interconnected application services that are just too complex to manually monitor, operate, and manage. Container orchestrators help in this regard. They automate most of the typical tasks, such as reconciling a desired state, or collecting and aggregating key metrics of the system. Humans cannot react quick enough to make such an application elastic or self-healing. Software support is needed for this in the form of the mentioned container orchestrators.

2. A container orchestrator frees us from mundane and cumbersome tasks such as the following:
   - Scaling services up and down
   - Load balancing requests
   - Routing requests to the desired target
   - Monitoring the health of service instances
   - Securing a distributed application

3. The winner in this space is Kubernetes, which is open sourced and owned by the CNCF. It was originally developed by Google. We also have Docker Swarm, which is proprietary and has been developed by Docker. AWS offers a container service called ECS, which is also proprietary and tightly integrated into the AWS ecosystem. Finally, Microsoft offers AKS, which has the same pros and cons as AWS ECS.

Chapter 13

Here are some sample answers to the questions presented in this chapter:

1. The correct answer is as follows:

```
$ docker swarm init [--advertise-addr <IP address>]
```

The `--advertise-addr` is optional and is only needed if you the host have more than one IP address.

2. On the worker node that you want to remove, execute the following command:

```
$ docker swarm leave
```

On one of the master nodes, execute the command `$ docker node rm -f<node ID>`, where `<node ID>` is the ID of the worker node to remove.

3. The correct answer is as follows:

```
$ docker network create \
    --driver overlay \
    --attachable \
    front-tier
```

4. The correct answer is as follows:

```
$ docker service create --name web \
    --network front-tier \
    --replicas 5 \
    -p 3000:80 \
    nginx:alpine
```

5. The correct answer is as follows:

```
$ docker service update --replicas 3 web
```

Chapter 14

Here are some sample answers to the questions presented in this chapter:

1. Zero-downtime deployment means that a new version of a service in a distributed application is updated to a new version without the application needing to stop working. Usually, with Docker SwarmKit or Kubernetes (as we will see), this is done in a rolling fashion. A service consists of multiple instances and those are updated in batches so that the majority of the instances are up and running at all times.
2. By default, Docker SwarmKit uses a rolling updated strategy to achieve zero-downtime deployments.
3. Containers are self-contained units of deployment. If a new version of a service is deployed and does not work as expected, we (or the system) need to only roll back to the previous version. The previous version of the service is also deployed in the form of self-contained containers. Conceptually, there is no difference in rolling forward (update) or backward (rollback). One version of a container is replaced by another one. The host itself is not affected by such changes in any way.

4. Docker secrets are encrypted at rest. They are only transferred to the services and containers that use the secrets. Secrets are transferred encrypted due to the fact that the communication between swarm nodes uses mutual TLS. Secrets are never physically stored on a worker node.

5. The command to achieve this is as follows:

```
$ docker service update --image acme/inventory:2.1 \
    --update-parallelism 2 \
    --update-delay 60s \
    inventory
```

6. First, we need to remove the old secret from the service, and then we need to add the new version to it (directly updating a secret is not possible):

```
$ docker service update \
    --secret-rm MYSQL_PASSWORD \
    inventory
$ docker service update \
    --secret-add source=MYSQL_PASSWORD_V2, target=MYSQL_PASSWORD \
    inventory
```

Chapter 15

Here are some sample answers to the questions presented in this chapter:

1. The Kubernetes master is responsible for managing the cluster. All requests to create objects, reschedule pods, manage ReplicaSets, and more happen on the master. The master does not run the application workload in a production or production-like cluster.

2. On each worker node, we have the kubelet, the proxy, and container runtime.

3. The answer is A. **Yes.** You cannot run standalone containers on a Kubernetes cluster. Pods are the atomic units of deployment in such a cluster.

4. All containers running inside a pod share the same Linux kernel network namespace. Thus, all processes running inside those containers can communicate with each other through localhost in a similar way to how processes or applications directly running on the host can communicate with each other through localhost.

5. The `pause` container's sole role is to reserve the namespaces of the pod for containers that run in it.

6. This is a bad idea since all containers of a pod are co-located, which means they run on the same cluster node. Also, if multiple containers run in the same pod, they can only be scaled up or down all at once. However, the different components of the application (that is, `web`, `inventory`, and `db`) usually have very different requirements with regard to scalability or resource consumption. The `web` component might need to be scaled up and down depending on the traffic and the `db` component, in turn, has special requirements regarding storage that the others don't have. If we do run every component in its own pod, we are much more flexible in this regard.

7. We need a mechanism in order to run multiple instances of a pod in a cluster and make sure that the actual number of pods running always corresponds to the desired number, even when individual pods crash or disappear due to network partition or cluster node failures. The ReplicaSet is the mechanism that provides scalability and self-healing to any application service.

8. We need deployment objects whenever we want to update an application service in a Kubernetes cluster without causing downtime to the service. Deployment objects add rolling updates and rollback capabilities to ReplicaSets.

9. Kubernetes service objects are used to make application services participate in service discovery. They provide a stable endpoint to a set of pods (normally governed by a ReplicaSet or a deployment). Kube services are abstractions that define a logical set of pods and a policy regarding how to access them. There are four types of Kube service:

    - **ClusterIP**: Exposes the service on an IP address that's only accessible from inside the cluster; this is a virtual IP (VIP).
    - **NodePort**: Publishes a port in the range 30,000–32,767 on every cluster node.
    - **LoadBalancer**: This type exposes the application service externally using a cloud provider's load balancer, such as ELB on AWS.
    - **ExternalName**: Used when you need to define a proxy for a cluster's external service such as a database.

Chapter 16

Here are some sample answers to the questions presented in this chapter:

1. Assuming we have a Docker image in a registry for the two application services, the web API and Mongo DB, we then need to do the following:

   - Define a deployment for Mongo DB using a StatefulSet; let's call this deployment `db-deployment`. The StatefulSet should have one replica (replicating Mongo DB is a bit more involved and is outside the scope of this book).

   - Define a Kubernetes service called `db` of the `ClusterIP` type for `db-deployment`.

   - Define a deployment for the web API; let's call it `web-deployment`. Let's scale this service to three instances.

   - Define a Kubernetes service called `api` of the `NodePort` type for `web-deployment`.

   - If we use secrets, then define those secrets directly in the cluster using kubectl.

   - Deploy the application using kubectl.

2. To implement layer 7 routing for an application, we ideally use an IngressController. The IngressController is a reverse proxy such as Nginx that has a sidecar listening on the Kubernetes Server API for relevant changes and updating the reverse proxy's configuration and restarting it if such a change has been detected. Then, we need to define Ingress resources in the cluster that define the routing, for example, from a context-based route such as `https://example.com/pets` to `<a service name>/<port>` or a pair such as `api/32001`. The moment Kubernetes creates or changes this Ingress object, the IngressController's sidecar picks it up and updates the proxy's routing configuration.

3. Assuming this is a cluster internal inventory service, then we do the following:

   - When deploying version 1.0, we define a deployment called `inventory-deployment-blue` and label the pods with a label of `color: blue`.

   - We deploy the Kubernetes service of the `ClusterIP` type called inventory for the preceding deployment with the selector containing `color: blue`.

- When we're ready to deploy the new version of the payments service, we define a deployment for version 2.0 of the service and call it `inventory-deployment-green`. We add a label of `color: green` to the pods.
- We can now smoke test the "green" service and when everything is OK, we can update the inventory service so that the selector contains `color: green`.

2. Some forms of information that are confidential and thus should be provided to services through Kubernetes secrets include passwords, certificates, API key IDs, API key secrets, and tokens.

3. Sources for secret values can be files or base64-encoded values.

Chapter 17

Here are some sample answers to the questions presented in this chapter:

1. We cannot do any live debugging on a production system for performance and security reasons. This includes interactive or remote debugging. Yet application services can show unexpected behavior to code defects or other infrastructure-related issues such as network glitches or external services that are not available. To quickly pinpoint the reason for the misbehavior or failure of a service, we need as much logging information as possible. This information should give us a clue about, and guide us to, the root cause of the error. When we instrument a service, we do exactly this — we produce as much information as reasonable in the form of log entries and published metrics.

2. Prometheus is a service that is used to collect functional or non-functional metrics that are provided by other infrastructure services and most importantly by application services. Since Prometheus itself is pulling those metrics periodically from all configured services, the services themselves do not have to worry about sending data. Prometheus also defines the format in which the metrics are to be presented by the producers.

3. To instrument a Node.js-based application service we need to do the following four steps:

    1. Add a Prometheus adapter to the project. The maintainers of Prometheus recommend the library called `siimon/prom-client`.
    2. Configure the Prometheus client during startup of the application. This includes the definition of a metrics registry.
    3. Expose an HTTP GET endpoint/metrics where we return the collection of metrics defined in the metrics registry.
    4. Finally, we define custom metrics of the `counter`, `gauge`, or `histogram` type, and use them in our code; for example, we increase a metric of the `counter` type each time a certain endpoint is called.

4. Normally in production, a Kubernetes cluster node only contains a minimal OS to keep its attack surface as limited as possible and to not waste precious resources. Thus we cannot assume that the tools typically used to troubleshoot applications or processes are available on the respective host. A powerful and recommended way to troubleshoot is to run a special tools or troubleshoot container as part of an ad hoc pod. This container can then be used as a bastion from which we can investigate network and other issues with the troubled service. A container that has been successfully used by many Docker field engineers at their customers site is `netshoot`.

Chapter 18

Here are some sample answers to the questions presented in this chapter:

1. To install UCP in AWS, we do the following:
    - Create a VPC with subnets and an SG.
    - Then, provision a cluster of Linux VMs, possibly as part of an ASG. Many Linux distributions are supported, such as CentOS, RHEL, and Ubuntu.
    - Next, install Docker on each VM.
    - Finally, select one VM on which to install UCP using the `docker/ucp` image.
    - Once UCP is installed, join the other VMs to the cluster either as worker nodes or manager nodes.

2. Here are a few reasons to consider a hosted Kubernetes offering:
   - You do not want to, or do not have the resources to, install and manage a Kubernetes cluster.
   - You want to concentrate on what brings value to your business, which in most cases is the applications that are supposed to run on Kubernetes and not Kubernetes itself.
   - You prefer a cost model where you pay only for what you need.
   - The nodes of your Kubernetes cluster are automatically patched and updated.
   - Upgrading the version of Kubernetes with zero downtime is easy and straightforward.

3. The two main reasons to host container images on the cloud provider's container registry (such as ACR on Microsoft Azure) are these:
   - The images are geographically close to your Kubernetes cluster and thus the latency and transfer network costs are minimal.
   - Production or production-like clusters are ideally sealed from the internet, and thus the Kubernetes cluster nodes cannot access Docker Hub directly.

Other Books You May Enjoy

If you enjoyed this book, you may be interested in these other books by Packt:

Continuous Delivery with Docker and Jenkins - Second Edition
Rafał Leszko

ISBN: 978-1-83855-218-3

Learn how to clean your data and ready it for analysis

- Get to grips with docker fundamentals and how to dockerize an application for the CD process
- Learn how to use Jenkins on the Cloud environments
- Scale a pool of Docker servers using Kubernetes
- Create multi-container applications using Docker Compose
- Write acceptance tests using Cucumber and run them in the Docker ecosystem using Jenkins
- Publish a built Docker image to a Docker Registry and deploy cycles of Jenkins pipelines using community best practices

Mastering Docker Enterprise
Mark Panthofer

ISBN: 978-1-78961-207-3

- Understand why containers are important to an enterprise
- Understand the features and components of Docker Enterprise 2
- Find out about the PoC, pilot, and production adoption phases
- Get to know the best practices for installing and operating Docker Enterprise
- Understand what is important for a Docker Enterprise in production
- Run Kubernetes on Docker Enterprise

Leave a review - let other readers know what you think

Please share your thoughts on this book with others by leaving a review on the site that you bought it from. If you purchased the book from Amazon, please leave us an honest review on this book's Amazon page. This is vital so that other potential readers can see and use your unbiased opinion to make purchasing decisions, we can understand what our customers think about our products, and our authors can see your feedback on the title that they have worked with Packt to create. It will only take a few minutes of your time, but is valuable to other potential customers, our authors, and Packt. Thank you!

Index

C